DATE DUE

HIGHSMITH   45231

DIVIDED
WE FALL

ALSO BY HAYNES JOHNSON

Sleepwalking Through History
(1991)
In the Absence of Power
(1980)
The Working White House
(1975)
The Bay of Pigs
(1964)
Dusk at the Mountain
(1963)

Lyndon, with Richard Harwood
(1973)
Army in Anguish, with George C. Wilson
(1972)
The Unions, with Nick Kotz
(1972)
Fulbright: The Dissenter, with Bernard M. Gwertzman
(1968)

FICTION
The Landing, with Howard Simons
(1986)

DIVIDED
WE FALL

GAMBLING
WITH HISTORY
IN THE NINETIES

HAYNES JOHNSON

W. W. NORTON & COMPANY
NEW YORK·LONDON

65600

The text of this book is composed in 11/14 Times Roman with the display set in Augustea.
Composition and manufacturing by The Haddon Craftsmen, Inc.
Book design by Charlotte Staub.

Excerpt from "America" by Paul Simon. Copyright © 1968
by Paul Simon. Used by permission of the publisher.

Library of Congress Cataloging-in-Publication Data

Johnson, Haynes Bonner, 1931–
Divided we fall : gambling with history in the nineties / by
Haynes Johnson.
p.   cm.
Includes bibliographical references and index.
1. United States—Politics and government—1993–   2. United
States—Economic conditions—1981–   3. United States—Social
conditions—1980–   I. Title.
E885.J65   1994
973.929—dc20   93-45713

ISBN 0-393-03629-4

W. W. Norton & Company, Inc., 500 Fifth Avenue, New York, N.Y. 10110
W. W. Norton & Comapny Ltd., 10 Coptic Street, London WC1A 1PU

1 2 3 4 5 6 7 8 9 0

CAROL HOUCK SMITH
who believed

And for the Tierneys of Maine
and all the others who shared
with me the feelings
of their hearts

CONTENTS

EPILOGUE
Journey's End   385

The Clock   399

In America, I saw more than America; I sought the image of democracy itself, with its inclinations, its character, its prejudices, and its passions, in order to learn what we have to fear or hope from its progress.

—Alexis de Tocqueville, *Democracy in America*

The genius of the United States is not best or most in its executives or legislatures, nor in its ambassadors or authors or colleges or churches or parlors, nor even in its newspapers or inventors . . . but always most in the common people.

—Walt Whitman, Preface to *Leaves of Grass*

DIVIDED
WE FALL

THE CLOCK

Midtown Manhattan, high noon, January 20, 1992, gray and cold, with snow squalls swirling about skyscrapers shrouded in mist:

Shining faintly through the gloom, suspended above the city from outside an office building at Forty-third Street and Sixth Avenue, are pale yellow numbers from a flashing electronic billboard. Above the constantly tumbling numbers are the words "Our National Debt." At this moment, the debt stands at $3,804,653,000,968.

Millisecond after millisecond the electronic clock tabulates the ever-escalating debt of the United States of America. The clock possesses a life of its own. Its numbers are directly linked and yet far removed from the activities of people on the street below and from the lives of millions of others throughout America.

It is exactly one year before the first presidential inaugural ceremonies of the 1990s are scheduled to begin and the beginning, too, of a personal journey around America that will end a year later when the next president takes his oath in Washington.

Washington, high noon, January 20, 1993, fresh and mild, with brilliant sunshine illuminating an inaugural platform beneath a Capitol dome framed against a cloudless blue sky:

A vast throng, silent, motionless, anticipating, stretches as far as the eye can see toward the Washington Monument. A stir, then a cheer, as the oath is administered. The cheering continues as the thunder of a twenty-one-gun salute echoes off the Capitol walls. The new president faces west toward the people and begins to speak. "We have heard the trumpets, we have changed the guard," he says. "There is nothing wrong with America that cannot be cured by what is right with America."

At this moment in New York, the numbers on the National Debt Clock stand at $4,177,365,738,326. In exactly one year, the national debt has increased by $372,712,737,358, rising at a rate of $13,000 per second, at an annual interest cost to the nation of $292 billion. The average American family's share of the national obligation now stands at $55,716.

PROLOGUE

THE JOURNEY

I did not set out to write a treatise on the public debt when I stood peering up at those stupefying numbers in midtown Manhattan on January 20, 1992. Nor, a few days later, did I think I was embarking on a romantic journey across America when I drove off from my home in Washington at four o'clock on a frigid morning and headed north to New England.

By the time I reached the New Jersey Turnpike, the skies were streaked with the vivid reds and yellows of a winter sunrise and an old Simon and Garfunkel tape was blaring out the closing lyrics to "America" over my car radio: *Counting the cars on the New Jersey Turnpike: They've all come to look for America, all come to look for America, all come to look for America.*

I was looking for America too, and inspired by the lyrics, I started counting—not the numbers of cars, but their make. Far more were Japanese than American. My car was not American-made, either. Small symbol of America's changing condition.

That was the beginning of a year's look at my country, in a trip that took me region by region from Maine to the Mexican border with a southern California grappling with the hardest economic times since the Great Depression. It turned out to be a journey of intense emotions as I reacted day after day to the lives of people I met. Nothing in my previous experience of traveling across America prepared me for the depth of feelings—the fear, the doubt, the anger,

the *rage*—I encountered everywhere. Strongest of all was a feeling of
bewilderment, a troubling sense that the assurances of the old America were passing and that the uncertain new America emerging
promises to be far more unsettling. Never before have the worlds of
political Washington and journalism seemed more disconnected
from the world beyond the capital. They were, in fact, directly connected; but that forms another part of this story.

This book grows out of a conviction that the United States, whose
history has been one long turning point, is approaching an epoch that
requires it to make more than a turn in direction; it means the United
States must leap an abyss into an uncharted future. If this opportunity is seized, and genuine economic, political, and social change
results, America will be in a stronger position to deal with its growing internal problems and with the challenges of a turbulent post–
Cold War world in which the old rules no longer apply. If Americans
and their leaders do not create change, one of their best chances to
put their national house in order will have been lost.

It could be the last chance for the traditional political system. I
believe President Bill Clinton is correct when he says it's "make or
break time" for America in the Nineties.

The challenge involves more than how Democrats and Republicans in Washington respond to economic and social policies that one
president proposes. More crucial is whether Americans can overcome the narrow competing interests that divide and make them
increasingly incapable of resolving problems. These negative tenden-
cies have surfaced again during Clinton's first year in office, producing further evidence of inability to act to resolve long-term national
issues. Failure will almost surely lead to more fragmentation, to
more public frustration and cynicism, to more Ross Perot–type protest movements that make consensus more difficult. For Americans
facing a long-term crisis of change, divided we fall.

It is against that background, and out of that belief, that this book
is written. It also grows out of a conviction I formed while writing
Sleepwalking Through History, a narrative of America in the Reagan
years: that the political, economic, and social consequences of the
1980s would inevitably lead to a critical test of the American people
and their political-economic systems in the 1990s. With that in mind,
in these pages I shall address the problems President Clinton faced

during his first year, and assess the success or failure of what he described to me as "the great gamble with history" he is taking in dealing with some of them; examine the underlying structure of the regions through which I traveled; and, in the heart of this book, portray the frayed American fabric of the 1990s.

I sought out many of the Americans who appear here in advance and put much care into letting them speak as clearly as possible for themselves. I did so in the hope that their views and experiences would illuminate the way we live now as we face economic restructuring, the passage from defense to civilian spending, the ordeal of public education, joblessness, race, crime, urban decay, growing generational conflict over scarce resources for health care and retirement benefits.

In many of the places explored, I renewed contacts with people I have reported on during thirty years as a journalist and author. In others, as in Los Angeles, I met many remarkable people for the first time. Nine months before the riots there, I started making contacts to examine tensions between three target groups: blacks, Koreans, and Latinos. In each area I visited, the natural course of my inquiries led me from old to new acquaintances.

Here you will meet this American procession: public officials and private citizens, mayors and police chiefs, cops on the beat and parish priests, heads of corporations and universities, high school principals and elementary school teachers, illegal aliens and members of inner-city gangs, high-flying savings and loan executives who profited—then crashed—in the boom of the Eighties and those who helped bring them down, demographers and scholars, judges and social workers, retired citizens and farmers, erstwhile antagonists in Southern civil rights struggles, high school seniors and graduating college students, union members and business executives.

I asked them to reflect on their jobs and aspirations, their families and communities, their country and its economic and political systems. I also asked how each person felt about the presidential election and how his or her hopes for change affected feelings about the nation and its future—and how, when I spoke to many of these people a year after that election, they felt political leaders had responded to their desire for change.

What I heard at the beginning in the below-zero shadows of

Maine was what I heard at the end in the broiling sunshine of San Ysidro, California, where U.S. Border Patrol members vainly tried to check a tidal wave of illegal immigrants entering from Tijuana, Mexico: that America was in trouble, that it needed to change, that it faced more disturbing questions than anyone could remember. This belief was held even by those who survived the Great Depression and World War II.

Based on what I found, failure to address America's increasing racial and ethnic tensions, economic inequities, and the rapidly widening gap between the haves and have-nots will inevitably result in new and greater explosions. The Los Angeles riots of April 1992 were not an aberration.

During the Depression and World War II, Americans understood the stark choices involved: jump out the window, as some stockbrokers did after the crash in 1929, or unite and work to change the system. Give up, after bombs fell on Pearl Harbor, or fight.

The present condition is less obvious and thus more difficult. It represents the most fundamental testing of the American system, and the American people, since Franklin Roosevelt assumed power in 1933; but it takes place without the unifying sense of a clear enemy. It also makes Clinton's attempt to create what amounts to a *new* New Deal—a reordering not only of the nation's economic and social priorities but of the role of government itself—more daunting because it is undertaken with a people wearied by their long-term challenges without being energized by the need to act at once to prepare for the new world of the next century.

On the surface, America faces a test of its ability to govern itself as internal forces threaten to divide and pull it apart. On a deeper level, it comes down to an ultimate test of the American character: can we make the hard choices to ensure that the country will survive and prosper?

BOOK ONE

THE PEOPLE
AND THE DREAM

CHAPTER 1

THE PEOPLE

High on the hills of Oakland, overlooking San Francisco Bay and the Golden Gate, rises a cluster of elegant houses, the homes of judges, doctors, lawyers, architects, business executives, and university officials. All races and backgrounds are represented there. Success is their common denominator.

In the fall of 1991, a great fire swept the hills, leveling many homes and reducing others to blackened shells. No sooner had the smoke and flames subsided than the very poor of the inner-city flatlands of Oakland swarmed up to loot, invading even some houses that had survived the fire and were still occupied. One of the hill people took to sitting at night in his living room with a baseball bat to ward off the looters. He's seventy years old, a man of distinction in government and university circles, and someone I've known for years.

"It's more than drugs and crime," he says of the problems he sees afflicting America, "it's deterioration of the fabric of life altogether. I have always been upbeat, superpatriotic. But I'm depressed. If Alvin Toffler is right that change increases at an ever-accelerating rate, and if the British Empire lasted five hundred years, maybe the post–World War II American Empire will only last seventy-five years."

He pauses, then talks about his reaction to televised scenes of plundering after a Florida hurricane that fall. "Now whenever I see a looter, I say shoot the bastard," he says. "I don't care if they shoot the fuckers"—and he's not a profane man.

A thousand miles to the south, in the Hollywood Hills, a black filmmaker, a success by any standard, speaks of the ferment among less fortunate African-Americans. In so doing, he addresses some of the reasons for the spontaneous pillaging that periodically erupts throughout America as those at the bottom seek to get their share of the American Dream by taking from those at the top.

"People don't have a stake in their own life," he says. "From the time they are born they are processed. You are welfare recipient No. 89995, you live in Section 8 House No. 00001. On the first and fifteenth of every month you get check No. 11111. You will go to dysfunctional school and learn nothing. You will then be tossed out into the street where you can gain no employment. So their lives have no value, but because people are resilient they take alternative means: 'Well, I'm going to get mine. I'm going to rob somebody. I'm going to sell dope. I'm going to steal cars.' You create your own culture as a functional necessity. You don't just sit there and die.

"I tell you, the problem lies right out there in the inner city of Detroit, in the inner city of New York, in the inner city of Los Angeles. The solution to the problem begins there, not in Washington. That's why I believe we're either in the decline or the rebirth of America."

In south-central Los Angeles, where the riots flared that spring, an illegal immigrant from El Salvador talks about the odyssey that brought him to southern California two and a half years before. Abandoning his law studies, he fled Salvadoran oppression and was led hundreds of miles through a network of checkpoints in Mexico by a half-crazed "coyote" smuggler to whom he and thirty others paid $1,300 apiece. They also paid cash bribes to Mexican federal police every time they were stopped on their way to the American border. After racing past U.S. patrols and then lying under stacks of lumber in a pickup truck heading north on the freeway, this man finally arrived, with only the clothes on his back, in Los Angeles.

"My dream was to come over here to work and study," he says in Spanish, "and I imagined a country that was full of opportunity. I suffered a great disillusionment. There is poverty just like in my country. There's social injustice here, just like in my country. There is tremendous economic development, but it's in the hands of two or three people. Before I came here, I was much more of a dreamer, an idealist. Now I'm much more hardened. If I'm walking down the street and someone asks me for a quarter, I don't have anything to eat myself, so I don't give him anything."

In Peoria, Illinois, a twenty-six-year-old fifth-grade public school teacher is called in by her principal and given a pink slip. She has been teaching one year, then becomes one of nine teachers laid off because of a budget crisis. All of those let go have the least seniority. With a $10,000 student loan to pay off, she is unable to meet rent, car, and health insurance payments after her school benefits run out. She moves back into her parents' home. To earn money to go back to school and start over, she answers an ad in the paper for blackjack operators on a new gambling riverboat, the *Paradise,* in the Illinois River off Peoria. "I feel I did everything the way I was supposed to," she says, explaining why she believes the American Dream is dead. "I worked hard in high school. I worked hard in college. I always made the honor roll. I did my job well, and the bottom just fell out. So here I am. I want to be a teacher and what am I doing? I'm going to blackjack school!"

Also in Peoria, a much-traveled chief executive officer of a management and business corporation is struck by the way cities are becoming "the new reservations of America." Everywhere he goes he sees fearful haves setting up barricades against threatening have-nots. He visits his son in suburban Dallas and finds him living behind high fences in an area patrolled by a private police force. "Everyone lives behind those fences to make sure that those who have not aren't going to come in and take it away from them," he says. "And I say to myself, 'What a way to live!' At my cousin's wedding in Riverside, California, it was the same thing. I was jogging along this road and I see these high fences and beautiful homes up there and signs: 'Beware of Dogs.' We're living in medieval fortresses. Lift up the drawbridge. We're secluded, we have all this nice comfort in this little area, but we know there's *danger* out there."

In Santee, South Carolina, in a walled community halfway between Miami and New York off Interstate Highway 95, a retirement enclave of ranch-style homes fronting on a lake presents a scene of peace and harmony. Yet fear of violence pervades this quiet place too. "For the first time I have a couple of pistols," says a former auto executive. "I've loaded 'em and I keep 'em where it would be strategic for me." An even deeper concern unsettles these Americans: that they no longer will be able to afford their retirement Utopia, that their pensions and health benefits may dissolve in the wake of continuing mergers of American corporations, that their middle class is in decline, that they will fall victim to economic forces that could negate their lifetime of careful planning.

"It's a horrible period of life," says a former professor, seated beside his wife in a living room overlooking a golf course, "because you don't have any group rates for anything. An enormous amount of our retirement income is for health insurance. And we're not even sure that insurance is going to continue to work. Between the cost of health insurance and other insurance—car insurance, home insurance—these are serious threats when you're on a fixed retirement income." They talk about the nation at large. "For a couple of decades I've thought that America needed to look at its values so that we can spread out the resources of the country," says his wife, a former college dean. "What I see happening is quite the opposite. Rather than a growing middle class I see a dwindling one where people are dropping behind and others, greedy as the Lord can ever make anyone greedy, are going in the other direction."

In Waverly, Iowa, a small town in the middle of the Farmbelt, a Lutheran minister describes the uneasiness among his congregation and the townspeople. Even though the farm crisis of the Eighties has passed, he says people are afraid; they still fear that "the big conglomerates are going to have us all." But this man's greatest worry is that accumulating frustrations could lead to "a situation in America where we'd be ripe for a dictatorship. People's fears and apprehensions are reaching a point where the call for a strong leader could develop very quickly."

In Arlington, Texas, halfway between Dallas and Fort Worth, a proud father keeps a large color photograph of his son on the wall behind his desk. It looks like a recruiting poster: a handsome young man in Marine camouflage uniform, his face streaked, his weapon at the ready, posing before a sand dune in the desert. The young hero of Desert Storm.

In his parents' living room, the young man recalls the way people cheered as his troop ship left San Diego harbor bound for Kuwait and then how shocked he was to learn, after the desert war, that he could not reenlist in his present position because of military cutbacks. He remembers the tumultuous homecoming ceremonies: the crowds blowing kisses at New York's JFK Airport, the pilot relaying words of welcome over the intercom from air controllers in cities below while flying back to California, the near-hysterical mobs upon landing, the parades back home in Texas. Painfully, angrily, he remembers his search for work: opening the newspaper every morning, reading want ads, going to employment offices, applying to a local police force and being put on a waiting list with more than two hundred applicants. Months later, he files for unemployment. "I felt worthless," he says. "You'd meet friends and they'd say, 'What do you do?' and you'd say, 'Well, I just got out of the military,' just to change the subject of being unemployed."

In Charleston, South Carolina, a Catholic priest in his late forties who marched in civil rights demonstrations during the Sixties worries about Americans who increasingly seek to elevate their "rights" at the expense of the rights of the greater community. "I had high expectations for our country after the civil rights movement," he says. "Then Vietnam and Watergate happened, and Irangate. When you think of all the ways in which our government and our institutions—and even my church—have always shown themselves to be less than we hoped them to be, I'm fearful we'll have more of the same. I'm not sure what will make a difference from everybody protecting their own rights and privileges to moving to a common sense of purpose, a more community sense. I keep saying this is a critical time, this is a critical time, and yet we get more of the same. That's my biggest fear, that we're going to reach the millennium and we're going to still allow the differences among us, which are real, to become sources of division and not sources of diversity. This is a crucial period, and the longer it goes on, the more crucial it becomes."

In Durham, North Carolina, a young law student at Duke University, about to graduate at the top of his class, reflects on a widespread feeling among his age group: that his generation will not be able to enjoy the life-style of their parents. This makes them feel cheated, he says, of a living standard it was assumed they would achieve. "For the first time," he says, "I feel that a group of Americans is going to have to deal with the idea that they're not going to live as well as their parents. To even live at their parents' level they're going to have to rely on their parents and their parents' money—which is very frustrating for a nation that prides itself so much on self-sufficiency."

His view, which is repeated across the nation, is echoed by parents as well. "Life is going to be a lot tougher for our kids than it was for us," says a father of two young children in Oakland, California. "We've borrowed their future to party it up for the last decade. I don't know how the hell they're going to dig their way out of it. Ironically, the globalization of the economy is making happen exactly what we wanted to happen when we were liberal, hippie college students, which was: our greedy American industrial society is being forced to share the wealth. The problem is we're doing it by giving away all the jobs to *other* parts of the world. That is going to make the standard of living and life in this country a lot tougher for our children. They're never going to be as well off as their parents were."

In New York, in a skyscraper overlooking Wall Street and the waterfront, a top executive of one of the world's leading construction firms cites America's failure to repair its crumbling infrastructure of bridges, highways, and transportation systems as a typical American desire to put off action on long-term problems. Only a crisis, he says, galvanizes the people into long-term concerted action. He recalls his initial shock after going underground in one of the subway tunnels that makes the city run. "It was chilling to me that something as grand as the subway system could have gotten to the point that it did," he says. "There was seepage everywhere. You were literally in a Venice-like environment. It was just rotting away."

We talk about this man's role in rebuilding that system, and of my own experience in going hundreds of feet below New York to where a tunnel is being built to provide the city's water. When completed, it will permit reconstruction of two other tunnels that date far back into the nineteenth century. One of them, I'm told, is so bad that inspectors don't turn the valves for fear they will collapse or malfunction. "It's no wonder that basic infrastructure gets ignored," the construction executive says. "In the short run, why care about it? Why is it necessary? As long as you can get to and from work, and as long as there's some hope of being able to drive your car where you'd like to, and as long as your house is still standing, and as long as the dams are still standing, fine. Let someone else worry about it. I'm one who actually believes that crises are what make the country. In a democracy, that's about all that can galvanize people—either a real crisis or one that's manufactured. But I've been saying this to myself for twenty years and the crisis still hasn't happened. Or maybe we've been in one for the last twenty years and don't want to face it."

In Topsham, Maine, I snap off the tape recorder and thank the two teachers at the Woodside Elementary School. As I prepare to get up from the little desk at which I am seated, I ask if they want to add anything else to what I believe has been a reassuring, highly optimistic conversation in a cheerful classroom.

A strange look crosses the face of the younger teacher, a man in his late twenties. He didn't think he was going to tell me this, he says, particularly after saying how proud he is to be an American and to be at the school, but he and his wife are thinking of leaving—not just Woodside Elementary, but the United States.

I turn the recorder back on.

That weekend he and his wife had attended a four-day conference in Boston at which recruiters from one hundred countries interviewed American teachers interested in jobs in other lands. He was interviewed for a teaching position in Tokyo. "It's ironic," he says, "because here we are talking about how we can make America great, and how we want to have our children grow up and be aware, and my wife and I are talking about making a decision—even with a two-year-old and one that's not even born yet—to go someplace where we will be financially set, where we will get everything we need, where the schools will have everything we could possibly want."

His colleague is listening intently, and she, too, has a strange look. It turns out that she and her husband have also been talking about leaving the United States, in their case after reacting to news reports of increasing crime and economic hardship.

I'm stunned, and tell them so. Nothing in our conversation has given any hint of this kind of vexed and troubled shift.

"My God," I finally exclaim. "Help me understand this better. Here we are in Topsham, Maine, looking out on a scene of pastoral beauty and tranquillity, in a place that has to be as far removed from the problems of urban America as anyone can imagine. I mean, we're not talking about escaping the Bronx or Harlem."

The young man speaks up first. "No," he says, "but the whole isn't good, and because you're afraid the whole will start to infect—"

His colleague interrupts. "You're afraid the Bronx will have spread into all areas," she says.

"It's like a disease," he explains. "It's going to catch on."

In Norwich, Connecticut, outside superior court on foreclosure day, a lawyer friend prepares me for what I'll see. Like a scene out of Dickens, he says, describing the explosive rate of home foreclosures in that part of the state. We step off the elevator into a sea of people. All are waiting for their cases to be called. Young women with babies, young men, well-dressed professional women, a woman with an artificial leg, an elderly couple holding hands while leaning against a marble wall—all are thrown together in a quick moment of chance. There's little conversation. Most people stare and wait.

"It used to be fun to practice law," a lawyer says, glancing at his clipboard with its extensive list of foreclosure cases to be called that morning. "You could put together deals. But now I deal with people who have been successes, who've done everything right, who saved, who made their payments. And all of a sudden, through forces beyond their control, they're losing them. They are desperate people."

Many are leaving this area, he continues. "Every day you'll see cars with Connecticut license plates with belongings strapped to the roof."

Like the Okies? I ask.

"Just like the Okies," he replies. "Reread the book, reread *The Grapes of Wrath*. The only thing different is instead of wicker chairs, you'll see VCRs strapped to the side. They're heading to places like

California where they aren't known. If you're well-known and successful, you know, there's a stigma of having failed."

In Mystic, Connecticut, at Ashby's Tavern, the lean young man with a sandy mustache joins a group of friends and neighbors who gather for a Sunday-afternoon jazz session—and a conversation that has become all too familiar to me begins. It deals with the notion that Americans have only themselves to blame for their problems, and it's up to them to solve them.

Many of those around the table have spent their lives building nuclear submarines at the installation in nearby Groton. Some come from families who built whaling ships there in the early 1800s. The young man with the mustache is from an old family in the area, too; he represents the fifth generation to make and sell velvet fabrics throughout the world. He's just returned the night before from a business trip to London, and he joins our conversation about the heavy impact of defense cuts in the New London–Groton area.

He listens, then says: "Maybe it's the best thing that ever happened to us. It's our own fault. We don't have anybody else to blame. We can't blame Reagan, we can't blame Bush, we can't blame the Japanese. We ought to stop blaming everybody else and face it. It's our problem. You know, we had a paradise here, but we're not taking care of it. Americans are just like water—we take the path of least resistance. We go downhill. We're becoming a nation of waiters and waitresses, and I don't look good in an apron."

CHAPTER 2

THE DREAM

$\mathbb{B}$y the early 1990s, the United States was mired in its eighth recession since 1950. In human and statistical terms, it did not approach the wreckage of the Great Depression, when one-fourth of the work force was unemployed, when no governmental safety net sustained the jobless and homeless, no governmental agency guaranteed bank deposits, and the nation's real gross national product fell by 50 percent over a four-year period. Nonetheless, the recession of the Nineties reveals underlying structural flaws that place it among historic economic tides that have reshaped the United States—like that of the nineteenth century when millions of Americans left the farm, and that of the early twentieth century when millions more moved from town and city sweatshops to new mass-production factory assembly lines.

Now the United States is being shaken by similar great change. "Restructuring," it's called, inadequately. It is a far-reaching, fundamental phenomenon the likes of which post–World War II America has not experienced. It affects every region of the country and raises questions about whether an era of unlimited American expansion is passing, and with it a way of life. Traditionally optimistic Americans, who believed in progress, in themselves, and in the American Dream, find themselves anxiously wondering if their old belief that tomorrow will always be better than today is still valid. To increasing numbers, it is not.

There is nothing new about the forces reshaping America. For nearly two decades, talk of "restructuring," "cutbacks," and "consolidation" filled boardrooms and provided grist for scholarly analysis and commentary.

First came the restructuring wave of the 1970s that crashed over America's manufacturing base and enveloped the Rustbelt, or "Smokestack America." That old industrial base eroded in the face of greater foreign competition and inefficient labor and management practices. The "downsizing," or "hollowing out," of corporate America caused heavy job losses.

Then, in the recession of the early Eighties, 4.2 million jobs were lost between June 1981 and January 1983. Job losses in the recession of the Nineties were even greater than during the early Eighties, and occurred over a shorter period. From June 1990 to January 1992, 4.5 million jobs were lost, 300,000 more than the losses during a comparable period a decade before. These were not cyclical layoffs; these were permanent.

Day after day during the presidential campaign year of 1992 such industrial giants as General Motors, General Electric, IBM, AT&T, Xerox, Sears, Unisys, DuPont, and TRW announced major reductions in plant and personnel. As only two examples of the severity of these cutbacks, IBM went through five major restructurings in which the jobs of 100,000 of its workers were eliminated, a quarter of its factories closed, and the company sustained its first annual loss of nearly $3 billion, and General Motors cut 74,000 jobs, announced plans to close twenty-one more factories, and slashed capital spending.

Those kinds of losses continued after President Clinton took office. In the first week after his inauguration, four more corporate giants—Boeing, McDonnell Douglas, United Technologies, and Sears, Roebuck—announced the elimination of 100,000 "good" jobs providing full-time work at high wages with full benefits. Housing sales fell nearly 14 percent in the month after Clinton became president, the sharpest drop in eleven years, and new government figures showed a further dismaying widening of the distances between Americans along economic lines: more than 10 percent of all Americans were receiving welfare food-stamp assistance, the Agriculture Department reported, the largest percentage of Americans to use the program since it began in 1964.

New convulsions continued to shake IBM and GM, with tens of thousands more job cutbacks announced. And on the day after President Clinton's State of the Union address, in which he laid out his program for economic revival, Boeing announced the elimination of still another 23,000 jobs, with 5,000 more to come in 1994.

Those Boeing cuts underscored the long-term restructuring problem facing the American economy. Boeing's wages were the highest in the state of Washington, and, as in similar job losses, there was a ripple effect. For every Boeing job lost, it was estimated that another three would be lost in related businesses serving the huge aircraft manufacturer.

Until the recession of the Nineties, the rapidly expanding service sector was thought to embody the growth of the future: a largely white-collar base composed of diversified industries that moved beyond the old factories into such fields as airlines, finance, accounting, trucking, telecommunications, advertising, health care, real estate, entertainment, and computer, sales, and information businesses.

This was believed to be the foundation upon which postindustrial America would be built, and it constituted the largest segment of the economy. Whereas by the Nineties the manufacturing sector employed about 20 percent of the American work force, the service sector employed more than 60 percent.

Service sector growth fueled the boom of the Eighties, generating nearly twenty million new jobs in that decade. It was expected to provide even greater growth after the recessionary cycle of the early Nineties ran its course. Instead, something ominous occurred. Leading banks, insurance companies, airlines, and accounting and legal firms were forced to grapple with the same brutal problems—ranging from reorganization to outright bankruptcy and failure—that for years had diminished the industrial base. Even strong service sector companies found they were not immune to wrenching change. Among them were such service sector giants as BankAmerica, Pac-Tel, Peat Marwick, and Skadden Arps. The banking industry alone estimated the loss of 100,000 jobs in 1992.

Some economic studies laid out a staggering forecast. They estimated that four million fewer service sector jobs would be created by 1997 than the growth patterns of the past fifteen years had indicated. This at a time when the good jobs that provide the way up for Americans, offering opportunity to purchase homes and send children to college while giving health and pension protection for retirement years, are rapidly becoming relics of the past. Now, "temporary" jobs—those with no benefits, no security, and minimal wages—are the wave of the future. When Clinton became president, the government projected there would be 35 million such "temp" jobs by the year 2000. Half of all workers would fall into that category, and two-thirds of all women workers.

There are economists, too, who believe the United States now stands at the beginning of one of the economic "long-wave downturns" which occur at intervals of forty-five to sixty years. These take place when the economy emerges from a period of great overexpansion of capital plant and large accumulation of debt from that expansion—as in the Twenties and the Eighties—to a period resembling a great depression. That is when the debt is repaid and there is no need for additional construction because the industries involved in that construction have fallen on hard times. As consumers and businesses pay back their debt, the money supply is reduced and thus the demand for it. The country therefore faces falling demand in the face of excess capacity—a condition that produces major economic stresses like those of the Nineties.

Compounding all these long-term forces are two other factors. The first involves spending for defense. With the Cold War over and the ranks of the permanent military establishment facing reductions of a fourth or more of its strength, a crucial underpinning that has sustained the U.S. economy for nearly half a century is being removed. This means further difficult restructuring of the industries, and the high-wage jobs that filled them, upon which a significant sector of the American economy has rested. The second factor involves the increasingly pessimistic attitudes of the people about their future, especially about the jobs they and their children can expect to have.

There are many reasons for the pervasive doubts that I encountered during my journey, and not all of them spring from the obvious economic problems. Everywhere, people express a gnawing uneasiness about what kind of country America is becoming. Everywhere, they are concerned about the purposes and values of the society. They know America has failed to face up to long-festering problems of crime and random violence in its cities and in the deterioration of its public schools; that it has yet to find a way to deal honestly and openly with race relations and with the other cultural and ethnic conflicts that divide the nation; that the very diversity Americans rightly view as a source of national strength and pride can also become a liability under group pressures to conform to new standards of "political correctness" and "multiculturalism"; that the breakdown of families, neighborhoods, and communities and the accompanying erosion of personal responsibility are symptoms of national decline. They know, too, that the special place America has occupied since the end of World War II is fast changing, that the rate of change is accelerating rapidly, leaving them feeling the postwar world they so signally helped fashion is outstripping them and that they must struggle ever harder to catch up.

But more than anything else it is fear over the economic future that most powerfully affects Americans. At the most elemental level, it is a fear that the American standard of living no longer can be sustained.

Long before the Nineties, that process of decline was already taking place. For two decades the American standard of living has been declining as real incomes—wages and salaries adjusted for inflation—stagnated. From the end of World War II to the early 1970s, the U.S. economy grew at a rate that enabled its people to double their standards of living over a generation. Over the next twenty years, as the restructuring of basic industries was underway, America's growth rate was so low that it will take a century to double standards of living.

The consequences of the Eighties, with explosive rising levels of public and private debt and dramatic transfer of wealth, accelerated these trends and intensified the public feelings about them. During the Eighties, those at the top profited immensely at the expense of the eroding middle class and the rising numbers of Americans at the bottom.

A study of U.S. income trends in the 1980s by the Center on Budget and Policy Priorities in Washington, based on detailed data from the bipartisan Congressional Budget Office,* concludes that "income disparities between wealthy and other Americans have widened significantly." It adds: "The most affluent Americans reaped exceptionally large income gains during that decade, while middle income Americans gained little and low income Americans fell further behind. As a result of these trends, the richest 1 percent of all Americans now receive nearly as much income after taxes as the bottom 40 percent of Americans combined. Stated another way, the richest 2.5 million people now have nearly as much income as the 100 million Americans with the lowest incomes."

The study also notes that the widening gap between the wealthiest Americans and the rest is only a relatively recent phenomenon. Between 1950 and 1970, it says, income disparities actually *narrowed.* "This pattern reversed itself in the 1970s," the study states, "as disparities began to grow modestly. Disparities then grew more sharply in the 1980s."

In the Eighties, too, wealthiest Americans benefited the most from tax cuts. The effective tax rate on the wealthiest 10 percent of the population dropped by about a seventh, declining from 28.6 percent in 1980 to 24.5 percent in 1985.† Another shift intensified the economic inequity. By the Nineties, heads of American corporations were earning more than *ninety* times as much as industrial workers, a stunning disparity that had more than doubled in a decade—in 1980, they were earning *forty* times more than workers.

Not by coincidence, it was during the same period of massive "restructuring" of the industrial and service sectors and the further dramatic shifts in wealth that increasing numbers of Americans began to feel something fundamental had gone wrong with the country. By the 1992 election, for example, national opinion surveys con-

*The CBO data tables, upon which this study rests, are based on data from four sources: the annual population survey of the Census Bureau; annual income statistics compiled by the Internal Revenue Service; a consumer expenditure survey by the Bureau of Labor Statistics; and the National Income and Product Accounts.

†Kevin Phillips, in his important *Boiling Point: Democrats, Republicans, and the Decline of Middle-Class Prosperity* (New York: Random House, 1993), persuasively documents the plight of the middle class, and writes: "The ultimate fiscal truth of the early 1990s was that for America's two or three hundred thousand somewhat rich or genuinely rich families, combined taxes as a share of income were probably at their lowest point in more than sixty years, whereas for middle-class families, combined federal, state and local taxes took a higher portion of income than ever before and were rising steadily."

sistently reported that seven out of ten Americans believed the country was on the wrong track. Out of fears that the American Dream was fading were forged the actions of voters that determined the presidential election.

It was against this background that William Jefferson Clinton, the forty-second president of the United States, strode down the packed aisles of the House of Representatives a month after his inauguration to deliver one of the most somber presidential domestic challenges to the American political and economic systems since the depths of the Great Depression.

Clinton's nationally televised message to a joint session of Congress was distinguished not because he called for a new direction for America. Every new president does. It was notable for the starkness of the economic portrait he drew and for the degree of the sacrifice he said was needed to remedy it.

"Unless we have the courage to start building our future and stop borrowing from it," he said, "we are condemning ourselves to years of stagnation, interrupted only by recession, to slow growth in jobs, no growth in incomes, and more debt and disappointment. . . . If we don't act now, you and I might not even recognize this government ten years from now. If we just stay with the same trends of the last four years, by the end of the decade the deficit will be $635 billion a year, almost eighty percent of our gross national product, and paying interest on that debt will be the costliest government program of all. We'll still be the world's largest debtor, and when members of Congress come here they'll be devoting twenty cents on the dollar to interest payments, more than half of the budget to health care and to other entitlements, and you'll come here and argue over six or seven cents on the dollar, no matter what America's problems are."

Within a week, Clinton laid out the other side of his plan: how the United States' role in international commerce would have to change, and the steps he proposed to achieve it. His speech at American University in Washington, D.C., was an attempt to link America's domestic economic problems with the tides of international commerce.

Saying that America stands "at the third great moment of decision in the twentieth century," he posed the question for the nation as whether it would repeat the mistakes of the 1920s and 1930s by turning inward or repeat the successes of the 1940s and 1950s "by reaching outward and improving ourselves as well."

Clinton's description of the post–Cold War world in which America found itself was one that people I met throughout the nation would instantly recognize, and had worried about, for in one way or another they all knew their lives were being affected by that world beyond America's borders:

> Whether we see it or not, our daily lives are touched everywhere by the flows of commerce that cross national borders as inextricably as the weather. . . . When a firm wants to build a new factory, it can turn to financial markets, now open twenty-four hours a day, from London to Tokyo, from New York to Singapore. . . . Now if you buy an American car, it may be an American car built with some parts from Taiwan, designed by Germans, sold with British-made advertisements, or a combination of others in a different mix. Services have become global. The accounting firm that keeps the books for a small business in Wichita may also be helping new entrepreneurs in Warsaw. . . .

In the early weeks of Clinton's presidency, as he carried his case for change to the country, the shape of an even more ambitious presidential effort emerged. What Clinton held forth before the American people made it seem as if he were proposing sweeping action: a far more activist role for the federal government, reversing the social and economic policies of the Ronald Reagan/George Bush years; an industrial policy, though not called by that name, in which the government would attempt to play a leading part in assisting specific American industries to compete more effectively around the world; a major reordering of federal spending by transferring billions of research and development funds that went for defense during the Cold War into spurring U.S. high-tech industries; a multibillion-dollar effort to retrain defense workers for other kinds of jobs; an infusion of additional billions into the nation's long-neglected infrastructure of roads, bridges, dams, aqueducts, and air and rail facilities; and a reversal of federal land policy, which for more than a century has benefited private developers at the expense of the public. Clinton's approach placed greater priority on conservation and protecting the environment.

In addition to these initiatives, Clinton sought to change the social context in which national treasure is spent and allocated. He proposed to do far more, for example, for children, for immunization, for research, for public health clinics (including, by issuance of an executive order, removing the previous administration's ban against abortion counseling at such facilities).

Most difficult of all to achieve was his goal of reordering the entire national health care system to ensure that it provides, nearly half a century after Harry Truman first called for it, a genuine national health insurance system available to every American.

These changes, if implemented, would indeed produce a new relationship between the government and the people. They would reverse the trend, which crested with the Ronald Reagan presidency in the Eighties, of a minimalist government bent on privatizing formerly vital public functions and, through employing the old concepts of laissez-faire, letting the private marketplace be the dominant force that determines the nation's course.

Clinton's stated approach was the opposite: a more activist government, one that attempts to rekindle not only the U.S. economy but the U.S. spirit by encouraging new involvement in public service. His proposal to create a domestic version of the Peace Corps would make it possible for Americans, through financing like the G.I. Bill before it, to have their college educations subsidized by the federal government in return for their later service as teachers or policemen.

Taken together, all of this left the impression that he was attempting nothing less than a restructuring of the entire American political and economic system. In reality, he offered considerably less—and even what he did propose became imperiled by his own early missteps and by the political forces that quickly formed to oppose and thwart him.

Bill Clinton came to power out of the political mainstream. His models are political improvisers like FDR, absorbers of information like JFK, students of political power and governance like Senator J. William Fulbright of Arkansas. Clinton had worked for Fulbright as a young aide while attending Georgetown University before winning the Rhodes Scholarship that—as happened with Fulbright himself decades before—profoundly influenced his life.*

Not since Lyndon Johnson has a president been so avid a student of the political process, and particularly of the intricacy and interplay of domestic issues. At the core of his belief, growing out of his own experience of poverty and personal hardships from a broken home, is a conviction that government should play a major role in alleviating social inequity and expanding economic opportunities. These convictions represent much more than easy political sloganeering so often employed by presidents; they are, people who know him best are certain, deeply held beliefs. Clinton also came to office as the first president in sixty years not shaped by the two great events that created modern America: the Depression and World War II.

In the twenty-eight years from 1933 to 1961, the United States was led by three presidents. They were the great commanders of World War II: Franklin D. Roosevelt, Harry S Truman, Dwight D. Eisenhower. Each of them was forged by the difficult times of the Depression. In the next thirty-two years, from 1961 to 1993, and reflecting the increasing destruction of national leadership, seven men sat in the White House: John F. Kennedy, Lyndon B. Johnson, Richard M. Nixon, Gerald R. Ford, Jimmy Carter, Ronald Reagan, George Bush.† Each of them wore the uniform during World War II; each came of age during the Depression. Much was made of the generational shift of power from Eisenhower to Kennedy. In fact, as Kennedy himself remarked, it was more a case of junior officers of the war assuming control from the old generals of that conflict. Until Clinton, these men were all also strongly shaped by the mentality— and the realities—of the Cold War.

With Clinton, the nation marks the first true generational shift in

---

*I am not one of those who claims to be a "Friend of Bill," but I do have strong recollections of the young Clinton who was a Fulbright aide in the mid-1960s during the year I worked out of that same office preparing a biography of Fulbright. I had no sense, of course, that here was a future president, but I do remember that he impressed everyone as being bright, hardworking, and ambitious.

†The toll of this destruction can be measured by the fate of these seven presidents: one was assassinated, one driven from office by an unpopular war, one forced to resign under threat of impeachment, three turned out of office by the voters after one term. Only one, Reagan, was given a full two terms in which to govern.

a lifetime. Everything in Clinton's life bespeaks those new circumstances. He was born in 1946, exactly at the point when the United
States possessed the largest share of the world's resources and was
the unquestioned international leader economically. It was during
his formative years that the notion of American decline began to take
hold. Clinton was still in his twenties when America's international
competitive position weakened notably in the early 1970s with the
move of manufacturers offshore. In that same period, the increasing
vulnerability of the United States was driven home by the shock of
the Arab oil embargo that ignited an inflationary cycle resulting in
the highest interest rates since the Civil War. By the late 1980s, the
idea of an America in historic, perhaps irreversible, decline became
more fashionable through the writings of such academic "declinists"
as Yale's Paul Kennedy, author of *The Rise and Fall of the Great
Powers.* The major economic restructuring of America's industrial
and service sectors that was the backdrop for the 1992 election reinforced that gloomy proposition.

Clinton is also the first American president to come to power
during the post-atomic age—the first to be born after Hiroshima, the
first fully to face a world in which the two great superpowers of the
United States and the Soviet Union no longer divide and dominate
the globe. He is the first, too, to reach maturity during the acrimoni-
ous Vietnam War that so divided the nation and his own generation
along class and ideological lines. Like many of his age and college
background, Clinton opposed the war, protested against it, and successfully avoided service. While many professional military officers
and enlisted personnel resented him as having been a "draft dodger"
while they were fighting in the jungles of Southeast Asia and their
colleagues were dying, an equal if not greater number of his fellow
citizens who had been influenced by that same experience did not.

Nor did they judge his private life according to the strict moral—
and often hypocritical—codes of the past. Invariably, people I talked
to on my journey did not care that much about Clinton's personal life
or the fact that he had had problems in his marriage—or used marijuana, either. So what? was the typical reaction. Herein, too, lies a
significant generational change: baby boomers like Clinton are the
first group to come of age in a society in which fixed concepts of
marriage and infidelity are no longer so resolute. All too many Amer-

icans have firsthand experience of divorce and the difficulties of living together. John Wayne long since has passed as the quintessential
American hero. Now it is more an antihero like Jack Nicholson who
sets the national tone.

Generational change also breeds new generational conflict.
Young Americans, facing a national debt they did not create, resent
being asked to pay for older Americans—and more of them—when
they themselves doubt they can expect similar support in their retirement years. They are aware that by the time one more generation
reaches maturity, the proportion of Americans aged sixty-five and
older will have increased from one in every eight persons to one in
five. Misunderstanding and conflict have always divided generations,
but in the world younger Americans will inherit, they see fewer jobs,
more domestic strife, more failure to pay for the changes that keep
American society functioning effectively.

Younger Americans are becoming increasingly aware—and
angry—that the supposed surplus of hundreds of billions of dollars in
Social Security trust funds set aside for their retirement years does
not exist. Instead of accumulating to $4 trillion by the year 2015, as
grandly announced after a 1982 Washington Social Security "summit
crisis" conference, the supposed surplus has actually been *spent* to
cover the federal government's annual general operating deficits. No
surplus exists.

This sets the stage for a fiscal crisis of unprecedented proportions
about the time Bill Clinton's baby boomer generation reaches retirement age. It also intensifies the struggle over who wins and who loses
in the allocation of limited resources. Not the least of the pain involved in this looming "entitlement" struggle will come over the
battle to reverse the present national priority that provides $14 in
benefits for the elderly to every $1 that goes for children.

Generational change also extends to the way politics is perceived—and played. Clinton is the first president, for example, to
employ all devices of the electronic age. If Roosevelt was the first to
use the medium of radio to forge powerful political bonds with the
people, Kennedy the first to embrace television on a regular basis,
and Reagan the first to govern through the electronic airwaves by
staging virtually every public event for the cameras, Clinton is the
first to go beyond the traditional networks to reach young Americans

of the MTV generation, the Cable Network News talk-show outlets like *The Larry King Show,* and the entertainment programs like Arsenio Hall's. The result is a new "talk-show democracy" that combines show-business-personality approaches to public issues with appeals for instantaneous action—and gratification—by pressure groups best able to take advantage of the connection between the mass electronic culture and the political class.

All of this symbolizes major change in American life, and it was that theme of change—at least the desire for change, if not the will to make the hard choices necessary—that determined Clinton's election. I was convinced, after only one week of talking with voters in Maine as the presidential year began, that George Bush would not be reelected. The only caveat lay in the Democratic Party's penchant to devour its own or again offer a candidate who could not win. But from the earliest days of my journey, the feelings I heard expressed about George Bush were so strong—and from lifelong Republicans who had voted for him and for Ronald Reagan twice—that it was obvious his reelection prospects were, at best, seriously imperiled. People did not hate Bush. He was not subjected to the venom that had been directed against Lyndon Johnson and Richard Nixon. Bush was simply seen as being hopelessly out of touch with the lives of Americans and with the hard new realities of American life. He was seen as irrelevant. Nothing more clearly demonstrated that to people than the highly publicized time—promoted, no less, by the White House!—when he went to a shopping mall, bought two pairs of athletic socks, and cited that as an example of how Americans could reverse the recession by purchasing more consumer goods. This was also the time when he expressed amazement—again for the TV cameras!—at the working of the supermarket checkout. He never recovered from that episode. From that point on, disparaging comments about him were legion, and from a wide segment of the electorate, not least among Republicans.

Bush faced another handicap. To a public feeling increasingly alienated from all politics, he was viewed as representing the most distrusted group of politicians—those in Washington, D.C., who were seen as ever more remote from their constituents and more beholden to the wishes of the special interests whose political donations enabled them to maintain their power.

Resentment of the capital is not new. Americans have repeatedly expressed their contempt for the workings of Washington, relishing and repeating such sardonic observations as Mark Twain's "There is no distinctly native American criminal class except Congress." But public attitudes about the performance of Washington have grown notably more negative.

Part of the reason for rising cynicism is the historic destruction of leadership that has rent the nation since John F. Kennedy was assassinated in 1963. Never before have so many strong voices, representing the widest range of political thought and belief, been removed so suddenly and tragically. The murders of the Kennedy brothers, John and Robert, and of the black leaders Martin Luther King and Malcolm X took four of the most compelling figures while they were still young men with their potential for greatest influence ahead of them. The forcing out of two other strong presidents, Lyndon Johnson and Richard Nixon, one over the foreign crisis of Vietnam, the other over the domestic turmoil of Watergate, further contributed to the sense of destruction of political leadership.

All of those events, coming against the backdrop of domestic unrest and uneasiness about America's economic future, had two significant results: they intensified a belief in national conspiracies and they made voters increasingly look beyond their capital in choosing their presidents.

Not by chance did Americans turn to governors from states as different as Georgia and California for their presidents in the years following the Nixon impeachment process.* Nor was it by chance that in 1992 they again looked outside their capital to pick their leader. Outsiders, presumably less contaminated with the sins of capital insiders, became the candidates who attracted the most favorable public attention beginning with the presidential primaries in New England. The more independent the candidate of Washington, the greater his public appeal.

Among Democrats, neither Paul Tsongas of Massachusetts nor Jerry Brown of California had held elective office for years. They ran as outsiders who sounded repeated warnings about the failures of the

---

*I exclude Bush from this because his 1988 victory over another Democratic presidential nominee who came out of the gubernatorial ranks, Michael Dukakis of Massachusetts, represented more of an extension of Ronald Reagan than a triumph in his own right.

traditional political system, including those of their own party. Among Republicans, Pat Buchanan had never held elective office and he, too, ran an insurgent's campaign that deeply wounded the GOP incumbent, George Bush.

Of all the candidates, the man who struck the most sparks was the one who claimed to be totally independent of the normal political process, Ross Perot of Texas. Perot's greatest appeal, which he skillfully exploited through the mass media, was his image as a person of such great wealth and demonstrated business success that he could not be bought by the special interests that supposedly held all of Washington in their grip. Like Paul Tsongas, he employed homely metaphors that appealed to the electorate. And like Tsongas, he was credited with bringing refreshing candor to the political discourse through a repeated mantra about the depth of America's long-term problems and the need for fundamental, even radical, change to resolve them. The engine's broke, and we have to get under the hood to fix it, Perot said over and over in the single most powerful metaphor of the political year.

In a matter of weeks, the relatively unknown Texan had ignited a spectacular grass-roots movement. That it was accomplished through the spending of his own vast wealth and through his extensive national exposure on talk shows does not depreciate the power of his appeal.

By late spring, as Perot became more of a force, I was encountering the most remarkable voter response to a candidate that I have witnessed in some thirty years of writing about national politics. The Perot appeal was not, as some suggested then and later, narrowly based. It extended across the ideological spectrum, embracing liberals and conservatives, Democrats, Republicans, and Independents. It attracted support from normally opposite groups of race and class. Nor was it limited by age or by region. I met Perot supporters who had been ardent backers of Barry Goldwater and Richard Nixon— and of Robert Kennedy and Martin Luther King. I found him appealing to students about to graduate from college and to retired professionals.

Two examples, of many, are typical.

In the retirement community of Santee, South Carolina, Jack Gates, a former partner in an upstate New York law firm, became so enamored of Perot that he helped organize a Perot-for-president movement, becoming its voluntary legal adviser and posting a "Perot for President Committee" sign on his front door. His motivation was America's growing debt—"a Frankenstein monster," in his words— and his belief that Perot offered the "best hope of getting this mess straightened out."

Seated in his living room, with his wife, Win, joining in the conversation, Gates produced a letter he had just written a son. Reading aloud, he said:

" 'My latest project is trying to get people to sign petitions to get the name of H. Ross Perot on the ballot so he can have a chance at least to get to Washington and try to straighten out the mess our beloved politicians have gotten us into. I feel sorry for you children and your children's children, to whom we have left a legacy of a debt which currently is four trillion dollars.' "

Looking up from his letter, he said: "I had never written out a trillion. It's twelve zeroes." Then, continuing, he read: " 'And growing this year at a rate of about thirty billion.' " Again, an aside: "It turns out it's actually closer to four hundred billion. My calculator went wrong." Then, still reading:

" 'In analyzing the effect the projected 1992 deficit of four hundred billion dollars will have on the current national debt, we find out we're adding at the rate of one billion, ninety-six million dollars a day, forty-five million, six hundred and sixty-two thousand, one hundred dollars each hour, which amounts to seven hundred and sixty-one thousand dollars a minute, which means we are plunging deeper into debt at the rate of twelve thousand, six hundred and eighty-four dollars every second and the clock ticks thirty-one million, five hundred and sixty thousand times a year. Each second the clock ticks we run up more debt than many millions of our population exist on for a year. In 1991, the interest payments on the national debt amounted to about thirty dollars for every hundred dollars of taxes collected. It's time we put a businessman in charge of the Oval Office, and it certainly won't be easy when you think of all the mealy-mouthed crooks we call congressmen who'll be in there trying to do business as usual for all their wealthy pals and contributors.' "

Therein was the voice of the authentic Perot protester expressing a host of grievances against the political system and those who led it in Washington. The Perot protesters were motivated by what they saw as the need for radical reform to save an America whose politicians were permitting it to sink dangerously into decline.

More complicated was the view of Raphael Winick, who was about to graduate from Duke University Law School.

He spoke from the viewpoint of a generation deeply conditioned to cynicism about political leaders and accepting, almost without question, the notion of conspiracies to explain some of the tragic episodes of recent American history. To his generation, he said, the Oliver Stone film *JFK*—perhaps the most extreme example of misstating of historical fact to spin undocumented conspiracy theories about a cabal of top government officials to kill Kennedy—rang exactly true. "Of course, that's what happened," he said. "We knew that. Why is this such big news? It didn't strike us as shocking. It was another story about some insider conspiracy and cover-up. For our generation, we've grown used to that stuff."

Winick's own experience deepened that sense of cynicism. He grew up in New York with private school classmates who were the children of such symbols of the Eighties as Ivan Boesky and Calvin Klein. "Our values were the most Eighties values you could possibly imagine," he said. "Like people would show up in ninth grade wearing Rolexes. That was the kind of thing we thought life should revolve around—wearing the newest Polo shirts, driving to school in Porsches."

He remembers hearing Boesky speak at his high school graduation; at the time he idealized Boesky. "We all knew who he was, and everyone knew how successful he was," he says. "Then in my freshman year in college he got indicted and was on the cover of *Time* magazine as being the biggest crook around. That really changed it; it did something in the back of my mind."

Other legacies of the Eighties made an equally strong imprint on Winick and, he believes, his generation. "When Len Bias, the basketball player, died of a drug overdose," he says, "just as John Belushi had done earlier, we all gave up drugs then. He was an athlete, in perfect health, and I know a lot of people my age who started eating healthy and changed their philosophies of life after that. The *Challenger* explosion was another thing that changed our lives. For my generation, everyone will remember that the same way your generation will remember where they were when Kennedy was killed. The *Challenger* explosion was something that said we're not as great as we thought we were. We invested so much of our self-worth in that, and then it failed.

"As an undergraduate I worked at a law firm as a paralegal in mergers and acquisitions. I worked on the RJR Nabisco deal, the Kraft deal, one of the big Robert Maxwell takeovers, and a lot of the deals I worked on eventually went into bankruptcies after hostile takeovers. It was all incredibly fast-paced, a lot of money going back and forth, no expense spared. And part of my job on RJR Nabisco was to go down to Winston-Salem and evaluate antitrust problems with the company. The workers knew who we were and they also knew the reason the deal was going to happen was so the company could be downsized and be more efficient, which meant they would get fired. We had nothing to do with firing them, but they thought we did. You could see the fear in their faces.

"We have morally ambiguous presidents and leaders who give us no direction," Winick went on, "which is the one thing you need. There's no one to say, 'Do this, this is the goal you should have, this is the direction you should take.' "

That was the political background that made Perot seem appealing to him. "America obviously made a lot of mistakes during the Eighties," he said, "and more important, I think it knows it. This year's campaign and the distaste for incumbents and the establishment is making the nation say, 'Look, let's take responsibility for some of the errors we've made.' On the other hand, the nation still doesn't know what's right and what's wrong. It's a nation that on the one hand will love the Gulf War, but a year later think of it as almost entertainment. It was good entertainment and made the country feel good for four months and that was it. It was a temporary diversion from other problems."

As for politics, he held a view that was typical of countless Americans of all ages and backgrounds: the political system was almost beyond redemption. "The most talented people of my generation are sitting it out," he said, "which is really too bad. We don't want to get involved. We grew up during the Reagan administration, when there were such transparent failures and such transparent fraud. So there's a sense of why bother."

In fact, Winick and millions of others *did* care enough to be involved. In the end, they turned out in the greatest numbers in a generation, reversing the steadily downward trend in every presidential election since 1960, when Kennedy narrowly defeated Nixon. Like so many others, Raphael Winick was looking for someone in whom to place trust. Initially, many like Winick were attracted to Perot, whom he described as "what everyone wants—an outsider, unlimited amount of money, doesn't play by the rules, a billionaire who's a real maverick."

Yet even then, while the campaign was still in its early stages, the way was open for a Bill Clinton kind of candidacy. As Winick said: "The nation would rally around anyone who finally had access to power who said I'm going to change. Clinton uses the word 'change' in every sentence he says. The cynics of my generation say, 'Well, how much is he really going to change anything?' But the nation would rally around an FDR kind of figure, a JFK figure—a *real* leader who wouldn't take any shit. Everybody is looking for a guy who would stand up and say, 'I'll take responsibility and I'm going to change everything.' That's why somebody like Perot seems to be getting so much support so quickly."

When Perot destroyed his own prospects by removing himself from the race within hours of Clinton's nomination in New York, thereby disillusioning innumerable people, he cleared the way for Clinton. Clinton was another outsider, but less threatening than a Perot, who even at the peak of his appeal stirred fears that he contained the seeds of an authoritarian figure, if not a dictator.

In the end, with Perot's subsequent in-and-out campaign actions during the election year and his increasingly prickly responses to any criticisms—which raised as many questions about Perot's character and temperament as they answered—Clinton was able to overcome doubts about himself by concentrating with single-minded intensity on the problems that most Americans wanted addressed: the nature of the economy, the shape of the future.

That is why so many people departed from their normal voting behavior to support him.

In his autobiography, *The Line of Fire,* published in 1993, Admiral William J. Crowe, Jr., chairman of the Joint Chiefs of Staff during the Reagan-Bush era, perfectly articulated this kind of attitude.

"I was dismayed by our lack of a sensible industrial policy, by our educational failings, and by the terrible divisiveness isolating so many citizens from the great American community that makes us a people rather than an assortment of factions," he wrote, in explaining why he broke ranks with the Bush administration to support Clinton. "I found myself increasingly disturbed by the Republican Party's tendency to exclude certain groups from the mainstream of American life and exploit antagonisms within the society. It seemed to me that our economic and industrial deterioration had replaced superpower confrontation as the greatest threat to our national security."

For all these reasons, the admiral said, he believed Clinton to be the candidate best able to "shake off cold war habits."

Clinton won, in part, because enough people shared Admiral Crowe's concerns. In signaling their strong desire for change, Clinton and Perot voters were also saying they understood that the price of change would probably be high and painful to them personally.

Judging by the people I met, not only did they understand that, they *expected* their president to propose truly strong action to deal with America's long-term problems, and particularly two of them: the rising debt and the shortage of jobs. Realistically, they understood that the process of real change would likely mean higher taxes and personal sacrifice. They also realized that results would not be achieved easily or swiftly. But they were ready to answer a call for concerted action.

Clinton had spoken repeatedly of the need for long-term solutions. Yet Clinton fell prey to the candidate's instinct to soften his message. He promised there would be no middle-class tax increase. He made no explicit calls for sacrifice. Unlike FDR or Churchill— or, for that matter, Perot—he issued no summons to unite in fighting a national danger as threatening as war itself. Neither did he attempt to prepare the public, as had FDR and Churchill confronting their crises, that conditions might worsen before they improved. It is possible he thereby missed a historic opportunity for a radical restructuring of the American economy and its governmental system; but the answer to that question will not be known until the success or failure of all his policies is judged much later in the decade.

There is no doubt why Bill Clinton won. His ability to strike the same notes day after day of the need for basic change and to do so in a reassuring, nonthreatening manner reminiscent of FDR enabled him to win a broad-based victory no Democrat had achieved since Lyndon Johnson in 1964: winning back blue-collar workers lost to Nixon and Reagan candidacies; carrying suburban and Independent voters who also had been defecting from the Democrats; sweeping the West Coast, taking states like Montana and New Mexico, dominating the Midwest, and forging a solid victory in the Northeast and the major industrial states like Pennsylvania, Ohio, Michigan, and Illinois. His victory was broad in range and in number of electoral votes, but narrow in popular vote, which was split three ways between himself, Bush, and Perot. Perot carried nearly 20 percent of the votes in registering the strongest third-party showing since Theodore Roosevelt's break from the Republican Party enabled Woodrow Wilson to win in 1912. As had John Kennedy before him (JFK defeated Nixon by one-tenth of a percentage point and carried only 49.7 percent of the vote), Clinton began his presidency with a shaky political base.

He *had* won a chance to govern and to see if he could fulfill his promise for change, but his victory did not banish the discontent with which Americans view their political system of gridlock and stalemate. And as public expectations had been raised, the stakes were higher.

Clinton's performance during his early months in office resembled a rocket—at times soaring, at others sputtering, at still others tumbling erratically. The outpouring of enthusiasm for the new young president at the time of his inauguration underscored the deep yearning in Americans to believe in their nation again and to have confidence in the future. To *The New Yorker*'s Philip Hamburger, who has written about fourteen presidential inaugurations starting with Franklin Roosevelt's first in 1933, Clinton's took place amid the "largest crush of hopeful humankind in my experience."

Bill Clinton's early days in power dashed some of that enthusiasm. His agenda of economic change immediately became diverted by intense controversy over his proposal to permit gays and lesbians in the military, prompting extraordinary comments of open contempt toward their commander in chief from officers and enlisted personnel on active duty. He was further deflected by embarrassing stumbles over two failed nominees for attorney general, each a young woman with little or no Justice Department experience. These failures resulted in large measure from Clinton's insistence on a cabinet that would resemble the diversity of America—a worthy goal, but foolish if that meant satisfying pressures to fill ethnic, racial, gender, and geographical quotas rather than excellence of the candidate. Because of these early missteps, Clinton appeared unusually slow to fill major appointments, adding to a sense of drift and lack of direction throughout the federal government. It was difficult to generate urgency about change without a governing team in place.

He found, too, as have all presidents before him, that no matter how determined he might be to focus on his main goal—in his case, restoring the economy—he could not escape the pressures of outside events. Some could have been anticipated. In the former Yugoslavia, daily televised scenes of carnage horrified Americans as Serbian forces continued their brutal "ethnic cleansing" of ancient Muslim foes in Bosnia, forcing the new president into an agonized and time-consuming—and, in the end, inconclusive—debate on whether to commit U.S. forces in conjunction with those of its allies to try to stop the slaughter.

In Russia, euphoria over the fall of communism faded fast amid rapidly deteriorating economic conditions and growing opposition to President Boris N. Yeltsin. Clinton was forced to devote more time and effort to assist Yeltsin through new U.S. economic aid. Other crises demanding his attention were unexpected—the terrorist bombing of the New York World Trade Center, and the disastrous governmental mishandling of a standoff between federal agents and cult members of the Branch Davidians in Waco, Texas, that resulted in the fiery deaths of men, women, and children.

Amid all these diversions and initial signs of political weakness, strong elements within official Washington began to take Clinton's measure and to react against him. Washington had been shaken by the election and the overwhelming evidence of growing public anger against it. For decades the capital had acted like the outpost of privilege and power that the American public so resented. Despite regular attempts at political reform, the connection between the lobbyists and the legislators grew stronger election after election. Costs of campaigns kept increasing; the lobbyists provided the money neces-

sary to win election through their political action committees. Once
elected, members of Congress had been virtually guaranteed reelection. The all-incumbent Congress was a fact, not a slogan; incumbents had been retaining their seats in over 96 percent of all elections.

All of these factors, plus the special rules and privileges the members enjoyed, contributed to a political climate in which the status
quo prevailed. Another factor worked against accomplishing real
change. The American political system, with its carefully crafted
constitutional checks and balances, was designed to make change
more difficult by deliberately setting up competing interests. The rise
of the political parties further institutionalized the forces of political
division along party lines. By the time Clinton became president,
divided government had become an accepted fact of life in Washington. Democrats had controlled Congress almost continuously since
the New Deal. Republicans, with the single exception of 1976 when
Jimmy Carter won by carrying only 49.98 percent of all ballots cast,
had controlled the White House since 1969.

Throughout this long period of divided powers, and despite the
increase in presidential authority during that time, Congress had
become accustomed to getting its way regardless of the White House
occupant. As Hubert Humphrey told me, in a conversation we had
about the problems Democrat Jimmy Carter was having with the
Democratic Congress in 1977: "Congress has asserted itself again. I
can't overemphasize the importance of this. Congress is no longer
afraid of the executive—particularly when you look at things like the
budget. I've heard dozens of people up here say, 'Well, I know that
Carter's got that in *his* budget, but what's *our* budget say?' And I'll
tell you something I hear people say now that you never heard
before: 'I've seen them come and go, and I'm still here.' They're
talking about presidents, you know. I've run through seven of them
myself."*

That attitude was shaken by the results of the 1992 election, when
anti-incumbency fever led to the greatest turnover in congressional
seats since 1948, broke the Republican lock on the electoral college,
and ended the GOP hold on the White House. In restoring one-party

*This conversation, tape-recorded in the months before Humphrey's death, is cited in my
account of the Carter presidency, *In the Absence of Power: Governing America* (New York:
Viking, 1980), p. 168.

control over both ends of Pennsylvania Avenue, the voters sent a message that all politicians were forced to ponder. They did, but their interpretation of that message differed markedly. Both parties recognized that some action—symbolic or real—would have to be taken to reduce the deficit. Clinton and the Democrats confronted the fears of their past about raising taxes—fears that were skillfully exploited by Ronald Reagan—and argued that increased taxes were essential to any real deficit reduction. Republicans bent slightly from the antitax sentiments of the Reagan years and publicly acknowledged that new taxes *might* be necessary—but only as a last resort and only after sharp spending cuts. Privately, they intended to unify their own badly splintered ranks, riven with ideological conflicts emanating from the Reagan era and recriminations over the Bush defeat, by branding Democrats with the epithet that had worked in the past: as "tax-and-spend" Democrats. They were aided in this approach by the magnitude of the new taxes Clinton proposed, taxes that, campaign promises notwithstanding, were to fall heavily on the middle class.

Clinton's initial stumbles, plus the awareness of political Washington about how narrow his victory had been—he won with only 43 percent of the votes and ran *behind* the winning margins of *nearly every* congressional member—opened the way for many of the old elements of the status quo to challenge him. He therefore began his presidency in a considerably weaker condition than Ronald Reagan had twelve years earlier. Reagan ran *ahead* of his party members in Congress and ahead of congressional Democrats, sweeping Republicans into control of the Senate for the first time since 1952. Reagan's popular appeal with voters produced the kind of political fear that caused surviving Democrats to break ranks and support his legislative program. That was not the case with Clinton.

From within Clinton's own party, barons of the Hill like Senator Sam Nunn of Georgia, who had flirted with becoming a presidential candidate in previous election cycles and was widely believed to be nourishing hard feelings for not being appointed Clinton's secretary of state, strongly and repeatedly criticized the new president's stated intention to remove the ban on gays in the military—a Clinton campaign promise that generated intense controversy when the president moved to fulfill it in his first week in office. From the Republican

ranks, Senate Minority Leader Bob Dole of Kansas, a dour man of
sardonic wit tinged with deep bitterness, had publicly signaled on the
very day of Clinton's inauguration that there would be no honeymoon for him from the opposition.

Dole, who had failed to win his party's presidential nomination in
1980, 1988, and 1992 and was a losing vice-presidential candidate in
1976, aggressively began to formulate a Republican strategy of resistance, based upon the use of the filibuster, to deny passage of Clinton's
program. During the Bush presidency, it was the veto that enabled
Republicans to thwart Democratic congressional majorities. Now, in
the Clinton era, it was to be the filibuster, the ultimate political tool
of obstruction. Even though Democrats had the numbers to pass
Clinton's program if put to a vote, they lacked the sixty Senate votes
necessary to kill a filibuster and thus were denied even an opportunity to give the measures a yes-or-no vote. The filibuster was not
foolproof—after a series of successes in blocking Clinton and the
Democrats' legislative proposals, six Republicans broke ranks on a
bill to simplify and increase voter registration by adding as many as
fifty million new voters to the rolls—but the threat of further GOP
filibusters continued to darken Clinton's early prospects. Dole's hand
was strengthened in this legislative tactic by Clinton's own failure to
appoint any Republican to his cabinet as a bipartisan gesture. This
would have enabled Clinton to tell the public that the American
economic crisis demanded an end to political partisanship and gridlock.

Unlike the last Democratic president, Jimmy Carter, who had
been unable to gain the support of even greater Democratic majorities in Congress than those enjoyed by Clinton, the new president
initially did forge a unified party front that enabled him to win swift
passage of the general outlines of his new budget proposals calling for
tax increases and reduced spending. His tax proposals also cleared
their first hurdle in the House of Representatives with good prospect
of passage. Privately, Democratic leaders in Congress said they understood their fortunes were tied to Clinton's. That is, they knew the
voters were expecting them to work together and produce real
changes. Congressional Democrats recognized they were on trial no
less than the Democratic president.

Outsider though he was, Clinton was seen by them as a far more

skillful politician than Jimmy Carter and someone with greater potential for effective national leadership. Further, Clinton demonstrated a capacity to connect effectively with people outside of Washington in televised town meetings and forums in which he made his
case for change. But he became mired again by the magnitude of the
changes he sought and by the desire to accomplish too many goals
within a short period.

"If I have one strong criticism to make about this administration," said a key Democratic leader after Clinton had been in office
four months, "it is that they are trying to govern by deadline. When
they don't meet the deadlines, they create a strong feeling among the
public that they have failed."

Actually, this leader had more than one criticism to make, adding that Clinton had made the mistake of rewarding his campaign
aides with important White House and administration jobs. In some
cases that was fine, he said. They were able people, even if inexperienced in Washington; but a president should not confuse the
skills necessary to win election with those needed to govern. Presidents must *govern;* politicians must *run.* There is a crucial difference.
Failure to recognize it can be politically disastrous. These criticisms
came from a major figure who wanted Clinton to succeed.

Similar concerns had already been sounded before the inauguration, when Clinton was starting to form his new administration. In
Minneapolis, where he was then practicing law, Walter F. Mondale
was alarmed when he saw a newspaper photograph of Clinton's new
White House aides, many young and inexperienced. Recalling his
own experience as vice president under Jimmy Carter and his many
years as a leading U.S. senator dealing with White House staffs and
presidents during times of crisis, Mondale viewed the Clinton team's
lack of experience as a major potential problem.

Mondale told me later that he immediately picked up the phone
and called the vice president–designate, Albert Gore, Jr., with whom
he had served in the Senate and had established close ties during his
own bid for the presidency in 1984. Clinton was making a big mistake, Mondale told Gore. He should pick senior advisers with solid
White House experience. A successful president *must* have seasoned
people around him. Clinton *needs* them, he went on, urging Gore to
appeal to Clinton to select from among many available people who

had served John Kennedy, Lyndon Johnson, or Jimmy Carter well. It did not happen, and Clinton paid a price as early initiatives began colliding and a sense of confusion of purpose and priority escalated.

Clinton *had* overloaded the system, he *had* set unnecessarily stringent deadlines—the health care plan was to be announced publicly by May 1, for example, one of numerous goals not achieved— and he *had* created an impression of someone trying to do too much too fast and in too scattered a fashion.

Beyond these problems, he faced growing questions about the wisdom of his many new proposals. Increasingly strident attacks from Ross Perot further added to the sense of new political fragmentation. Perot had formed a grass-roots political organization that within only two months was reported to have a membership exceeding one million, larger than either the Democratic or the Republican national committee had attained during the presidential election. Perot was again buying network time in half-hour blocks costing $382,000 to criticize the Clinton economic plans as being riddled with "Mickey Mouse stuff," and urging his supporters to place greater pressure for change on the administration and Congress. His critique of Clinton's economic program and presidential performance was scathing as he warned voters in a prime-time "infomercial": "You're going to sacrifice, pay more taxes, the budget will not be balanced, the debt will not be paid down, and spending is going to go through the roof." Even before Clinton's critical health care plan was announced, Perot again went on network television to warn that the president's plan could be doomed to "catastrophic failure."

Perot was also holding forth the prospect that he would be available to challenge Clinton in 1996. With this, Perot's own approval ratings rose dramatically; the number of those who said they might vote for him for president had more than doubled since the election. Ross Perot was the "real winner" in the first hundred-day shakedown period of Clinton's presidency, said the Democratic pollster Celinda Lake, who had conducted extensive polling for Clinton during his presidential campaign. Citing the evidence of public opinion survey results about Perot's appeal at the hundred-day mark, she said that "a whopping forty-six percent of voters, up from one-third, say they would consider voting for him, twenty-seven percent strongly. Majorities of Republicans, younger voters, younger men, non-college men, rural voters, and union households say they would consider voting for Perot."

Problems from Perot and Republicans aside, many of the criticisms of Clinton went beyond partisanship. Should he not cut much more spending before raising taxes and seeking funds for new programs? Would his program really *reduce* the national debt as advertised or substantially *increase* it by another $1 trillion as his own budget figures indicated at completion of his first term?* Was he acting as boldly as the conditions demanded and as the public wanted? Was he allowing himself to be seen as another politician who wished to please everyone?

Piece by piece he gave way: giving in to pressures from Democratic Western senators not to impose fees on grazing land and mining rights, thereby leaving conservationists feeling betrayed; scaling back his already small economic stimulus program from $19 billion to $16 billion and then to $12 billion before ultimately losing the entire package in humiliating defeat from a solid Republican filibuster which made the stimulus seem unnecessary and filled with pork-barrel political projects. Thus the centerpiece of his program was stripped from the agenda he presented to the public.

Further, he was forced to drop crucial parts of his proposal for the federal government to buy and distribute free all childhood vaccines in the United States; to drop his plan for an investment incentive tax break for small businesses; to alter his proposal for an energy tax; to scale back significantly the scope of his political campaign reform bill to curb special-interest spending by political action committees; to reduce similarly the dimension of his public service plan both in the number of those eligible and the amount of money to fund it; and to give way on imposing some of the proposed new taxes on the middle class that had alienated voters who believed he had broken his campaign promise.

As these setbacks occurred, the permanent power brokers of Washington—the lobbyists and the representatives of the special interests—began moving more aggressively to check Clinton. Some had been in a state of shock at the sweep of the changes Clinton

---

*Despite Clinton's insistence that his plan would reduce the national debt by nearly $500 billion, his own budget submitted to Congress projected annual budget deficits for his first four years of $264 billion, $247 billion, $212 billion, and $214 billion.

proposed, especially the reinstitution of federal regulations and reimposition of heavy new taxes. Now they took comfort in the belief they might continue to prevail as in the past—despite the new president and his ambitious program, despite all those new members of Congress who presumably had been elected to carry out real political and economic change.

One incident underscored the depth of Clinton's problems. At a White House meeting between Clinton and members of Congress, Richard K. Armey, a hard-right Republican conservative from Texas, stunned those present by mocking the Clinton program to his face. With contempt, Armey then predicted that Clinton would be a one-term president—this after less than three months in office. Former Senate Majority Leader Robert Byrd of West Virginia, a white-haired figure given to quoting the classics, responded indignantly. In his forty years as a member of Congress, Byrd said, raising his arm and pointing toward Armey, he had never heard anyone address a president of the United States in such a manner. Byrd then recalled battles of ancient Greece, warning Armey that those who draw the sword had better be prepared for war.

By the time Clinton reached his first hundred days in office, Clinton's own budget director, Leon Panetta, was publicly stating that his program was in serious trouble on Capitol Hill, and some of it was virtually dead. Privately, Democratic congressional leaders sounded even bleaker. "His program is in desperate trouble up here," one of them told me.

Clinton himself ruefully admitted to making mistakes and misjudgments. He acknowledged the need for a "tighter focus" on his political priorities as he regathered his forces by shaking up his White House staff for the greater battles to come. The greatest of these was over health care reform, and deep uneasiness over the massive cost of that process—estimated, inaccurately, in press speculation to require as much as $150 billion in new taxes—had settled over the administration and stirred new opposition among public and private interest groups and politicians. Clinton then, in effect, launched the second phase of his presidency by making regular appearances out of Washington. He appealed for public support to break the gridlock in Washington—and its gridlock mentality—and shifted the focus to deficit reduction rather than spending increases by endorsing legislation to create a new trust which would dispense federal tax revenue derived from spending cuts only for deficit reduction. And he urged Americans to stand with him to create the long-term changes he proposed. He acknowledged his own mistakes and conceded he might have misjudged the enormity of the task before him; change of the magnitude he sought takes time and cannot be accomplished easily.

In closing an Oval Office session with a group of *Washington Post* reporters, Clinton said he meant to read something to them. Then standing, and holding a sheet of paper, he began reading aloud from Machiavelli's *The Prince:* "It must be considered that there is nothing more difficult to carry out or more doubtful of success, nor dangerous to handle, than to initiate a new order of things. For the reformer has enemies . . . and only lukewarm defenders. . . ."

Here was a remarkably revealing glimpse of Clinton's thinking: the reformer battling his enemies and being hampered at the same time by lukewarm supporters. But he was determined to keep pressing for change, he said, and expressed confidence that in the end he would prevail with the backing of the American people.

Yet his words and defensive manner contributed to an impression of a new somberness at the White House. Public opinion polls again showed the American people becoming more cynical and distrustful of the Washington politicians. This came as government statistics showed a still-faltering economy—growth slowed markedly during the first quarter of his term, registering an anemic gain of only 1.8 percent. This was quickly followed by more bad economic news: the government's principal economic forecasting gauge, the "index of leading economic indicators" that projects economic trends six to nine months in the future, registered its sharpest drop since the depths of the recession two years earlier, igniting fears that another downturn was underway. As in the election year, seven out of ten Americans surveyed in a *Washington Post/* ABC News poll on Clinton's one hundredth day were again expressing the glum belief that the country was headed in the wrong direction—a sharp reversal from the optimism that greeted Clinton upon his inauguration.

There was one consolation for Clinton in these early findings. He still enjoyed the support of three out of every five Americans, and the greatest target of public scorn was Congress, particularly the Republicans, who were viewed as obstructing his efforts to create change.

This was significant, for while the battles that Clinton had begun over economic restructuring, debt reduction, health care, education, and welfare reform were being fought at the national level, their ultimate resolution will depend upon the support of those who live in the cities and towns and countryside of America. It was also true that Clinton had set the stage for a contest of historic proportions. By attempting to force Americans to confront hard choices and unpleasant truths, instead of accepting the illusions and outright lies that have characterized much of political discourse for years, he had triggered the first great national debate over America's direction and priorities in at least a generation, if not since 1933. With all its flaws and despite its initial setbacks, his was an exceedingly ambitious agenda that offered a vision of a different, and better, America in the years to come.

In the end, something more important than the success or failure of specific legislative, economic proposals in Washington is at stake. Adequate response to the deep underlying structural problems of American society must come from the people themselves, from outside Washington. Clinton's test is to reconnect the capital and the country in common purpose. The country's test is to find reason to believe the American Dream is no longer fading; either to work to reclaim the Dream or to invent a new one. As a teacher in Texas told me, "We're in a mess, but is anybody really hungry? Yes, we're hungry for a dream."

The Rev. Dennis Dickman, sitting quietly in his study in St. Paul's Lutheran Church in Waverly, Iowa, put into words as well as anyone I met the larger stakes for the United States in this critical transitional era.

"We've got to redefine who we are and what kind of people we want to be," he said. "We can no longer be what we once were. We could be much richer, much better. It's a unique time. I haven't seen anything like this before."

BOOK TWO

WINNING WARS, LOSING EPICS

CHAPTER 3

"THE JOBS AREN'T THERE"

*"It's like nobody's in charge of the other side any more.
I miss it," he says. "The Cold War. It gave you a
reason to get up in the morning."*
—John Updike, *Rabbit at Rest*

Over the decades, the Cold War did more than give people "a reason to get up in the morning," as John Updike's character exclaims. It was the central fact of American life.

Millions of Americans served in uniform during the Cold War, millions more made their living from it. New industries and new technologies, backed by some of America's most talented scientists and engineers, sprang up because of it. By far the greatest amount of money went for weapons development—the missiles and satellites and nuclear air and naval fleets—to sustain the newly emerging National Security State. At its peak, 70 percent of all money spent for national research and development came from the federal government, and the greatest proportion of that went for defense. By comparison, in the late Eighties the federal government was allocating only five-tenths of 1 percent of its research and development money for environmental protection and two-tenths of 1 percent for industrial development.

When it was over, when the $11 trillion it had cost was tabulated as the single greatest expenditure of treasure in the nation's history, Americans awoke to find that they and their leaders had made no plans, short- or long-term, for conversion of jobs, skills, and resources from defense into domestic purposes. It became painfully clear that a heavy price would be paid for their failure to anticipate that conversion and for the massive debts and internal disintegration they allowed to accumulate to support the long contest.

They discovered that the end of the Cold War removed the threat of a common enemy around which national consensus and unity of purpose could be achieved. In the absence of a Hitler, a Stalin, the Bomb, or communism and its "evil empire," Americans were left to ponder the wisdom of Walt Kelly's Pogo: the enemy is us.

Americans also confronted an old truth: it is harder to secure the peace than to win the war. Or as Tom Saturley, a young entrepreneur in Maine, remarked of America's tendency to live for the moment and not plan for the long-term future: "We can win wars, but I'm not sure that we can win sagas, and epics are real important."

The United States is a nation, but also a union of regions of immense variety and range. In America, on the same day, different people experience a fifty-degree-below-zero arctic blizzard in Alaska, bake in the heat of the Southwestern desert, and bathe in the waters of the Gulf of Mexico. These physical differences are unchanging, but in many ways what's distinctive about the regions is disappearing. What remains are swings of prosperity and recession, not always moving through all regions at the same time. However these cycles may differ, all regions have lost the ability to control their own destinies. The underlying structural problems they all face now are national and international in scope and long-term, not short-term, in duration. This means that Americans, the most migratory of people, may be discovering at last that they've nearly run out of space in which to escape from their problems. By the time they pick up stakes and follow the old path west, the region is filling up, the competition for jobs is at least as severe as in the places they left, and the struggles of daily life are much the same.

In the Northeast, where I began my travels, a depression, not a recession, gripped the region. The giddy Eighties, when speculators capitalized on soaring housing and land prices and when banks competed aggressively to extend credit for further residential and commercial expansion, were gone. New England had seen its real estate market collapse, its banks were failing at the greatest rate since the 1930s, its defense industries were being cut back severely, and the high-tech industries upon which much of its new prosperity rested were foundering. In less than three years, ninety banks failed in New England; and that figure does not include the savings and loan institutions that went under during the same period. Bank loans came to a virtual standstill. No credit was available, even to the best banking customers.

Gritty old towns like Lowell, Massachusetts, where the American industrial revolution was born through manufacture of textiles and which had been cited worldwide for its economic comeback in the 1980s after decades of decline, sank into even worse times—all the more so because it was so sudden.

Ten years before, I had visited Lowell to write about it as a new model of success. This time I found Lowell's condition desperate, and worsening. At three o'clock on the afternoon of my arrival, at the end of banking hours, federal and state regulators seized and closed the Central Savings Bank, an institution that had been doing business in Lowell for 121 years.

Customers began gathering outside, peering at notices taped to the front doors informing them that the bank and its seven branches had been closed and its assets turned over to MassBank for Savings, doing business in Reading. "I just hope I can get my money," Mary Zabbo, seventy-eight, kept repeating as she walked back and forth in front of the bank.

At that point approximately 80 percent of Lowell's banking structure had been wiped out. Banks that had marched in step with Lowell, helping finance its growth and prosperity, were gone. The Lowell Institution of Savings, which survived the financial panic of the late 1830s, the crisis brought by the Civil War when the supply of cotton was cut off from the mills, the bank crashes of the 1890s that led to the agrarian revolt and Progressive Era of reform, the Great Depression of the 1930s, and all the wars, large and small, and all the recessions, long and short, was forced to close its doors in late 1991.

Gone, too, was Commonwealth Fed, which had been the largest underwriter of mortgages in New England; the Union National Bank, which became part of the Bank of New England, which also failed; and the Lowell Bank and Trust. The high-tech business upon which Lowell had depended too heavily for its rebirth a decade

before was devastated,* defense budget cuts were affecting the manufacture of Patriot missiles in Lowell, and state and local governments
were going broke, laying off employees, cutting services. "That's like
having all four corners of the stool collapse at once," said George
Duncan, chairman of one of the few remaining success stories in
Lowell, the Enterprise Bank and Trust Co. "To me, that's what's
happened to New England."

The lessons of Lowell are not limited to Lowell. As someone
there told me: "Lowell is just Lowell. There are a million Lowells in
the country. They're desperately searching for a leader."

When he looks at Lowell, banker George Duncan is heartsick.
"It's not so much the unemployment figures," he says, "but what
goes with that. I had a customer in here not too long ago and I was
talking with his attorney, and he said, 'Jeez, George, you've got to
talk to him, because he's going to take the .357 solution if you don't
sit down and talk with him. I'm not saying make the loan or not, but
he just needs someone to talk to.' I guess the .357 is a .357 Magnum.
There have been suicides. Kids have been pulled out of college.
Wives have gone back to work if they could find menial jobs. The
losses are incredible. I'll be coming down Main Street and I'll see the
empty stores and I'll remember who the shopkeepers were and people who worked there."

In the past, local bankers who knew and respected their customers would advance credit in the strong belief that the businesses
would survive cyclical recessions and personal setbacks. They did so
out of a conviction that in the long run this was in their, and their
customers', mutual interest. But the days of the local banks were
over. Replacing them was a network of interstate banks that changed
the way financial business was transacted. The interstate banks themselves were part of the problem, for in the boom days they encouraged real estate speculation and eagerly granted easy loans. When
hard times arrived, they withheld credit even from their best customers and pressed for payment, a process that often led to bankruptcy. I

---

*Wang Laboratories was then on a tailspin toward extinction, having cut its work force
from fourteen thousand to three thousand and battling debts of more than $500 million.
Subsequently, it declared bankruptcy, then announced in mid-1993 a reorganization plan calling for the "reinvention of Wang"—a reinvention that would require the permanent elimination of one-third of Wang's remaining work force.

found examples of this short-sighted, and short-term, business mentality everywhere I went.

Major industrial cities like Bridgeport, Connecticut, long the financial center of southern Connecticut and once home to many Fortune 500 companies, reflected all these problems and more. In 1991, Bridgeport became the first city of its size to file for federal bankruptcy protection since Congress passed Chapter 9 provisions during the Great Depression—and this a city that is also the seat of one of the wealthiest counties in the United States, located in the wealthiest state.

In three years, Bridgeport's unemployment doubled, the city lost between eight and ten thousand jobs as companies folded or relocated, and citizens found themselves facing a deficit of $60 million that continued to rise as real estate values further eroded their tax base. By the time I arrived in Bridgeport, 15 percent of the population were on welfare, and their numbers were increasing. Four of the twenty banks that had failed in Connecticut were in Bridgeport. The city resembled a bombed-out Bangladesh: deteriorating streets and buildings, shuttered stores, increasing violence, and an air of palpable despair.

"From Portsmouth, New Hampshire, down to Norfolk, Virginia, maybe fifty miles wide, this is Uni-City," says Sam Marks, a third-generation businessman in Bridgeport. "It's one city, just one strip of millions of millions of people. And Boston is in trouble and New Haven is in trouble and Bridgeport's in trouble and New York's in trouble and Newark's in trouble and Philadelphia's in trouble, and we're all in it together."

He was right. The same grim conditions prevailed in all that area. During our conversation, Marks described how it felt to awaken at two o'clock in the morning, sit straight up, then fall back again as the weight of his problems hit him. "Behind the belly button, it's turmoil," he says. "You've got to be strong, because your people are holding on to you and you're trying to do everything you can not to let them down."

Marks is an example of a familiar American story: the family-owned business that prospers through generations of hard work and by constantly saving and reinvesting. His grandparents immigrated from Russia, started a company that sold kosher food, and branched out into a hardware store that survived as part of a larger $12 million family construction equipment business operating throughout Connecticut and the Northeast. When I asked what he thinks happened, he replied:

"Connecticut was technology. Connecticut built the best nuclear submarines. We had sophisticated radar detection things that can drop the bomb down your smokestack. We've got attack helicopters that have been the talk of several wars. We built tank engines here. We build jet engines in this state for the most sophisticated aircraft.

"The market is shrinking for that stuff. And the tax base in Connecticut went from a surplus to a negative, a billion-dollar swing in the blink of an eye. Connecticut has been providing these magnificently technical systems and things, nuclear submarines that can go under the ice pack and stay there for ninety days and never come up for a breath of air. Well, maybe they've got to learn how to build triple-hulled supertankers up there.

"Who is to blame, who is to blame? I don't want to dwell on the past, but what a gem we had here in Bridgeport. What a gem. I mean, with GE, with Columbia Records, with Underwood, with Remington Arms, with a lot of other well-known companies, really top-drawer stuff. We've got to change, and it's going to be painful. You ask what has happened, and I answer with a question. What has happened? Some basic thing has been moved out of place."

Months after we talked, Sam Marks was bankrupt.

There are, of course, successes, and examples of people's triumph over adversity. As in the American past, the lessons of their success are timeless. They succeed by personal initiative, hard work, individual attention to building a business, and pinpointing the audience they wish to reach.

On Main Street in Brunswick, Maine, two brothers in their mid-twenties, out of college and facing a bleak job market, had been "doing a little bit of everything," as one of them said. They did landscape work, sold Christmas trees, made holiday wreaths for customers in New Jersey. After studying the market in Brunswick, they opened their own video store.

They faced strong competition from a national video chain that already had established three outlets in Brunswick, and was, they

learned, renting between one and two thousand movies each week-
end among them. The brothers, Matt and Dave Cost, calculated that
out of Brunswick's estimated twenty thousand households there was
a potential market of five thousand VCR rentals per weekend. With
energy and enthusiasm, they raised the capital—that alone an impressive feat given the lack of loan money available—to open their
own Matt and Dave's Video Store. They stocked the store with foreign films and classics as well as the standard action-adventure-
porno fare. They cut prices, advertised overnight specials, "two movies for the price of one," and opened for business.

Matt and Dave's had been operating successfully for a month
when I stopped by. It was attracting precisely the additional customers the brothers had anticipated. A year later, it was still doing a
thriving business.

Also in Maine, a five-minute drive from the coastal resort of
Kennebunkport where George Bush vacations, I found an example
of the way the pressure of economic crisis can forge new cooperation
and sacrifice to create change. The John Roberts clothing factory
appeared to be going out of business when a bank announced foreclosure, threatening the loss of 170 jobs. Most of the workers were
women who did piecework—making men's suits, coats, and sport
jackets for customers as far away as Florida and California. It was
low-wage work, with hourly wages ranging from $6 to $9 in an industry competing directly with even lower-wage operations in Mexico
and overseas.

Instead of becoming another statistic of decline, the workers at
the plant, led by the union officials and with the backing of outside
investors, bought and operated the plant themselves.

The driving force in this venture is Mike Cavanaugh, representative of the Clothing and Textile Workers Union in Biddeford. At
forty, he's one of those Americans whose lives were shaped by the
college antiwar movement of the Sixties, but unlike many of his
peers, he has remained active in social causes.

Cavanaugh presented his idea to union members at the plant, and
they responded by raising several thousand dollars to hire a lawyer
and begin an appraisal of the factory and its assets. Women whose
previous experience had been as clothing stitchers joined with outside appraisers to study the company's financial records. Workers

agreed to 6 percent pay cuts, gave up all holidays, and changed their pension plan. Only health benefits were left untouched; protecting them was their bottom line.

Local banks were solicited for loans, but without success. Two outside entrepreneurs who had started a venture called Shared Ownership and Management, Inc., seeking to work with unions to form worker-ownership operations, agreed to put up $150,000. Shared Ownership operates under the management philosophy of W. Edwards Deming, the U.S. business pioneer whose ideas of stressing the quality of the work force were initially rejected by Detroit but embraced by Tokyo.

Later, a $600,000 loan was obtained from the National Cooperative Bank Development Corporation in Washington, D.C., which was established to deal with worker-owned enterprises.

When I visited the factory I saw a large poster with bold red letters that read: FEAR. Under it was a quote from Deming: "The job of management is to drive out fear." After nine months, results were positive. No workers had been laid off; the factory was making a small profit.

Ethel Beaudoin, who started working at the factory in the early Sixties and in the years since has operated a machine that attaches the welt (a man's small top pocket) to a suit coat, said she'll never forget the moment when they learned the factory was about to go out of business.

"A lot of us are single parents," she said, "and it was devastating to think, now what? What's going to happen to me? Am I going to work a different craft? Am I going to get a job at all? You go back to your machine and you start thinking, what if I don't get a job at all at my age? I'm fifty-three. And for a couple of days until the union stepped in and gave us an alternative, everybody was depressed and confused about what would happen."

In the year after the workers began operating the plant, Beaudoin's income dropped from $16,500 to $12,500, "so that's a big chunk out of my standard of living, but I still *have* a standard of living." As for the work, "It's a nice feeling to be part of the process . . . of deciding what this company buys for machinery and to know the customers more intimately. They're *our* customers, and it's a nicer feeling when the customers know that the coat that we put out is made by owners. It's almost like you're making it more personal."

These examples of underlying strength and perseverance are heartening, but they do not address the deeper economic problems which have made America so vulnerable in the Nineties. There is no mystery about these problems. They come down to what products America makes and what kinds of jobs Americans can expect to have in the increasingly more competitive future. Every American understands these facts, and, in one way or another, virtually everyone I met expressed growing concern about them.

In Brunswick, Maine, the experience—and the emotions—of Warren and Eileen McFadden are typical. Now retired, he at seventy-one, she at sixty-eight, the McFaddens are part of a vanishing generation shaped by the hardships of the Depression and World War II. They remain unabashedly patriotic. As one way of demonstrating this, they try to buy American-made goods whenever they can, but this has led to some frustrating experiences.

In buying a tape recorder, they debated whether to purchase a Sony or one made by General Electric. "We figured, well, they both look pretty near alike and they cost pretty near alike, so we bought the General Electric," McFadden recalls. "We get home and it's made in Malaysia! You can't buy anything electronic made in this country anymore. We bought a little television set, Magnavox. That's an American company. And we get that home and it was made in Mexico! It doesn't say any place where it's made except on a little corner on the box. We don't *make* anything. This new furnace I put in, the oil tank has got a sign on it, 'Made in Canada,' and all the pipes are made in Canada. I don't object to doing business with Canada, but it just seems that we ought to make *something*. And I don't see that we make anything anymore."

Their common frustration underscores a related, and greater, one: the anxiety and fear of people who are being trained for jobs that don't exist. In the immediate past, for instance, virtually everyone who graduated from the Central Maine Technical College in Auburn found work—and in the state of Maine. Not anymore. If the new graduates want work, they have to relocate, but they soon find that severe job shortages are nationwide, not just regional. Those still in school face another unsettling fact: the age composition of their classes. In Carl Hinkley's first-year automotive class, the ages range from the usual eighteen-year-olds to one man of fifty-eight. "He got laid off from the shoe factory up in Williston—Bass Shoe," Hinkley explains. "We're getting a lot of people who are coming here at a late age in life because their industries or their mills have shut down."

Bill Frayer, who has been an instructor at the Auburn technical school for fifteen years and now heads its communications department, sees many older students in his classes. "Some of them are very tentative and concerned," he says. "They don't have a lot of confidence, and I wonder how well some of them are going to do when they get out. Imagine going back to school at the age of fifty-five! It's such an adjustment."

But the more difficult problem is the one that Roger Bertrand, who chairs the electronics department, identifies: they are training and retraining people for work that no longer exists, not only in Maine, but throughout the United States. As he says, what good does it does do "to train people for jobs if the jobs aren't there?" The answer is self-evident. All it does is raise—and then crush—people's hopes, leaving them more despondent and embittered than when they began their new retraining process.

Clinton's new labor secretary, Robert Reich of Harvard, alluded to this problem when he acknowledged publicly during the early months of the administration that it would be "cruel" to train workers for jobs that don't exist. Yet that is exactly what is happening across America. All the trends indicate that this condition will get worse as automation and further restructuring of the U.S. economic base accelerate, producing more and more temporary—or "disposable"—workers who move from one part-time job to another. Such concerns, driven by fears of greater job losses to come, fueled working-class opposition to the North American Free Trade Agreement (NAFTA) with Mexico and Canada at the end of Clinton's first year in office.

By the time Clinton had completed sending his economic program to Congress, with its abortive jobs creation proposal that failed to survive the Republican filibuster, there was new evidence of the magnitude of the long-term problem. Beginning in March 1991, when the government determined the recession to have ended officially, and during the next two years of supposed recovery, the number of jobs nationally increased by only eight-tenths of 1 percent—the most dismal performance in any period of national recovery from recession dating back to the early 1950s. Of 1.66 million private-sector jobs lost during the recession of the Nineties, less than a third—510,000— had been recovered. At the same time, the Labor Department reported that temporary hirings made up two-thirds of all private-sector job growth. These "temporary" jobs, with low pay and no benefits, were not limited to the blue-collar work force; they encompassed new college graduates and increasing numbers of white-collar workers. In fact, as senior economic analyst Stephen S. Roach of Morgan Stanley & Co. notes, for the first time in the American experience white-collar unemployment was exceeding blue-collar joblessness by some 200,000 workers.

The failed Clinton jobs bill did not fundamentally address the problem that Roach describes as "the new silent majority suffering from white-collar shock." Its essential purpose was to create summer jobs for inner-city youths and to put blue-collar construction workers to rebuilding the infrastructure. Even had the stimulus program passed as proposed, it was so small and short-term that it would not address the greater problem that people like the McFaddens and the teachers at the Auburn technical school raise: what are the products that America will make that the world wants and what kinds of decent jobs can humans, not robots, expect to perform?

In the ebb and flow of American life, the industrial North and the agricultural South had long since begun to change places, with dramatic economic effects. While the Northeast battled stagnation and decline, the South prospered and rose. From the end of World War II to 1970, the South experienced its greatest growth, going from the nation's poorest and most backward region into a national symbol of economic rebirth. The South became the "Sunbelt." It glowed with new prosperity and optimism. It came to think of itself as free, if not immune, from the problems that plagued the old industrial North.

As is always the case, labels are misleading. The Sunbelt was always part reality and part myth. Reality is the unquestioned economic advance the region made. By adopting an informal industrial policy, the South aggressively courted industries to relocate there. In no small part, it accomplished this because its economy was based on low-wage, nonunion labor, low-cost land, and low taxes. This attracted mass-production businesses from the Northeastern mill towns and Midwestern Rustbelt factories.

By the time I arrived in the South in the spring of 1992, the area still stood in welcome relief to the depressing scenes I had witnessed throughout the crumbling Uni-City of the Northeast. Major international manufacturing entities dotted the countryside—a Mitsubishi plant or a Burroughs-Wellcome—taking their places alongside computer and high-tech forest products facilities. In eastern North Carolina, Weyerhaeuser boasted of having the highest-technology sawmill in the world. Weyerhaeuser was able to cut down trees in North Carolina, turn them into high-quality paper, and sell the product in Sweden for less than what Swedish paper cost. In Asheville, at Wilson Art Laminate, 25 percent of the countertops made were sold outside the United States.

Workers understood their linkage to a greater world beyond. They would tell you how this order was going to Australia, this to France, this to Germany, this to Brazil, this to Panama. They knew, too, that their jobs depended on their ability to be more competitive than their foreign rivals.

At the famous Research Triangle Park, located between the major universities of Duke, North Carolina, and North Carolina State and the cities of Raleigh, Durham, and Chapel Hill, fifty-eight major research facilities employed 34,000 people, generating a combined payroll of more than $1 billion. More significant, the Research Triangle was accomplishing exactly what its creators hoped a generation before: it was spawning other jobs around the state. The park itself has become part of the global economy; half of its employment came from multinational firms. Its areas of greatest growth were in businesses of the future: telecommunications, pharmaceutical, chemical, and biotechnology companies.

By any measure, the Research Triangle was a success—and a lesson. "One of the great things about this area is that between the three universities and the Research Triangle Institute there is something over half a billion dollars a year in research contracts that are virtually all nondefense," says Jim Roberson, president of the Research Triangle Foundation, which runs the Research Triangle Park. "They are very much concerned with health. If you look at the other major research centers and research universities in the country, enormous amounts of money they've received have essentially been for defense. That is now their problem."

At the same time, Roberson pointed to another reality—what some people call the lengthening shadows on the Sunbelt. "While the Research Triangle area encompasses about seven hundred thousand people," he says, "the rest of the state is suffering. In the eastern part of the state, and in the western part of the state, our public education is just absolutely in shambles."

The universities in North Carolina, like those throughout the nation, were experiencing enormous new financial pressures. Funding cutbacks had reached such a point that libraries of the major public universities were unable to subscribe to desired scientific journals. In the long run, of course, this affects the research work of scholars who are working to create new technologies.

This problem was directly attributable to the economic crisis of the Nineties, driven by the recession and the debts that were forcing public and private institutions to retrench and restructure. Longerterm forces were also at work that put the Sunbelt in a far more vulnerable position than many of its people at first understood.

Underneath the prosperity of places like the Research Triangle lies a deeply rooted structural problem of the Southern economy—its historic failure to invest adequately in its human resources. In North Carolina, for instance, George Autry, head of MDC Corporation, a distinguished Southern "think tank," cites a startling figure. "The productivity of our skilled workers in the Saturn plant and Honda and Toyota plants is as good as in Japan," he says. "But we've got more functionally illiterate adults in North Carolina than does all of Japan—and Japan's got ninety-five million more adults than North Carolina. That's one of our Achilles' heels."

While the Sunbelt was changing in the years after World War II, assisted by new industries and the showering of federal programs and money on the region as the old segregated system finally collapsed under sustained national pressure for change, the underpinnings of its economic life were also shifting, with profound implications for its future. Beginning in the 1970s, what had been assets for the Sunbelt— its low wages, its low taxes, and the rest—suddenly became liabilities. Like New England before it, the South found itself competing with far cheaper labor, this time offshore in places like Singapore and Mexico. As Autry says, "The years when we had an unlimited number of Yankee plants eager to relocate here are gone. Those plants are going overseas these days."

The result has been an increasingly unstable Southern economy as that "other South"—largely rural, undereducated, underproductive, underpaid—threatens to become a permanent drag on the region's economy. During the 1980s, for example, unemployment rates of the South along the Atlantic Seaboard were consistently *below* the national average, although they, too, rose to the highest levels in twenty years during the recession. But inland, from the coast to the Gulf of Mexico, the South's unemployment rates were consistently *above* the national average. These areas continued to lose ground.

At the same time, the great black migration out of the South that began in the 1940s and continued throughout the 1950s and 1960s had ended. Now a reverse tide was taking place. As manufacturing declined in the Rustbelt and Northeast, surviving firms employed far fewer people. By the Nineties, the South was experiencing what the North had already undergone: an increased capacity to produce through better technology, but to do so with fewer workers.

In one of history's ironies, many blacks were moving back to the South in search of greater opportunities; but this time they were moving into urban areas instead of rural communities. Some brought with them many of the behavioral habits of the inner cities: crime, drugs, and gangs.

The South faces a paradox. Until recently, what distinguished it from the rest of the nation was its rural problem in contrast to the North's urban problem. Now thoughtful Southerners are aware that they face urban problems similar to those that have plagued the North. The danger is that the deteriorating conditions of the Lowells and Bridgeports will be recreated in a South that—again like the North—has an increasing capacity to produce products and a decreasing capacity to employ people.

"What we've got today is a backlog of people who are underemployed, a lot of them working for low wages," says Charles E. Bishop, a business consultant whose posts have included president of the University of Arkansas and at one point adviser to President

Lyndon B. Johnson on Southern rural poverty. "We're finally beginning to realize that we botched it. When I say 'botched it,' I mean
we're recognizing we have not developed our key resource, which is
our people."

CHAPTER 4

OF BOOM
AND BUST

No other area of America exhibits more of a boom-and-bust mentality than the Southwest, and no other state has swung so wildly between good and bad times as Texas, where, not surprisingly, the savings and loan scandals first flourished.

The impact of that disaster—by far the single costliest in American history, placing a levy on U.S. taxpayers of at least $200 billion—is inescapable in Texas. In only a few years, nearly two hundred S&Ls either failed or were merged. More than a hundred banks closed throughout the state. Texans, who had boasted they were financing their own destiny through Texas banks owned by Texans, were left with a banking system in which most of the major banks were no longer locally owned. They were controlled by outside interests. As in New England, bank loans became almost impossible to obtain. The real estate market was devastated.

In the downtown Dallas area, office-building occupancy rates stood at only 40 percent when I visited there. One realtor estimated that 35 million square feet of office space was vacant and said the price of land had dropped to its lowest point in thirty years. North Dallas property that sold for $50 or $60 a square foot in the boom times of the Eighties was selling for only a few dollars a square foot. "Ten dollars would be the max you would pay over there right now," a developer said. "Before, you thought you were getting a buy if you got it at fifty bucks a foot."

Along Interstate Highway I-30, where much of the S&L debacle began, shopping centers stood empty, concrete building slabs were plowed under by federal regulators who seized properties and returned the prairies to their original condition, and "For Sale, Federal Property" signs dotted an area where billboards still touted sales of the past. "Fabulous Lakeway," one read.

These were artifacts of a recently vanished era, an era that literally transformed Texas and affected every American taxpayer. Danny Faulkner, a former illiterate housepainter who became fabulously wealthy before he was convicted of racketeering and conspiracy in the S&L scandals, symbolizes the era perfectly. He was charged with stealing $150 million in loans intended for condo developments along that I-30 corridor running east and curling north from downtown Dallas.

"We're in an appeals situation now," he says, in his headquarters at Faulkner's Point overlooking a lake. On the walls are color photographs of people he posed with when times were good: Ronald and Nancy Reagan, George and Barbara Bush, Edwin Meese, Billy Graham, Jerry Falwell, Roger Staubach. Among the pictures are framed invitations for events in Washington. One photo shows Faulkner with Bob Dole and other Senate Republican leaders; an inscription thanks him for helping elect the new Republican majority in 1980. Others show him standing beside Democratic politicians—former Speaker Jim Wright of Texas and Texas Governor Mark White. "Those are some of my friends back when the money was real good," he says. "Some of 'em are still my friends. Some of 'em are political people that I used to contribute to. If I liked the Democrat, I'd contribute even if he wasn't a Republican. But it sure dries up if you have problems."

At his peak, Faulkner had a Learjet, two helicopters that he used to go from his office to lunches in downtown Dallas, four Rolls-Royces, a fleet of limousines, and personal property that included an eight-hundred-acre ranch in East Texas, with several lakes and hundreds of deer behind deerproof fences.

His second-story glass-enclosed office at Faulkner Point overlooks a racquetball court and the heliport. In the center Faulkner sits with his son and business partner; signs designate their desks as belonging to Big Danny and Little Danny. "There were a lot of good

stories written about him," Little Danny says of his father. "He was
the American Dream, yes, because he was a kid that couldn't read or
write."

Big Danny talks about his legal situation, and walks across to a
plate glass window. Below, filling a huge area, are sixty-three filing
cabinets. On top of them are stacked box upon box. Those, he says,
are the results of everything that had to do with his trial—financial
records, statements, testimony—the product of years of investiga-
tions by, he says, twenty-five FBI agents and eight U.S. attorneys at a
cost to the government of more than $20 million.

"I might have to serve twenty years in the penitentiary," he says
calmly, "and forfeit forty million dollars. Yes, forty million. But let
me tell you, what I bought for forty million ain't worth forty million
now because everything went down. Just about everything collapsed
in Texas and all the savings and loans collapsed. Most people in
Texas are going to have a tough bankruptcy. Those that haven't are
just hanging on by their teeth.

"It was wonderful, you know, couldn't have been no better.
Being in the ultimate land boom. Nobody else had ever built any
condos out here before we started. And you know, I certainly didn't
think it was anything wrong with it. I built my office here. I built my
home here. We probably spent ninety-five percent of the money we
made out here. Now the rest of the guys took their money and went
overseas and hid it in foreign banks and they ain't been able to get
that money yet. Ours is in property, it ain't in money."

Little Danny speaks up. "Everybody was of the opinion that
those times were never going to end," he says. "It wasn't like a cycle
where we had to get it quick because it's fixing to be over. It was like
this is our life-style from now on and nobody prepared for the rainy
day. It was spend spend spend and invest in everything.

"There's no way you can lose in real estate. It was a no-end-in-
sight philosophy. Texas was the place to be, and we were going to
slide past all those recessions. Couldn't happen here. So we've been
proven wrong. It happened to us first. Now it's taken the whole
country over."

The Faulkners blame their problems on the times and on people
who betrayed them. Those who helped unravel that complex series of
financial disasters naturally disagree. They see the S&L scandals as

cutting to the core of American political and personal values, and as offering major lessons for the American future—if, that is, those lessons will be learned and acted upon by the people and the politicians they elect.

"It was a myriad of failures," says Joe Selby, who became chief regulator for the Resolution Trust Corp. in Texas in the spring of 1986 after a thirty-two-year federal government career in the Office of the Comptroller of the Currency in Washington, D.C. "It was a failure of deregulation that started in the Carter years and became even more in the Reagan years when Reagan came in as the great deregulator. It was also fueled by a banking system making outrageous loans creating a balloon effect and then you had this group of unscrupulous 'entrepreneurs'—as they called themselves—who came in and found it very advantageous to buy thrift institutions because they had deregulated the asset side of thrifts.

"They saw that as an easy way of developing real estate, particularly their real estate. It was a failure of Congress. To them, the thrift industry was motherhood and apple pie, financing homeownership, the American Dream. So the thrifts basically got everything they wanted. The regulators were not regulating the thrift industry because the industry was very powerful and did not want to be regulated. So all of a sudden all of this rapid growth and these bad loans and false appraisals and outright fraud came to a head. Then the economy went down and it burst."

When Selby came home to Texas, he discovered the S&Ls had not even been examined in three years. He immediately became aware of the dimensions of the problem. Within six months, he knew that the billions and billions of dollars in Texas S&L losses in federally insured deposits would eventually have to be paid by the government and the American taxpayers.

It was equally apparent that massive fraud had taken place. The sheer amount of it was shocking even to the most sophisticated regulators. Mary Kieswetter's experience as a regulator is typical.

"About eight months after we started," she recalls, "my husband and I, as we did in those days, went out to a bar. I was drinking my martini and we started talking about work and I said—if you'll excuse my language—'We're in deep shit.' By the time we could figure out what was going on and get a grasp of not only what happened but what we could do about it, all the politics slammed in our face.

"Basically, what we and our examiners were finding was that people were buying properties and arranging to sell them to straw borrowers or others of their friends at higher profits, so you were seeing an artificial income stream and really no capital. Very few of those acquirers put much of their own money in. They were pretty much allowed to come in and acquire these savings and loans. So there was not much for them to lose, and it was all starting to come around.

"We were also discovering what we now know to have been a lot of illegal activity. A lot of flying around on jet planes. We were finding things that people a few years later shrieked about—you know, the hunting lodges for S&L executives. One thrift I was working on did an around-the-world Concorde trip within twenty-four hours. They wanted to stay in daylight for twenty-four hours and play golf at the best golf courses around the globe. That was their game. Of course, they charged it as a business expense because they took their clients. Those are the kinds of things that we gassed over every night over our drinks."

When I ask Selby, a mild, soft-spoken man, whether the lessons of the S&Ls have been learned, he becomes indignant.

"It's already forgotten," he says angrily. "It's forgotten in Texas. Danny Faulkner's trial comes up and it's kind of ho-hum now. The only evidence of it is the inability of people to get jobs here, particularly in the financial area. We've had so many bank failures, so many S&L failures, and the people who worked there are desperate. I have a banker friend who's been unemployed for five or six years. Can't get a job. And FDIC and RTC are hiring people on contract at minimal salaries.

"How significant was it? It was the most incredible disruption I have seen in my lifetime, in my professional career. The problem is, we didn't learn. It's a very sore spot with me, because I thought the benefit of it all was that everybody understood the blame and what was wrong. Congress. The regulators. The administration. Everybody. But we didn't resolve the problems.

"There was a lot that could have been done. We talked for years about the federal regulatory system, the financial regulatory system—we didn't resolve that. It would have been a wonderful time to have said, okay, here's how it's going to work in the future. But we didn't do it. We passed some laws but we just tinkered with this and tinkered with that.

"Now two years later it's started again with the banks. A mirror of what happened in 1986: hide stuff, don't solve the problem, give 'em time, blame the regulators, blame the examiners. Congress hasn't learned. They're doing the same thing."

When he speaks of the banks, Selby refers to what he believes are underlying problems affecting the entire American banking system, including big brokerage houses, investment banking firms, and major insurance companies. Those, he believes, pose an economic threat similar to that of the S&Ls in the Eighties. Interestingly, some of the S&L operators agree. That is the case with Tommy Gaubert, Sr., a former treasurer of the Democratic Party in Texas and a multimillion-dollar S&L operator. Gaubert was tried and acquitted in an S&L scandal case that he says cost him $35 million in attorneys' fees and forced him into bankruptcy. During dinner one night in Dallas, Gaubert says the S&Ls are "only the tip of the iceberg. If they do with the banks like they did with the savings and loans and they do with the insurance companies like they do with the banks, they'll devalue the United States of America."

Devaluing of America has already taken place, and not only in the wreckage of the S&L debacle. For at least the remainder of the decade, the nation will be paying a heavy price for permitting the S&L drain on the public treasury to occur even as the burden of the rising national debt makes it more difficult for businesses to obtain funds for new enterprises, expanding markets, investment in research, and for government at all levels to provide services for increasing numbers of Americans who have been left behind as their companies restructure by reducing the work force.

Much of the blame for this cumulative disaster can be laid on Washington policymakers and legislators who looked the other way when it was clear what the damaging long-term consequences would be. They were seduced by a vision that dominated much of the 1980s in both Washington and Wall Street: of the magic of the marketplace and the economic wonders that would result from a return to laissez-faire and deregulation. "Getting government off our backs" became a rallying cry and an operative philosophy, economically and politically, in the capital. But in a deeper sense, Washington was merely reflecting the boom-and-bust attitudes that permeated regions like the Southwest, fueling the speculative fever and hunger for quick profits.

Not that the Southwest was unique in this respect. With no little irony, the American Midwest had experienced its own cycle of boom and bust. Just a decade before, the Rustbelt and the Farmbelt were in dire condition. Factories closed amid the declining fortunes of America's heavy industrial manufacturing base. Farmers who believed the boom in land values would never cease—Midwestern farmland had risen from an average price of $193 to $725 an acre during the Seventies, leading to greater and greater speculation in it—were forced from land that some had held for generations. Many of these Midwesterners flocked to Texas in search of new opportunities, and many were greeted there with a contempt born out of regional pride that Texas was immune from cyclical swings of the national economy. Bumper stickers belittling these Rustbelt/Farmbelt migrants sprouted throughout the state. "Freeze a Yankee in the Dark," read one I saw then.

Now, in the Nineties, it was the Southwest that suffered while the Midwest, where the unemployment rate had been double that in the rest of the nation, was recovering.

For American manufacturing in the Rustbelt, the industries that survived were more efficient and productive, thus more competitive worldwide. For Americans in the Farmbelt, the overall economic environment of the Nineties stood in welcome contrast to the gloom of the previous decade. Still, in neither sector did I find great optimism. As in the Northeast, the South, and the Southwest, underlying doubt and wariness were evident. Yes, they had survived, people would say. Yes, they were better off than the East and West Coasts and the Southwest. But they believed they still faced considerable long-term economic questions. For many, it was not even a case of survival; they were still falling farther behind. That was particularly true in the Rustbelt. The situation in Peoria, Illinois, world headquarters of Caterpillar, provided a perfect example of current labor-management relations.

In the early 1980s, the United Auto Workers and the management of Caterpillar had engaged in a long and bitter strike. It was the kind of labor-management struggle that had repeatedly been acted out across the United States, in which neither side fully understood the other, and certainly did not appreciate the consequences of a new world economic order. Each side applied the power devices of the past out of an attitude that said, in effect, crush me and I'll crush you. When the strike was over, Caterpillar's work force was cut in half, from 36,000 to 18,000. As in nearly all major U.S. strikes in recent years, the union and its workers were the losers. Deep bitterness lingered.

Ten years later, the unions and management clashed again. This time the conflict was even more uneven. Caterpillar, like so many major U.S. industrial firms, had diversified and taken aggressive steps to improve its worldwide competitive position. "We are an international company," says Jerry Flaherty, Caterpillar's president. "We have seen our competition change drastically. Fifteen years ago our competitors would have been U.S.-based companies. They no longer are. We, as a company, had to make a decision, and that was how we were going to compete on a worldwide basis. Even though we have located facilities in other parts of the world, to compete from a U.S. base we had to sell around the world and ship from the U.S. So we modernized our facilities and restructured our company. We've looked at our costs and spent a lot of dollars. We feel we can continue to be competitive from a U.S. base."

One way of accomplishing that was by further reducing the work force. Worldwide, Caterpillar employment dropped from 89,000 employees in 1979 to about 51,000 in the early Nineties. In Peoria, where another disastrous strike was underway when I was there, the work force was down to approximately 16,500, and still declining.

"I feel like we were stabbed in the back—the union was," says Jerry Brown, UAW local president in Peoria. "We bent over backwards to help the company. We bought the global competitiveness bullshit. We bought it clear back in '82 and '83 during that strike. We struck for seven months. The company was saying the same crap then: we've got to be globally competitive, we've got to make these hard changes. After that long strike, I bought it hook, line, and sinker. And it didn't come easy. I had a lot of opposition. People threatened to kill me because we combined job classes, which eliminates jobs. We made those hardline sacrifices, we gave up the work rules from the old days. We eliminated people. These were my friends and neighbors, and I helped eliminate their jobs in the interest of making the company globally competitive. I promoted and pushed for employee involvement programs—we call it ESP, employee satisfaction process. There were people out there saying, 'Brown, you're nuts. They're going to screw you. All they care about is the bottom line.' Turns out they were pretty much right, weren't they? The company doesn't give a shit about the workers. They just want to dump us and replace us with new hires for seven-fifty an hour."

Workers raging at owners is hardly new. What is different among the workers I met is the way they recognize the deeper dimensions of their economic plight and talk candidly of their own degree of responsibility for it. Throughout days of conversations with workers in Peoria, and later with UAW members in Willow Run, Michigan, and Arlington, Texas, I heard workers acknowledge that management in years past was often right in criticizing poor quality of work. These workers also understood the new competitive pressures affecting every U.S. business, and they realized that change was necessary. But they also felt passionately that they *had* changed, had improved quality, had sacrificed to ensure the company's, and their, survival. And, in fact, business executives generally agreed about this.

The deepening fury of the workers came from their belief—again, passionately felt and almost always expressed—that they were being treated unfairly and then discarded. "In this strike, the company has shown me that they have absolutely no feelings at all for me," says Ken Mounts, a Caterpillar product assembler with nearly twenty-five years of experience. "I am a disposable commodity. That hurts, that really does. Granted, I don't think I'm the best worker, but I've never said no, I've done everything they've ever asked me to, I've volunteered a lot for them, I was an emergency medical technician for them. We've done a lot for the company and it's turnaround and now I see what they think of me."

The more Mounts talked, the angrier he became. Finally, he erupted in a more generalized grievance. "This country right now is controlled by the almighty dollar. One percent of the people control ninety percent of the wealth. The service industries have grown so much in the last ten years, but the services are being cut. The prices are not going down, but the services are being cut. You don't get near the quality of service when you go someplace to buy something. Instead of people being there to serve you, the customer's there for their convenience. If the union goes, so goes the middle class. There'll be the rich down to the seven-dollar-an-hour worker. No middle class. All of these big companies are going broke. The airlines are going out of business left and right. They have no customers. How many people making five and six dollars an hour can afford to fly anywhere? The auto industry's going down the tubes. How many people making five and six dollars an hour can afford to afford to buy a fifteen-thousand-dollar car, which these days is a mid-size, basic piece of transportation?

"The little man has been stepped on long enough, and we're getting mad. We're not young kids anymore. We're not gullible. We're more educated than our parents were. They can't stand there and tell me I'm making too much money and the chairman can make five hundred thousand dollars and also sit on the board of other companies. We're not dumb enough or stupid enough or ignorant enough to believe the lies that they told our parents. My dad doesn't have a grade-school education. He worked at Caterpillar and he's retired now. He was brought up to respect your elders, do what your boss tells you without questioning. His values are not mine. If the companies don't realize they need us as much as we need them, we're going to have a revolt, because we're tired."

Such talk of "revolt" is neither unusual nor casual. The more I traveled, the more I heard people raise this prospect—and I am not talking here about those who live in the inner cities where violence is a daily occurrence. I am talking about those Americans who feel they have been falling out of the middle class and who are increasingly angry about it.

Not surprisingly, this is particularly evident among blue-collar workers like those at Caterpillar whose high wages and good benefits are evaporating. Perhaps even more striking, echoes of this attitude are heard on the Main Streets of small Farmbelt communities where, on the surface, life appears pleasant and well ordered and the reasons for the kinds of resentment heard in the industrial Rustbelt cities would seem to be absent. It is not, even if the tone of the conversation is generally more muted.

One of the reasons for the continued anxiety—and anger—is the concern that despite its improvement the Farmbelt is not yet out of the crisis it experienced in the last decade.

At the First National Bank on Main Street, in Waverly, Iowa, David J. Huser, executive vice president and senior loan officer, says the recession—or depression—of the Eighties resulted in 20 to 25 percent of farms either going under or having to reduce operations. "I don't think it's over with," he says. "I would say across the state of Iowa there are still twenty percent that are living on the edge, that cannot withstand a major drought or a sharp rise in interest rates. They cannot withstand any more severe problems. They're edgy because they know things have got to work and if it doesn't it's going to collapse on them."*

Such uneasiness stems from more than fear that conditions might worsen. People in the Midwest, like those in the other regions, are all too aware that the good jobs like those at Caterpillar or John Deere are disappearing, and with them a comfortable standard of living. Huser, the banker, cites the example of his own wife. After graduating from college in 1979 with a business administration degree, she worked for John Deere's factory operations in Waterloo, Iowa. "Deere hired her," her husband recalls, "then turned around and trained her to be an engineer. She worked till '85, then got laid off, and took a lump severance payment because they basically said she'd never be able to work again for Deere because of their economic troubles. One year later they hired her back through a leasing company because it was cheaper to hire her that way."

Larry Pugh, who manages a major hospital in Waterloo that serves a wide region in the Farmbelt, points to his son's experience. "He graduated from college a year and a half ago and he applied and applied and applied until he finally got a job driving one of those Frito-Lay trucks," he says. "He started part-time filling in. If you go to work for Frito-Lay you must start at the bottom. But he gets benefits. Now I have relatives who didn't go to college who say, 'Isn't that great, John's driving a Frito-Lay truck.' Well, that's fine. John is doing the best he can. He's got a job, and he tells other guys, 'Hey,

---

*Fears of more severe problems were tragically realized when the great floods of the summer of 1993, the worst recorded, devastated the entire Midwest and hit farmers especially hard.

I've got a job.' Lots of those kids, their parents are still having to support 'em. Or they're back at home.

"I see a serious deterioration, almost an eradication, of the middle class that I grew up in. What we have are lots more rich and lots more poor and fewer of the middle. The Rustbelt, what did it get rid of? It got rid of the Midwest. It got rid of all those hundreds of thousands of workers who made good wages. We lost our craftsmen, we lost our builders, the trade workers. Everywhere I go socially I see people who're all retired, people who had to take early retirement—fifty-year-olds, fifty-five-year-olds, people my age and younger, all retired, doing nothing.

"When I was in college and my brothers-in-law were working in factories, I used to say, 'Man, the money they're making.' They'd buy cars and they'd buy campers and they'd buy guns and boats and they lived great. They bought new homes. That's gone. I mean, there used to be seventeen thousand five hundred people working here at Deere. Now there are six thousand. Those people spent their money. They bought the cars. They bought the houses. They were replaced by people that are at the minimum wage—seven or eight dollars an hour, not fifteen or twenty dollars an hour. These people can hardly eke out a living at today's wages.

"All the companies are cutting the benefits, cutting the packages. And big companies like Sears that led the way in this are eliminating more and more full-time employees who qualify for benefits. Fewer and fewer employees at the big companies around here are full-time workers who get full-time benefits. They have to pay for those benefits themselves. Well, they don't have the money to pay for them. Isn't this a horrendous thing that in the richest nation in the world we've got all these people with no benefits."

Even American agriculture, an amazingly efficient business capable of supplying the food needs for the entire world with only 3 percent of the U.S. population engaged in farming, is not immune from the economic forces reshaping the United States and the world in the Nineties.

Aside from the further threat that the huge conglomerates, many of them owned internationally, will exercise even greater control over American agribusiness, farmers face a more daunting competitive struggle. They operate in a world that desperately needs their commodities but one in which many of the nations most in need—from Somalia to Russia—lack the money to pay for them. One danger, farmers told me, is that American agriculture could again face a crisis of overproduction in which its very efficiency becomes counterproductive by creating surpluses that drive down prices.

They also face the same problem confronting the manufacturing sector—tougher international competition.

"If you take the farming business, and commodities in general, Japan used to buy about seventy percent of the soybeans from the U.S.," says Dave Seegers, who with his partner, Jay Ranard, operates a John Deere dealership in Waverly. "They've now reduced that down to about thirty-six percent. That's a shocking number to me. There's two reasons that's happening: mostly Japan is buying their soybeans from Brazil and Argentina and they're doing that because the quality of soybeans from Brazil and Argentina is a lot higher. That really surprises me, because I always said we had at least as good or better quality leaving this country than any other country. But that's not the case. The same thing has happened in Europe. We've lost about half the commodities market that we had in Europe."

His partner, Jay Ranard, talks about the other side of farming—the heavy-machinery tractors and combines, plows, cultivators, and planters, that they sell at prices of $110,000 and higher and that traditionally were the best in the world.

"I see our ag business on a trend to follow the same patterns we have in our manufacturing industries," he says. "Once we were the leader, and we became complacent and tried to follow the same methods for doing business that we did thirty-five years ago. The whole business has got to change. Inferior quality isn't going to work anymore. People don't have to buy that. Japan does not have to buy dirty grain. And they won't. Our customers don't have to buy an inferior product—and they won't. Costs of our products are becoming prohibitive to our customers, and somebody will fill that void. I look at it with Dave: we're on really shaky ground and we have to be able to revamp how this business is being done in a way that works for us and works for our customers."

Those are practical concerns, rooted in the reality of changing economic conditions and new competitive pressures facing all of the

OF BOOM AND BUST

United States. Other concerns are more personal, growing out of troubling changes in people's own lives and aspirations. David Huser, the bank loan officer, recalls the agony of the Eighties when families lost their farms, their assets, their independence, their way of life.

"They were losing farms that may have been in the family for generations," he remembers, echoing the comments of his banking counterpart George Duncan in Lowell, Massachusetts. "We had threats. I had people call me up and say, 'I'm going to be there with a gun, I'm not going to let you put me through this hassle any longer.' I've had people sit at my desk and say, 'Maybe the best thing to do is commit suicide. I've got plenty of insurance; the rest of my family will survive.' I know a number of bankers that got out of banking altogether. They couldn't withstand the pressures. I know bankers that ended up in divorce situations because their families couldn't put up with the pressure they were going through. So it affected not only the farmers but also the local business people, because the farmers didn't have the money to spend."

The aftermath of that experience weighs heavily in the Farmbelt. Based on my conversations, it has changed people, and, from what I heard, in many ways it has made them stronger. Those that survived often found they could do so only with the support of others in their same situation. At the same time, their mutual hardships made them, as it was said to me, more skeptical and cautious, less trusting. They were much less willing to assume new debt; almost desperately anxious, in fact, to pay down as much debt as possible and then remain, as one farmer told me, "as debt-free as you can be. We don't want debt." He repeated the words, with stronger emphasis: "We don't want to take on *any* debt."

They also found they had to reexamine, and rethink, many other assumptions about their lives—and not only about farming. They learned that they no longer could depend on the big concerns like Caterpillar and John Deere to provide Farmbelt jobs for those in the community not actually engaged in farming. In Waterloo, Iowa, for instance, not only John Deere had drastically cut back its work force; the other staple of Waterloo's economy, the Rath meat-packing plant, servicing the entire nation, went bankrupt in the farm crisis of the Eighties.

Painfully, people in the area learned that their future lay in small businesses that were employing five to ten people. That was happening in Waterloo when I was there, and the business climate, though still tentative, was beginning to turn around. At the Rath packing plant, too, the land was in the process of being parceled out for new small businesses.

Not only that, but after many years of declining population, the Farmbelt was experiencing gains in people entering the area. The nature of the people on the land was changing fundamentally too. For the first time in Iowa's history, a majority of the people who lived in rural areas were not engaged in farming. How great a shift this was can be seen in the U.S. Census figures. In 1940, the rural population of Iowa included 917,000 members of farm families and 66,000 nonfarmers. Fifty years later, the number of rural residents who made their living from farming had dropped to 257,000 while the number of rural nonfarmers had increased to 371,000. The 1990 census tracked the movement of 52,000 people who came to rural areas *not* to farm. This significant movement provided further evidence of the way America's regions experience waves of cyclical ups and downs, and seldom simultaneously. In the early Eighties, the East and West Coasts were enjoying a boom while the farm and factory communities were experiencing their worst times since the Great Depression. By the Nineties, that had been reversed.

All of this reflects the larger American community, which is being tested just as severely and with the same kinds of wrenching dislocations in the Nineties as the Midwest experienced earlier. In this, too, the people of the Midwest I met whose fiber and character have been sorely tested have something to say to the nation at large.

While staying at the farm of Fran and Howard Mueller, near Waverly, Iowa, I spent many hours one night around a dining table with five farm families who call themselves "the Winners' Circle." They began meeting regularly in the mid-1980s as an informal support group to help each other during their mutual difficulties. It was support that went beyond helping them endure, and survive, hard times. They counseled each other on the strategy to employ when going to banks that were foreclosing other farm families, on seeking legal advice, on how to approach governmental units directly involved in the farm communities. Less tangibly, but maybe more substantially, they made them feel they were not alone, and that they could count on others to help them.

Their group took form when two of the women, Fran Mueller and Austa White, discussed how neither they nor their husbands were sleeping well at night. They were seized with worries about the declining value of their land and their ability to pay their debts as their equity kept dropping. Whereupon gradually these couples ranging in age from sixty to the late forties began to meet and compare notes regularly about their traumatic experiences.

"I was fearful as we worked through those next few years and restructured our debt twice," Austa White says, "but I was angry as well because of the banking situation. We had been in this bank for twenty-eight years as a customer and all of a sudden that twenty-eight years of history and good customer relationships and good payment of debt made absolutely no difference. Personally, I haven't gotten over the anger yet of the banking situation."

Their group met, as she explains, to share ideas and offer practical assistance to each other, not to hang crepe. But they also experienced a great deal of fear and anger. "Fear from the standpoint that we knew of marriages that were collapsing, families that were in trouble, suicides, teenagers who didn't understand what parents were going through," she says. "I found out a lot more about the stress of families and the fact that farm families were having to go on food stamps! In fact, one of our group had to go on food stamps, and that opened his eyes as to how people were treated in that system."

Many farmers, like real estate speculators, became trapped after having purchased high-priced land amid the boom and then watched helplessly as the values collapsed. That was the position in which Bruce and Becky Bixby, the youngest members of the group, found themselves. "We went through many nights when you'd go to bed tired at ten or eleven o'clock at night and you'd wake up at two o'clock in the morning and be sitting at the kitchen table pushing a pencil and trying to figure out how you can make this work," he remembers.

When conditions worsened, they sat down at the kitchen table with their children and said, "One thing we're going to do is keep the family together. We might not have the farm when we come out of this, but we will keep the family together." Becky Bixby worked as a cook at the Red Fox Inn in Waverly. Their boys started trucking grain. Their daughter, in the eighth grade, attended to the farrowing of the hogs. "We made it through this thing," Bruce Bixby says. "But I'm a bitter person today. I'm a bitter person. Not better, bitter. Very much more cautious, very much more cautious about dealing with people."

Howard Mueller agrees. "We are all hardworking," he says. "We relish doing a good job, we enjoy healthy animals and good crops, so when we're humbled it's a very painful experience. The decade past has been very painful to all of us." It was he who added: "It's made us more skeptical, more cautious certainly. Wiser. Less trusting. We appreciate the trust relationships we have developed. But we're not as open as we once were."

Shirley Miller talks about another painful subject—the impact on her own marriage. "We went through some really tough times in our marriage," she says, sitting near her husband, Jim, "and looking back we learned a lot about each other. With the farm crisis and money problems, Jim took it personally that he was not a good farmer anymore. Pride, I think, you know. We just became more distant. We didn't talk anymore. Didn't discuss things because we didn't agree. I would have given up farming in a minute. It just wasn't worth what it was doing to us. On the other hand, the only thing he ever wanted to do was farm. So we made it through. We're stronger for it, but it wasn't easy."

Becky Bixby sees another, longer-lasting consequence. "One of the saddest things to come out of this for the Midwest and for the whole country," she says, "is that we have lost a whole generation of farmers. We all have sons who want to farm and we're trying to help them, but the people who were in their twenties and thirties when this thing hit could not hang on and are gone from the farm. There will be farms and nobody to farm 'em. Pretty soon we're going to have a lot more big business for agriculture, which is going to be a bad thing for the American people because they're going to have to start paying for their food what the rest of the world is paying. And they're not going to like it."

In the end, they kept their homes and their farms and in so doing demonstrated impressive strength, self-sufficiency, and willingness to work together to help solve common problems—necessary traits that obviously apply to the plight of a nation as much as to a farm town. Looking back on their experience, they sounded almost surprised to discover how much it seemed to resemble what was happening throughout their state—and nation. "Our state of Iowa is starting to go through what agriculture went through," said Don White. "The teachers want more money. It's not there anymore. They're going to have to make do just the way we did. They're going to have to do without a lot of things. Our state doesn't have the money, and I don't think as a whole it's yet come to grips with the fact that if the buck isn't there you don't spend it. Farming's a long way from being healthy, and I don't think anybody has any idea of the hurt that's going on out there yet today. And I don't have any idea where it's going to end. But all of our society is starting to unload the way we unloaded in the Eighties."

Witnessing what I saw in the regions of America, I could not disagree.

CHAPTER 5

CALIFORNIA, HERE WE GO

With a combination of envy and admiration, Americans have thought of California as a place apart. Until the very recent past, even Californians believed this. They gloried in their state's position as America's Promised Land.

In reality, California has always been much more of a mirror for what was happening to America nationally. It was the pacesetter, the place where national cultural and political trends started. But in one vital respect, California *was* different: it enjoyed the nation's most vibrant economy. At land's end of the continental frontier was where the good life reigned, and more and more Americans uprooted themselves to share in it.

While the Midwest suffered in the Seventies and Eighties, while the Northeast rose and fell in the same period, while the South saw its own jobs begin to move offshore, and while the Sunbelt underwent more cycles of boom and bust, California ran counter to all national trends. It sailed ahead on its own.

It was the nation-state, the place in which more than one out of every eight Americans lived. Its infrastructure, its public facilities, its parks, its educational system, and its job base were the envy not only of the nation, but of the world—a fact noted often by Ronald Reagan, who liked to boast that California had an economy larger than all but six countries.

By the early Nineties, California, more than any other place in

America, presents vivid proof of how regional differences that once distinguished the nation have disappeared. No other place more perfectly reflects all the strains that course through contemporary America, none exhibits change more swiftly, and, most critical, none illustrates more dramatically how America's economic fortunes have shifted. California's sudden economic free-fall symbolizes what is happening to America.

No longer could people run from the recession in other regions by escaping to California's good life. "California for so long was like the last-ditch state," says a nineteen-year-old sophomore at Berkeley as she describes how she and her family moved from Connecticut to California. "If you were in a recession state, you could go to California, because they weren't being touched by it. But that's not true anymore. All of a sudden it hit, and it was here. I'm afraid I won't be able to get a job. I don't know where else to go at this point."

Change, in fact, did come almost overnight for California. In 1988, its unemployment rate was around 5 percent. By the time of Bill Clinton's inauguration that rate had nearly doubled, leaving California with more unemployed people than any other major industrial state. For the first time, Californians were forced to acknowledge that unemployment was a major long-term concern for them—not just for the distant Rustbelt and floundering oil patches of America.

Some of the reasons are obvious. California's defense and aerospace industries paid the price for cutbacks after the Cold War ended. Every section of the nation was affected, of course, but two regions most severely: New England and California. They received 2.2 and 1.5 times respectively the amount of defense spending per capita than the rest of the nation received. Defense cuts in the early Nineties were expected to continue throughout the decade. The Office of Technology Assessment in Washington, a research arm of Congress, estimates that two and a half million workers will have lost their jobs by the year 2000 as defense spending declines to its lowest levels since the Cold War began.

California's recession was deep and severe—so severe that 800,000 jobs were lost in just two years, 80,000 of them aerospace workers alone. An additional 300,000 defense jobs are expected to be lost in California by the end of the decade. Of *all* jobs lost in the nationwide recession, a third were in California. Its businesses failed at four times the national average, its once-burgeoning real estate market collapsed, and its budget crisis, the worst ever experienced by any state, forced the legislature to pass record tax increases. This in the state that scarcely a decade before led the national tax-cut rebellion through passage of the famous Proposition 13.

At the same time, something else was happening that symbolized even greater long-term problems for California. For the first time in memory, people were moving *out* of California. By early 1993 the state's Demographic Research Unit reported that 41,000 more people had left California for other states during the previous year than had moved into it from elsewhere.

Explosive growth had propelled California in the past. Continued growth would permit the state to pay for its roads and schools and other facilities. Or so it was believed. Instead, California learned that it could no longer rely on growing.

As the recession lengthened, the numbers of Californians leaving their Golden State increased. For the first time in twenty years, more driver's licenses were expiring than were being renewed—354,800 drivers left California in 1991–92 while 341,800 drivers transferred their licenses to California from other states. For the first time, moving-van companies reported they were moving more people out of the state than into it. For the first time, one-way rental companies like U-Haul found themselves short of vehicles in California.

Despite the movement of native Californians out of the state, California was still growing, but it was growth that carried a cost. Offsetting California's outmigration was a record influx of immigrants: 303,000, mainly Latino and Asian, an increase of 22 percent in only a year, according to official 1993 figures. Here lay the seeds of a demographic time bomb.

This flood of *legal* immigration, in contrast to far greater numbers of illegal immigrants also pouring into California, placed an additional burden on a state already reeling under a multibillion-dollar deficit. Many of the new immigrants do not speak English and are in need of special services, which the state is expected to supply.

By 1993, these dramatic demographic figures caused California's Republican governor, Pete Wilson, to begin lobbying the Clinton administration and Congress to give the state $1.45 billion to help pay for services to new immigrants. In this, too, California was reflecting national trends. Similar pleas for federal assistance were being made by officials in New York City, swamped by their own growing welfare problems, caused, in part, by a very similar human flood.

This new type of growth was overwhelming California's environment. No longer did the state have the funds to provide for its prisons, its parks, its schools, and its transportation system and to clean up its air from man-made pollution.

California was also losing manufacturing plants and jobs to other areas—and countries. In the five-year period from 1987 to 1992, 708 manufacturing plants relocated from California, these alone displacing 107,000 manufacturing jobs. Mexico was the greatest beneficiary of this exodus, capturing 21 percent of the transferred facilities and 18 percent of the jobs.

Nor were those plants likely to come back to California. A local official in Silicon Valley told me of a luncheon conversation with a top executive of Hewlett-Packard who said, "Don't worry, we're not going to leave Palo Alto. That will be our headquarters, but we're never going to build another plant in California." "Now that's a California company," expressed the official. "HP was born and bred in California. So I feel very pessimistic, I *really* do."

Once again, it's the high-wage jobs that are being lost. Of California's manufacturing job losses, 73 percent fell upon industries with wages above the average for the state's total private-sector employment. By 1993, one of every two jobs in the state had been affected by companies that were "downsizing," and the state braced for further such reductions.

So difficult were California's budget problems—its annual deficit reached a historic high of nearly $15 billion followed by a shortfall approaching $9 billion even *after* tax increases and major cuts in personnel and services—that the legislature was forced into the humiliating position of authorizing the issue of IOUs instead of checks.

These problems made California an intensive example of the nation in ways that scarcely anyone could have anticipated. "We are, for the first time, strongly reflecting [negative] national trends and magnifying them to a degree," says Bruce Cain, a former Rhodes scholar and professor of political science at the University of California, Berkeley. Cain, one of the most knowledgeable scholars of the politics and structure of California, refers to that trend as California's "echo chamber" effect.

California moves from an era of surpluses and tax cuts into one of rising deficits and increasing taxes. In the same time span, a mere decade, America moves from the world's leading creditor nation to the world's leading debtor. California struggles with the consequences of political gridlock and divided government between Republican governors and Democratic state legislatures for most of a twenty-year period just as Washington does until Clinton's election restores one-party control of White House and Congress for the first time in twelve years. So severe are these forces of division that they prompt a strong move for separatism, indeed, for the ultimate division of California into three new states of the Union. This movement gathers strength as California learns that it no longer has the resources to support its once-splendid system of public services and initiates draconian cutbacks even as other states slash their services. California, which stands with New York as historically the most progressive state with immigrant strains most reflecting the American ideal of the melting pot, awakens to its boiling racial and ethnic tensions and widening economic class divisions—conditions that pose critical questions for all America.

An example of how California's problems intertwine with those of the nation came on the night that Bill Clinton laid before Congress and the people his program aimed at restoring the U.S. economy by tax increases and spending cuts that were supposed to reduce the deficit by $325 billion over a four-year period. That same day in Los Angeles, California's political and economic leaders were meeting in a highly publicized summit over how to regain their state's long-term economic growth. Nothing like it had been seen in California before.

Two nights before his State of the Union address, Clinton underscored the critical link between California's well-being and America's in a nationwide television address by saying that the U.S. economy cannot recover "unless California recovers."

After delivering his address to the nation with its challenge to both the Congress and the country, Clinton took his case directly to the people—and traveled to California. Again, he linked California's recovery with America's. "Unless California is renewed," he said, "the nation cannot recover economically."

He sharpened that point by saying: "This whole part of the country, which has been the beacon of hope for decades for Americans, is now under great stress. And the economic problems aggravate the underlying social difficulties that you find in every big city in America: more and more poor people, more and more single-parent households, more and more children forgotten and left behind."

The president also chided the nation, and indirectly his predecessors, for failing to have a conversion plan to deal with the transition from a heavy component of defense spending to an economy less dependent on defense employment. It was time, he said, that America adopted and acted upon a real long-term conversion plan to retrain workers, reallocate national resources, and work toward creating what he kept describing as "high-wage, high-growth" jobs—precisely those kinds of jobs that California and the nation were losing.

California's economy, like the nation's, has witnessed a dramatic change in its work force. In Los Angeles, for example, a significant transition is underway in the industrial sector as former high-wage factory jobs—auto, steel, rubber, and, of course, aerospace and defense—disappear. Workers who commanded $15-an-hour-and-up jobs find their pay cut in half—assuming they still have jobs. Much of the remaining industrial work force is being concentrated in smaller, light-industry work that typically pays in the $5-an-hour range. Normally, those factories don't provide health insurance benefits to their employees.

Into that volatile mix, with more and more people competing for work, flow an extraordinary number of new immigrants, many of them illegal aliens with false identity cards. Factories in Los Angeles are an immigrant rainbow—Asian, South American, Vietnamese, Filipino, Cambodian. Most Vietnamese workers and many Latinos speak limited English, if any. Thrown together in factories, competing for positions, fearful of their future, they cannot speak to each other. Inevitable resentment, jealousy, and friction result as one nationality fears that another is given favorable treatment by the employer.

Intensifying an already explosive situation are racial tensions. When I visited Los Angeles, a black man was leading a so-called Brotherhood Crusade by mounting protests at construction sites in south-central L.A. and demanding that African-American workers be hired in preference to Latino workers. Naturally, Latino organizations struck back and began their own protests. Their people needed jobs, too, and they expressed bitter resentment at discriminatory hiring quotas.

Thus new divisions arise not only between the haves and the have-nots of America but also among people at the bottom of the heap. In California, this offers one more sign that frictions between racial and ethnic groups, particularly in Los Angeles, will escalate even more in the 1990s. If nothing else, the demographics of California virtually guarantee that such tensions will continue to intensify.

By the year 2000, whites are likely to be approaching minority status in California. By then, population projections estimate, Latinos will number about 30 percent of the state's inhabitants, Asians close to 14 percent, and African-Americans just below 7 percent.

In another ten years, the white population is expected to drop from 50 to 45 percent as those rising nonwhite demographic trends continue to accelerate. Nearly all of California's new residents in that first decade of the twenty-first century are expected to be Latino and Asian—as is the case in the Nineties.

Despite their rapidly approaching majority status, nonwhites in no way possess the political power to which their numbers should entitle them. This is partly because of their low propensity to vote, but it is also because the present white majority is aggressively asserting and adding to its power. "Whites make our tax policy," says Bruce Cain, the California scholar. "Whites make our insurance policy. We make our reforms, all by the mechanism of at-large elections called referenda and initiatives. These are undercutting the power of the legislature at a time when the legislature is incorporating more and more minorities. So there's this frustration. Just as these groups are arriving in the legislature, their power is undercut by the fact that we're conducting business statewide by referendum."

Cain sees another trend in California politics that makes change more difficult. That's what he calls "middle-class denial"—a phenomenon that also exists throughout the nation.

"We've got a problem in that it's very hard to get resources out of the middle class," Cain says. "The middle class is in a quandary everywhere. On the one hand, they see certain services that they want. On the other hand, there's an unwillingness to pay for those services. If you look at the ongoing property-tax revolt that we've had in California since 1978, it crops up in various forms. You have, literally, a pathological fear on the part of politicians in this state of raising taxes, except in subtle ways. That is, pick on particular classes of taxpayers—on drivers, on smokers. You raise fees. You increase the bonded indebtedness of the state. You find ways to raise taxes that don't look like taxes either, because the payment is in the future or because it's on a particular class of taxpayers. So the basic theme is a confused middle class with a lot of denial going on."

That, in turn, further exacerbates tensions between the dwindling white majority and the rising nonwhite population. In California, as in the nation, whites have abandoned the inner cities for the suburbs. New white enclaves continue to form throughout the state—in San Bernardino and Riverside and Sacramento and Contra Costa. In the so-called I-80 (Highway) Corridor from the San Francisco Bay to Sacramento, the area is filling up with the white middle class—professional families fleeing the problems of inner cities like Oakland. Economically and socially they draw farther apart from the nonwhite population they leave behind.

During our conversation about this phenomenon, Cain says the continuing development of these new white enclaves "dovetails nicely with the cutting back of state funds and letting communities do their own thing." Just as the federal government has devolved a lot of responsibilities onto the states, so the states have devolved a lot of responsibilities onto the counties. "We're getting away from the sense of collective responsibility for social problems that was developed in the Sixties," Cain says. "We're getting back to the notion that decentralization means that you get to keep *your* resources, you get to concentrate on *your* thing."

So the economic problems prompt people either to leave California or to build new enclaves on the state's frontier. This, in turn, adds to the burden of providing needed services from increasingly scarce tax revenues and leads to even more dispersion.

Yet no matter how far away they move, the problems move with them. In California, as in America, the terrors of the inner cities extend into the suburbs. The violence of Los Angeles, for example, spreads into the San Fernando Valley and into the San Gabriel Valley as the drug-dealing of the inner city moves outward, bringing higher crime rates with it. As it does, it heightens the sense that California's quality of life is declining, and not only because of the weakened economy, but also because people fear that their enclaves are no longer safe. In the end, they discover they have no place to escape.

BOOK THREE

AMERICAN FABRIC

CHAPTER 6

SERVICES: FALLING THROUGH THE NET

Whe the hard times came, with businesses failing and tax revenues declining, the city of Lowell, Massachusetts, began to charge private citizens and businesses for trash removal. It was the first time that charge had been levied, and there was, I was told, a public outcry. Not surprising, to be sure: no one likes to pay for services that have been free. More striking was the *absence* of protest about other, more severe cuts in public services. In Lowell, as in Sherlock Holmes's England, it was the dog that didn't bark that was most revealing of public attitudes.

Jim Cook calls this "the outrage issue." More accurately, it's the lack-of-outrage issue. "I don't know if I'm using the best word," Cook was saying to me, "but 'outrage' is the only word I can think of. If people are not outraged by what's happening, they're not going to do anything about it."

Cook, a city planner and executive director of the Lowell Plan, the nonprofit business coalition instrumental in Lowell's rebirth during the 1980s, sees the trash collection issue as a symbol:

"Lowell was talking about cutting four million dollars out of the school system. Not a peep of protest, except from teachers and the special-interest people. Not a peep. Same thing on cutting police and fire—one hundred policemen and firemen. Not a peep from the community. The only people that come out when you cut fire are the fire unions. The only people that come out when you cut police are the police unions. The only people that come out when you cut school departments are the teachers. Not the public. There is no outrage. But if you tell the people their trash won't be picked up once a week anymore, that it will be picked up every *two* weeks, and that they'll have to *pay* for it, you won't be able to get near city hall with the people coming down! Where are our priorities? Are they in throwing trash out on the street or are they in putting good-quality people in our school systems? If you don't hit people in their homes, they're not affected, and they don't care."

During the Reagan era of supply-side tax cuts and privatization of public services, an inconclusive ideological debate raged in Washington and around the country. At issue was whether cuts in government services were imposing undue hardships on people in most need or whether they were protected by the "safety net" of existing social welfare programs.

That a fundamental shifting of the burden from Washington to the states and localities was taking place was never in doubt. Federal grants to states fell by more than half in the Eighties, and the percentage of state and local budgets that came directly from Washington dropped from 25 percent at the end of the Seventies to 17 percent in 1990. Such numbers, aside from indicating a major shift in allocation of funds, did not prove the case about new personal hardships either way.

By the Nineties, there was no longer any doubt about what had happened. The safety net had developed gaping holes, and more and more Americans were falling through it. It wasn't only the social welfare recipients who were suffering; every element of American society was being affected by major cutbacks in police and fire protection, schools, and hospitals.

No area of the nation was exempt. Everywhere I went I found examples of suffering, of worsening conditions, of growing anger and fear—among the citizens most directly affected, and among those responsible for providing basic services. The more I traveled, the more I wished the politicians of Washington from the president down—and, yes, my colleagues in the press who report on them— could experience the emotions I heard expressed daily.

Maine's example was sadly typical. After having stressed the state's rosy future during his gubernatorial campaign, the governor declared a civil emergency and shut down all government services except basic health and public safety operations. He also detailed major budget cuts affecting everything from education to mental health—emergency cuts that became even more severe as the state's budget crisis worsened.

In Lowell, mammoth across-the-board cuts hit every city department whether treasury, tax collector, auditor, or personnel. The city's recreation and public works departments were cut drastically, the human services department was eliminated, water and sewer fees were increased. Little League teams had to pay for permits to use the city's playing fields. If they played at night, they were charged for electricity. Schools, hospitals, and police and fire departments were also severely cut. Classroom sizes increased from twenty-five to forty pupils, and Lowell's high school was without an athletic director and a band instructor. Much worse was to come.

Lowell's new city manager, Richard Johnson, hired from outside to make the difficult cuts, told me that he had drafted plans to reduce the total city work force by 25 percent within six months. Among those affected were sixty-one firefighters, fifty-seven police officers, and 135 teachers.

What it meant for Lowell, he said, was simple and brutal: "They're going to have less police protection, less fire protection. Fewer recreation programs. Fewer services for the elderly. They're going to pay higher taxes with less services. We haven't had to close public buildings at this point. But—as an example—if I don't get the fee package, I'll probably have to close the library. We'll cut all of our recreation programs.

"It's incredible. I was hired here because people wanted change. When you come from out of town, you're called a 'Blow-In' here. So I'm a Blow-In. It doesn't matter that I was born here and lived here for fourteen years of my life. It's a helluva lot easier for me to lay off the firefighters than for a local person who knows the families. These guys would be the last guys hired. They're the young guys, they've got new families, they've probably got big mortgages and young kids. Where are they going to find a job with benefits in this market? They're not."

In Bridgeport, in just three years, 1,000 of the city's 4,500 municipal workers lost their jobs. Parks that were once the pride of Bridgeport, having been designed by the great nineteenth-century landscape architect Frederick Law Olmsted, who created New York's
Central Park, were tended by twenty-eight workers instead of the
former staff of 250. Many parks were forced to close as the budget
was cut in half. Some people advocated selling all the city's parkland—the most extensive in the state—to reduce the city's deficit.

As for the parks themselves, they were in a state of ruin. Along
the waterfront, broken picnic tables lay alongside trash and debris.
In the outlying areas of the city, what had been among the grandest
municipal parkland for a city of its size was now a desolate patch of
deteriorating acres. Roads circling through them were potholed and
in need of major repair. Curbs were broken, storm drains were inop-
erable, the land itself was overgrown. It had taken generations to
create this system; now it was falling apart before your eyes. In all of
the park areas, grass no longer was mowed and trash accumulated.
The same devastation was apparent in all areas of the city. Streets
were no longer swept. Snow no longer was plowed. All city recreation programs were eliminated, including lifeguards for the municipal beach. The library budget was cut by 60 percent. Services for the
city's growing elderly population were sliced in half. Police and fire
departments were severely cut.

Bridgeport's fire chief, Gerald Grover, had been on the job only
six months when I talked to him. In front of his desk, he gazed at a
huge sign that proclaimed: THINK POSITIVE.

After listening to him, I understood why he needed that daily
reminder.

"Right now I need two aerial trucks, two ladder companies," he
said. "It's almost an emergency state, but we can't get the capital
funds. I have two fire trucks that were built in 1956. I was in eighth
grade in 1956. I don't know where you were. The mayor wasn't even
born in 1956. In the city of Bridgeport, these trucks run ten runs a
day. It's not like being in the suburbs or a volunteer environment
where the fire trucks are not busy. Here, they're virtually falling
apart. A couple of weeks ago the tiller wheel—you know, the back of
the fire engine that you drive—came off in a fellow's hand.

"A year and a half ago they closed one firehouse. Engine 2. That saved them twenty-five fighters. We're talking about closing two others, maybe more. It's going to compromise safety even more. However, there's no money, so you do what you have to do. Prior to that, between 1985 and 1990, they closed two additional houses."

A similar situation exists in other communities. In South Carolina, the state with the nation's second-highest infant mortality rate, some communities no longer could afford to buy textbooks for their children. Some school buses were so antiquated that they posed a hazard. While the number of public employees for prisons increased—South Carolina was earning the unenviable nickname "the Detention State" because of the number of prison facilities being constructed—key environmental agencies in a state with a major nuclear waste disposal problem were being cut back sharply.

In Peoria, Illinois, aside from drastic cuts affecting education, the state's fiscal crisis was so severe that local drugstores were going out of business because the state hadn't paid its bills, in part because of a backlog of six-month-old Medicaid bills. Nursing homes were also being affected by the same failure of the state to pay long-overdue obligations. At the time of my visit, a new women's center for the treatment of substance abuse had not received a state payment in seven months. More and more doctors and pharmacies were turning away Medicaid patients because they could no longer afford to float the state of Illinois.

Barbara Drake, editor of the editorial page of the *Peoria Journal Star,* said: "The state is a big scofflaw. It's not paying its bills and it refuses to raise the taxes that would be necessary to pay off its debts.

"Every time the state doesn't pay what it owes to the Peoria school district, the Peoria school district has to borrow money somewhere to meet its contracts with teachers. So the Peoria school district is forced to borrow, not because of mismanagement, but to keep the schools open. The whole system is pyramiding and collapsing, and that's scary."

A Peoria doctor, David C. Holden, also spoke with bitterness. "I've lived here since I was four," he said. "The health care system is bankrupt financially. Perhaps morally, too, but that's a more loaded question. From the financial point of view the system we've got has run wild. With a large company like Caterpillar, if they have enough clout they can negotiate deals which would seem to be in their best

interests. But the smaller employer has increasing difficulty providing employee services and coverage, and it just moves right on down
the system.

"What happens to the people? If you've got insurance, then everyone's part of the problem, because the doctors take advantage of
the system, the patients take advantage of the system, the insurance
companies take advantage of the system. The hospitals take advantage of the system, the attorneys take advantage of the system. Everyone gets their pound of flesh. If you don't have coverage you're in
horrible trouble. And there's a big population that has—forgive me
for saying it—fallen through the cracks. If they don't qualify for
public assistance because they have some kind of job, they don't have
the means for adequate insurance. And it's astronomically expensive."

I asked him what he saw in his practice.

"I'm a family doctor," he said. "I see people with renal failure
who literally need to be on the waiting list for kidney transplants, but
they can't even afford to come in because they can't pay for an office
call. I see that routinely.

"The response of the medical society has been hilariously inadequate," he added. "They bought a building from the retired bishop of
Peoria and put up a clinic which is open two and a half days a week
and manned by one hundred fifty doctors in shifts. In those hours per
week you're supposed to meet the needs of the medically indigent. I
don't know what happens to those people the other hours in the
week."

What Dr. Holden was describing about health care problems in
Peoria was true for the entire United States. For Americans, no single issue was more personal, and more controversial, than health
care. About none was there broader public agreement on the need for
radical change. Yet beyond that general agreement, fundamental disagreement raged over what to do about the nation's health care system. Americans wanted it changed—and feared the changes it might
bring.

The reasons for crisis were evident. For a generation, health care
costs had been rising dramatically as the number of older Americans
kept increasing. To put the problem in perspective, start with this
primer. In 1970, America's health care costs amounted to 7.3 percent

of the nation's gross domestic product (GDP). Ten years later, when Reagan defeated Carter, the percentage had moved up to 9.2. Up to 1990, it rose even more rapidly, then momentarily came to rest at 12.1 percent. From there, the projections become ever more frightening. By the year 2000, health care costs will consume 18.1 percent of the U.S. GDP. By 2010, when the first of the baby boomers reach their retirement age of sixty-five, the estimated percentage is 22. By 2020, it's expected to hit 26.5 percent. Finally, in 2030, the year when Bill Clinton, that representative baby boomer, will be celebrating his eighty-fourth birthday, America will be spending virtually one-third—32 percent—of its GDP on health care.

These are disturbing figures, but there's even more to ponder. Health care costs are consuming more and more of the nation's collective treasure and represent a seventh of the entire United States economy. In 1965, for example, at the crest of Lyndon Johnson's Great Society era of increased spending for U.S. domestic needs, federal spending for health care amounted to only 4.2 percent of the total budget. A generation later, in 1990, it was consuming 17.9 percent of the federal budget, or nearly $800 billion. By the year 2000, it is expected to eat up nearly 30 percent of the budget, and keep on rising into the future. When the soaring interest on the national debt is added to this equation, plus money spent for national defense, this means there will be barely *any* money left to spend on *any* other government efforts to improve the quality of American life.

Other statistics sharpen the dimension of the crisis. A prime example involves spending on Medicaid, the government program that assists the poor. Medicaid was a key element in Lyndon Johnson's Great Society. After its enactment in 1965, federal and state spending for Medicaid rose by a relatively modest $13 billion. Within ten more years, the federal government and the states were spending $41 billion for Medicaid. By 1995, that total figure is expected to more than quadruple, to an estimated $189 billion annually.

Not only is Medicaid spending adding substantially to the annual federal deficit, it places heavy burdens on already severely strained state budgets—rising from an average of 7 percent of state budgets to a projected 25 percent of the average state's budget in 1996. By the mid-Nineties, Medicaid represented the second-largest component of state budgets, ranking only behind education in total amounts spent, and ahead of money for transportation and prisons. No wonder that Florida's Governor Lawton Chiles, a Democrat, remarked during this period, "Medical costs are the Pac-Man that eats everything. We're becoming a government that has no money for education, for parks, for prisons, because all of it is going to medical care."

Adding to these problems is another factor—the "graying of America." The figures tell the story. In 1970, there were 20.1 million Americans aged sixty-five and older, but of them only 1.4 million were eighty-five and older. Twenty years later, the over-sixty-five population had grown to 31.6 million. By 2030, that number will have increased to nearly 70 million. Of those, 8.4 million will be eighty-five and older.

Add to these demographics two other sets of figures: the rising costs of all health care and the increasing numbers of older people whose health care costs are far higher than those of younger Americans. To take the 1992 presidential campaign year as a base, the average amount then spent on health care for those under the age of sixty-five was $2,349. For Americans sixty-five and older, the average amount was almost four times higher—$9,125.

Then consider the plight of those 37 million Americans—15 percent of the entire population—who have no health insurance coverage and the additional 72 million Americans who lack insurance coverage for prescription drugs.

When all of these facts are combined, it's apparent that Americans are paying far too much for their health care and it is covering far too few. And the costs of each component continue to soar—and will keep on soaring until the entire system is reformed.

Americans I met everywhere were deeply worried or angry about the rising costs of their coverage—assuming they had some—and especially apprehensive about maintaining that coverage, amid pervasive fears of job losses and cutbacks in benefits. In some ways, however, the most emotional responses I heard were from those professionals who had taken their benefits for granted, only to suddenly feel vulnerable. That was the case with two of the people I spoke to at MIT.

Willard Johnson, a black professor of political science, was reflecting on the upward path his life had taken from a hard childhood in a segregated society. "I've always felt that my own personal future was going to get better and better," he says, "and it has." He lives a comfortable life, provides well for his children, and holds a position that brings him prestige and respect. Nonetheless, he speaks of feeling battered by serious new concerns.

"My parents both died of cancer, and my father's was a cancer that could have been treated," he said. "It wasn't, because he thought that if he were to get the treatment, he'd lose his house. It's a very real problem, even when you're well covered." MIT's health benefits no longer seemed so secure, Johnson said, as costs kept rising. Circumstances could arise in which his health benefits would not cover an illness, wrecking his hard-earned place in the black middle class and placing terrible burdens on his children.

At the time we spoke, MIT had been forced to slash subsidies for its Blue Cross health plan. A friend there described over dinner his feeling of desperation at the burden of these escalating costs, especially when added to a different cost for which no government benefits exist: the extraordinary expenses of maintaining a loved one in a nursing home. This man's father, then ninety-three, a former successful banker, had already gone through all his life's savings and was then in a good private nursing home in Connecticut. That cost seventy thousand dollars a year. My friend, who faced college expenses in the range of twenty thousand dollars a year and rising health insurance costs, was also forced to try to cover his father's expenses. He had no alternative, he said, to selling his splendid old Victorian house in Brookline. The problem and the worry exist at all levels of society.

Belief that Clinton would achieve basic health care reform contributed significantly to his election. Once in office, he quickly moved to fulfill that promise, and did so in a bold and unprecedented fashion. He named his wife, Hillary, to head the President's Task Force on National Health Care Reform and pledged that it would report with its preliminary findings and legislative recommendations by May 1, 1993, not even four months after his inauguration—another example of Clinton's ambitious vision coupled with his penchant for setting unrealistic deadlines.

Under Mrs. Clinton's direction, the task force of officials, academics, and some health care providers began an intensive—and

secretive—health care study that operated on a crash basis from
early morning to late evening as it attempted to reach a consensus on
what to recommend. Everyone agreed on three goals: control costs,
increase insurance coverage, maintain quality of services. But after
this, consensus began to fall apart. Simply to control costs was an
immense and complex undertaking. Aside from waste, mismanagement, and price gouging, costs were soaring because of advances in
life-sustaining equipment and other sophisticated technologies which
prolonged life, but at far greater expense. By the mid-Nineties, for
instance, the total cost of treating eight uncured diseases—osteopo-
rosis, diabetes, stroke, depression, arthritis, Alzheimer's, cancer, and
cardiovascular diseases—was an astounding $419 billion a year. This
did not include the tens of additional billions being spent for AIDS,
another rapidly growing disease for which no cure had been found.

In appointing his wife to a position of such influence over such a
critical national issue, Clinton elevated the stakes for his health initiative and focused intensive public attention on it. The secrecy that
at first surrounded the sessions of Mrs. Clinton's task force, a secrecy
that extended even to the names of its members and the time and
place of its meetings, naturally increased public curiosity—and criticism, especially from the hundreds of thousands of medical practi-
tioners and other health care providers who were not included but
would be profoundly affected by any changes.

Trial balloons and inevitable "leaks" to the press about the proceedings of the task force heightened the sense of controversy, and
the reform's estimated costs as reported in the media, often inaccurately, rose to as high as $150 billion. Public uneasiness increased
even more after some administration officials talked openly about the
need for new and higher taxes to finance the program, and budget
officials such as Robert D. Reischauer, director of the nonpartisan
Congressional Budget Office, testified on Capitol Hill that "cost controls are likely to be more painful than many envision, requiring
consumers to accept some real limits on the quality or quantity of
medical care that is available."

In such a climate, many Americans began wondering if they were
not better off with what they already had, however imperfect, than
with a "reform" of uncertain application and certainly greater cost.
Besides, to gather from the initial political and press commentary

about health care reform, it was beginning to sound as if Washington was hatching another tax-and-spend big-government program. Millions of citizens had come to have little faith in these. In fact, the Clinton health task force was engaged in one of the most exhaustive, and comprehensive, governmental efforts ever to fashion a proposal that would reform the nation's health care system and guarantee coverage for the first time to every American. Before the task force completed its final proposals and the president made them public during a nationally televised address to a joint session of Congress, it had held eleven hundred meetings with various interest groups involved and begun to generate enormous pressure for real change.

Hillary Rodham Clinton's team was aided in this effort by increasing public clamor for action. Americans understood that the health care system, if permitted to continue on its current course, could bankrupt the nation and diminish lives. For this reason alone, the success or failure of Bill Clinton's presidency will likely rest upon the eventual resolution of his health care plan—the greatest such struggle in decades—and the way Americans judge his handling of it.

They also realize that health care represents only part—albeit a huge segment—of the way in which America's cumulative budget crisis affects every level of government in providing those services that enable society to function. In Oakland, Judge Demetrios Agretelis speaks of California's financial dilemma and its effects on the court system.

"Nobody would have dreamed, if you were a career district prosecutor in a metropolitan county in a rich state like California, that you'd lose your job," he says. "Twenty or thirty people have been laid off in the district attorney's office because we don't have enough money. County government employees, sheriffs, district attorneys, prosecutors, are all being laid off. The state judges' retirement system—which, by the way, was designed to be very generous to judges—is unfunded. It needs about a billion dollars to fund it. It's beginning to occur to me that the retirement system—a safety net like Social Security—might be substantially dismantled or go completely under. It's possible. It's staggering.

"There are fewer and fewer resources and more and more demands on the courts, as if the courts were in a position to solve all social problems, which they're not and shouldn't be. Public resources

seem to be crumbling. Walk around Berkeley at night—not just
Berkeley and Oakland, it's worse in San Francisco—and you'll see
people sleeping on the sidewalks. We used to recognize that we have
a moral responsibility to these people. Now the idea seems to be, if
I can make it, *they* can make it."

Another northern California judge, Stanley Golde, deals almost
exclusively with the criminal sector. He sees people who represent
the "ills of society, the hopelessness, the despair, the inability to work
or really partake in the society." For good reason, he has more people on death row than any other judge in California: he tries more
death penalty cases. And his bitterness is even greater than that of
Judge Agretelis. "Here comes the budget," he says, "here comes the
totally irresponsible legislature, the totally irresponsible governors
and executives who are strictly elected by the various lobbyists. And
the lobby with the *least* effect is public protection, because we have
no clout. We don't have the same clout that the lumbermen have,
that the unions have, and so forth. So when it comes to the budget
they take away our support staff."

Judge Golde expects the newest round of cuts to eliminate counseling. "We have already lost things like the volunteer bureau, where
instead of sending someone to jail, I can have him work. That's gone.
It looks like guards for the county jail will be cut. We have two
county facilities. If you close one because you don't have people to
staff it, where do I put the people who are sentenced to jail?

"Let's take juveniles. If I don't have a county jail facility, I'm
going to do one of two things. The person who's a minor irritant but
not a threat, he's going to go out. The person who probably should be
in the county jail for a year will go to the state penitentiary. So there's
no way in the world you can salvage the human being. No way in the
world! After forty-plus years in this business—a criminal defense
lawyer for twenty-five years, a judge for twenty—I'm ending up
worthless. My life isn't worth a thing."

I asked Judge Golde what I had asked the others: what happened
to us in America to create these conditions?

"Okay," he said briskly. "There's the egocentricity—the selfishness—of the power structure. They're only concerned with themselves. Then, as the economy has tightened, we're having the haves
and have-nots. It's like the European countries, like the South Amer-

ican countries. We don't care. As long as *I'm* protected, as long as I can live in a good area, in the hill area in Beverly Hills instead of central L.A., if I can live in Westwood instead of on Compton Avenue, then I don't care."

In the Martin Luther King/Charles Drew Hospital in south-central Los Angeles, in the very center of the area where the riots flared in 1992, Joseph Israel talks of having to "operate smart" in the emergency room because of reduced staff. More cuts in preventive medicine services were then being proposed in Los Angeles County. "Unfortunately," he says, "we're not investing in our future." Others there describe how understaffing intensifies tensions with patients. "There's a longer waiting period for these people, who then get frustrated and try to take their frustration out on the employees," says Alejandro Stephens. "After a long wait they become edgy. You have to be sympathetic to them. They're sick. At the same time you know that the system is to blame. We cannot continue to provide the services without the money."

A similar refrain pervades the conversations at the King/Drew center, a huge complex of concrete structures that took form when the Great Society was pouring money into domestic programs and seeking to improve the nation's health and welfare systems. The hospital is part of the Los Angeles County health care system and contains one of the area's major trauma centers. Because of the growing indigent population in Los Angeles and the decrease in funds coming from the state of California, the King center has suffered major cutbacks. There are many more patients to be served and many fewer health care professionals to serve them, and with fewer resources, from medical supplies to equipment.

When you enter the hospital, the waiting room and hallways are jammed with people waiting to see medical personnel. These are the people from the inner city, and they, as usual, are paying the heaviest price for reduced services.

Ethel Edmond, a young black who works in the hospital's trauma center and who also attends nursing school, offers another aspect of the problem: the increasing severity and number of cases. "Nine years ago," she says, "I saw mainly stab wounds. Once we saw a lot of assault-type rifle wounds. That slowed down. Now you see more and more gunshot wounds, the fatal type now—shots to the head and neck and chest. It's like these people are more trained, more advanced. Like they're practicing at the shooting range, because their aim is getting better."

Lidia M. Duron, a Latina at the hospital who had previously worked for twenty years with Los Angeles County social services, told me that the stress of the job makes her want to take early retirement even though she will have a reduced pension and less income. She feels burned out by the desperation she sees every day. "I have a patient who had twin girls. I asked her about the babies' father, and I didn't think I heard her right the first time, because she looked like a very nice lady," Duron says. "She said she prostituted herself to get money for her kids. I said, 'Why do you do this to yourself?' And she said, 'My kids needed the food.' So there's people doing things they probably never would have done before. When I worked for social services we were idealistic. We tried to serve. Now I feel sorry for anyone who has to go to social services, because the service isn't there."

Reasons vary for the severe strain on vital public services across America. In each area, you find different causes; but they all represent a larger national symptom: the erosion of public support for public problems.

In Lowell, a contributing factor to the cuts in services was the city's failure to deal with its own municipal unions.

"We procrastinated in dealing with the issue two years before," says Richard Howe, twice mayor, formerly a public-school teacher and member of the Lowell city council since 1965, and a practicing lawyer. "The police in Lowell were the fifth-highest-paid in the country," he says. "I think Miami is first, then Los Angeles, Chicago, Boston, and Lowell. If you look at our public safety payroll, it's staggering.

"Instead of confronting the public employee unions, we simply vacillated. Salaries did level off, but there was no cutting back, and that is something we had to face and did not face. It was very clear what was happening and what we should be doing about it. We just didn't do anything. Our unemployment was going up ten to fifteen percent, yet we're paying police officers a minimum salary of fifty thousand dollars. The average superior officer in Lowell gets close to seventy thousand dollars with his overtime. It's actually obscene what we pay police and fire."

The glaring contrasts between America's private wealth and public poverty are most sharply drawn in Bridgeport and in surrounding Fairfield County. When Bridgeport filed for bankruptcy, the Bridgeport-Stamford-Norwalk-Danbury area boasted the highest personal income—$31,438 per capita—of any metropolitan region in the nation. Fairfield County was first in personal income, just as Connecticut had the highest average personal income of any state. Because Connecticut did not then have an income tax, local governments were forced to rely mainly on real estate taxes for their revenues.

As businesses left, about 60 percent of Bridgeport's total tax revenue came from residential property owners. Their property tax rates were nearly twice those of surrounding suburbanites, who did not have to bear the rising expense of a deteriorating inner city and its soaring social services costs for homeless shelters, public housing units, and drug treatment centers and greater crime and fire prevention expenses. A house selling for $130,000 in Bridgeport was taxed at $3,171. Identically priced houses in wealthier nearby suburban Trumbull and Stratford were taxed at $2,816. Suburban residents made double the average income of city dwellers—$20,954 per capita in Fairfield versus $10,534 in Bridgeport—yet paid far less in taxes for far better services.

In Peoria, the cuts were compounded by the state of Illinois's failure to pay its own bills when faced with a rising deficit. In California, the tax-cut fever of the previous decade contributed to a reluctance—or unwillingness—of citizens to fund institutions that assist those in most need.

All of these varied situations, reflecting local conditions and circumstances from coast to coast, add up to a larger national truth: that America faces something new in its experience, a population that no longer advances materially but falls behind, and a population that requires more assistance exactly when the nation's ability to provide it diminishes. These pose critical tests for every element of government: town, county, and state. How well, or poorly, those tests are being met becomes disturbingly clear in the place where my journey began, Maine.

In Maine, the state's crisis stemmed as much from a state of mind as from specific decisions made when the recession hit. Throughout the Eighties, Maine, like the nation, grew economically beyond anyone's expectations. Wealthy executives from as far away as Texas snapped up oceanfront land for new vacation homes and condos. With the influx of such people, driven by the boom of the decade, came new state revenues through increased sales and income taxes. Along the shoreline of southern Maine, local officials boasted of "zero unemployment." Spending increased, savings declined, but no matter—each month state revenues exceeded those of the previous one, and each month housing and land prices rose. At one point during those years, the governor turned to Jim Tierney, then the attorney general, and said, "Jim, this is a money machine; it won't quit."

By 1989, the feeling of success was so strong that the National Alliance of Business singled out Maine as its "State of the Year." So sanguine were the prospects, so rosy the economic assumptions, that Maine even returned $61 million to its citizens in tax rebates. At the same time the state obligated itself through bonds to spend similar millions for capital construction projects for which the citizens would pay over the next thirty years. "Can you imagine more irresponsible or preposterous management?" Tierney says. "But that's the way the state ran its household. We would borrow sixty million and give away more than sixty million for short-term gain. Amazing."

Businesses hired more people than they needed for the long term because they were getting more orders than they could handle for the short term. Housing developments, malls, industrial parks, office buildings all were built far beyond the need. Suddenly, the boom stopped—dead.

At first Maine went through a period of denial, from the statehouse down. Maine's economy was sound. What it was experiencing was only a temporary financial setback, a blip that would swiftly disappear. Yes, there were problems in neighboring Massachusetts; but that was because its governor, Mike Dukakis, spent too much money. Yes, there were problems in Connecticut; but that's because it also spent too much money.

Tierney remembers: "Even when it became absurdly clear that there was no money in Maine—which was the summer of 1990 when

I started to do cost savings in my own department—the rest of the state government continued to hire, continued to give raises, and the unions got more raises and they kept demanding more. The *Titanic*'s starting to tip up, and the band is playing, but they're still negotiating and getting raises just like nothing happened."

By the fall of 1990, austerity became the order of the day. An era of brutal cuts began. By 1992, Maine's personal-income growth sank to last among the fifty states. As the state's deficit continued to soar, more emergency cuts were needed. "All of a sudden there was no place you could hide," Tierney says. "All of a sudden every public official in every community in Maine was faced with a terrible reality. They had to raise taxes and cut services. That's it for the Nineties, and maybe forever."

In 1988, when Lucille Jeffery became director of welfare services in the town of Topsham, Maine, she worked twelve hours a week. Four years later, she worked full-time and was on call seven days a week, twenty-four hours a day. In that last year alone, her caseload had increased 40 percent and she dealt with a new class of clientele: unemployed professionals entering a welfare office for the first time in their lives.

Many of these people were about her age, in their mid-forties, and reflected one of the most important demographic facts about America: many two-income families of working husbands and wives— struggling even on the double income to meet mortgage payments, tuition, car payments, and taxes—were suddenly becoming *one*-income families, with financial obligations they couldn't meet. "They don't know where to begin," Jeffery says. "They're embarrassed to come in to see me. They don't want to be seen when they come in here. It's quite a shock. It really is."

She sits behind her desk surrounded by supplies stacked on shelves filled with canned goods—milk, tomatoes, baked beans, split peas, vinegar, salad dressing, apples, baby food—and a variety of clothing from new and secondhand adult wear to diapers either on those same shelves or in cartons piled high throughout the office. If people tell her they're out of food, she lets them help themselves, no questions asked. If they need assistance getting food stamps, or help with unpaid light bills or fuel or rent or child support or the loss of critical family medical insurance, Jeffery provides what service she can or points them toward other agencies.

Jeffery deals with people "all dressed up to all dressed down," from "the ones that come in with their briefcase and their nice coats" to those ill dressed and ill housed who form the ranks of the permanent poor. The numbers in all categories, Jeffery points out, are increasing.

"What do *I* see?" she says. "I see people who have drained the college funds for their kids, who have drained their savings, their retirement, their CDs, everything. And they are trying to hold on to their homes. I see the poor getting poorer. The programs are being taken away from them, the people that really need it. I see the elderly being taxed out of their homes. I see an increase in crime, because if you lose a chunk of income you start worrying about bills and having tiffs that turn into big arguments. Calls to the police have increased, absolutely.

"I see a lot of people moving in with their families like the old days, moving in with parents or grandparents or brothers or sisters because they can't afford to be on their own. That's the only way they can live, pooling their money."

She also sees something else—or feels it. "Everybody's having a hard time," she explains. "That's why everybody's ugly. I try not to take it personally, but a lot of them get really ugly with me, with the system the way it is."

One man did not understand when Jeffery told him that family assistance grants had been slashed by $300 a month. "He did not understand how come he had qualified before and this time he did not," she says. "I explained that the governor had changed the system and I showed him my charts and my laws, and he got ugly. That happens a lot. Sometimes I think they're going to reach out and choke me. They don't know what to do; they don't know where to turn. People who are usually calm and could deal with crisis, they're at the end of their rope. I can see where people might think about suicide. One couple who were in here talked about it. A few weeks ago another lady said, 'Well, I may as well commit suicide.' And I said, 'I hope you're not really thinking about that.' A woman of forty-three, younger than I am."

That kind of experience is being played out across America as individuals turn to agencies that can ever less assist them. Every recession produces terrible stories of hardships, and the recession of the Nineties has been no different. What *is* different is the magnitude of the suffering and the rising frustration among those in need of help and those who are there to help them. Like the economy, these problems are not transitory; the damage is deep and long-lasting, because of the long-term fiscal crisis confronting government at all levels.

I saw this most powerfully at the second level of government in Maine. The temperatures were plunging below zero, and an icy wind carrying gusts of snow whipped across the parking lot when I pulled up behind the Tri-County Mental Health Clinic at night in Auburn, Maine. Inside, a welcome warmth and brightness eased the harshness of outdoors and set a tone of informality among the group of clinicians and managers drinking coffee around a conference table in the back of the clinic.

These were impressive men and women, thoughtful, measured, not given to rash judgments, and they spoke calmly about how they felt about their clients and themselves. As I listened to them, one after another, the voices began to have a disturbing emotional power of their own. Caseloads of clinical mental illness were rising, the incidents of depression and violent behavior increasing. In just three years, the clinic's waiting list had soared from ten to 150; people once saw a professional on the day they called for an appointment, but now a month might pass before a scheduled appointment. There were new personal pressures, new stresses, for their own budget had been cut sharply, their own dental and drug prescription benefits reduced, and they were expected to do more with less. "We have much more demand for service than we can ever meet with the available resources," Nancy Essex, a manager, says. "They keep taking money away and keep expecting more in return for less money." It was not said with anger, but rather with disappointment and a tone of despair.

"What strikes me is the level of hopelessness of the people coming in here," says Susan Sayer, a clinical social worker. "This week I've had at least three people talking about cuts. A woman who lives with someone else on general assistance, they've cut her rent payment because she's single and childless. So the other person now has to pay the bulk of the rent out of his Social Security disability benefits. The food stamps are being cut. Another young woman whose retarded child's program was cut is afraid it will be cut again, and we simply can't see any more people at this point."

After a long conversation, a consensus is reached: that the severity of the problems will force America to change, but change won't occur until conditions get worse. "When enough people are hurt and enough people are tired of the way things are, there will be a groundswell," Nancy Essex says. "It's like the civil rights movement and the women's movement, with which I was intimately involved. You've got to wait till it hurts bad enough before people are willing to stand up and say, 'I've had enough.' "

Susan Sayer, who began our conversation, closes it. "You know," she says, "our politicians talk about the end of the Cold War. But what's going on here feels like it's going to be as deep a restructuring in America as it is in Russia. I think we'll look back and say, 'Oh my God, we really went through an earthquake here.' "

At the third level of government examined in Maine, Sabra Burdick, head of the Maine Bureau of Income and Maintenance, already had experienced her own personal earthquake when I talked with her. In only a year and a half her agency had experienced a 30 percent rise in caseloads of food stamp beneficiaries and a 25 percent increase in Aid to Families with Dependent Children (AFDC) rolls, and all this while its welfare services and its own work force were being cut.

It was a grim situation, but philosophically Burdick supported the conservative Republican governor, John McKernan, for whose reelection she had worked hard the year before, as he made his budgetary and personnel cuts. Her breaking point came when he publicly proposed denying AFDC benefits to single women who have additional children. Burdick then resigned, ending an eighteen-year public service career with the state, the last five with welfare services. She gave up her $57,000 salary with its five weeks of annual vacation and fully paid health insurance and retirement and an important job supervising an agency of some nine hundred employees with an annual budget of $34 million.

Her resignation wasn't a big story, certainly not the kind that attracts national news coverage. I learned of it through an item in the

Augusta newspaper, and shortly thereafter arranged to meet her one afternoon at Papa Gino's Pizza Parlor in the Auburn Shopping Mall.

Sabra Burdick turned out to be as reluctant to talk about herself in person as she had been on the phone earlier. Slowly, hesitantly, while seated at a back table amid shouted pizza orders, she explained how someone like herself—a Baptist from a small-town Republican family whose only previous public protests involved a few antiwar marches in the Sixties—took the action she did.

"Ideologically and philosophically, I came to terms with the fact that even the poorest of the poor have to help solve the country's problems," she says. "I always thought that I was trying to help people make their lives better, and I know some people need an awful lot of help. They don't have the skills—and probably aren't ever going to have them—to be what the rest of the world would call 'productive members' of society. But they need help to be as productive as they *can* be. I also think welfare parents should be working as soon as they can. I'm conservative enough to want that to happen.

"What the governor's policy says is something different. This is a philosophical switch from trying to help people who are in need to blaming them for their condition and on top of that punishing the children for the mistakes of their parents. That was unconscionable to me. Trying behavior modification on adults is something I'm not sure we should be doing. But certainly punishing kids for the fact that their mother slept with somebody—that is just plain wrong. And that is a position I could not honorably defend."

The next day Burdick was going to Boston to meet with friends in the federal government. "It's like, 'Goodbye and here's my résumé,' " she said. "It's pretty scary." I asked how she thought of herself now. The question seemed to disturb her. After a long silence, she answered, speaking even more slowly and deliberately:

"I've always seen myself as a public servant, and now I don't have that anymore, so I'm not sure what I am. I've lost a sense of identity. And that brings tears to my eyes."

With that, she began to cry. Upset at displaying such emotion, in public and before a stranger, she remarked again on the lack of identity she felt. Then, smiling slightly, she added: "As a nation, we may have the same loss of identity that I now feel as a person."

The crisis in which the United States finds itself over providing basic services for its citizens did not come about overnight, and it will not be solved quickly or easily. For more than a decade, the United States in effect has sold its assets to attempt to maintain its standard of living. The nation has been like the person who finances an expensive vacation by selling his house. When he comes home, his standard of living has been reduced.

In general, that's what Americans have been doing. They have borrowed on their credit cards and home equity loans to live beyond their incomes. American cities, counties, and states have done the same. So has the United States government. While individual Americans and their governments have been borrowing continually over many years, the total debt has been gradually accumulating. Inevitably, interest payments on that rising debt loom larger and larger and make the ability to borrow more difficult. Merely to pay interest on the debt requires living below one's income—and lowering one's standard of living.

When that reality hits home, as it has in the Nineties, it comes as a shock to discover that the hard choices people face are limiting, long-term—and inescapable. If America lived *above* its means for a decade or two, it will have to live *below* its income levels for at least that long to pay back its debts and put its house in order. This is an exceedingly difficult transition for a nation that has always taken tomorrow for granted. Not the least of the difficulties will be how to accomplish that goal while still attending to those who have fallen through the safety net.

There is little that Bill Clinton—or any president—can do immediately to restore equity and economic health to the social welfare system. Even if they had been enacted as introduced, the blizzard of legislative proposals Clinton sent to Congress in his first year would not have shown results until long after passage. Most programs are long-term, such as his near-revolutionary welfare reform, which for the first time would tie benefits to work performed and set limits on how long welfare recipients can receive public assistance.

The key ingredient, deficit reduction, will not begin to take place—if Clinton's assumptions are correct—until after four years have passed. And even then, the deficit will not actually be *reduced;* only the *rate of increase* will be slowed. The nation's deficit—and its debt—will still be rising. In the meantime, the underlying problems that have caused the crisis in basic services continues. Jobs are still being lost, state and local budgets are even more strained, more cutbacks are occurring. Across the nation, public libraries continue to close or severely curtail their hours of operation. In California, for instance, half the school libraries in the state have been closed in the last decade, librarians continue to be laid off, and money to buy books keeps dwindling. The fears I heard expressed from Judges Demetrios Agretelis and Stanley Golde of even more crippling cuts in their judicial and criminal operations in Alameda County, California, unfortunately were being realized a year later as the sheriff there faced the prospect of laying off 338 of his workforce of 1,300. In Los Angeles County, Fire Chief Michael Freeman said new cuts resulted in a one-third curtailment of operations.

By late spring of 1993, reacting against further massive California cuts in services, county sheriffs and fire chiefs—traditionally among the most conservative people in government—began organizing a revolt against Republican Governor Pete Wilson's state budget priorities. Their plans for a march on the state capitol in Sacramento came after the governor proposed shifting $2.6 billion from the counties and cities to education, threatening the layoff of deputies and firefighters, closing of jails, and release of inmates. "Over the years when the budget had to be cut, it was the libraries, parks, and general public services, that bore the brunt," Sacramento Fire Chief Gary Costamanga told *The Los Angeles Times.* "They've already cut those to the bone in many cases. Now it's public safety that's being impacted."

To the north, in the state of Washington, a nearly $2 billion budget deficit forced the closing of a mental health program in Skagit County, a 25 percent reduction in funds for counseling services for victims of crimes, major cuts in drug abuse programs and in-school security services, and a 20 percent increase in tuition at community colleges and universities. "The middle class probably won't feel the cuts in the budget," Representative Gary Locke, the top budget writer in the Seattle house, said. "The poor, the mentally ill, or some businessman waiting for some inspection probably will. Agencies won't be able to hire many workers, serve people as quickly, or serve everybody."

Across the nation, local governments, desperate for relief from being required by their states to provide services that the state was not funding, began introducing constitutional amendments prohibiting such mandates. By mid-1993, ten states, a number of which I visited, had adopted such amendments—California, Florida, Hawaii, Louisiana, Maine, Michigan, Missouri, Montana, New Mexico, and Tennessee. Other states were expected to follow, making the battle for provision of services even more severe as the cutbacks that first began from the federal to the state now worked down to the lowest levels of American government. A disintegration of the ability—or the willingness—of government to provide services was accelerating across America. Local supporters of these constitutional amendments argued that they were only forcing the states to accept responsibility for services they required the local jurisdictions to provide. But it also meant that the states were losing their ability to require that minimum standards be set for education, infrastructure, the environment, and health and human services.*

Also across the nation, the number of people applying for Aid to Families with Dependent Children (AFDC) assistance continues to rise, showing an increase of 1.2 million Americans in the years from 1976 through 1992.

The conditions I encountered in Maine appear to be as difficult, if not worse, a year later. Two of the state's major cities, Portland and Bangor, filed suit against the state, charging that financially strapped state mental hospitals are "dumping" severely disturbed patients into the streets. This came after it was disclosed that a mental health institute in the state capital of Augusta and another major institution for the mentally retarded were being forced by the state's budget crisis to reduce their operations and discharge increasing numbers of patients. Portland also threatened to drop its entire welfare program if it became a magnet for the poor from towns that abandoned their programs. The two cities bringing the legal suit were seeking to require community-based care for "deinstitutionalized" psychiatric patients who are straining already overtaxed homeless shelters.

In denying that Maine was "dumping" mental patients and fail-

---

*An excellent overview of this situation, from which I have drawn herein, is Linda Wagar's article "A Declaration of War," in the April 1993 issue of *State Government News*.

ing to provide proper facilities, an assistant attorney general of Maine, Richard Bergeron, virtually acknowledged that this in fact was taking place. "Like any other state, we don't have enough resources to meet the demand," he told William Claiborne of *The Washington Post*. Then, resorting to bureaucratic jargon, he added: "We are not dumping patients. We are creating a lot of community services while we downsize the institutions."

He may see a distinction between "dumping" and "downsizing," but it is doubtful that those patients on the streets or those who pity, fear, or are dismayed by them do. In any event, Maine's problems mirror those of the nation. Thirty other states were also reported to be cutting or consolidating their mental hospitals in 1993, and the number of patients in public mental hospitals had decreased by nearly half a million in the years from the mid-1950s to the early 1990s. That drop did not occur because America was providing *better* care for its mentally ill citizens. It occurred because America was less able—or less willing—to provide for them.

CHAPTER 7

SCHOOLS:
THE DUMPING
GROUND

They call it their Times Square, the central place through which all corridors cross and through which everyone passes at least once a day. As they move from class to class or go to the nearby cafeteria or congregate in the large circular amphitheater that bears the designation "Student Commons," each student sees the flags of many nations massed against the red brick wall and stirring in the currents of air. At least thirty of these national banners, in all their varied colors, fly from individual poles mounted on that commons wall: Vietnamese, Cambodian, Filipino, Japanese, Chinese, Korean, Mexican, Salvadoran, Guatemalan, Jordanian, Ethiopian, all these and many more are posted prominently to remind students of the composition of Oakland High School.

Once the school reflected a different Oakland, California, and a different America. On the wall in the principal's office are old framed photographs of teachers and students posing before the school's front steps. Everyone is white. In some of the photographs, men have flowing white beards. In others, young women in long dresses pose for a class picture. Athletic teams, again all white, are shown in uniforms that expose little skin—bloomers for the women, knee-high stockings for male basketball players—and holding equipment like medicine balls that seem like vestiges of a distant past. Now the volleyball team is Asian, the soccer team Hispanic, the football team mainly black with only two white players. Also on the wall, in places of honor, are photographs of graduates who left Oakland to become world-famous Americans—Jack London, the writer and adventurer; Gertrude Stein, the expatriate who gave the Lost Generation of the Twenties its name.

Today, through extraordinary demographic changes, Oakland High School has been transformed from a predominantly white to a predominantly black to a predominantly immigrant student body in which Asians and Hispanics now number three-fourths of the population.

Teachers deal with a problem their predecessors could never have imagined: to supply primary language support to students who are either bilingual or can barely speak ten words of English. As if that were not difficult enough, they also must instruct them, as mandated by law that requires ESL (English as a second language)—and not only teach in their various native languages, but also teach others in the same class by employing English. It is a testament to this California public school, and to its teachers and administrators, that it has an advanced algebra/trigonometry class that is taught in Cantonese. The teacher conducts the class first in English, then in Cantonese.

However difficult it may be to serve such a diverse student body, the school provides an education that permits a large proportion of its graduates to go to college. Some make it from Oakland High to Harvard, MIT, and Stanford, and in doing so make Oakland a public education success story at a time when such stories are harder and harder to find. They are becoming harder to find at Oakland High, too.

At the time I visited the school, Oakland High had an enrollment of 1,789 students. The City of Oakland was then providing money for only 1,666 students, a shortfall which meant that the school did not have enough funds to supply all the required textbooks, going short one hundred in physiology and quite a few in American history. For two years it had been without the services of a school nurse; budget cutbacks had slashed $30 million out of the city's school appropriation, with more reductions to come. The Oakland school district also had been forced to eliminate or sharply curtail music and art classes. Its vocational education program had been severely reduced. Class sizes were larger than they had ever been. And in all of the public schools, the greatest problem is not what takes place inside the classrooms but what goes on outside. Each school, especially if it's in the inner city, rises as an island surrounded by a sea of troubles.

Visiting public schools throughout Oakland, one after the other, from elementary to middle and then to high school, provides a study in the sociology of American neighborhoods—and of the tensions that flow through inner-city areas. The closer the school to the high-crime, high-drug districts, the more graffiti are scrawled on the school walls and playgrounds. The more evident, too, the problems of imposing discipline on loud or restless students who move about classrooms while teachers repeatedly ask them to be seated. In the worst areas, some school windows are boarded up because of repeated vandalism. Walking down the hallway of one school, the principal stops to talk to a woman holding a child. She tells him she picked up the child, a boy, after he was hurled from a window of a drug house. She intends to keep him in her care until a foster home can be found. In higher-income areas, the sense of tension eases, the atmosphere inside the school seems less forbidding. Yet in all the problems of the inner city are inescapable.

"We talk about boys and girls coming to school with no breakfast," says Carol Quan, assistant superintendent for support services for the Oakland school system, who escorted me from school to school as we visited classrooms, talking to teachers and principals. "Boys and girls have to walk over syringes and bullets and even condoms before they can get to the classroom. Boys and girls enter real terror zones. They're concerned from the moment they leave their front doors to the time when they reach the doorstep of the schoolhouse. The students are coming in with so much anger, and the parents have so much anger—not so much directed at schools as at society in general. How do we deal with those kinds of community needs and attitudes? We have a very high rate of dropouts with our Hispanic students. We have a large dropout rate with our African-American students, and more and more dropout students with our Southeast Asians."

Ethnic and racial tensions are inevitable among such a range of backgrounds and competing diverse groups. Teachers say the major strains arise out of conflicts between English-speaking and non-English-speaking students: between American-born Chinese unhappy with their immigrant cousins; between Vietnamese and Cam-

bodians; between Laotians and other Asian groups; between those of
differing Middle Eastern backgrounds; between those of two rival
Ethiopian groups who continue to wage their national battles in their
new land. Intensifying these rivalries is the old resentment between
the more established groups and the most recent poorer immigrants
occupying the bottom rung of the ladder. And further terrible pressures of the inner city press in from the gangs and the violence that lie
beyond the school's boundaries.

"Our students grow up—or attempt to grow up—under terrible
conditions," says Joanne Grimm, Oakland High's principal. "We
have students who are the main financial support for their family.
Approximately eighty percent of our students go to school all day
and then work another eight hours because that money provides for
their entire family. They need the money either to put aside for college or simply to survive. Some of them don't even have the twenty
dollars a month it costs for a school bus pass just to get here. They
work in a restaurant, or a sweatshop, or a garage, or as maids in a
hotel. We have students who have their own children to support. We
have children taking care of dysfunctional parents; they're really the
adults in the family. We have students who go home to a neighborhood full of gunshots, with crack dealers, whatever. We have kids
who have seen their friends killed. If you're an urban principal, you
go to a lot of funerals."

I asked Joanne Grimm to elaborate on that. She sighed, then said:

"I've been to a lot of student funerals. Both in junior high and
senior high. Last year I went to three, including the funeral of a staff
member who was murdered. These were all murders. The most difficult one was a young Asian girl who was murdered in her home. I
don't know if they ever found who killed her. She graduated in June
and was killed in September. This was a girl who worked in our
office, whom I saw every day, who hadn't done anything wrong. It
makes you cry, I'll tell you. I do a lot of that. I don't know how the
men handle it. I cry a lot in private.

"Your focus at the funeral is on the rest of the students; you have
to let them know this doesn't necessarily have to happen to them. As
principals and teachers, we walk around and listen to whatever kids
have to say. We talk to them. We're hoping that they'll remember the
way we treated them and that at some point they will treat somebody

else this way. We have this statement around here which is: 'First Do
No Harm.' We want to send everybody back into society better than
they were when they got here. You do the best you can with what you
have for as long as you can. Sometimes you have to cut your losses.
Sometimes you can't help this kid anymore. And that's hard. But for
them, life goes on. They're accustomed to the funerals. That's the
bad part."

When we left Oakland High on our way to another school, Carol
Quan raised the larger question. "What we're facing in Oakland, and
it's the same in any urban center," she said, "is the need for more
services at the same time we're getting less money. We can't afford to
have lawmakers whose children have graduated from school or go to
private schools dictate how we're going to allocate revenue to the
large urban areas. Right now, we're all at a disadvantage, even the
rural public schools. How do we turn that around? What do we need
to do so that *each* child has equal access to education in its finest
sense?

"Here's the issue: can public education as we have known it in the
United States survive the present fiscal environment, what with pulling out the props from public education and issuing vouchers so that
parents can choose whether their children go to public or private
schools? What's going to happen to public education? How are we
going to educate the great majority of our people—and will we be
able to do it?"

The need for quality public education in America has never been
greater, but the difficulty of achieving it has probably never been
greater. This stems from three principal causes: increasing violence
in urban schools, the erosion of scholastic standards, and the diminishing support for public schools by the middle and upper classes.
These, as well as the obvious question of racism, are the principal
factors behind the long flight of parents away from public education.
"Unfortunately, the predominant culture in our schools now is the
one of the underclass, of rebellion," says Sheilah Jordan, a member of
the Oakland school board. "That group of kids is becoming larger,
number one, and more severely disturbed, number two."

Jordan and many others describe how the pressure to conform to the standards of behavior of the most troubled, or violent, students gradually affects the performance of the more capable pupils. Bright students deliberately fail to work up to their potential because their peers disparage scholastic achievement. This is particularly true among black youths from the inner-city ghettoes. To them, academic success is derided as "acting white."*

Sheilah Jordan tells of one such bright young male who was, as she says, "a secret student." In his room at home, he could produce powerfully written pieces, but he would not turn them in to class for fear of being called not "tough enough."

Such incidents contribute to the belief that public education has failed. They also further weaken support for public education: through rejection of school bond measures, which forces school districts to cut services and staff; and through acceleration of the flight to private schools, which makes middle-class parents even more reluctant to pay taxes for public schools.

These problems, serious enough in themselves, mask a greater one that bears on the future of public education in America. Despite the perception that public education is a failure, the schools are expected to solve the worst of society's problems arising out of broken families, the drug culture, and the criminal world of the inner cities. Teachers are expected to be social welfare counselors and police officers as well—and to do so with fewer resources.† This leads to further overcrowding, to greater difficulty in achieving scholastic results, and more distancing between the public schools and the public.

The unpleasant truth is that the public schools, once the glory of

---

*Berkeley anthropologist John Ogbu, who coined the term as applying to behavior of black inner-city pupils, finds many black students consider success in school as "acting white" by the time they reach high school. Believing the rules of the game rigged against them, they apply peer pressure *against* getting good grades, speaking standard English, participating in volunteer work, and being on time. His work is cited in the Business–Higher Education Forum's report *Minority Life in the United States.*

†Kevin Phillips, in *Boiling Point,* notes: "Even in prosperous 1987, spending by all levels of government on public and private education had totaled just 5.1 percent of the U.S. Gross National Product, putting the United States a weak tenth among fifteen advanced nations, far behind leaders like Denmark (7.6 percent), Sweden (7.2 percent), Canada (7.1 percent) and the Netherlands (6.8 percent), albeit on a rough par with Japan and Britain (5.0 percent)." And this was before the recession and federal, state, and local budget crises forced greater spending cutbacks, curtailing services and resulting in layoffs of tens of thousands of teachers in the early 1990s.

American democracy, the way to a better life for generations of immigrants and the binding glue of economic and social classes, have become society's dumping ground.

In the years ahead, that problem almost certainly will become worse. Demographics tell the story. In the twenty-year period from 1990 to 2010, U.S. census figures estimate, America's nonwhite youth population will increase by 4.4 million. At the same time, the student population of white youths will decline by 3.8 million. In that same span, minority students will compose 40 percent of the entire U.S. public school population, up from 30 percent. America's inner-city schools, already predominantly black and Hispanic, will become even more separate. Nearly half of all minority students are poor: 40 percent of African-Americans under the age of eighteen are growing up in poverty, including 50 percent under age six and 53 percent under age three.

Without major changes in the system—and in our priorities—we can expect their plight to become worse. And the problem exists not only for inner-city schools but for all schools. In my travels, Peoria's example was vivid and typical. There, failure of the public to bankroll the public schools led to dismissal of talented young teachers at a period when their skills were most needed. The problem went beyond the local to the state level, where an Illinois budget crisis caused cutbacks in school-district subsidies. These were the forces that combined to force Debbie Quisenberry to accept a job as a blackjack operator in the new gambling ship *Paradise* to raise money for graduate school. She's the young elementary school teacher who was given a pink slip from her $19,600-a-year position at the Parkview Middle School in Creve Coeur, a mainly white, lower-income working-class community across the Illinois River from downtown Peoria.

Even before she and other junior teachers were dismissed, her school had experienced drastic cutbacks. Plans for new computers and band equipment had already been scrapped. The sports program was virtually eliminated.

"Eighty percent of the funding for this school is dependent upon the state, and our state just cut education funding," Quisenberry said. "They asked for a tax referendum and the community would not pass it. Teachers wrote letters to the school board saying, please,

please, help us out. The school board said we can't create money that's not there. You have to help us get a tax referendum passed. So we formed committees. We called our students' parents and said what is going on at your school; please vote yes for the tax referendum. If you do not vote yes, these cuts will occur. The tax referendum failed. People don't value education. If they did, our schools would be a lot different.

"There are no sports," she said. "There's no basketball. There's no football. There's no track. There's nothing after school at all. Our textbooks are falling apart. Seriously. Physically falling apart. The kids' desks are broken down. We've got seats that are too low and they can't be raised because they've been soldered on. Seats are cracked down the middle. The kids have to watch how they sit down so they don't get pinched. Screws are falling out—they've been replaced so many times the holes are stripped. Class sizes are going to jump. Money for classroom supplies is cut from one hundred twenty-five dollars a year to twenty-five dollars a year. That's supposed to pay for your pencils, your paper, your pens, all your art supplies for a year! I spent out of my own paycheck for supplies all the time; it's just part of what you do."

Quisenberry's school was in a relatively poor district. But the best public school district in Peoria was also hard hit. At the Richwood Community High School, you pull up to the front door and park in open ample public space. These doors are open; no security guard watches your entry. All around the school are the substantial homes and well-tended lawns that tell you this stands as one of Peoria's upper-income neighborhoods. But once inside, the story becomes all too familiar: more hardship, more cutbacks, more long-term difficulties.

Jay McCormack, the principal, says, "We've wiped out our first-year teachers for next year. They've been given an 'honorable dismissal.' I have three first-year math teachers—all young, energetic, potentially great teachers—yet all three have been released for next year."

McCormack pulled out a sheet of paper and ran down a list of figures: one of four administrative positions in his office, *cut;* one of five guidance counselors, *cut;* two teaching positions, in addition to the three math teachers, *cut;* one of two library assistants, *cut.* He also cut $14,500 from his equipment budget for such items as test tubes, cut the nonathletic intramural program, cut some cultural programs.

I related Debbie Quisenberry's story, how she had gone to her father, after losing her teaching job, and said: "Dad, don't talk to me about the American Dream. The American Dream's over, dead, and your generation's responsible." How did that make McCormack feel as a veteran public school educator?

He answered with a nod, and what seemed like a weary shrug. "I live in a very sheltered world with a very good school," he replied. "This is the best, and not just in Peoria. You can go to the suburban Chicago area and find some that are bigger and maybe as good, but this is about as good as you get." Then he shifted the focus of my question to a more general concern about American public education. In the last year, he had been able to examine the workings of the "magnet" schools in Chicago and Philadelphia that some experts are citing as the hope for the future. These are the schools into which substantial money is being poured to promote "quality education." And that is fine as far as it goes, McCormack went on, but it's certain to exacerbate the divisions between economic and racial groups in the public schools. "The magnet schools are not really a way of promoting science or health or mathematics," he says. "They are a way of skimming off the quality kids that still want an education and getting them into a better learning environment—a safe school. So we've got ten magnet schools that are safe and have a good educational environment for the kids. And then we've got the teachers and the students in the other twenty-six schools that are like the old blackboard jungle."

As for his own school in Peoria, he went on, "I don't live in a school where you lock the door when the bell rings and nobody gets in or out until fifty minutes later when the bell rings again. My nephew does at Farragut High School, in a lower-income area of the city, and he and I talk about what he does there and what I do here. And our days are completely different."

Later, I spoke to another high school principal in Peoria about the situation in which young teachers dismissed from their jobs find themselves. David Barnwell, whose Woodruff High School stands in the inner city surrounded by a large fence with all but one of the doors locked and padlocked and security guards watching the one open entry, was more personal in his response. He already had to give pink slips to five first-year teachers because of the budget crisis, he said, and it was a heartbreaking experience. "Yet the horror stories you hear about good, young people who get pink slips, who thought they'd prepared themselves to be part of the American Dream only to find their dreams at least temporarily smashed, are not just in education, and not just in our school," he said. "They're in so many of our industries. It makes people turn off and say to themselves, 'I'm going to take care of myself. I've lost my desire to do something for others in this world.' More and more it seems like—and maybe this is an overgeneralization—people are saying they don't have the spirit to do things for the benefit of mankind. They've got to find a way to make money and take care of number one.

"If we lose the idealism that young people have and the drive that they have, more than just our educational system is in trouble. You know, when hard times come, the youngest and brightest are often the first to go, and those are the people we desperately need to mix with some of us older people"—Barnwell is in his mid-forties. "We don't have the mix of faculty we used to have at any of our schools. We're top-heavy with people in that forty-five-to-sixty age bracket. There's not the turnover there used to be. Seldom do we get a chance to hire some good young people straight out of college."

Like his fellow principal Jay McCormack, David Barnwell believes that public schools in Peoria are doing an excellent job preparing their best students for college. But he worries about two other groups: the 20 to 25 percent of students who drop out and become lost to productive society, and those in the middle academically who *do* graduate. "I'm concerned about how prepared they are to face the real world," he says. "They have a diploma, which doesn't mean very much, and I don't know what they're going to do. Somehow we've got to develop a more relevant curriculum for those kids who are not going to go on and earn a college degree."

That requires much more: a new national consensus on how best to educate and train young Americans for that "real" world. But money is also essential to create any new educational system, and the painful lesson of my journey is that public schools across the nation are not only having to lay off teachers and curtail programs, they're also having to scrounge for basics taken for granted in American schoolrooms for more than a century. That situation became instantly apparent in the suburban bedroom community of Arlington, Texas, halfway between Dallas and Fort Worth.

When I walked into the Roquemore Elementary School to talk with Jeanne Paull, the principal, and Diane Patrick, outgoing head of the Arlington County school board, I noticed two coin machines in the front hallway in which students could put quarters to buy pencils and notebooks. I had not seen that before, and I asked the principal about it.

"Well, I provide most of my students with supplies through charity organizations," she said. "I have an awful lot of Adopt-a-School people that give money. If the students are able to buy the pencils and notebooks, they're there. If they can't, I'll get them one way or another."

In other words, she has to scrounge—beg or borrow—for them. The reason is again familiar: the school fiscal crisis in Texas forced her to cut the school supply budget first 10 percent, then 25 percent, then 50 percent; it was agreed to cut another 25 percent if necessary. These actions came about because the Arlington school district was in the midst of massive cuts driven by a $10 million shortfall after voters rejected an attempt to raise taxes for schools. "We were very surprised because we thought our community really supported education," the principal said. "When this happened, and with a loss of at least eight million dollars and probably more, we had to look hard at our programs."

It wasn't just the people of Arlington who rejected spending on public schools. All of the 3.2 million children in the Texas school system—the nation's largest, after California—were being adversely affected because of the unwillingness of citizens to pass school-funding measures. As in Illinois, Texas local school districts were suffering from state budgetary cuts—again caused by voters rejecting tax increases for schools.

"We do a great deal of forecasting, and we tell the school administration to do three-year financial forecasting," said Diane Patrick, who won election to the Arlington school board as a Republican. "That's become a joke, because it's impossible to know what our shortfall's going to be because of the state funding crisis. We're now looking at a shortfall of about five and a half million dollars. Next year they've told us to estimate something in the neighborhood of a thirteen-million-dollar shortfall."

She produced a chart that showed a stunning disparity. In ten years from 1983 to 1993, the Arlington school district student population had increased from 13,000 to 47,000. While this explosive growth was occurring, Texas state aid per student dropped from $1,012 in 1984 to $740 in 1992. There were nearly four times as many students and 25 percent less money to spend for each student's education.

It seems inevitable, I said, that more drastic cuts are going to have to be made.

Yes, she said. They were trying to keep their cuts limited to "what might be described as nonessential." At that moment they were involved in a budget review process with a newly established citizens' advisory committee. Hearings were held and citizens were asked to examine the budget and establish critical priorities. "Basically what's happened at the hearings is that every person has come in and said, 'Don't cut my program. I know this other program's important, but it's not as important as what my child does.' "

Just like Washington, I said.

"Special interests!" she said, laughing. "We have 'em right here in Arlington, Texas."

What was all this saying about what was happening to America? I asked her.

"It says that we've got to get our priorities rearranged to be sure that education is our number one priority," she replied. "Nothing is more important for the future of the country."

How high a priority Texas places on public education became depressingly clear a year later. A proposed amendment to the Texas constitution that would have forced wealthier school districts to share tax money with poorer ones was defeated by two to one.

This vote came after the Texas supreme court ordered that changes be made in the way public school funds were allocated because it had found that the present system led to egregious disparities that violated the constitution's guarantee of "an efficient system" for "the general diffusion of knowledge." This also came after Texas Governor Ann W. Richards had campaigned vigorously for the constitutional amendment, about which Texas voters had been debating

for a quarter of a century. Its defeat led to a threat by the court to
shut down *all* Texas public schools unless a new method of dividing
state educational money more fairly was immediately implemented.

It was a victory for antitax, anti-public-education forces—those
beyond-the-Washington-Beltway "special interests" again. And it
came even as Bill Clinton's new education secretary, Richard Riley,
a former governor of South Carolina who has earned a national reputation as an innovative education reformer, was presenting the administration's educational reform package to Congress calling for a
series of goals to be achieved by the year 2000.

There was, in this Texas development, another element of high
symbolism: it delineated the value the public places on education and
its willingness to expend public treasure to create change. On the
same day that 2.04 million voters of Texas went to the polls to deliver
their negative verdict on the school-funding issue, three times as
many Texans lined up to pay for a chance to win the $50 million state
lottery.

Considering the massive problems teachers face, the marvel is
that so many continue to be devoted to the principle of public education. This is true everywhere, but it's most striking among those who
teach in the inner city.

In south-central Los Angeles, in the center of the riot area, Cathy
Silva is an assistant principal of James Foshay Junior High, another
school whose demographics have changed from predominantly black
to Latino. Silva is white. "In all the years I've been in education—
and this is my twenty-eighth year—my time in the inner city has been
the most rewarding and exciting and meaningful to me," she says.
"People used to say, 'Oh, how can you work down there? It's scary.
Aren't you afraid you're going to be killed or beaten up?' And none
of it's true. It's not true for me personally. I *chose* to go to the inner
city, I wasn't transferred there. I was glad to be able to stay and do
something."

Not that Silva doesn't feel the common frustrations of others in
public education. In Los Angeles, too, there have been major cutbacks with teachers and administrators facing salary reductions of
up to 18 percent. Silva equates the unwillingness of society to pay
more for its teachers and administrators to underlying sexism. "It's a

female's job," she says sarcastically, "therefore why pay more? The people want a by-product that can go into the twenty-first century: reading, writing, doing all the wonderful things that they like to see. But they don't want to pay for this. They're not willing to give teachers class sizes that are less than thirty-three or thirty-five. They're not giving them enough money for instructional materials. They want to send the kids to private schools and there aren't enough private schools. So we're in schools with just minority students. And everybody knows—and I'm being very sarcastic—minority students can't succeed."

Another assistant principal at Foshay, Nora Corbett, also white, put it this way: "We've been saddled with trying to take on society's problems as a whole, and we can't solve the problems of the family, the drug culture, and the things that are breaking down around us. What we're trying to do at Foshay—and I'm sure at every other school—is build a safe environment where we can do a decent instructional program. But then you come back to the question: for what? If we don't answer that question, then we're going to give up, and that's what I'm afraid is happening. If we don't believe our kids have a future, why are we coming to work every day? I come to work because I want to believe that they have a future. If we don't believe that, maybe we shouldn't be in education."

At Crenshaw High, also in south-central Los Angeles, Yvonne Noble had been principal for barely a month when I spoke with her. She is black, and that fact powerfully affects her outlook. Despite the severity of present educational problems, she says, with teachers having to mortgage their souls and being treated like beggars, there is still proof that the public educational system has worked—and her experience as a black woman exemplifies it. When she began teaching in the early 1960s, she remarks, no student would have had an African-American principal as a model of achievement. "So a lot of things did change," she says, "although I think we are slowly creeping back to the place where we were. That's why public education is the only way we've been able to give people parity. Without public education, there would be no Yvonne Noble in this society."

Then there's Gail Hojo, in Oakland, whose life and career show the way that society has consigned greater roles to teachers—or at least foisted far greater societal responsibilities on them, whether they seek them or not. Teachers now are often expected to be family counselors, crisis negotiators, even keepers of the peace between rival gangs. Gail Hojo's all of these things and more.

She was born in one of the infamous relocation camps for Japanese-American citizens during World War II; then, at the age of two, she was sent to a government housing project near U.S. military bases in Alameda, California. She still remembers the squat shape and cement floors of the building where she and her family lived. Nearly half a century later, she believes the children in her charge—even the black kids—at the Claremont Middle School in Oakland, California, don't understand what real prejudice is. "It was just blatant," she says. " 'No Japs Allowed.' We couldn't go into certain restaurants, we couldn't go into certain movie houses. 'No Japs Allowed'—I saw those signs all over the place. So I know what exclusion means—real exclusion. I know what it means to go to an elementary school and not have anybody to play with, and to be called names."

Oddly enough, the experience didn't embitter Gail Hojo. Her family moved to East Oakland, a mixed neighborhood, where she went to public schools from elementary through high school. In 1965, she graduated from Berkeley. Two years later, during the Vietnam War, she earned her teaching credentials and married a Japanese-American like herself.

They joined the Peace Corps and served for two and a half years in Thailand, bordering Cambodia, placing them at the edge of the expanding Vietnam War. When she returned to Oakland in the early Seventies to resume her teaching career, Gail Hojo experienced more than culture shock. The world she had known in Oakland was gone; the schools showed it. They were occupied by inner-city blacks, many of whom began life with three strikes against them. The test scores in her school were sinking year after year, and had dropped to the twentieth percentile (the fiftieth percentile is regarded as average grade level). In her sixth-grade classes, Hojo found herself dealing with pupils who regularly reported to their "POs," or parole officers.

Nonetheless, Hojo remained a dedicated teacher. As she said, the actual teaching is the easiest part of her job. More difficult is dealing with angry children, angry parents, school bureaucracy, political dictates imposed from "downtown." Even harder is watching students fail and drop out. "Most of them want to do their best," Hojo says, "but let's be honest. Some of our kids are lost. They're lost to us as a society, and we have to acknowledge that. We try so hard, and we've got to keep trying hard. But we're not going to do it for everybody. We'll lose them at eleven or lose them at twelve."

After a generation in the Oakland public schools, Hojo continues to be an optimist; but she's also a realist. She views her own school with pride. It is a positive example of what an urban school can accomplish, and not just by new programs or techniques. Its success was achieved the old-fashioned way: through sheer hard work, dedication to excellence, and insistence upon high standards in the classroom; through generating a climate of enthusiasm throughout the school and striving for as close connections as possible between students and teachers. In recent years, achievement scores rose from the low twentieth percentile to the sixtieth and seventieth. It's hard to tell whether the students are actually improving scholastically, however. There have been ethnic and political pressures to remove standardized tests and grades that work to the disadvantage of many minority students. Statewide tests to measure student achievement have been eliminated in the belief they were racially and culturally biased and fail to gauge a pupil's real ability to solve problems. When we talked, the school had *no* standard base with which to measure performance.

"I can't give you a clue as to *how* we're doing for the past two or three years," Hojo says, "because we really don't test."

She describes a situation in which students come to her middle school having been led to believe they are doing satisfactory work when in fact they are far behind. "It's really a shame," she says, "because it threatens their esteem. They thought they were doing well at elementary school. They say, 'Damn, I can't read those words. *They* told me I was okay.'

"We try not to be condescending—don't give them second-, third-, and fourth-grade readers if they're in seventh or eighth grade. We give them seventh- and eighth-grade readers. We try to bring them up to that level, because it's not good to tell them, 'You're doing so well, you're doing so well.' And dammit, they're *not* doing well! They're reading at third-grade levels and they're sixth-graders.

"In elementary school we're giving them Gs and Es because their effort is good at a third-grade level. That doesn't say a thing. When they get here—*bam!*—reality hits. They say, 'Hey, I can't go on.' There is this great gap, and how do we bridge that gap? We don't even want to look at their elementary report cards. What's an S? Satisfactory. What does that mean? Satisfactory in math. That doesn't mean anything. Satisfactory at what level? A G, a good, an E, an excellent, what does that mean? It means absolutely *nothing* to us. It gives us *no* information. Thank goodness, most of them have *some* test scores so we can see at what level they're functioning."

Hojo also feels strongly about California requirements for bilingual education. "It's not possible," she says. "We don't even have enough teachers. We're never going to meet that requirement. At some point, we've got to say we can't do this. There is not one district in California that can meet those state requirements.* I've tried to devise a program that makes sense for my kids who are limited in English. I don't have people who can teach in nine to thirteen languages. But I *can* try to see that the kids get a good education in English. By God, we can teach them English! It's very condescending to teach ESL math and ESL this and ESL that and have them go on to high school and think they can get in college. *Ha!* Do they have to pass the SATs [Scholastic Aptitude Tests] at other students' level? Yes they do! Colleges and universities are not looking for ESL math. They're looking for achievement in geometry, trig, calculus. So there's a problem, a big problem. I don't have the answers, but I can identify the problem."

Another problem Hojo cannot solve, but must deal with, involves trying to keep the criminal and gang behavior out of the classroom. At times, in an attempt to avoid territorial conflicts that might spread into the school, she finds herself negotiating with rival gang leaders outside of school. She also has met with people involved in drug deals to try to keep them out of the area and, most crucially, the

---

*Joanne Grimm, principal of Oakland High, makes a similar point. "The students were never asked," she says of directives for bilingual education. "The students are not interested in learning in their native language. Their parents may be interested and the state may be interested but the students are not. They want to speak English as quickly as possible. They'll come in and rant and rave about being in ESL classes. It's considered a failure to be in these classes, and nobody ever asks the kids why they feel that way."

school. Once, while she was negotiating with rival gang members, a phone call came through warning that a youth with a gun was coming to see her. She expressed her alarm to some of the gang members. "I got really scared," she said. "I thought, I don't want to die. I want to see my daughter graduate from high school and college."

The young men listened to her concerns, then one said: "Man, that's part of it, Mrs. Hojo. You take your chances. If you die, you die."

"But you've got to make your chances so you *don't* have to die," she insisted.

"Hey," she was told, "that's just the way things are."

That's the saddest thing, she said, this acceptance of early violent death. "It's easier for some of my kids to get a gun on the street than it is to get a stupid library card. That makes no sense to me. When they go to the library they give them all kinds of hassle about filling in the form. But, 'You want a gun? Five dollars, man, I'll give you a gun.' That's it. Sometimes they don't even have to pay for it."

When Bill and Hillary Clinton came to Washington they faced a choice that millions of other American parents must make: whether to put their child in public school. Their decision was the one made by countless other citizens. They sent their daughter, Chelsea, to a private school.

Lynne and Steve Spickard have much in common with the Clintons. They are well-educated baby boomers who share the liberal values of many of their neighbors in the San Francisco Bay area. The Spickards' public-or-private-school dilemma is even more telling than that of the Clinton family, whose lives are constrained by questions of security. For the Spickards and others of their generation, the choice of schools has become an overriding issue.

When the Spickards moved into their Oakland neighborhood they had not made the decision to become parents, but if they did they knew that the quality of the schools would be of central concern. Steve, an economist who plans ahead, called the state education office shortly after their move to obtain California Assessment Program (CAP) scores for the local schools. They were in the 30 to 40 percent range: below average, but, as Steve said, "not horrible." He and Lynne, an artist and product of Oakland's public school system, concluded that the score results would probably improve, given the area's emphasis on education.

Five years later, Lynne became pregnant. Should they move to an area where the schools were better or stick it out? Again, Steve obtained the state CAP scores. The results had dropped even more. Even so, the Spickards decided to stay. When the time came for their first child to go to kindergarten, Steve checked out the schools again. He was dismayed to learn they had dropped into the low twenties. "For two graduate-student types like us," he said, "the idea of sending your kid to a school that scores in the bottom fifth of the state was untenable."

Yet they stayed, and planned to put their son in the public school.

Steve said, "We had this Sixties radical idea that we would all get together and take over the school and make it in our own image even if we had to do it grade by grade starting with kindergarten."

With other young couples in the area, the Spickards formed a neighborhood parents' association. They attended school board meetings, talked to officials, went door to door in their neighborhood to generate support for their ideas to change the school curriculum and make the educational environment more challenging. This meant raising money to buy computers—there were only two, both locked up, when the parents toured the school—and also getting funding for additional teaching assistants and better classroom equipment. Through their new parents' group, they believed they had sufficient strength and support to, as Steve said, "basically pack a kindergarten class with our kids and change policy."

One night, their parents' group attended an open house in the school. "We saw the little play and the performance that the kids put on, talked to the teachers, looked at the classrooms, examined the kids' work," Steve recalled, "and it was sad. As we were walking back up the street, all the parents were shaking their heads." They had seen teachers struggling to maintain discipline—because an Oakland day-care center adjoined the school, inner-city children were bused to it and also permitted to attend the school—had found almost no parental involvement for the ghetto children, and had encountered what seemed a clear lack of interest from the principal in their ideas for regenerating the school. As Steve said of the parents' group, "It was clear their decision was, no way we could change that. It was too much. The school board seemed insensitive. We were going to kill ourselves trying to do this grass-roots thing, and for what?"

As a result, all the parents who walked back from the school that night sent their children to private schools.

"We all supported the public school system, we wanted our kids to go to public school," Lynne said, leaning forward intently during our conversation, "but—"

"Yeah," Steve interjected, "every single one of us was a product of the public school system, most of them from California, a bunch of them from the Bay area."

Steve wanted to make sure I understood the depth of their feelings. "Once we had kids," he said, "the consuming factor in our life-planning has been: how the hell are we going to get them educated?"

After their disillusionment with the neighborhood public school, the Spickards began to study available school choices. They were immediately attracted to the four "magnet" schools in Oakland, those public schools that emphasize quality education and select top students. But because of the popularity of these schools, there were far more applicants than the schools could accommodate. Oakland's solution was to admit students through a lottery drawing. At a public meeting at the magnet school where Steve and Lynne hoped their son would go, the principal said that after the lottery numbers were chosen "we would have to equalize it demographically." What did that mean? one parent asked. The composition of the incoming kindergarten class would have to be comparable to that of the city of Oakland, the principal explained.

"That means," Steve said, "they're going to take one white boy and one white girl and all the rest are going to be minorities or else it won't balance. I thought, wait a minute, I've got one chance in fifty of winning the lottery and if I do win the lottery my kid's going to be the only white boy in the entire class? That wasn't exactly what I was looking for either. Besides, you couldn't deal with the uncertainty. If you waited to get in but you didn't, then it would be too late to get into any public school—or private school."

They began an exhaustive process to select a private school they could afford. Neither of them wanted their son to go to "a snooty-type school. What we really wanted was what we had as kids: a basic plebeian public school." Soon they discovered that instead of interviewing the school authorities about the institution, the officials were interviewing *them*. "It's like applying to college," Steve said, "and for a kindergartner! It's insane. Plus it costs a lot more than going to UC Berkeley. The standard joke at my office was: 'I can't wait till my kid gets to college so his tuition will finally go down to a normal level.' "

Their son Gregory got into their second choice of private school, at $4,700 a year. By the time their second child was ready for kindergarten, the combined tuition was $7,000 a year, a heavy burden for a couple in their late thirties. In the end, the Spickards sold their house and bought another in a more expensive area adjacent to Oakland where the public school was, if not as good as the private one their older son was attending, better than the public school where they had been living.

What did their experience say about public education and where it's going? I asked.

"You mean once you get past the anger," Steve replied.

"I wish we could have stayed in our neighborhood," Lynne said, "and gone through schools that were integrated, where my kids could learn more about ethnicities and cultures and study with blue-collar workers and white-collar workers and all live together in harmony. But it's just not working out like that."

No school can escape the financial and societal forces that beset American education in the Nineties. They affect the great private universities like MIT and Yale and the great public institutions like the University of Michigan and the University of California at Berkeley. And what the Association of Governing Boards of Universities and Colleges describes as "the new depression in higher education" will last for years, reflecting the state not only of education but of the United States.

"When I was young, everyone looked to the United States as a place of golden opportunities," said Chang-Lin Tien, who came to this country as a refugee from China after World War II. In 1991 he became the first Chinese-American chancellor at the University of

California at Berkeley. "Now you are sharing the wealth with many other countries, and that's a tough adjustment for the United States."

Berkeley had already made many painful adjustments. Department budgets were cut, and many faculty members were forced to take early retirements. Fees and tuition were raised. In just three years, the chancellor said, the university had to raise fees and tuition by 85 percent. Thirty years ago, the University of California's nine-campus system—then widely regarded as the best such system in the world—received 70 percent of its funds from the state. At the time we talked, in the fall of 1992, that had dropped to 24 percent. A year later, when the state's 1993–94 budget was adopted, it was given $400 million less to operate than it had received three years earlier—and less than had been appropriated in 1986–87. In the seven years since then, inflation and student enrollment had increased by 40 percent. In other words, there were 40 percent more California students and they were receiving less aid than students got seven years earlier!

The same thing had happened in Michigan, whose public university system was also world-renowned. As the automobile industry declined, so did the Michigan economy. With it came sharply reduced state financial support for the university. By the early Nineties, the University of Michigan was receiving only 17 percent of its money from the state. Neither Michigan nor Berkeley was truly a publicly supported university system any longer. Each had to rely on outside sources for funds. Berkeley, for instance, was raising more than $100 million annually through fund-raising efforts—a fivefold increase in just a decade.

Dimensions of the financial crisis facing higher education are astounding. For twenty years preceding Bill Clinton's presidency, tuition, fees, books, and housing costs at America's 3,500 public and private colleges and universities rose an average of 8 percent each year—faster than inflation or after-tax income, placing all institutions under greater and greater pressures. If the annual costs keep increasing by 8 percent, students attending kindergarten when Clinton was inaugurated will be faced with a total expense of $300,000—and $85,000 for the senior year alone—for four years at a premium institution like Harvard. As Daniel S. Cheever, Jr., president of the American Student Assistance Corporation and former president of

Boston's Wheelock College, notes in *Harvard Magazine,* that cumulative $300,000 figure is only the cost to a student's family. The full cost, Cheever adds, is more than twice as much at well-endowed institutions where the differences are made up through alumni gifts, endowment income, and other sources.

Using the same College Board formula for an "average" private college, Cheever estimates the cost of a degree at $200,000. "It will be cheaper—but still very expensive—to attend a public university," he writes, "where the cost of educating a student is not much lower than at a private college. Tuition is less because the taxpayer picks up about 80 percent of the tab. If today's kindergartner chooses to attend a public college like the University of Massachusetts, it could cost that student $75,000 and the taxpayer four times that amount."

Cheever, whose corporation is a guarantor of federal student loans, adds: "Regardless of whether these tuition projections prove correct, the real problem is that tuition may consume a greater portion of family income. From 1980 to 1987, after adjusting for inflation, family incomes rose only 6 percent while public college tuition increased 30 percent and private college tuition jumped 50 percent in real dollars. . . . For middle-class families, median family income adjusted for inflation has risen only $2,000 since 1970, and that small gain is largely because of the entry of women into the labor market. That's why these tuition projections for today's kindergartner are not adjusted for inflation. There is no point adjusting for inflation if family incomes do not grow. The real measure of college affordability is the rate of increase in after-tax family income. Few of us dare predict significant increases in the Nineties, burdened as we are with $4 trillion of national debt, the elimination of many jobs during the recession, and enormous unmet needs in such areas as medical care and human services."

Even the most optimistic scenarios—with after-tax disposable family incomes rising, say, at the unlikely rate of 4 percent a year— the projections remain worrisome. Cheever estimates that costs for a four-year private college would exceed $175,000, and for a public college would exceed $60,000. He also observes that "the bad news gets worse." Other college costs—from faculty and staff salaries to employee benefits and maintenance and intensifying pressure to provide greater financial aid—drive tuition even higher. And this when those tuitions already are rapidly rising to offset lost state revenues from budget cuts.

Much more than a financial crisis is at hand. Other problems afflicting American education are placing the nation's future at risk. A disturbing example of the immensity of the challenges can be seen in relation to scientific achievement. Despite the growing importance of science in national life, and at a time when scientific advances in the next generation will dwarf the changes of the last quarter-century, the United States continues to fall behind its competitors in producing scientific and technological leaders. Since 1960, the proportion of undergraduate degrees in science and engineering has stagnated, according to the Association of Governing Boards of Universities and Colleges. Since 1982 the number of freshmen planning to enter engineering has dropped by 25 percent, and only 60 percent of freshmen planning a career in science or engineering receive a B.S. degree. Undergraduate degrees in engineering and the physical sciences have dropped steadily throughout the 1980s, and the report adds: "The number of advanced degrees in science awarded to Americans has plummeted, and the number of advanced degrees in science awarded to minority Americans is pitifully small. Most years, American universities can count the number of African-Americans awarded the Ph.D. in mathematics on the fingers of one hand."

However critical these challenges, they do not begin to convey the personal anguish of parents who fear that their children's lives will not be as good as theirs, and who worry most about two things: the ability to provide good educations for their children, and their children's eventual prospects of finding rewarding work. The two, of course, are inseparable: education is the foundation for the good life, and the good job. Through shortsighted actions like those described here, America is shortchanging the next generation—both those who attend the best public schools and those who attend the worst. It is also endangering the colleges and universities that have always been the vehicle to move from the bottom to the top.

Many college graduates I met who despaired of their prospects when Bill Clinton was running for president never found work in their fields. They were forced to take whatever opportunity presented itself. And even then, these were the fortunate ones. A full year later, many were still searching for work and competing with the next

wave of college graduates about to enter an even gloomier job market. College placement officials said that 1993 graduates faced the
most dismal job prospects since the end of World War II. More than
35 percent were taking jobs that did not require a degree. For some,
this meant competing with high school graduates for increasingly
scarce factory jobs. For others, it meant further swelling the ranks of
America's "temp" workers.

"A bachelor's degree today is worth the equivalent of a permanent incomplete," a nationally respected educator, Milton Stern of
Berkeley, told me. "We are witnessing something America has not
seen before—a new class, the educated poor, downwardly mobile,
overqualified, and with diminished prospects of finding jobs for
which they were trained. Nor is this a temporary phenomenon. It is
likely to continue well into the next century."

As Stern says, all this raises doubts about the value of a college
degree, and about what kind of country America is becoming. There
is a new term for what graduates encounter: "outsourcing." Companies will hire highly qualified employees, often at good wages, but for
only two days a week and with no benefits. As a result, more and
more people will hold more than one job, work in smaller units, and
often work from their homes. For graduates with tens of thousands
of dollars in college loans, the situation is crucial. Many who tried to
"ride out the recession" by going further into debt and entering graduate schools are even more in the hole after receiving their degrees,
and still without work. This is another reason why Clinton's public
service plan, permitting students to repay government loans for college by serving as teachers or in police and fire departments for two
years after graduation, makes good sense.

As for higher education's financial crisis, eminent public universities like Berkeley and Michigan will survive and prosper, and so
will more munificently endowed private ones like Harvard and
Princeton. Others, less fortunate, will not.*

Of all the schools and universities I visited, the saddest example
of decline was the University of Bridgeport. For sixty-five years, it
had fulfilled its educational mission well. It is situated in an area of

---

*Between 1960 and 1990, 323 U.S. institutions of higher education went out of business.
Most of them were private and quite a few were entrepreneurial—intended to be profitable.

Connecticut graced by private universities like Yale but with no schools comparable in quality to the public colleges and universities of the Midwest and West. UB, as it is called, provided a good private education at reasonable cost. Over the years, it became a way up for sons and daughters of immigrants and for increasing numbers of foreign students. UB and the city for which it was named were good for each other. A graduate from a blue-collar family in the Sixties told me, "I never would have made it in the world if UB was not there." Physically, the university's location was superb: eighty-six acres fronting on Long Island Sound. Academically, in its best days, it was a place of high morale and had an excellent faculty.

By the time I arrived in Bridgeport, UB was perhaps the most visible symbol of the ills that had overtaken the city. Cut off from the center of Bridgeport by freeways that bisect the city, the campus had deteriorated into a dangerous slum. All around it were ugly faded red-brick projects, dismal testimony to the failure of public housing in America. Graffiti and obscene insults were everywhere. "Fuck the bitches," read one crudely scrawled message on a project wall.

As I parked in the center of the campus and got out of my car, I saw littered streets, broken windows, formerly dignified college buildings in disrepair. A few blocks to the south, one of Bridgeport's once-grand parks was now a haven for drug dealers. As I entered an administration building, I saw two signs. One read: "Auto Theft Alert. Incidents of theft of vehicles parked in our lots have increased dramatically. Don't wait for something to happen before calling." Another, in bold uppercase letters, read: "P.S. DO NOT WALK ALONE. CALL 4911 PUBLIC SAFETY FOR AN ESCORT. DON'T TAKE CHANCES."

The university, like the city, was broke and struggling to stay alive.

As Bridgeport had declined, so had the university. Its problems intensified in the mid-Eighties when enrollment dropped and smaller-than-anticipated freshmen classes registered, bringing tuition revenues sharply down. At the same time, the university was obligated to pay what turned out to be overgenerous salary and benefits to its unionized faculty and staff.

UB also faced demographic problems common to every American institution of higher learning. As more and more Americans attended college, the cost of college rose along with the number of people needing financial aid. UB's tuition of $12,000 was approximately half that of the Ivy League schools, but its average student received from $3,000 to $4,000 annually in financial grants. A 1987 strike that began after a faculty union contract expired made the financial strains greater.

UB's shaky financial condition worsened as the recession ravaged the Northeast. Officials began an intensive cost-cutting effort and discussed proposals to sell part of the university's land and buildings. By 1992, the law school, started only in 1977, announced plans to separate from the school and affiliate with another private university outside Bridgeport.

Not long before my visit, UB's board of directors had been conducting secret talks with foreign governments, among them those of Japan and Israel, with the idea of having those nations assume its debts and provide additional revenues in return for programs tailored for their students. These talks failed. UB then turned to another secret source: the Unification Church, based in Korea—the ultraright group known as the Moonies. (Months later, the Moonies bought the school.)

"We do not have high morale among the students, among the faculty, among the staff, anywhere," Edwin Eiger, UB's president, wearily told me. "People are wondering if tomorrow they're going to have a job or not. Students are wondering if they're ever going to be able to finish their program. We reduced salaries across the board. Everybody is earning less now than they were two years ago by a considerable amount."

I asked Eiger, a native of St. Louis who did his postgraduate work at MIT, to what extent he thought the university's plight was representative of education nationwide, both public and private.

"The University of Bridgeport is just a little bit ahead of other institutions in this regard," he answered. "My suspicion is that there will be many other institutions facing the same problems. Those that are smarter and learn by watching others might be able to do something a little earlier than we did and maybe avoid the extreme conditions that we faced, but more and more are going to be in this situation. I have not met anybody in higher education over the past two years who seemed to think that things were in good shape anywhere in the country. People are more seriously concerned about the future than I can ever remember."

He proved to be correct. While I traveled, a wave of resignations of key university officials—and superintendents of major public school systems—swept the nation. In a relatively brief period, some three hundred presidents of American colleges and universities resigned. At Yale the president, the provost, and the academic dean all resigned. So did the presidents of Columbia, Stanford, Chicago, and Duke. At the same time, financial conditions worsened and more evidence emerged that the academic quality of entering college freshmen was declining, in many cases requiring more remedial classes for them.

As if all this were not cause enough for concern, colleges and universities face growing racial and ethnic polarization that compound their financial problems. In separate conversations, conducted months apart on two coasts, two of the nation's most respected educational leaders expressed concern. The first conversation was with Charles (Chuck) Vest, president of MIT, the other with Chancellor Tien at Berkeley.

When he completed his first year as president of MIT in the fall of 1991, Vest issued a formal status report on what he called the "host of challenging external forces" facing the university, forces he described as potentially seriously damaging. Universities are not immune to the strains present in American society, he observed, and the battle over allocation of scarce resources holds profound implications for great research institutions like MIT. "These are treacherous times," he concluded.

When I talked with Vest, he sounded even more disturbed by the disparity between what needs to be done and the resources to do it. But he was equally concerned about the huge demographic changes. Diversity of cultures is America's long-term strength, he says, but for the present the United States is "going through some difficult periods in which racially, ethnically, and in terms of gender, we're pulling apart and not communicating enough."

Dividing, not uniting? I asked.

Exactly, he replied.

At Berkeley, Chancellor Tien, too, was troubled by the widening divisions among groups. "The greatest challenge," he said, "is how to change the campus atmosphere. Racial tensions are one area. But it's not just racial tensions. There is an institutional balkanization in higher education. We have various constituencies, just like politics. You have a board of regents, a board of trustees, you have alumni, you have administrations, you have faculty, you have staff, you have students—all fighting for their own. Totally factionalized. And there's no common campus feeling."

In other words, I said, we're all so separated no one can agree about a common goal. Is that what he meant?

"Exactly, exactly," he said. "People say the major challenge in higher education is financial. Financial problems come and go. The greater problem, I think, is this factionalization or balkanization. And that applies to all society."

One year later, well into the Clinton presidency, Chancellor Tien was less philosophical about the ebb and flow of financial problems. Facing even greater cuts than called for in the state budget, and reflecting the continuing—and in many cases accelerating—financial crisis on campuses nationwide, he threatened to resign during a private meeting of the chancellors of all nine University of California campuses if another round of reductions, including further inducements for professors to retire early, were carried out. Berkeley had already lost 15 percent of its faculty to early retirement. Five percent pay cuts were imposed across the board. Graduate admissions for Berkeley's drama department and library school were suspended. The English department debated whether to eliminate its master's degree program. The engineering college lost 21 percent of its faculty. One-fourth of the nutritional sciences faculty were gone, forcing students to spend an extra year to become registered dieticians. The anthropology department was reduced by 17 percent, and Berkeley had to slash 40 percent of its daily supply and operations budget. In addition, it lost 26 percent of its physics department—ranked among the best in the world—and one-fifth of its mathematics department, rated number one in the nation.

Throughout the university, these losses meant elimination of numerous undergraduate and graduate courses, the creation of larger classes, fewer workshops, and less counseling for students. Student placement services, designed to help find jobs upon graduation, were cut by a third. One job outreach program for Bay area companies was eliminated. The university health center no longer offered twenty-four-hour emergency services, and the waiting list for students seeking psychological counseling rose to one hundred. Full-service library hours were curtailed, subscriptions and acquisitions cut back, and new subscriptions reduced by four thousand.

All of this took place when Berkeley was celebrating its 125th anniversary. Some faculty members and administrators began to fear that the university might lose what it had taken a century and a quarter to create. It was against that background that Chancellor Tien threatened to resign.

He then took his case to the public. "We are facing a historical, unprecedented challenge," he said at a campus news conference. "We have to let people know what's at stake." He appealed to the public to let lawmakers know that the standard of excellence at America's preeminent public university would be imperiled if further reductions were forced on it, a prospect that Berkeley and all universities will continue to face for years.

CHAPTER 8

RACE: "CAN WE ALL GET ALONG?"

The call came in the night, while I was sleeping. "Haynes," the urgent voice said in the familiar Southern drawl, "turn on the television set. They're burning L.A.!"

It was Joe Smitherman on the line. In 1965 Smitherman was the young mayor of Selma, Alabama. A segregationist, lean, almost gaunt in those days, he had stood beside Jim Clark, the potbellied sheriff with the dark glasses, helmet, billy club and boots, in the black section of Selma to block Martin Luther King, Jr., and the civil rights protesters from marching to the courthouse to register to vote. Twenty-seven years later, Smitherman was still the mayor of Selma. Seven times he had run for reelection. Each time he had won with the support of black voters—this in the town where the last legal vestiges of segregation fell after the bloody events in Selma led to passage of the Voting Rights Act, which opened the doors of public office to blacks throughout the South.

After hanging up the phone, I stumbled across the room in the old Southern mansion, now converted to a bed and breakfast a block off Selma's Main Street. Turning on the small TV set, I could hear the excited newscaster's voice. "There's another fire over there!" He was speaking against the backdrop of chattering blades from an "action news" chopper hovering overhead. Flames shot high into the sky from a group of small low-lying buildings that had just been torched. Again the camera panned. Down the street hundreds of looters were running. The sharp crackle of gunfire, *pap, pap, pap,* mingled with the sounds of the chopper blades, *whup, whup, whup.* I stood transfixed, feeling numb and empty. Like a recurring bad dream, it was happening again.

Twenty-seven years earlier, in that hopeful spring when blacks and whites suffered together in Selma to end the great wrong of American history, Martin Luther King's dream of racial reconciliation had stirred the world. America, it seemed, had changed. One bright moment that summer strengthened the belief. It came on August 6, 1965, when Lyndon Johnson, the first Southern president since the Civil War, who had forcefully allied himself with the cause of civil rights during the violence in Selma by telling the nation that "we shall overcome," signed the historic Voting Rights Act.

Five days later the dream turned into a nightmare. On August 11, blacks in the Watts section of central Los Angeles arose in an outburst of rage and pillage, dashing hopes for nonviolent protest, ushering in the urban riots that swept the nation in succeeding years, and leading to more racial violence, including the assassination of Dr. King. Instead of racial reconciliation, there was growing racial hostility. For me, and for other reporters who had covered the events in Selma, those flames in Watts were a conflagration that drew us, mothlike. From that spring in Selma to that summer in Los Angeles, we chronicled the rise and fall of America's civil rights movement. Now, before my eyes, on my first time back to Selma, history seemed to be repeating itself.

I had arrived in Selma that afternoon of April 29, 1992, traveling from Birmingham, another symbol of historic racial conflict. Immediately, I renewed a contact with Smitherman that had been at best uneasy and at worst hostile when I had reported on the struggle a generation ago. Our conversation lasted for hours into the evening, at times becoming so emotional that Smitherman choked back tears. He had been wrong, he kept saying, but he and Selma had changed for the better. And not, he insisted, simply because blacks now held important positions where before there were none: half of the city council, three of five elected county commissioners, the police chief, the superintendent of schools, the president of the community junior

college, the high school principal, the postmaster, the heads of the
human resources office and the housing authority, and many other
public officials were black.

His point to me was that Selma's blacks and whites together had
made *real* progress in easing racial animosities. More important perhaps, in an existential way *he* had come to understand how much his
own experience as a poor white in the rural South resembled that of
the poor blacks he had once tried to suppress. "I've been called white
trash, white trash, get back on the other side of the tracks, white
trash," he said. "You carry that with you. So I can relate to what the
blacks felt. You see, Haynes, I grew up in a family of six children. My
oldest brother had TB. Couldn't work. My father was gone. There
was no work. The whites wouldn't take the menial jobs around because they had too much pride. The blacks became the maids or
worked in the laundry. So as a result you went hungry because of
white pride. My God, when I think what my mother went through!
She would get up in the morning and figure out how we were going to
eat dinner. We'd make a meal out of potatoes. Back then, whites did
what the blacks do today. They came back to live with relatives
because they couldn't find work. So I've come to have a different view
of things."

By the time Smitherman dropped me off at my lodging, the recall
of some of the most emotional moments of our lives had left me
spent, as I'm sure it did him. I fell into bed, to be roused by his call.
Only this time the violence three thousand miles away was even
graver, more extensive, and more destructive.

David Johnson, a union organizer, was driving through downtown Los Angeles on the Santa Ana Freeway. It was surreal, he
thought. Normally at that time of day the freeway would be jammed
with cars. Now he could see only three or four. There was something
even more startling: a setting sun burning red through huge clouds of
black smoke. All over the city, pillars of smoke billowed. The acrid
smell burned his nostrils. Over the car radio came a stream of frantic,
near-hysterical news reports. He leaned forward to listen as an-
nouncers described how they had "an incident" here—and there—
and there. They switched from scene to scene to give details of casualties. It was like being in a war zone, Johnson thought. Johnson,

who is white, found himself glancing from side to side looking for snipers on street corners.

High in the hills overlooking downtown Los Angeles, in Echo Park, Katarina del Balle had just come home from work, where she deals mainly with Latino and black hospital employees in the inner city. From her window she saw what seemed to be an extraordinary cloud formation ominously dark in the east. Black masses moved rapidly across the horizon. This isn't the time of year for that kind of storm, she thought. She saw that neighbors had gone outside to look. And then she realized those weren't thunderheads. She turned on the television and for the second time in her life saw Los Angeles burning. As she heard reports of the simultaneous torching of so many different parts of the city, she said to herself: This is worse than Watts. We're in a lot deeper trouble than any of us have grasped.

At Crenshaw High, in south-central L.A., Yvonne Noble, the principal, who is black, was practicing her serve on the tennis court after school. Suddenly, police helicopters began circling over the school. Noble felt a tremor of apprehension. My God, she thought, somebody they're looking for is loose. Others, students and teachers, ran from the school and watched as the smoke began rising less than a mile away. As she drove home, Noble saw people running in the streets, surrounding and stopping vehicles. Once safely home, she sat riveted before the TV. This is wrong, this is wrong, she kept thinking, what they're doing is wrong. She also thought: These people are really pissed off. They are more pissed off than I ever thought they were.

At the University of California branch campus in Santa Barbara, Marcia Choo had finished the speech the college administration had invited her to give on Japan-bashing and hate crimes against Asian Americans. Choo, twenty-seven, a Korean-American graduate of UCLA in social psychology and sociology who immigrated to the United States at the age of five, was a crisis mediation expert working with a group called the Black-Korean Alliance, whose purpose was to reduce tensions between the African-American and Korean-American communities. On the freeway toward home, she turned on the car radio. An all-white jury in suburban Simi Valley, adjoining Los Angeles, had just acquitted four white policemen charged with brutally beating a black man, Rodney King. The case had become notorious, because the beating was captured by a private citizen on videotape and had been played repeatedly over television. The sight and sound of those blows from the police batons—*thwack, thwack, thwack, thwack, thwack*—striking King fifty-six times in eighty-one seconds as he lay on the ground, played over and over in slow motion and in stop action on America's TV screens, had burned the episode into the national consciousness.

A wave of emotion, part rage, part hopelessness, swept over Choo. She was sure there was violence to come. By the time she arrived home and turned on her TV set, Los Angeles was in flames. Then the black mayor and the white police chief, who had not been talking to each other, came on, unconvincingly trying to explain the situation away. There's no leadership, she thought bitterly—in the city, or the county, or the state, or in Washington, D.C.

In south-central Los Angeles, an illegal alien who had escaped oppression in El Salvador by bribing Mexican police and paying a "coyote" escort all the money he and his family could scrape together was about to enter his apartment after finishing work as a janitor. He saw a group of young blacks approaching, ten to twenty, he couldn't be sure in the darkness. One of them grabbed him and tore his shirt as he struggled to free himself. Running for his life, with the mob in pursuit from both sides of the street, he was caught once more, and tripped. After rolling on the ground with his assailant, again he broke free. He saved himself by jumping onto a passing pickup truck. In Salvador, this man had often witnessed violence with people being shot for no apparent reason. It was like this, he thought.

Not far from this scene, Elder Hwang, a Korean-American merchant who had arrived in the United States in 1964 and earned a master's degree in business from the University of Southern California, grew alarmed. Closing his dry-cleaning business, he stepped out into a mob of more than a hundred people. Two shots were fired at him; he could feel a burning where a bullet singed his right arm. Hwang escaped, but his store did not; it was looted and burned. His whole life's work was gone. He had no insurance. Hwang felt a murderous rage; his initial reaction was to seek revenge, to knock down and kill blacks.

In Berkeley, Eunice Baek, a twenty-two-year-old Korean and

recent graduate at Berkeley who could not speak English when she arrived in California in 1975, heard the Rodney King verdict over TV. Koreans are going to be in big trouble, she thought, aware of anger between Koreans and blacks in Los Angeles. As scenes of rioting began, she watched in dread. TV cameras showed Koreans fighting back with semiautomatic weapons from behind cars and on the roofs of buildings. Many wore military fatigues, with headbands and sunglasses. Eunice Baek is a sensitive young woman, burdened by her ethnicity and ambivalent "cultural baggage" or "self-hate," as she sometimes describes it. Deep embarrassment mingled with horror as she watched the violence. She called her father in Los Angeles. It was wrong for Koreans to be shown over television—all over the world—as ready to kill and fighting violence with violence, she told him. People would think that those angry, militant Koreans valued merchandise more than human lives. Naively, she implored her father to call people in the Korean community and make them stop. They had no recourse, her father replied: the police weren't there and many of the Koreans had no insurance. Their entire livelihood was in jeopardy.

When it was over, when the death toll and the damage figures were tabulated, the Los Angeles riots of April 1992 were ranked as the single greatest spasm of domestic violence in modern United States history.* Soon afterward, the inevitable postmortems began. One took place a month later in the Los Angeles school district in which the Foshay inner-city school is located.

The goal was crisis intervention. It was to be an informal group therapy session—for the school district's parents, teachers, staff, and administrators. People were encouraged to express their true feelings. Cathy Silva, an assistant principal who is white, was shocked by

*More than fifty people died, more than fifteen hundred buildings were destroyed or damaged, and more than two thousand people were hospitalized in Los Angeles alone in the riots, which caused over $1 billion in property damage. During the summer riots of 1967, forty-three people were killed in Detroit, thirty-four in Los Angeles in a replay of the Watts riots there two years earlier, and twenty-six died in Newark, but property damage, though extensive in all those riots, did not come close to L.A. in 1992. However, the L.A. riots were not as deadly, or as extensive, as the four days of pillaging and lynching of blacks by mainly Irish-American mobs in New York City's Civil War Draft Riots in July 1863, an uprising that left more than four hundred dead, thousands beaten, wounded, or otherwise assaulted, and far greater public and private property damage over a more extensive area, comparably speaking.

the emotions and attitudes exposed, especially from the black community. One black man in particular was full of hate. "I know that I never really liked whites," he told the group. "Now I know I hate them all."

Listening to him, Silva thought to herself: Why is it all right for you to say this publicly and not for a white to say this publicly? She tried to empathize with the black man, but had a hard time. "It was really awful," she said later.

The comments of a white woman teacher were no less disturbing. She was married to a black man, and had never felt a racial strain between them before. But suddenly, she confessed, she felt distanced from her husband, and that frightened her.

Another white teacher said that she had a lot of guilt about what had happened in the King case and doubted that she would be able to relate to her black pupils anymore. After admitting this, she began to sob. When the meeting concluded, after three hours, the situation was unresolved. Raw emotions hung in the air. There was no follow-up; the group never met again.

But the intensely complicated questions about race and personal and professional relationships did not subside. Cathy Silva found herself wondering why none of the white people in the room had challenged the black man who said he hated all whites. "It was as if we were afraid to speak out," she said. "It's all right for a minority person to say some things and not for an Anglo."

She recalled two incidents that had taken place in successive years during their regional school meetings. In the first, a regional school superintendent, who was black, opened the session by stating to the other teachers and administrators, a third of whom were white, that only black teachers and administrators could make a difference with black children. A year later, he said the same thing, only this time he added Hispanics to the racial/ethnic mix. Only African-Americans and Hispanics, or blacks and browns, can deal effectively with black and Hispanic students, he said.

"The second year we got angry and upset," Silva said, "but who's got the guts to say anything?"

A protest *was* made, anonymously by phone, to the school superintendent's office, which led to an apology by an administrative assistant. There had been a misunderstanding. What the regional superintendent meant was that blacks and browns should be role models. "None of us bought it," Silva said. "We ended up by writing on our evaluations: 'If this is how you feel, why don't you bus us out?' If such a thing was being said about blacks by a white superintendent in the valley, the NAACP would be here and God knows who else, and the man would've been fired. We were too chicken to say anything for fear of losing our jobs, I suppose."

She felt the same way about those occasions when she was accused of racism after having criticized someone's professional work. "I get so tired of the cop-out," she said. "I don't think that blacks and browns should only have blacks and browns working with them. I think it's wrong. This society is not just black and brown."

In the aftermath of the riots, similar questioning and confrontations were taking place all over Los Angeles—and America. During a community relations hearing at UCLA, Marcia Choo, the Korean-American crisis mediation expert, found herself on a panel with an African-American attorney.

"Basically," she said, "what he told me was that I was like an alcoholic in denial because I could not admit that Korean-Americans had a problem, that they came over here as foreigners who learned the evil ways of the white man and decided they too were going to lord it over black folks. I was not acknowledging that. And he said, how can I be a person who's trying to fix the problems when I won't admit what the problem is? The problem was that Koreans did not know how to be grateful to African-Americans such as themselves who came to liberate us during the Korean War."

On hearing this, Choo had lost her temper. "I refuse to sit here and take this," she told her accuser. "I can't believe you're telling me this when in fact the riots are all about four hundred years of racial oppression—and you continue to buy into pitting our communities against each other. If you're going to blame the Korean merchants for the riots and the rebellions of 1992, how are you going to explain 1965 and the Watts rebellion—before Korean merchants were in that part of town?"

Choo made a point of saying she didn't deny that tensions exist. She gave the lawyer her business card and said she'd like to continue their dialogue. They needed to talk more, she said. She never heard from him.

Later, in talking to me, she said: "This country has never honestly dealt with the issue of race and racism. This country has never acknowledged the history of oppression against communities of color. People of color, their contributions have never been acknowledged and welcomed, and that's what this was about. Certainly the Rodney King verdict, outrageous as it was, was a spark that ignited the flames, but the riots are about a lot more things than people care to talk about. It's much easier to characterize it as a black-Korean conflict. When you simplify it that way, it's easy for people to absolve themselves of their responsibilities.

"Too many people say, 'Well, I'm not Korean and I'm not black and I'm not an immigrant. I can go to my home on the hill.' That's where people are sadly mistaken. It didn't happen overnight, and it's not going to be solved in one or two days, or decades."

As usual, John Hope Franklin, the eminent black historian, put the problem in proper perspective.

"In 1902, W.E.B. Du Bois, the very distinguished African-American scholar, said the problem of the color line will be the problem of the twentieth century," Franklin remarked during our lunch in Durham, North Carolina, where he is a professor at Duke University. "We've done so little in dealing with the problem in a fundamental sense that it's going to be the problem of the twenty-first century, too. It's still the most powerful force in our national thinking.*

"I'm not saying we haven't done anything. But I don't believe we have dug deep enough into our national psyche to come to grips with the problem. We have still not confronted our past. These little Band-Aids, including civil rights acts, are not going to relieve us of the problems. We Americans have a view of everything that we can fix it. Got a flat tire, need a tuneup? Eventually, we will fix it. Having done that, we sit back and can't understand why things aren't all right, why they don't work, because we fixed it. The fact that it *isn't* fixed, that there are all these manifestations of it not being fixed, simply adds to the impatience and disgust of the general public."

Franklin reflects those emotions himself, and from a deeply per-

*At the time we talked, Professor Franklin was employing the same argument for a series of lectures at the University of Missouri. They were published in 1993 as *The Color Line: Legacy for the Twenty-first Century* (University of Missouri Press).

sonal perspective. During our conversation, I was struck by what seemed an uncharacteristic pessimism. Was I right in thinking that? I asked. Yes, he replied, and went on to describe how he had changed. "Everyone says my recent writing shows a kind of anger that I did not have ten, fifteen, years ago," he said. "I thought we were on our way, that we were going somewhere. Take Thurgood [Marshall] and all that crowd. I thought we all were moving up in the world, so to speak.

"Well, the terrible thing is that we've moved up very, very selectively. A white high school graduate still has a better chance at a particular job than a black college graduate. We've moved up enough to salve a conscience, but that's about all. So when a black kid becomes the first to enter a great university, or becomes vice president of his company, or sits in the president's cabinet, we say, well, everything's fine. We got used to finally getting a fresh start, like [Supreme Court Justice] Clarence Thomas did when he was seven years old. You were on your way; everything comes in due course.

"The tragedy is that the racial experience we've had in this country has caused considerable numbers of blacks to grow up hating themselves. Clarence Thomas is an example of it. I suspect that when you get not only Thomas but people like him in high places forgetting who they are, where they come from, it's an example of self-hate, an example of wanting to escape from one class to another."

John Hope Franklin and other blacks have every reason for dismay over what has happened in the years since the glory days of the civil rights movement. But the civil rights acts of the Sixties and beyond—achieved as much through strife and bloodshed as through appeals to the American conscience—did represent more than a Band-Aid on America's racial problems. Racial conditions in America did change in ways that even the most cursory examination of places like Birmingham and Selma demonstrates.

Birmingham, in particular, is almost unrecognizable from the city of Bull Connor a generation before. Then, it personified racism at its most extreme, a place where churches were bombed and police used clubs and dogs and fire hoses against nonviolent civil rights demonstrators. Now, in Bull Connor's place is a black police chief who joined the force the second day the police department was integrated back in the Sixties. Chief Johnnie Johnson supervises many of the older white members who, as staunch segregationists, bitterly opposed blacks holding *any* public positions in Birmingham. "Those folks now work for me," he says, "but I cannot harbor any hostilities because I've got a job to do. Underneath, I know there's still some feeling of animosity. We have a captain here who always says the tail doesn't wag the dog, the dog wags the tail. So whatever we see in society, we're going to see portions of it here."

In Birmingham, as in Selma and in cities and towns across the South, blacks hold major positions where before they held none: at the time of my visit the mayor and school superintendent were black and the city council was predominantly black, as were important boards and commissions in city and county government. As many had predicted years before, the South has done better in ameliorating racial tensions than urban areas of the North, and the evidence is all around you as you revisit places that had been datelines signifying racial strife. During the civil rights days, if you traveled to Birmingham or Selma or Montgomery or Bogalusa, Louisiana, or Meridian, Mississippi, where the forces of segregation and integration were colliding, a sense of fear and tension pervaded those places. It was as heavy as the humid Southern atmosphere. You could see it in people's faces, in the way they warily sized up a stranger, in the suspicious way, even, they examined you as you checked into a motel. On both sides of the color line, distrust and even paranoia abounded. A generation later, the openness and the cheerfulness, the civility and the courtesy, between the races stand in marked contrast to the more brooding, often angry, encounters between blacks and whites in the urban north.

At the same time, as leading blacks and whites frankly acknowledge, racial polarization is increasing all across the nation. The problem stems from questions of class and caste as much as race; but race remains central, especially racial strains between blacks and whites. Undercurrents of mutual anger, resentment, and hatred are more complicated as both races react to the failure of public education, and doubts about—if not rejection of—an integrated society, and new moves toward separatism among both blacks and whites.

Among older blacks, particularly those in the Deep South who participated in the civil rights movement, some cling to the old belief in integration, but even there it is notably muted. "What integration really meant to us was the swallowing up of what was once predominantly black by that which is all white. Also, the control has been maintained by the whites," said the Rev. Abraham Woods of St. Joseph's Baptist Church in Birmingham, Alabama. As a leader of the Southern Christian Leadership Conference, Woods had worked closely with King in the Fifties and Sixties. "We didn't intend for integration to mean that blacks would be disenfranchised. Integration was a worthwhile goal but the way it is being carried out, racism is still very much alive. Our leaders in high places have helped create the kind of climate where racism would grow again."

In Selma, F. D. Reese, who as chairman of the Dallas County Voter League in 1965 cosponsored the marches led by King, reemphasized that point. "I don't know whether or not we could say that integration was a goal," he said. "What we were talking about were opportunities, and it was through integration that those opportunities could be experienced."

In general, blacks of his age and background were strongly opposed to the growing black separatist movement. In Boston, to take only one example, a secessionist movement was agitating to have part of the city renamed Mandela after the black South African leader. "Separatism does not make any sense to me," said Selma's J. L. Chestnut, the leading black lawyer there. "That's just unacceptable to Americans. Hell, it's pie-in-the-sky. You have to deal with something that's real. That's why I go back to economics and pooling our resources."

At the same time, blacks like Chestnut feel increasingly alienated and sympathetic to those new separatist strains. As he said, "I have not felt included in the American discussion since Lyndon Johnson said, 'I'm not gonna run again.' I have felt more and more the outsider, less and less the American. I don't know whether you can understand. It's very disturbing to me. There's no way I can be an African. But I've never quite been an American in the sense that you are. Sometimes I'm reading novels about a man who's stateless and I think, Lord, I'm not stateless. My position is different from that. But I really don't know how. All my life, except for about twenty years, the government has not been responsive to me. It's harsh to say, but for those twenty years the gates were open. They let a few of my kind through and then the gates closed. That's part of the rage you see out there in L.A. It goes far beyond Rodney King and what the L.A. police did."

Chestnut's young law partner, Hank Sanders, tends to view integration along legal lines. "It's an important goal to break down de facto and de jure separation," he says. "If there's a law that prevents that, I'm for removing it. But just to have integration as a goal, there is a serious problem with that. What we're talking about is getting rid of the obstacles and then let's see what's going to happen. There are natural affinities in communities, whether they are based on race, status, education, or background. When you make integration a goal, that means you've got to force folks to be in proximity with one another. That's at the heart of some people's perception that blacks are getting more than their share."

Speaking also for younger professional blacks, Sanders expresses doubt about the concept of nonviolence espoused by leaders like King or older African-Americans. "There was always a dichotomy in that," he says. "Most blacks saw nonviolence as a tactic, and King saw it as a philosophy. There's a world of difference. Then you had a powerful magnetic national leader who was saying it's a philosophy. I don't think most black people, even during that period, felt that. They simply felt this was a tactic that could be used to try and accomplish their end. When black people see nonviolence accomplishing that, they will pursue it. But when they see it as not effective, they're less likely to pursue it."

Ending segregation was always the easiest part of resolving America's racial dilemma. Achieving racial harmony is infinitely more difficult, for a variety of reasons: intense competition for good jobs when such jobs are diminishing and minorities are left, as always, in a less favorable position; changing demographics, creating new tensions between racial and ethnic groups, not least between blacks and faster-growing immigrants, principally Latinos and Asians; widening gaps between America's haves and have-nots.

New racial polarization is intensified by frustration among blacks who feel that despite their economic advances, they still occupy the bottom rung in society. Despite the end of legal segregation, de facto segregation still exists. The public schools of Birmingham and Selma, for instance, are 90 percent black. Whites have fled the city public schools for either white-majority suburban schools or private schools. Racial crimes and acts of violence still occur. While I was in Birmingham, the white "skinheads," a neo-Nazi descendant group of the Ku Klux Klan, were holding rallies and attracting extensive news coverage. One of their members had just been arrested for the murder of a homeless black person, an assault that authorities said was racially motivated.

Blacks who aggressively challenge authority and attack racism often find themselves accused, as in the old days, of being provocateurs or subversives. That's what happened in Selma in the Eighties and early Nineties to a remarkable young black couple, Hank and Rose Sanders. Both graduated from Harvard Law School and were active in leading economic boycotts and lawsuits in Selma on behalf of blacks. "Here in Selma, if you fight racism, and you're black, you're called a racist," said Hank Sanders, then running for a congressional seat that would have made him the first black to represent the rural "black belt" of Alabama since Reconstruction. "I never heard of a firefighter being called an arsonist. But if you speak out against racism, if you fight it, if you try to change it, if you try to include more people, then you are attacked and called a racist."

In his own life, Sanders offers proof to any doubters that the American Dream still can fulfill its promise. He grew up in desperate poverty, the second of thirteen children in a three-room wooden house without glass windows in rural Baldwin County, Alabama, near Mobile on the Gulf. His father, who never went beyond the third grade, could not read or write. His mother, who had a seventh-grade segregated education, loved to read and encouraged her children to do so. However difficult their personal circumstances, both parents instilled their children with hope. "We were kind of outcasts," Sanders recalls, "because we were from such a large family and we were so poor. But I had a mother and a father who kept saying you can do anything you want to. You can do it. They bred and nourished that spirit in us."

Race was not a crippling factor in Sanders's mind. Growing up surrounded by poor blacks, and with little contact with whites, he was nearly out of high school before he realized blacks were not the majority. His heroes, whom he read or heard about, were blacks: Frederick Douglass, Martin Luther King, Supreme Court Justice

Thurgood Marshall, though he remembers being also strongly influenced by impressions of Jefferson and Lincoln. But Justice Mar-
shall was the one who had the greatest impact on his life. By the time
Sanders was in the seventh grade, his ambition was to be a lawyer like
Marshall. He remembers how his seventh-grade teacher would ask
each of the students to stand and say what they were going to be.
"When they got to me," he recalls, "I said I was going to be a lawyer.
Somebody next to me started snickering. After a while the whole
class was laughing, because it was outlandish that a black boy from
Baldwin County was talking about being a lawyer. And I stood there
and cried. It was such a painful experience for me that it wasn't until
I was a junior in college that I would ever tell anybody again that I
was going to be a lawyer. That's how painful it was; they'd never seen
a lawyer, and they'd certainly never seen a black lawyer."

Upon graduation from his segregated high school, Sanders
worked at a sawmill, then went to New York, where for several years
he was a janitor, an elevator operator, a shipping clerk, and eventually an electronics technician, a position he earned after attending
night courses and taking algebra and geometry, neither of which he
had studied in his Southern segregated school. He returned to the
South and entered Talladega College. There he was befriended by a
white woman who encouraged him to apply for a special summer
program at Harvard. He was accepted; in the summer of 1965, between his sophomore and junior years, while the events in Selma and
Watts were reshaping U.S. racial history, Sanders was at Harvard.
He then went to Boston University, under another special program
aimed at assisting black Southern students. Later he won a Felix
Frankfurter Scholarship to Harvard Law School. "They say the
Frankfurter Scholarship goes to poor young men who show great
promise," Sanders says. "They weren't wrong about my being poor.
But I don't think I showed great promise."

After graduation, instead of pursuing a traditional legal career
path, Sanders spent a year in Africa, then returned to the rural South
to practice public interest law, working to create greater opportunities for blacks like himself. In this, his career deviates sharply from
that of Clarence Thomas, another impoverished black of his age who
rose to the United States Supreme Court after having won minority
scholarships to Northern colleges and help from other affirmative

action programs. "I was strongly opposed to Clarence Thomas," Sanders says. "I feel that it is imperative for those of us who get a break, who get a lift, who get affirmative action either from an institution or from our grandparents or from our community, to reach back and try to pull up folks—that we try to open the door wider instead of closing it. I went on radio and television in strong opposition to Thomas because I was convinced that he wasn't trying to pull anybody else in, that he was prepared to close the same door that he had walked through."

Against this context of optimism, my conversation with Sanders as it pertained to progress toward racial harmony became all the more arresting. For Sanders, who lost to a white candidate in his 1992 congressional bid, now expresses a fear—shared by nearly every black I met—that race relations in America are deteriorating. "We are at the most dangerous period since the end of Reconstruction," he said. "There's a second post-Reconstruction going on now. During Reconstruction, there was significant black progress in politics, some in education, some in business. Then along came the period where they were undermined on every front—the economic front, the political front, the legal front. Now there's a second Reconstruction and the question is whether we can avoid having history repeat itself.

"When I talk to whites there's a strong feeling that they have been wronged by affirmative action. Even though less than one percent may have been affected, the perception is that there's been a broad impact, that whites have been completely wronged. Whenever folks feel they've been wronged, whether they have been or not, they begin to react, and that's what's reflected in the reaction to the jury in Los Angeles. In time that's going to lead to more attacks on blacks all across the country. So I'm more frightened than I've ever been."

Blacks like Sanders believe they are still treated unfairly by the American justice system. Not just in the courts, but by the police, the prosecutors, and the all-white juries like the one in Simi Valley, California. They feel that African-Americans bear a special burden. They suffer most at the hands of criminals—from drug dealers to murderers—yet they are lumped in with the criminal class and branded as dangerous by the white majority merely because of their color. When they do find themselves involved in the justice system, they believe they receive punishment disproportionate to their crimes when compared with whites. In fact, they are right in all these assumptions; being treated fairly has not been the lot of blacks in America, and every thoughtful person knows it.

That is not to minimize the anger that whites increasingly express about what they see as reverse discrimination and false charges of racism by provocateurs like New York's Al Sharpton, the black minister and political candidate who has risen to public prominence by leading black demonstrations against the "white power structure." One of the strongest impressions of my journey is the degree to which moderate and liberal whites share this growing resentment. This includes many who have worked diligently for better race relations, sometimes at personal risk.

In Selma, Kathryn T. Windham, an author and racial progressive with a gentle, self-effacing manner who became famous in recent years through her regular commentaries for National Public Radio, worries about a decline in civility and an accompanying rise in hostility. "There's still an undercurrent of anger and resentment and hatred," she says, "and one of the things that distresses me is that I don't have any young black friends. I don't have any teenage black friends, or even those in their twenties or early thirties. And that lack of contact, of establishing friendships, hurts us, both black and white. One thing that saved us from greater violence in the Sixties was just pure, common courtesy. Growing up here together, both sides, whites and blacks, maintained a courtesy. And it's vanishing." She tells of being shaken when a young black schoolgirl called her a "white honkie bitch" while Windham's car was stopped in traffic and the girl was crossing the street with other students. "She didn't even know me and I had done nothing to antagonize her," Windham says.

In Birmingham, Natalie Davis, a dean at Birmingham Southern College who came there in 1972 as a George McGovern Democrat and remains politically active, describes the new racial polarization. "As resources diminish," she says, "the pie gets smaller and the choices harder. Somewhere in the process, people forget their common interest, or what's good for everybody. They get theirs and run like hell. You add the issue of race, and the problem exacerbates it.

"I live inside the city limits. I have no political power whatsoever.

That's different from twenty years ago. You can say turnabout's fair play, but a lot of whites in my generation are saying: 'Look, this isn't fair. We didn't create this situation. The generation that came before us did. Now we're having to pay for it in ways that *we* perceive are unfair.' Our generation has the best civil rights record of any generation, but our generation is also asking the hardest questions about fairness and affirmative action. I want everybody else to have equal opportunity, but I don't want something for nothing. No one gave me something for nothing."

The degree to which race continues to dominate attitudes in the South extends into every aspect of life, including organized religion. In Charleston, South Carolina, Father Sam Miglarese, the son of an Italian immigrant, recalls how his family arrived in South Carolina as members of a minority—Northerners who came South, Catholics who came to live among Baptists. "But it was a lot easier for us because we were not of color," he said. "Now why is that? Why is it easier for Americans to incorporate ethnicity than color? At first our family was discriminated against because we were different. Differences breed suspicion. But being white gave us an enormous edge in terms of being accepted.

"I don't know what it is about the color black that puts Americans on edge—it's guilt over slavery or the differences that flow out of culture. Our Roman Catholic church pushed hard for integration of schools; we were the first in the South to do that. But now we're being accused by our black Catholic members of having destroyed their schools. In the midst of this effort to integrate, there's been a sort of homeostasis: things go back the way they were. We have many black Catholic members in the cathedral parish. We had none when I came. But I worry that they don't feel welcome. So the color issue is a real concern.

"The bishop of Charleston, and I'm his executive assistant, has to walk down the hallways of his life with a lawyer on one side and a public relations officer on the other. Everybody wants a piece of his influence. You can't come out and say, I need to close a school even though it's predominantly black because the salaries are lousy, the education is crummy, the facilities are dangerous. The previous bishop would keep it open no matter *what,* because closing a school would be a sign of racism. Or a sign of not supporting the poor. The specter of racism hangs over everything that politicians and religious leaders do."

Father Miglarese, the white priest who marched for civil rights in the Sixties, and J. L. Chestnut, the black attorney in Selma who helped achieve those rights, are typical of Southerners who recognize that the most difficult racial challenges lie ahead.

In 1958, when Chestnut began practicing law in Selma, he was the only black attorney in a totally segregated society. Selma had black and white water fountains, black and white rest rooms. Chestnut's mother and other black women couldn't try on a hat in a downtown department store. No black person had ever served on a jury in Alabama. There were no black policemen, no black officials, no blacks other than delivery "boys" who worked in any downtown store.

Chestnut now looks back on all this with a sense of awe—but also with new anxiety. "I'm astonished how far we've come," he says, "but I'm overwhelmed by how far we have to go. The miles that lie ahead are infinitely more difficult than the ones we traveled the last thirty years—and I know how difficult the last thirty years have been.

"I see a black superintendent of education, I see this black law firm which once represented demonstrators and protesters now representing school boards and county commissions. *We* are now that 'establishment' that I started out throwing rocks at. And I've found out that it's infinitely more difficult to run a school system than it is to attack it.

"I look at all these things and I am astonished, but then I have to face the fact that we black folk—not merely in Selma, but all over the country—don't manufacture hardly anything except some hair products, and we consume everything. The dollar bills are not staying in the black community long enough to sneeze at. I don't think we will ever be truly free until we learn how to deal with the economics of a free society.

"We have made remarkable progress in politics, though I often tell Joe Smitherman that not one ounce of racial progress has come to this town voluntarily. All of it came either as a result of a court decree, the federal bayonet, or the threat of it, and boycotts and demonstrations.* But I don't see any corollary when I look at the economic front. As I go about the black belt from little town to little town, invariably there's the courthouse sitting in the square run by blacks, surrounded by white merchants who own and run everything else. More often than not, these two groups are not speaking, let alone cooperating.

"The whole country is at a standstill racially. I told my wife—and she had a fit—that I'm almost glad the jury did what they did in California. I don't know how else we can get the attention of the American people."

When Rodney King appeared before the television cameras in the midst of the rioting to appeal for calm in Los Angeles, he posed a challenge and a question for Americans. "People, I just want to say, you know, can we all get along? Can we get along? Can we stop making it horrible for the older people and the kids? . . . Please, we can get along here. We all can get along. I mean, we're all stuck here for a while. Let's try to work it out. Let's try to beat it. Let's try to work it out."

At the heart of his appeal, eloquent in its simplicity, lies an expression of hope that is uniquely American. It is also an expression of hope that is more a statement of faith than of fact. In part, it speaks to the belief, as John Hope Franklin put it, that ever-practical Americans can fix what's broken.

But Rodney King also speaks to a deeper strain in the American character. That is the belief that America stands for more than wealth and possessions and power. It represents a promise to do better for all its people. That's the essence of what Gunnar Myrdal, the sociologist, called the American Creed. "The ordinary American is the opposite of a cynic," he wrote. "He is on the average more of a believer and a defender of the faith in humanity. . . . We recognize the American, wherever we meet him, as a practical idealist."

---

*This point is often made by white Southerners who express pride in the advances their region has made when compared with the North. As Jess White, a former member of the Carter administration, said in Chapel Hill: "I believe in progress because I've seen so much of it in the South. On the other hand, you have to say that it would never have happened if it had not been forced on us, which leads to the question of what will be the force, the fundamental change, to address these national problems in the Nineties that we're talking about."

Myrdal wrote those words during World War II, when patriotic pride flourished and idealistic notions about America were commonly held. He evoked those strains to challenge Americans to resolve the issue expressed in his book title *An American Dilemma: The Negro Problem and Modern Democracy.* Half a century later, the legal aspects of "the Negro problem" have largely been resolved; but, as the Los Angeles riots of 1992 demonstrate, the resolution of the larger racial "problem" remains.

Without exception, people in Los Angeles I spoke to were more hostile, more angry, and more despairing six months *after* the riots than they had been before. That was true among Latinos, blacks, and Korean-Americans.

"There's more hate between blacks and us," said Miguel Canalas, a factory worker who came to the United States from Mexico as an illegal alien and qualified for legal status during the amnesty program for immigrants in the late 1980s. "Blacks think they're in the situation they're in because we Latinos have multiplied so many times. We've grown so rapidly. Since we come from other countries under a lot of pressure to try and feed our families, we work really hard. Sometimes we put a lot more work into the job than the black workers do. Blacks are also frustrated by the idea that we're taking their jobs. There's been a big media campaign to try and publicize that Latinos are taking jobs away from blacks and that there are a lot more Latinos than blacks in the factories. They use derogatory terms for us. Like 'dirty Mexicans,' you know. They assume we're all Mexicans, even though we're not."

A black entrepreneur, Bondi Gambrell, whose own jewelry store was looted and burned during the Watts riots in 1965, expressed a typical feeling of bitterness.

"There's confrontation all the time," he said. "I'd hate to be one of those kids in the public school system today. The Rodney King deal was just the straw that broke the camel's back. It had been festering since the Watts riots. Nothing was really done after that— only promises.

"Our leaders have failed us—our black leaders, our white leaders, in this city and in this country. When the riots happened, instead of saying we really failed the people, they started pointing fingers at each other again. So we're still not there. It's greed again. I think the white businesses that are involved in rebuilding L.A. see it as an opportunity for *them* to make some more money. It's the same old S&L scandal. These guys are ripping off all the stuff they're taking back. It's crazy. Billions of dollars and you can't find a billion dollars to stick into our inner cities."

When we talked about tensions between blacks and other minorities, especially Korean-Americans, Gambrell exploded: "I do a lot of business with the Koreans. I interact. It's business, okay, and I'm a businessman. But they don't understand our culture and we don't understand them. And they don't care whether we understand or not, because we're consumers and they use us. They want to interact with white people and identify with them and disregard us, kind of roll over us, because their opinions of us have been molded by what they've read and heard about us in their countries before they came here. And it's not very good. I don't see us mending our ways with them. That's too much to ask. Bullshit! It'll never happen. People separate, they're comfortable with their own kind. You can talk all you want about harmony in a city like L.A. Boy, a lot has to happen for that to happen, believe me. There's too much hurt going on. People are too poor."

He was reiterating, in modern idiom, the elements of an old story: people ignore appeals to improve race relations when they can't feed their children.

Tensions between blacks and Korean-Americans were escalating long before the Rodney King beating and trial triggered the riots. In one incident a teenage black girl named Latasha Harlin went into a liquor store owned by a Korean family and picked up a bottle of orange juice. The woman store owner, Soon-Ja Duh, confronted the girl and accused her of shoplifting. An angry argument ensued. The black girl slapped the store owner, slammed money down on the counter, and turned to walk out of the store. By then, the owner had pulled out a gun. She fired, striking the girl in the back and killing her.

Later, Soon-Ja Duh claimed the gun had a hair trigger that had been filed down, making the gun go off when she raised it. She said she had never fired a gun before.

In the black community, the death ignited angry protests. To many blacks, the shooting only proved the disregard of Korean merchants for black life. Emotions became even more inflamed when Soon-Ja Duh, after being tried, received only a fine and probation. This prompted more protests and accusations. Koreans were enraged when a black woman wrote an op-ed newspaper column saying that the Korean community equated the life of a black child with the cost of a $1.59 bottle of orange juice. The article seemed to imply that blacks would be justified in taking the lives of Koreans. A black "rapper," Ice-Cube, added to the tensions with a song that Koreans took as a summons to blacks to kill Korean merchants. Titled "Black Korea," from the Ice-Cube album *Death Certificate,* its lyrics offer a glimpse into the resentments and hatreds among African-Americans in the inner cities. They begin by expressing the anger of blacks who feel humiliated by the treatment they receive from Oriental "penny-countin' motha fuckah" storekeepers. From there, the lyrics build into a litany of resentment at the assumption that blacks are viewed as being on the take, must be watched at every turn lest they commit some criminal act—an assumption that makes "Nigga mad enuf to cause a little ruckus."

Directly addressing the Korean merchants, the lyrics go on to warn them not to follow the black customers up and down their market or else "their little Chop Suey ass will be a target."

The final verse concludes ominously—and foreshadows what took place during the riots—with a warning about respecting "the black fist" and burning the Korean markets "to a crisp."

Koreans had their own grievances. Their community had been subjected to numerous killings by blacks—thirty-two such homicides were listed in one edition of the *Korea Times* published in L.A. as having occurred between 1988 and 1991—but Koreans believed these facts, as published in their Korean-language paper, never were given wide exposure in the mainstream press.

Seven years earlier, relations between the two communities had grown so hostile that Korean merchants, reacting to inner-city violence and the murders of Koreans by blacks, pooled their money and hired an armed Korean security group to patrol their areas in cars. After community and city leaders met to try to avoid further violence, a so-called Watts Treaty agreement was reached between the two groups. Koreans pledged to disband their security patrols and to hire more inner-city black youths in their stores.

Further heightening racial tensions and adding to mutual misunderstanding are the great cultural differences that exist between Koreans and blacks. Culturally, Koreans are somewhat xenophobic, and with reason. As an old nation, with a history dating back some five thousand years, Koreans have always felt surrounded by enemies. They were twice the victims of Japanese aggression, suffered endless attacks of piracy, and for more than thirty years, beginning in 1910, were a brutalized Japanese colony. For hundreds of years, before the twentieth century, they were invaded by Mongols, subjugated by Chinese rulers from the Ming Dynasty to the Manchus, attacked repeatedly by Russians under the czars, by the French, and even by American Marines, who stormed and razed a system of river forts in the 1870s after a clash between U.S. and Korean naval forces in which an American ship, *General Sherman,* was burned and its crew slain in the Han River. Koreans began to feel, as one Korean told me, "like the Jews of Asia"—repeatedly assaulted, always struggling to avoid extermination.

Korean cultural differences also make them seem distant, and often hostile, to American blacks. In truth, Koreans are not nearly as open as Americans. Women, for instance, often don't make eye contact with men, and especially with strangers. Nor do they often touch other people's hands. There is a strong sense of hierarchy, with strict gradations in social order and status. The American notion of instant equality is, to many Koreans, totally foreign.

"Every Korean child grows up with the hierarchy in mind," said Eunice Baek, the recent graduate at Berkeley. "I hate to say this, but you know from the community who is preferable to whom. You should prefer your own kind—Korea is the greatest, Korea is our country. But if you have to deal with foreigners, then on top are the whites, below that the Hispanics, and on the bottom are blacks. Koreans pick this up through the *white* community. If you're going to survive, you have to assimilate. One of the things about assimilating is that you've got to take on 'their' values as well. With blacks at the bottom, and Koreans wanting to get ahead, they make sure they push themselves above the blacks."

The violent world of the inner city makes all these factors even more combustible. Korean merchants locate in the inner cities mainly because they cannot afford to do business elsewhere. They pool their community resources, raising money through their churches to make loans to Korean-American entrepreneurs,* and then set up shop where the rents are cheapest. Theirs is a frightening world, and they and other merchants of various ethnic backgrounds live in constant fear of violent crime.

Events in the families of James J. Lee and Jong Chil Lim, before and during the riots, are grimly typical. Lee came to Los Angeles in 1984 to help run his father-in-law's dry-cleaning business. Before his arrival, the father-in-law had sold a liquor store after he was held up and, with gun to head, locked in a refrigerator. Operating a dry-cleaning store would be safer, the older man thought. One night, as he was preparing to close up, two men entered the store, pulled out guns, killed him, took the money, and fled. They were never caught. "My wife, my sister-in-law, my sister, my brother-in-law, my mother-in-law, they hate blacks," Lee said.

During the riots, Jong Chil Lim was one of those whose family lost everything to looters and arsonists. They had no insurance; it is prohibitively expensive for merchants in the inner city. "We did our best," she said, still almost in tears months later, "working so hard, working for the children, trying to give them right direction—this is the right way, this is the wrong way, you know. Why did they take mine? Why? I'm working so hard. I came here seventeen years ago and feel like an immigrant again, you know. So we start all over again."

In the immediate aftermath of the Los Angeles riots, while the devastation became even more apparent through intensive television coverage, Americans were forced to confront their old problem of race more directly than in a generation. They did not do so out of goodwill or even, perhaps, because of guilt. Fear motivated them, fear of a racial apocalypse that has always lurked just beneath the surface of American life. Once more, events in Los Angeles forced that fear into the open. For the carnage in Los Angeles had touched

*Koreans usually don't seek bank loans: many have no financial history and will be turned down. They turn to their church for what are called *gaes,* a credit rotation system by which church contributions form a pool of money. From that, congregation members borrow money to begin businesses, paying back the pool in monthly installments. This enables people at the bottom, in most need, to get started. There is nothing comparable in the black community.

off riots in other cities—in Atlanta and Birmingham, in Chicago and Seattle. Two of the Koreans who were witnesses to those events in Los Angeles reacted to them in keeping with their temperament and background—one calmly and philosophically, the other more emotionally and urgently.

The Rev. Yoo Young speaks from a theological perspective. He came to the United States in 1971 at the age of eighteen, earned a theology degree from Princeton University, and became a minister of the Yong Nak Presbyterian Church, a congregation of seven thousand Korean-Americans in Los Angeles, where we spoke.

"There is no doubt that racism is ingrained in us," he says, "whether we're black, white, Korean, or whatever. It is ingrained in human beings. Because of their status as an oppressed people for so long, black Americans feel a lot of anger. We—Koreans—happened to be in the first line. That's all, I guess. We are not denying that there is a fault on our part, but we are saying that we just happened to be right there in front of them. This type of reaction between the Korean-American people and the black American people had to come. When you are oppressed so long, it has to come out somewhere. Unfortunately, it came out this way. How to resolve it? That's the big question. Allocating money for the disadvantaged, government programs, all those kinds of things are just bandage work. Unless you go deep down into the roots, you cannot resolve anything. Really, deep down, it requires a change of human nature."

Marcia Choo speaks from the vantage point of a community activist, of someone who believes that the solution to society's problems lie not just in a change in human *nature* but in a change in human *action*. America failed to get its act together after the racial violence of the Sixties, she says, and thirty years later it has been presented with one more chance, maybe its last, to demonstrate its ability to make fundamental changes. If it does not, she adds, there will be more uprisings, more riots, more rebellions. "I'd like to think that what has happened this time is a final wake-up call for America," she says. "I hope people answer this final wake-up call."

One year later, with April come again and a new president in the White House, the nation was suddenly fixated once more on Los Angeles. There, a second Rodney King jury was deliberating the fate of the same four white policemen whose acquittal had ignited the riots of 1992. This time, there were differences. Instead of a local, all-white suburban jury, this was a racially mixed federal panel that had been convened in central Los Angeles. Day after day, as this jury deliberated, the nation held its breath. As it did, the city and state mobilized their forces; United States military forces also stood in a state of readiness.

Then, despite a year's wait, and despite the old notion that justice delayed is justice denied, the conviction of two of the four policemen involved in the King beating by the second Los Angeles jury permitted the nation to believe in itself. It did not, of course, answer the question of whether human nature had changed or whether human action to address the underlying problems of racism and riots would now follow or again be postponed in the absence of an immediate crisis.

In that connection, I find myself thinking of two people whose lives were enveloped and changed by America's racial conflicts, one black, the other white, both in the Deep South.

Chris McNair, a tall courtly man in his mid-sixties, was intimately involved with Martin Luther King and the civil rights movement in the Birmingham protest days. McNair's young daughter, then his only child, was one of the four children who died when segregationists bombed a Birmingham church in 1963 during Sunday services, an act that horrified the world. Nearly thirty years later, we were seated in his study talking about Alabama and America. He was then a Birmingham environmental commissioner, widely admired in both the black and white communities, and seeking to become the first black United States senator from his state. Yes, he knows, he said, there are people who say, " 'Chris, you're crazy, the folk in Alabama haven't changed that much. They're still racist.' I contend I don't think they're any more racist in Alabama than they are anywhere else in the nation."

He shifted slightly and leaned forward. "You see, I think we are to the point in America now where we are drowning, and I don't believe anybody is going to worry about what color the hand is that is reaching out to pull you up. I see an America that is very frustrated—and this has nothing to do with race, nothing to do with ethnicity. I see an America that was laid-back and comfortable and had jobs people thought would be there forever. And now they see

GM laying off thousands of people, other companies laying off thousands, industries going down the drain, the whole thing going down the chute. There's no need for this to happen. It's going to take time to bring it back, but things *can* be done to make it come back."

Look what happened in Eastern Europe, he said. People said communism couldn't fall there, and it did—before our eyes. "All the experts were wrong, you see," he went on. "Then we sat down and watched television and saw the people of Russia—the *people*—" he raised his voice—"pull down the statue of Lenin. It just crumbled before our eyes, and no expert would ever have predicted that."

I found myself glancing at two small photographs on the wall beside McNair. They were of the daughter who died in the 1963 church bombing. In one photo, she was seated on a bed in a flannel nightgown holding a doll. In the other, she was waving into the camera, a beautiful young girl in a plaid pleated skirt and a white sweater. Behind her, posted prominently, was a sign that poignantly evoked that past: "Register to Vote."

Finally, I had to ask McNair the question I had kept wondering about while listening to him: how is it that he exhibits no bitterness or anger? He looked at me gravely. Then, slowly and with great dignity, he said: "I'm not going to sit here and tell you that I don't have the anger. That was my only child at the time. And I was crushed. I'm still crushed. I think about it every day. But instead of allowing myself to be consumed by anger, instead of getting lost in the loss of my daughter, I go from day to day trying to do things that are going to benefit humanity. At the same time, I'm not naive enough to think that humanity will ever be perfect. I'm not naive enough to think that you'll ever cut out conflict, that you will ever have peace. But I think these are things that human beings should strive for so they can have some semblance of balance and peace themselves. And also, if I let anger conquer, then I won't be of any service to myself, to my present family, or to other people. So with that in the back of my mind and in my heart, I'm able to move from day to day and go on to the next level."

He did not win his Senate race, but I have no doubt that he did not let disappointment or anger defeat him.

In Selma, Joe Smitherman was talking about the changes he sees since the days of racial strife. We've come a long way, and we've got a long way to go, he said. It isn't the racial divisions that separate people in Selma, though those are present, that strikes him most, but the common problems they all face. Selma reflects America: its economy in trouble, its welfare rolls rising, its jobs diminishing and hopscotching to Mexico, its infrastructure needing repair, its schools experiencing difficulties, its services being cut. "We've got a new ball game out there with the economy," he remarks, "with programs being cut and young blacks coming back and looking around and saying, 'Why the hell should I get an education when I can't get a job?' So they turn to drugs or crime or whatever. And we've got a lot of poor whites here with the same problem. So here we are and the future's very uncertain. Now the federal government's broke and the state government's broke and the people are frustrated and down on government. They want some leadership. With all the progress we've made, we still have the basic problems of jobs and education."

As he says, those were Selma's problems in the Sixties. They're still America's problems in the Nineties.

CHAPTER 9

CRIME:
FROM THE STREETS

Gus diZerega was heading home, to north of Oakland, one afternoon in his Honda. He had just pulled onto the freeway entry ramp when a pickup truck suddenly roared around him, cutting in front and forcing him to hit his brakes. DiZerega, an ebullient young man who has been an artist, a teacher, and a resident scholar with the Institute of Governmental Studies at Berkeley, and who works with community groups to improve inner-city areas like the flatlands of Oakland, saw three young black men in the truck. Two were in the cab. The other, in the bed of the truck, stared directly at him.

After the near-crash, his initial reaction was to "flip them the bird," the familiar obscene gesture. He did not. Be cool, he said to himself. He merely shook his head slightly and murmured to show his disapproval of their dangerous aggression. He was congratulating himself for holding his temper when he saw the young black in the back knock against the truck window and say something to the driver. Without turning around, the driver reached out the window and flipped the bird. DiZerega did not respond, either by gesture or grimace.

He continued following the pickup truck in the right lane of traffic, then moved into the left lane, feeling vaguely relieved that they didn't glance at him as he passed. Suddenly, they cut sharply from their lane and pulled up behind him. It was unsettling, but other than feeling a bit uneasy, DiZerega didn't think much of it.

At the Lake Shore–MacArthur–Grant exit, he left the freeway. They exited, too. His concern intensified. He began to check his rearview mirror. He crossed Grant, crossed Lake Shore, and started to go up MacArthur. The pickup continued behind him. For the first time, DiZerega felt a tremor of alarm. Most drivers turn on Lake Shore. They didn't. Clearly, they were pursuing him.

He began to feel panic. Should he keep driving until he saw a cop? he asked himself. And what would happen if he had to stop for a red light? Would they pull alongside, or stay behind? His mind racing, his body tensing, his hands tightly gripping the wheel, he continued up MacArthur behind another car. As he approached an intersection, he made a snap decision. Jamming his foot on the accelerator, he gunned his engine, passed the car in front, then cut sharply to the right and into the intersection. He regretted his own dangerous maneuver, but was relieved that it had worked. He had lost them. James Bond would have been impressed, he thought, as he sped down the block, then turned, and continued up the hill toward his home a few blocks away.

Just as he was beginning to relax, he saw the pickup truck coming over the top of the hill toward him from the opposite direction. Obviously, they were searching for him. This is crazy, he thought. As their vehicles approached, DiZerega thought he would try to break the tension by being friendly and waving as they passed. He never had the chance.

When they were some ten feet apart, he saw the driver's hand extended out of the window pointing toward him. It held a pistol. Oh, shit! DiZerega thought. He can't miss. Crouching down behind his wheel, his heart pounding, he waited to die. There was a sharp cracking sound. After a moment that seemed curiously suspended, DiZerega looked up. He was not hit. He looked around. The pickup truck was gone; it had vanished after the shot was fired.

Still in a state of shock, DiZerega pulled his car into his garage, where it could not be seen. Normally, he parks on the street. He got out, examined his car for bullet holes, found none, then began to shake uncontrollably.

Inside, he called police. Did he have their license number? he was asked. No, he said, but who would have thought something like that would escalate the way it did? By the time he knew what was happening, he was too involved to note the license number. There was nothing the police could do.

"It put a whole new color on daily life," DiZerega said later. "That's for sure. I could have been killed, and it would have gone down as a random shooting. Nobody would have known it was because I shook my head at somebody who cut me off in traffic."

In a class one day, he was amazed to learn that four of twenty people said they had experienced something similar. "Who knows how many others there are?" he said. "I read something that a third, or a quarter, of the cars in Oakland contain weapons. I don't know if that's true. How do you know? Do you take a poll? 'Show me your gun!' "

No subject generates more concern than violent crime, none touches people more deeply and personally, none triggers more emotion. More than any issue, including jobs and education, the growing specter of violence leads people to think that something fundamental has been broken in America. This is as true among blacks as among whites, among Asians as Latinos, among liberals as conservatives, among high-income professionals as low-income workers, among students as the elderly. It affects attitudes and behavior and becomes one of the motivating forces of American life. It influences where one goes, where one lives, where one attends school, how one looks at another person, how one parks, especially at night, and even how one dresses. Don't wear the colors of a rival gang in the inner city or you'll be shot. Don't wear a Raiders football jacket in certain areas; it could trigger violence even if it was given to you, a white professional, by the owner of the team. Do take martial arts courses. Do learn to use Mace, especially if you're a woman. Do, perhaps, buy a gun if you or your family or someone you know at work has been attacked.

When people are asked what they think can be done about "it," the answer that invariably comes back is either "I don't know" or "Nothing!" Crime is believed to be beyond the society's capacity to eliminate. So people turn inward, become more guarded and wary. With excellent reason, they discount—disbelieve—political promises to "do something" about America's "crime on the streets."

From its colonial period to the settling of the frontier and on to the establishment of its big cities, America has always experienced violence out of proportion to other societies. By the Nineties, its annual murder rate of over sixty thousand is by far the world's highest, and half of those deaths are the result of gunshot wounds. While most murders are still committed purposely, by people who know their victims, what increasingly disturbs Americans is the randomness and casualness of the violence—and the knowledge that it is spreading. That is not a belief; it is a fact.

The degree to which crime has spread comes over strongly wherever you travel. It is most striking—because it is not expected—in areas far removed from big inner-city ghettoes. In Waterloo, Iowa, and Peoria, Illinois, people worry about the infiltration of crack cocaine from the gangs of Chicago. In Selma, Alabama, there are also crack gangs. In Arlington, Texas, crack gangs from Los Angeles recruit fifth- and sixth-grade public school students to act as runners for them.

Two forces are at work in these, and other, areas: the overall increase in violent crimes and the organized nature of those crimes in the form of criminal gangs dealing in drugs.

Selma is a perfect example. "When I was a boy my mother went anywhere she wanted to in this town and she never locked the door," says J. L. Chestnut, the black lawyer who played a major role in ending segregation there. "Now I worry about somebody going in there and robbing and killing her.

"There are drugs everywhere in a little town like this. Basically, they come out of the ghettoes of Chicago and New York and Detroit. They're imported here. There is something fundamentally different between a black child who was reared in the Detroit ghetto and one who was reared across the street here. When I was a boy and we were coming home from school, if I was doing something wrong, anybody who saw me whipped me. When I got home, I got it again. The entire neighborhood was an extension of my family. You can't do that now. You whip a child and the mother will be here in this office within ten minutes to bring a lawsuit.

"That attitude is basically non-Southern. That's imported here from Chicago and Detroit. But it's here now. They brought it here. Another peculiar and dangerous twist on that that nobody has really looked at has to do with convicts. Years ago, a black person who spent five or ten years in the penitentiary in Alabama went straight to the bus station and headed north to New York or somewhere. The only thing he wanted to do was get out of Alabama. Now he wants to stay.

"For the first time, there's a cadre in every major city in Alabama, including Selma, of these ex-cons. There's a group here that calls themselves the Brotherhood. What they want most of all is to be accepted by the black middle class. They're not concerned about being accepted by whites. I have represented some of them, and they're a dangerous group. Their values are as alien to the black middle class as they are to the white middle class, who don't even know they exist. When I was a boy, we didn't have two murders in Selma all year. You may get two a month now."

However problems intensify in areas that were relatively free of violence, the core of the problem still lies in the pathology of the inner cities. There, not only is crime pervasive, it can become an act that lends status to those who commit it. In Washington, D.C., for instance, police arrested three inner-city youths who videotaped their crimes. One of the youths would carry a minicam, with appropriate lighting, as the youths selected victims in their neighborhood for vicious nighttime assaults. Then, standing over their victim, one of the two youths who savagely beat their victim would interview the other, as if he were an anchorman, while the third filmed the scene. They were arrested when police recovered a videocassette they had inadvertently dropped. This video, which I later saw in its entirety, provides a riveting glimpse into the violent behavior and attitudes of the ghettoes. Two cities, a continent apart, Bridgeport, Connecticut, and Oakland, California, provide other examples.

In Bridgeport the sense of fear is indescribable. It's just there, and not only in the housing projects where young men in Raiders jackets and new sneakers, most of them armed, openly sell crack cocaine on street corners in broad daylight. It's also present in the heart of the central business district.

In my journalistic career, I have covered urban riots and reported on urban violence across the United States, as well as wars abroad. Never have I felt such menace as I did when stepping out the front door of Bridgeport's only remaining downtown hotel, the Hilton, at night into a scene of totally deserted streets and shadowy figures standing on corners. On succeeding nights, the same eerie sense of unseen, but omnipresent, violence persisted as I traveled through deserted streets. Bridgeport then had the highest murder rate in the state and the fifth-highest rate of motor vehicle thefts in the nation. Awareness of those statistics affects everyone from business people to residents to students on the campus.

Students are among the most concerned. I met with four of them late in the afternoon in a room on campus, two men and two women. Two of them were black, one a Latino, and the other white. They all said they were unprepared for what they found at the University of Bridgeport.

"Coming from Washington, D.C.," said Wallace Southerland III, a black graduate, "I had this perception of college life: that I would go someplace where there would be grand, beautiful, manicured lawns. Colonial buildings. When I got here it was like being in certain parts of urban Washington, and I didn't want to deal with that again."

Mary Armstrong, a sophomore from Salem, New Hampshire, and the only white person in our group, had a similar reaction. "I was afraid to live in New York, coming from New Hampshire," she said, "and I thought this would be a nice little place where I could visit New York every now and then without living there."

And what did you find? I asked.

"I found a lot of people being mugged all the time, and cool things like that. Actually, I'm quite used to it now. I carry Mace and if anyone attacks me I'd like to see what Mace does to them."

She added, in a matter-of-fact tone, that she knew a student who had had a gun held to his head while surrounded by seven men who robbed him.

"The first month I was here our student council president was shot in the back right off campus," said Wanda Miranda, a psychology major and senior class president. "They held her up. Since then, more and more people are trying to get more security on campus."

These incidents may be more extreme than those on city campuses elsewhere, but Bridgeport's crime problems and the composition of its ethnic/racial groups is a microcosm of other cities. There are fifty-two ethnic groups in the city, 155 neighborhood groups or associations, and a variety of organized crime groups—Jamaicans, Dominicans, Colombians—with, police say, evidence of the Korean mafia in prostitution areas. Through the seaport, cocaine enters the city from canisters in the bottoms of ships.

"It's an amazing little city in a number of respects," says Thomas J. Sweeney, who at forty-eight is the first outsider hired as Bridgeport's police chief. "It surprised me how it represents a cross section of what you see in the major cities. Urban policing is a totally different world. You go across town lines here and it's like driving to another country. There's policing in the suburbs and then there's city policing. And there are different worlds out there at different times of the day or night.

"I tell our police commissioners, 'Come on with me at nighttime.' It's a hair-raising experience, because you take them through places they normally never go, never see. You know, when the lights go down, who comes out of the woodwork. It's also something of a culture shock for officers coming in here from our towns outside to hear the volume of radio traffic. If I turned the radio on now you'd hear a steady stream—shots fired, those kinds of calls. The level of 'hot calls' here is probably about twenty-five percent, which is more than most cities, and the level of violence calls is much higher."

The arrival of crack cocaine in the mid-Eighties made Bridgeport's situation infinitely worse. "You've got to understand," Sweeney says, "that in a city like this, seventy percent of the people we arrest for buying in the drug trade are from the suburbs. Yes, seventy percent! Some of these parents in the suburbs would be scared witless if they knew where their little Johnny and Jane were. These kids go into areas where a person in his right mind wouldn't go to buy drugs."

When Sweeney arrived in Bridgeport, major Colombian drug groups were attempting to corner the crack market in bars through the use of strongarm enforcers. Two groups of the Jamaican Posse, known as the Cats and the Rats, were also fighting over control of drug territory. In the early Nineties, smaller groups of gangs began to proliferate in Bridgeport. All of them were involved in shootings—notably a particularly ominous phenomenon called "leggings." That's when drug dealers enforce their discipline by shooting clients or people in the leg who may have welshed on deals.

Another major change is the number and type of weapons being used. From .22 and .32 caliber "Saturday-night special" handguns, the weapons became predominantly mint-condition 9mms, some .357s. The 9mm is the weapon of choice. In addition, the criminals use automatic weapons—the Intertex, the MAC-10s, automatic pistols, and AK-47s. Shotguns also are being used again with more regularity.

For a time, colorful sports paraphernalia and a preference for flashy gold became status symbols for gang members. "But the gun has increasingly become the status symbol," Chief Sweeney says, "so instead of buying the gold they're buying the gun."

At the end of 1990, Sweeney recalls, a study was published suggesting that while assault rates in the United States had not changed, the number of juveniles arrested for homicide had increased by 117 percent. The rise in homicide rates was caused by the sophistication of the weaponry involved. "The technology of the assault had improved," Sweeney says. "So instead of punching you out or beating you up or plinking at you with a .22, they're now using a 9mm or a high-quality automatic—and you ain't surviving. That suggests, one, there are more guns because more juveniles are coming in, and two, the technology of the assault has increased."

Children aged nine and ten carry—and use—weapons.

"They don't see living beyond twenty anyhow," Sweeney goes on. "They'd rather trade their whole life for five or six years of cars, women, money than live forty years in a tedious and dull job. You've got kids with a thirty percent dropout rate, some of them can hardly speak English, and they see a chance for big money, splash. What more could a guy ask for?"

Nine- or ten-year-olds are paid $50 a week by drug dealers to ride their bikes through the neighborhoods on the lookout for police. Some become rooftop spotters with two-way radios. From there they progress to running drugs or selling them under consignment. On a busy corner, some kids make $5,000 a week. All tax-free. "Some of these kids are not stupid," he says. "They're good businessmen. They see high money, quick flash, the American Dream right in front of them. It's very hard for families to protect their kids from that, and a lot of these kids are from broken homes."

Even getting arrested brings status. "Let me give you a stunning disconnect," Sweeney continues. "In the state of Connecticut, illegal possession of a handgun by a juvenile is not a serious juvenile offense. Possession of narcotics is a serious juvenile offense. Now which of the two is more dangerous? I'm not dismissing narcotics, but to me guns are far more dangerous. Yet we have people in the state legislature who cannot comprehend it as a problem. I've offered to take them on a walk any night they want here where the young people with guns are very, very unpredictable. That makes the officers' world far more dangerous.

"Most of the people that make up our state legislatures in every part of the country are defense lawyers. Most come from suburban and rural communities and have no concept of what's going on in the cities. They're dreaming. They're living in never-never land. Are they going to get serious at the federal level or the state level about dealing with the cities? Ha ha. Ha ha. That's my pessimistic side."

In Oakland, Judge Stanley Golde, who presides over five thousand criminal cases a year, described the changes he's seen in his twenty years on the bench.

"The use of drugs is the number one commercial endeavor in the ghetto economically," he says. "It serves the purpose of a doctor, of a psychiatrist, of a mother, of a father. It becomes the healer. You take it to ease the pain of living. Of these five thousand cases that I handle a year, probably sixty percent are narcotics offenses. They range from the pretty-good-sized dealer who sells to one ghetto person, selling to another ghetto person, a twenty-dollar bag of cocaine. He gets the twenty bucks. He buys some more. He gets a little bit for himself. It's like a dog, hitching his tail.

"Then you have the homicides, and there's a dramatic change. There is such hostility that you no longer have to have a reason for killing. If you're walking down the street and you inadvertently bump into somebody you may get shot, whereas before you'd say excuse me or pardon me. Now 'you've disrespected me,' and you get shot. There's also a lot of senseless beating for beating's sake. I've had murders where they didn't take anything from the guy. They've killed the man and left his watch and his money. Most of the crime is black on black.

"I've also had the opposite where they have killed somebody for a ten-dollar watch—and I mean a ten-dollar watch, not something you paid three hundred fifty for and it's not worth twenty. I'm talking about killing for a ten-dollar watch. There's no value on life. Life has no value whatsoever."

In 1965, Daniel Patrick Moynihan, the Harvard professor who then was an assistant secretary of labor and later a U.S. senator from New York, was excoriated as a racist after he warned of the problems that would result from growing numbers of black children being born to single mothers. In the past, Moynihan said, children abandoned by their fathers and raised by single women became disproportionately involved in violence and social disorder. The proportion of blacks born out of wedlock nationally was then 26 percent.

Little more than a decade later, half of all black children were born to single mothers, and in 1985, twenty years after Moynihan's warning, nearly two-thirds. In one generation, the rate of blacks born out of wedlock had tripled—and those numbers continued to rise, as Moynihan warned again in citing the latest figures at the end of Clinton's first year. And in their first four years of life, 8 percent of black children grew up in homes without either a mother or a father.*

By the Nineties, the statistics were worse. In a 1990 report compiled by the Business–Higher Education Forum, *Three Realities: Minority Life in the United States,* startling evidence was presented to document the virtual collapse of the two-parent black family. The forum, composed of chief executives and presidents of major U.S. corporations, universities, and colleges, reported that from 1940 to 1960, families headed by a husband and wife composed about 75 percent of all black families. For whites, the comparable figure was 85 percent. But from 1960 to the mid-1980s, census figures showed that 43 percent of all black families were headed by single women and 52 percent of black children under the age of eighteen were being raised by a single parent. Those figures took in *all* black families; the

*The number of women who became mothers without marrying also rose significantly among educated and professional women, according to Census Bureau figures released in the summer of 1993. Nearly a fourth of all unmarried women in the nation were becoming mothers, an increase of nearly 60 percent in just a decade. This dramatic shift notwithstanding, out-of-wedlock births were still predominantly among women who were poor, uneducated, and members of minorities.

proportions for blacks in the inner cities were much higher, and accelerating. For young black women, 78 percent of the births to fifteen- and nineteen-year-olds and 88 percent of the births of nine-teen-to-twenty-four-year-olds were out of wedlock.

Statistics about young Americans are arresting. Every thirty minutes in America, fifty young people drop out of school, eighty-five commit a violent crime, and twenty-seven teenage girls give birth, sixteen of them out of wedlock. That process continues, half hour after half hour, until by the end of a year a million students have dropped out of school, 1.3 million youths have committed a violent crime, and 478,000 teenagers have given birth.

The most disturbing demographic trends highlight the plight of young black males in the inner cities. As the forum report notes, they are in danger of becoming marginal citizens in their own communities—less likely than their sisters to graduate from high school or attend college, less likely to hold a job, and, even if they do have one, less likely to earn enough to support a family.

School officials in places like Oakland point to another symptom of the breakdown of the black family structure. That is the number of children, many with neither mother nor father, who come to school from a second-, third-, or fourth-generation family welfare background. "There is a large school population for whom the official guardian is a grandparent or a great-grandparent," says Carol Quan, an Oakland public school superintendent.

Others, like J. L. Chestnut in Selma, point to a breakdown in family values coinciding with the movement of blacks to the urban North during World War II and after. In Birmingham, Alabama, Police Chief Johnnie Johnson, also black, makes a similar point about family structure deterioration nationally in the post–World War II era. "Not only didn't we give them whippings, we didn't give them love," he says. "We didn't give them the attention and we certainly didn't give them the discipline they need. Now we find ourselves the grandparents of children who don't have good parents because of us. So that brings about a police problem. Our children need to know how to love themselves so they can love other people. This disregard for life has a lot to do with how they feel about their lives."

The problems of crime and violence that spread outward from

the inner cities are America's new-old racial dilemma. Just as when faced with the old racial dilemma, America chooses not to confront its new problem so long as it is confined to the inner cities. There, in a world apart, black families—descendants of those that withstood the ravages of slavery and segregation and the travail of the great migrations out of the rural South into the urban North—are foundering. Born into a dehumanizing environment that encompasses isolation, abuse, poverty, ignorance, despair, and disease, they live with midnight in their hearts.

Homicide has become the leading cause of death for young black men in the ghettoes; one out of every twenty black men can expect to die violently—a casualty rate not exceeded by participants in any American war.* This point is made by Adam Walinsky in detailing what he calls the deadly "arithmetic of American life."

In the years since he served as a young aide to Senator Robert F. Kennedy, when I first knew him, Walinsky has been a successful private New York attorney and for nearly twenty years has been engaged in a crusade to awaken America to its urban crisis. His idea for a domestic Police Corps that would put 100,000 college-educated police officers on America's streets by the year 1997, augmenting existing police forces and providing college scholarships for those who serve, was adopted by Bill Clinton as part of his crime bill that he presented to Congress in late 1993. It is an excellent idea and, if eventually adopted, could make a significant difference in providing more and better-trained police officers on the streets of America.

It will not, of course, resolve the deeper causes that signal the destruction of still another generation of young inner-city blacks. Theirs is a world of casual killings, many not even motivated by desire for money or material goods, but killing for killing—for an insult or a whim or a youthful rite of passage. It is a world in which the young do not expect to live long, in which prison holds no terrors,

*This was a theme that Clinton struck toward the end of his first year. Speaking from the Memphis pulpit where Martin Luther King had delivered his last sermon, he warned black ministers that the achievements of the civil rights movement were being diminished by a "great crisis of the spirit that is gripping America today," adding that if King were addressing them in the 1990s he might say: "I fought to stop white people from being so filled with hate that they would wreak violence on black people. I did not fight for the right of black people to murder other black people with reckless abandon."

in which the gun means status, and in which the operative family structure is the gang.

There is nothing new about gangs in America or the forces that create them. From the earliest days of the Republic, criminal gangs have existed. The Five Points area of lower Manhattan, the site today of New York's principal agencies for the administration of justice, was the spawning ground of gangs that terrorized the city for nearly a century. Out of the miserable mass of tenements, and on the same marshy ground where in colonial times an episode called the Slave Plot of 1741 led to execution of a score of blacks by hanging, burning, or breaking on the wheel—after they rose against their masters and attempted to burn and loot the city—came gangs such as the Forty Thieves and the Kerryonians (for County Kerry, Ireland) and the Plug Uglies and the Dead Rabbits. For generations, these gangs operated from places called Murderers' Alley and the Den of Thieves. The names were apt. Old records of New York indicate that for nearly fifteen years, murders in the Old Brewery area averaged one a night. Like today's gangs, those early gangs adopted distinctive garb and colors. The Roach Guards' battle uniform was marked by a blue stripe on their pantaloons. The Dead Rabbits wore a red stripe and formed behind a gang member carrying a dead rabbit impaled on a pike. And like their historical successors, these gangs constantly fought each other over territory and primacy of criminal operations.

Today's gangs adopt colors and leave their spray-can marks on the walls of their territories. "Tagging," they call this ritual; they put their tag on buildings and streets and bridges and freeway dividers to declare their turf. Such markers are no longer confined to the inner cities. Now they appear, often overnight, in schoolyards and on concrete walls in small towns of the rural Midwest and South and Pacific Northwest: this section DSG for Diamond Street Gang or that section as belonging to the Bloods or the Crips. Gangs exist literally everywhere in America.

While they still fight each other for territory, while racial and ethnic animosities still motivate them, while they still adopt their own rules and codes, contemporary gangs differ from their predecessors. Now they are often connected to international criminal operations, mainly narcotics, coordinated through coast-to-coast networks. Southeast Asian gangs are established in every port city from Hong Kong to seaports throughout the continental territory of the United States—in Seattle and San Francisco and Los Angeles and San Diego and Houston and Miami and Philadelphia and New York. They are, I am told by criminal justice officials, even better organized than the Mafia: they recruit in one area and dispatch their members to deal drugs and run prostitution rings in others.

Instead of the bludgeon, billy, or knife of past gangs, today's gang members carry assault weaponry. Sometimes they have more firepower than police. As the gangs proliferate and splinter within the urban areas, they become smaller, less organized, more free-lance—and more dangerous. Their violence is different from the organized criminal activity of, say, the era of Prohibition, when gangs battled over control and distribution of illegal alcohol, and from the equally well-organized gangs that control drugs today. The greatest danger comes when these heavily armed youths shoot each other—and anyone who might come in their way—often without reason.

"In Panama, we knew who the gang members were and we were taught to stay away from them," said Alejandro Stephens, who works at the Los Angeles King/Drew medical center in the center of the riot area. "But those gangs had more respect for their communities. Here it's a totally different mind-set. They don't value life, they don't value you, they don't give a damn. It's like you are nothing. They'll pull you out of a car when you stop at a stop sign."

He described a recent incident that had happened near the hospital. Two young men were trying to rob a woman. Stephens blew his horn and drove fast toward them. The woman held on to her purse; the two men fled. When Stephens got out of his car to see if she was all right, the woman drew back in fear. "Naturally, she's Hispanic and I'm black and she thinks I'm also part of the scene," he said. "After I spoke to her in Spanish and said, 'Look, don't get scared by my color,' everything was okay. That's part of the problem, too. Although I am Hispanic, I am also black, and the first thing they see is the color of your skin. They qualify you the same way."

Since he came to Los Angeles in 1962, Stephens has seen an evolution in the number of gangs and their use of force. For the first ten years or so, fistfights were more common between groups. "In the last fifteen years," he says, "since guns have become so available, it's no longer a matter of duking it out. It's a matter of getting a gun and having a shootout."

This was corroborated by Ethel Edmond, a young black studying for law school at nights while working in the King/Drew trauma center. "Back in my childhood, it was just gangs and turf," she says. "Now it's worse. You have to watch what colors you wear and where you wear them. Back then, we knew a lot of the gang members. They were our friends. They would come over and play with us. Two boys I knew were good friends. Both of 'em are dead now because they were in gangs. We knew they were bad people, we knew they had killed people, but it's something you deal with. You try to straighten them out, but there's not a whole lot you can do. Eventually, you grow apart, because you have your values and they have theirs. But it doesn't make you hate them. You still recognize them as human beings."

Estimates of the number of gangs and the numbers of gang members—including women—are frightening. In Los Angeles, the number of gangs may be one thousand, with total membership estimates varying from 60,000 to 100,000. Of those, the largest numbers involve Latinos, with anywhere from three to five hundred gangs. "The most acute problem in terms of gangs is—hands down—the Latino community," says Katarina del Balle, herself a Latina and a Los Angeles native who organizes Latino and other workers. "This has escaped the notice of the media. The gang culture and the gang-related culture is our most acute problem. The drug trade-off provides the only viable economic option for that community, and it goes beyond them to their families. Many family members are fully employed in the gang culture. Where the frustration of our youth used to be expressed through the Brown Berets, which was their version of the Black Panthers, now you don't find young people organized in any constructive or even hopeful political fashion."

Miguel Canalas, a Mexican-American factory worker in a steel wire plant, is one of countless parents who deplores the pressure put on young people to join gangs. "It begins at junior high," he says, "when they are about twelve years old. They get called names and they're also threatened if they don't join the group that's kind of a pre-gang thing. My oldest kid, who's fifteen, they were after him to join this little gang, and he didn't want to. They tried to intimidate him and pressure him and started beating him up. I'm lucky. He's a serious boy who likes to study, and I'm trying to encourage him to get involved with others like him who don't want to be in the gang.

"I was talking to my neighbor, who has a kid who's involved in gangs. By the time he was fourteen, these gangs had killed some people. When that kid across the street was thrown in jail for the murder of two people, we tried to tell our kids, look, this is the consequence of getting involved with a gang. The guy next door's son is sixteen. He's in jail, too. Three times already. And the guy next door was asking his kid why they're all getting in trouble. The kid answered, 'Well, all we're trying to do is protect our turf. This is our barrio and nobody's going to mess with it.' "

Canalas lives in the Temple Beaudry section, where small stucco homes perched on a hill are surrounded by the gleaming office towers of downtown Los Angeles. I asked him about guns in his neighborhood. "I've got a pistol back there," he said. "My neighbor's got guns, the guy across the street's got guns. We probably all have guns."

It's not surprising that gangs appeal powerfully to young people who have no structure in their lives; the gangs become their families. That is how Bubbles, as she is called in the Bloods, explains why she joined the gang. But she doesn't call it a gang. "It's a family," she says. Over the years, her brothers were "affiliated" with the Bloods, her husband was "affiliated," though he's been in jail for the last eleven years, and all the people in her neighborhood—or the 'hood, as she calls it—were either affiliated or wanted to be.

When Bubbles was twelve, living in south-central Los Angeles, she began "getting into little different things." She means fights or watching people drive by the 'hood shooting from cars. Her sister carried a hammer to school for protection; that was before people started carrying guns. As for herself, at the age of twenty-eight she has been through it all. "I've been shot at a hundred times," she says. "I've been shot in the leg, I was stabbed in my eye, stabbed in my back. I've been jumped on by men. I've been incarcerated for possession of a firearm and possession of cocaine for sale."

She says all this in a calm, low-keyed manner, and only pauses when I ask, "Did you ever shoot anybody yourself?"

"I've shot *at* somebody," she says after a long moment while she sizes me up, "but I don't think I hit him." Then she goes on, talking easily about her life with the Bloods in L.A. "Because of my size, I was automatically labeled a bully-type person," she says. "I mean, people saw that Bloods jacket and since everybody thought I was crazy, I started acting crazy. At first it was an act, but then it became *me*. After being the target for drive-bys and going through different things, that became my life-style. I started retaliating back and I got more involved. And I watched real close friends die. One of the homeboys that got killed was right before the rioting. I was standing next to him and the car drove by and shot and everybody ran except him. He ran so far and fell. And it was frightening, you know.

"It's exciting when you get away, it's something to go back to the 'hood and talk about, you know. Like we got away from what happened and you laugh, you know. But I've thought about it and I come to realize it's like we put on an act for each other."

Bubbles talks about the enmity between the Crips and Bloods. "There was no reason for it," she says. "I guess it was stuff that the OGs started. The OGs is the original gang. After a certain time in the 'hood you can say you're the OG, you know. They look up to you 'cause you're older and been around. My name is Bubbles, and there's a Little Bubbles and a Baby Bubbles. They look up to me; I'm their idol in the 'hood. Used to be I'd advise them, influence them, you know. Show me how hard you are and do this. Like start a fight with such-and-such and do a drive-by, you know. See that Crip standing on that corner? Go slap the hell out of him.

"Little Bubbles, she's seventeen years old. Not my daughter; I guess I'm her OG. And I tell her it's time to stop, you know, and I give her examples: see how Thunder died or Stone died. You know, don't go out like that. You're young, go to school, and they laugh and say I'm a sellout 'cause I don't hang out no more.

"But now it's kind of quietening down since the riots. I wouldn't exactly call it a truce, because nobody has put down their rags—I mean, that's what everybody fails to realize. We have not given up our colors. There is Crips and there is Bloods. We're not giving up what we are and what we are about."

That conversation with Bubbles—or Carolyn Hamilton-Ballard, which is her full name—took place in south-central L.A. in an area of hulking burned-out buildings, boarded storefronts, and fast-food shops marked everywhere by gang graffiti and hastily scrawled signs that say "Black-owned business." I was talking with present and former members of L.A. gangs who had been brought together for our conversation by the Community Youth Gang Services, a non-profit organization formed a decade earlier to defuse gang tensions and reach inner-city youths. With the proliferation of weapons in the area, the group's work had become infinitely more dangerous. Months after the riots, a tenuous gang truce had been struck, but still no major public and private aid was forthcoming. "Nothing has happened," Charles Rachal, a member of the Crips gang, said. "Just promises." Raised by his great-grandmother, he was one of eleven children from a broken family. Recently he had met a sister, then seventeen, whom he'd never seen before. "It made me feel good but it made me feel bad," he said, "because why did I have to wait this long? That always bugs me. Why did I have to be kept away from a part of my life?"

He, like the other gang members, had simply drifted into the gangs. "I'm a survivor, I'm a drifter," he said. "I can drift away and come back and just be all right."

The gangs represent security, attachment, belonging, despite the violence. "I had a little brother that got killed in a drive-by shooting in Los Angeles," Charles Rachal said. "I have homeys that got killed—people in my family, you know, they got killed. I've seen thirty to forty funerals. If you go through all the funerals I been to, and seen all the people laid in them caskets with their hands folded and just laying there—I mean, it's a hurting feeling."

"I love America," Rachal said later. "I ain't going nowhere out of America. Born and raised in America. I mean, the United States to me is a beautiful country. It's just who's running this country—the political side of this country—that ain't so beautiful."

The most eloquent of the group was an intense young black named Keith Washington, twenty-nine, who left the gang and was now a staff member at the Community Youth Gang Services. He, too, had been raised by a grandmother, had witnessed shootings and killings; he had narrowly escaped death himself at least twice while still a child. As for guns, you didn't have to buy one, he said; if you're a "homey," a member of the core gang, you could borrow one for the night.

I asked Keith Washington who he admired most in the world. "My hero is dead," he said. "King. I admire Martin Luther King because he tried to get to the core of some of the issues that are causing the setbacks of our nation. That hero's dead, but his spirit lives on."

The surveillance camera was trained on what they called "the house with the blue fence" in East Oakland, California. It was a slow Saturday in March, slow because the rain cut the number of customers to the blue house, and slow because of increased competition on the street.

Still, by any standard, business was brisk. In fifteen minutes, the two youngsters behind the blue fence—the one in beige pants was eleven years old, his brother with the umbrella was fourteen—were averaging one sale a minute of $10 packages of marijuana.

In drug argot, the boys are called "grinders" because of the fast pace of their work and the fierce competition they encounter. On a good day, each of them will earn up to $300 for a job that requires no skills and no education. Standing watch nearby, and continually keeping them supplied from "stash," were the boys' uncles. The customers, who pulled up in a steady stream, got out of their cars and quickly made their cash purchases, came from all over the San Francisco Bay area. They were middle-income people, professionals, suburban women in station wagons, citizens from the most affluent areas of Oakland. None of them would tolerate drug deals on *their* block. Their money, once handed over, was passed through an open window of the blue house to the sixty-two-year-old great-grandmother of the two boys.

That house stands at the center of a multimillion-dollar drug marketplace, a business that operates all day, every day, year in and out. So lucrative is the business that it would be the envy of any shopping center or retail mall in America. It is a business that attracts a steady stream of customers willing to pay the "market price" set by unskilled, untrained employees who work only on commission. No benefits are paid. There are no expenses for overhead, adver-

tising, training, or insurance. The business is pure supply and demand, and any business with this kind of demand will never be short
of supply. All tax-free, too.

This is an enterprise so valuable that people are willing to die for
it—and do.

In front of the blue house a young man was shot and paralyzed
for life after an "outsider" tried to do drug business there without
paying tribute to the established dealers. One month later that assailant was slain in retaliation. Not long after, a resident of the blue
house quarreled with one of the young grinders selling drugs in front
of the fence. The resident strolled around the fence, picked up a
shotgun hidden there, and shot the young grinder in the face, killing
him. Late one night, several blocks away, the cycle of murder continued. A brother of one of the grinders who was murdered was cut
down by an Uzi in a case of mistaken identity. The surviving brother
exacted his own vengeance; he gave the man suspected of slaying his
brother a deadly shotgun blast in the head while the victim was
playing a corner-store video game. Shortly after the Saturday in
March when the police took their video of twenty-four hours of business transactions, the woman who lives next door to the blue house,
one of the many grinders working that street, was murdered in her
driveway for giving up a bag of marijuana to the police.

All this is part of "normal" life in that Oakland neighborhood—
and it's by no means the worst. Crack cocaine houses are responsible
for even more human wreckage, but the house with the blue fence
does illuminate a critical problem that has become national. What
can be done about it? What will it take to rid these neighborhoods of
the drug dealers?

The answers lie not in Washington, but in the communities themselves, and it is in those communities that some of the most promising work is being done. Oakland itself demonstrates the best of those
efforts, just as Oakland's example shows how individual action can
make a difference.

When crack cocaine began to infiltrate inner-city Oakland in the
mid-Eighties, Police Sergeant Robert Crawford had nearly reached
retirement age after a career that included the directorship at the
Oakland Police Academy. But instead, he undertook a new kind of
police work, analyzing the tenacious problems of drugs and crime

from a different perspective. He knew that citizens felt terrorized by the violence and drug dealing that had turned their homes into danger zones. He also knew they had given up hope for change. Drug busts would occur, arrests would be made, but conditions would soon go back to "normal."

A different approach was desperately needed. The drug dealers had to be removed from their territories.

Sergeant Crawford began to concentrate on violations in city housing, building, sewage, zoning, wiring, and sanitation regulations at known crack houses. If the collective violations were enforced through inspections that led to fines and lengthy court proceedings, requiring the dealers to show up in court or go to jail, in time dealers would be forced to move—especially if the inspection process was repeated again and again. It was an untraditional way of addressing a problem that was being treated in a traditional police way—simply arresting the dealers for possession of drugs. "My God," Crawford says, "we were out there chasing our tails by creating all these temporary solutions. The temporary solution became part of the problem. It's like using bug spray. The bugs get immune to the spray. So then we bring in more spray when we should be removing the plants."

Beginning in 1987, Crawford began targeting the houses for violations through the combined efforts of various city agencies and their inspectors. When some crack houses were forced to close and the dealers moved away, community hopes rose. "We did it again and again," Crawford recalls, "and, one, things changed, and two, the community began to support the police like never before. In nearly twenty-five years of police work, I've been called 'pig' over and over and people have mistrusted me because of the uniform. Now that was beginning to change. People were coming out of their houses and saying, 'God bless you, thank you, please come back. It's about time somebody did something.' "

Crawford enlisted the support of the city manager, who provided funds for a special community unit, headed by Crawford, that would continue to target known drug houses. A community hotline number was established so people could report drug activity. Community meetings were held, in cooperation with other church, business, and community organizing groups. Residents were encouraged to take back their neighborhoods and report abuses anonymously.

Crawford's program stressed improved-quality-of-life issues: clean streets, removal of graffiti and litter, security. In printed material distributed throughout inner-city neighborhoods, he spoke to the residents. "The people of Oakland deserve the right to live their lives quietly and decently without the destruction of the drug dealers and their customers," one of his pamphlets read. "Gunshots, noise, speeding cars, cursing, fighting and other uncivilized behavior make life unbearable in drug-ridden communities. What can *you* do about a drug house in *your* neighborhood? Take control of the situation, talk to your neighbors and friends and get organized. There are many resources available."

In five years, Crawford's special unit of the Oakland police department closed seven hundred drug houses, and his efforts began to attract national attention. "It's an absolute blow-away success," he says. "We have a consensus of the community—government, police, churches, businessmen, everybody—saying this is a problem that's destroying us and we've got to do something about it."

Crawford was not boasting. I went with his unit into crack areas, saw how effective they were, and watched residents emerge from their homes and line their streets to signal approval after they saw the unit's vehicles arrive before a crack house. One midmorning's unannounced visit was typical. We pulled up before a small, unpainted house with a yard filled with litter, in a neighborhood of chain-link fences and many dogs. In our caravan of official cars were police and a variety of city inspectors. Inside the house a young man sprawled, asleep, on a broken-down sofa. Another man was slumped in a chair. A television set blared. Many cats prowled the living room; the smell was noxious. In the kitchen were piles of dirty dishes, roaches, open garbage. The toilet, filled with excrement, was not working. And in a bedroom, behind closed doors, a young man and woman were in bed. Three children, two boys and a girl, were in another room. The boys were dozing, the girl stared at a TV set.

Police found evidence of crack paraphernalia: pipe cleaners and double or triple matches that had been burned in a dish to heat up the base rock cocaine to ready it for smoking. They also found heroin balloons, which users swallow to avoid being caught with the drug; the heroin is recovered after the balloon is passed through a bowel movement.

Outside, in the welcome sunshine, inspectors noted the open sewer and tabulated the many housing, electrical, and sanitation-code violations they had discovered. Nearby, police and inspectors talked to the landlord, who had been summoned to the scene.

The landlord was told of the violations and what steps he would have to take to correct them—and at what probable cost. If conditions warrant it, as they clearly did in this case, the housing inspector is empowered to declare the premises unfit for human habitation and order the tenants—or owners—to vacate it immediately.

In some cases, children are taken under the custody of child protective services. Because of lack of funding, this is less likely to occur in today's economic climate. And there is another frustration: current laws are drafted to perpetuate the status quo. Legally, a home is declared unfit for children *only* when there's no food in the refrigerator. As long as there's food, the children remain in the house even if unsupervised, or if their parents or other adults are addicted to drugs. To the law, that environment does not qualify as an "unfit situation."

Still, the inspection process does disrupt the crack house's operations, does enlist neighborhood support for further action, does make a difference to others who live in the area. When the houses can be closed, the residents move somewhere else. The Oakland unit follows them and pressures them again and again until they leave the Oakland area entirely.

Sergeant Crawford, standing near the front door of this crack house as the operation was ending, was pleased with how it had gone. A few weeks before, he said, they had closed a crack house and found seven handguns along a fence, in the grass: .44 Magnums, Saturday-night specials, and a large eight-inch Magnum Force "Dirty Harry"–type weapon, all loaded and "ready to go." Those guns and the violence they imply are a separate issue from forcing the drug dealers from the neighborhoods. Crawford can confiscate the weapons; but he, and other local police officers, can do little to stop the flow of guns that flood into the inner cities through legal sales and a vast illegal arms traffic. He can only concentrate on helping neighborhoods to free themselves from the dealers themselves.

Inability to solve the greater problem doesn't discourage Crawford. He's an optimist. He sees his efforts at mobilizing many levels of society—from enlisting officials in city hall and its agencies to citizens in their neighborhoods—as an example of what a united America can achieve when it finds a clear goal around which it can rally. To Crawford, America's commitment of time, treasure, and energy in fighting and winning the Cold War against a commonly perceived enemy represents an example of what America can achieve when it wants to—and an example that can be applied to winning battles at home, if it also wants to.

"This country has greater things yet to come," he says. "I'm very positive about that. Look at what we accomplished in the Cold War. That was one hell of an accomplishment. If we could take those thirty-million-dollar jet planes and melt them down and take that aluminum and build something else with it, then let's do it! We can make better automobiles, we can make better TVs, we can make better computers, we can continue to be a world leader. Let's get on with it. It's the same way with people in these neighborhoods. They're talented human beings. There's work to be done here. It's just a matter of having the right leadership, of having the right direction."

Oakland is not the only example of how creative community work can begin to free neighborhoods from crime. In Bridgeport, Connecticut, Police Chief Thomas J. Sweeney has been a national pioneer in helping develop new methods of police patrols known as "community policing." After growing up in New York City and graduating in psychology from Manhattan College, Sweeney went to Berkeley during the Sixties. While many students protested against authority, he studied for a master's degree in criminology and then became assistant director of the San Francisco Crime Commission. After more academic study, and acting as a consultant to a number of police departments around the nation, Sweeney chose to become a beat policeman in a tough inner-city area of Portsmouth, Virginia. Before coming to a badly demoralized Bridgeport police department, he modernized the force in Yonkers, New York, and served as deputy police commissioner for surrounding Westchester County.

In Bridgeport, Sweeney has succeeded in giving his department a new sense of mission through early retirements, the hiring of young new recruits, and a new, more rigorous system of training. His tough-minded and practical approach challenges the community to work with, not against, him, just as he insists that members of his force must truly understand the communities they serve and become more directly linked to the people who live in them. That means more foot patrols in neighborhoods, less cruising in vehicles. It means establishing closer relationships with neighborhoods, from citizens' groups to youth organizations.

"We're teaching our officers: 'Empathize, identify with the community, understand their problems,'" he says. "Try to work 'em through but don't let your guard down.' We're telling the community: 'Hey, don't look to us to solve the crime problems. If I have twenty-five officers for four hundred street miles, let's stop the illusion. You've got to protect yourself. You've got to stand together. You've got to redevelop a sense of neighborhoods.'"

He was striking a familiar theme, one I heard in community after community: put aside your short-term cast of mind and address long-term problems. "The dilemma is how do you deal in a shallow political environment that's geared to quick answers and short-term payoffs," Sweeney asks. "The urban environment and the urban issues are long-term issues. They're not something you're going to change in a presidency or the two-year term of a mayor. You need long-range focus."

From Horatio Alger to the present, the notion of the self-made citizen beating the odds is part of the enduring American legend. Mythic or not, there's enough truth here to keep the American Dream alive—the belief that however flawed the society and however faint the Dream, America still provides the greatest opportunity for people to better their lives. In reality, the chances of that happening for inner-city youths, and particularly for black males, are exceedingly slim.

George Jackson beat those odds, and how he made it from Harlem to Harvard and then to Hollywood to become a success as a major film producer while in his early thirties provides a new twist on the old myth.

As we talked in Hollywood, Jackson was musing about his life and trying to figure why he had succeeded when so many others failed. A couple of days before, he said, he had read an article about one of the founders of the Bloods and was fascinated by this man's explanations that he got out of the gangs because he didn't go along with drive-by killings.

"He said something really profound," Jackson said. "He said when he was going to cheat a motherfucker out of his life, he didn't want to do it by sneaking up on him. The last words he wanted the guy to say was his name. He also talked about being taught respect for your elders. One of the most profound changes that I witnessed in the inner city was the total lack of respect by young people for their elders. I saw that change in the late Seventies and early Eighties as cocaine became very, very common in the inner city. After crack exploded, everybody was in the dope game and behavior changed.

"So I started asking myself why my life had taken a different turn. I have three or four cousins who died of drug overdoses, and my uncle was gunned down and shot by a couple of drug dealers. So I've been to the funerals, I've experienced the pain, I've buried people in my family as a result of this stuff. And I can remember lying in bed one night when I was in my teens after hanging out with a cousin, about my age, who was a drug dealer, and going with her to some really dangerous places. I lay awake in bed and I remember being troubled by the decision that I came to.

"I decided I'm not ruthless enough to kill somebody in cold blood. I could probably kill somebody if I was mad enough and my life depended on it, but my emotional foundation told me I can't be involved. So I made a decision that I wouldn't. Ever. It troubled me, because of peer pressure, the feeling I didn't measure up. But when I look back years later, I'm happy with the decision. Who knows where my life might have gone? My response was in part fueled by a moral foundation I got that made me say, this is wrong, this is wrong."

Jackson's life is worth examining for a number of reasons. Not least is what helped him escape the fate of other inner-city blacks. The single most dominant influence in Jackson's life was a strong mother who at an early age was determined that her children would have the best possible education and who worked to make them share the belief that education was the way out. In virtually every case, people I met who triumphed over terrible odds credited their success to a strong parent, or grandparent, or authority figure. In Jackson's case, it was all of these.

Though Jackson's father had left the family when he was an infant, his mother's two brothers were strong men whom he admired greatly. One was a decorated New York City police officer, the other—the one who was shot to death—was a numbers banker who, despite making a living from gambling, was unalterably opposed to the drug trade. These uncles and his mother—and their parents, an immigrant family who came from the Caribbean island of Monserrat—gave Jackson a strong sense of family values.

In the 1992 campaign, "family values" became a political foil. George Jackson will tell you that Vice President Dan Quayle and others who wrapped themselves in "family values" were right in raising it as an issue, but wrong in the way they applied it ideologically. "We do have a problem with family values," Jackson said, "but it ain't the shit Quayle talked about. We've got to love these kids who grew up the way I did consistently. We have to give their lives meaning. We have to eliminate the hopelessness and replace it with a rejuvenated kind of 'I can be somebody, I am somebody' feeling. If you don't value yourself you can't possibly value the life of another human being."

He remembers when the uncle who was later killed took him and his younger brother to Monserrat. "I'm taking you two on this trip because I want you to understand that you have a culture," he remembers his uncle saying, "and that you come from someplace, and that this bullshit that you see around you that you live in is *not* who you are." The uncle also told them he had insured each of them for $400,000 before their plane departed. "If anybody ever says to you what is the value of your life," he said, "you can tell them that you've been insured for four hundred thousand dollars."

Jackson also had the advantage of receiving a good education from Fordham Prep, a Catholic school in New York, where his athletic skills gave him all-city status in football and boxing. From there he went to Harvard on a scholarship, where he also played on the football team as a nose guard. "Harvard taught me that white people don't know everything and aren't the smartest people in the world. They have problems, too," he said.

His dream upon graduating in 1980 was to become a boxing promoter. It didn't work out, but he hustled and drove a cab. Then he became a management intern at Procter & Gamble, living in the nearly all-white Connecticut suburbs. He didn't like it, again tried boxing and television promotion, then learned of a film producers' training program in Hollywood. With barely $100 in his pocket, he drove from New York to California. For weeks he slept in his car and changed clothes and showered in a gym before going to work in the training program. A new acquaintance, learning of how he was living, let him sleep on the floor of his office. For nearly five months, Jackson did. Then came his big break.

The movie executive Lew Wasserman sent out a mandate to hire and train blacks to be executives. Jackson went through the interviewing process and was hired. By the age of twenty-four he was producing the first rap movie, *Crush Groove.* From there, he tapped into the phenomenon of rap music, before it became a craze, and began producing films. That led him to a partnership with Quincy Jones, the black composer and entertainment entrepreneur who produced the two Michael Jackson albums which became the most successful in the history of the music business.

In 1991, George Jackson was coproducer of the black film *New Jack City,* which became the highest-grossing African-American movie to that date. He has not, however, gone Hollywood or forgotten where he comes from. Hollywood, he says, is a hustle, a place where people lie every day, and where, despite the advances blacks have made in film and television productions, the reality of the black experience is still not presented to Americans.

The L.A. riots that he watched were part of the reality that he knows and seeks to portray.

"Part of our community—'our' being the black community—did not want to believe that this injustice would prevail," he said, referring to the first Rodney King verdict. "They wanted to believe that some modicum of justice would prevail. They wanted to believe that the kids who were being killed because of a government policy change that said you can't import foreign guns but that cheap gun manufacturers in America can flood the inner city with these cheap guns could be saved by a sense of justice. I'm talking about kids who are in the cemeteries and the morgues as a result of that policy change.

"But human beings are tremendous. We are resilient. Through all our adaptation before the riots, there was still a kernel of hope that justice would prevail. When that didn't happen, it was like taking a rubber band and stretching it till it either breaks or you lose control of it. Because people are so resilient, the rubber band didn't break. It snapped back.

"America has created an underclass that it tries to portray as black, but it is not black. It is multiracial, multicultural. Resources that could benefit that underclass have been misappropriated. If the pressures that are making the behavior of that underclass more violent and dangerous are not removed, our society will collapse. To quote Michael Corleone in *The Godfather,* if history has taught us anything, it has taught us that this pattern of abuse and neglect cannot prevail."

Once more, a year later, America waited, heart in mouth, for the Los Angeles verdict in the second Rodney King trial. This time, the jury provided Jackson's "modicum of justice" by convicting two of the four white police officers who beat King. The rubber band did not snap back, but the underlying causes that prompted the first explosion remain, a fact driven home again months later when another Los Angeles jury meted out light verdicts or acquittals to blacks charged with brutally beating a white truck driver, Reginald Denny, during the riots.

CHAPTER 10

CLASS: AMERICA DIVISIBLE

Fear of class warfare has haunted America since its inception. Race aside, no theme has attracted more attention, none has been more passionately debated. From the beginning of the American democratic experiment the central conflict, always expressed, never totally resolved, has been between the impulse toward greater democracy and toward privilege, between—less elegantly stated—the haves and have-nots, who have always coexisted uneasily.

Jefferson and Adams, those architects of the Revolution and of the Declaration of Independence, were united in believing themselves fashioners of a new and better democratic order in which liberty prevailed, but they differed fundamentally on how best to achieve that order. Jefferson believed in natural aristocrats of talent, but not in a natural aristocracy of power that maintained its control through inherited rank or wealth. Adams believed in a governing class and advocated adoption of titles for the elite to invest them with greater dignity. The differences of these two leaders over the question of class and the nature of democracy have echoed throughout American history. They are reflected in such great questions as the rights of man versus those of property.

Class differences have gone beyond legal redress and taken the form of insurrections and rebellions. In 1786, discontented Massachusetts farmers, failing to obtain relief from taxes in the state legislature when a depression led to foreclosure of their land, followed a former Revolutionary War captain named Daniel Shays and disrupted court sessions. They then attempted to seize the armory at Springfield. Shays's Rebellion was crushed when the dominant economic class led the effort to suppress it through the militia. In 1795, George Washington dispatched troops to western Pennsylvania to put down another uprising protesting federal taxes on whiskey. In Washington's view, the Whiskey Rebellion—or the "western insurrection," as he called it—represented a plot to overthrow the new central government. It, too, was put down.

Long before the American Revolution, fear of slave insurrections—real and imagined—sent tremors through the colonies. As we have seen, in the nearly forgotten Slave Plot of 1741 slaves rose against their masters in New York City and were executed after attempting to burn and loot the city. In 1822, another slave rebellion led by a free black named Denmark Vesey was crushed in Charleston, South Carolina, and thirty-seven people were executed. In 1831 the slave Nat Turner sent shock waves through Virginia and the South when he led an insurrection resulting in the slaughter of fifty-seven white men, women, and children in Southampton County, Virginia. After a manhunt tracked him down, Turner and twenty blacks were executed, and as many as one hundred other blacks killed. The bloodiest of all American episodes, the Civil War, was as much a struggle between economic interests as one over racial issues, though then as now, the two were inseparably joined.

Explosive combinations of race, rage, injustice, and economic discontent were all factors that led to the riots that transformed Washington, D.C., into a blazing battlefield in the summer of 1919 as thousands ran wild and blood literally flowed in the streets. Hundreds of police, U.S. cavalry, infantry, and Marines were not enough to stem the fury of the mob, which raged for three days across the capital and up to the very gates of the White House. Only after President Woodrow Wilson ordered two thousand more federal troops into the city and a providential rain swept Washington did the riots subside. But within a week, embers from that conflagration ignited similar racial riots in Chicago, followed by riots in Knoxville, Omaha, and Elaine, Arkansas. These deadly racial spasms were precursors to riots in Detroit during World War II, Watts in 1965, and cities across the nation after the assassination of Martin Luther King, Jr., on April 4, 1968.

Economic grievance was at the heart of the veterans' groups who descended on Washington in 1932 in the depths of the Depression. Their "Bonus March" on the Capitol turned violent and was suppressed by federal troops and tanks commanded by General Douglas MacArthur, assisted by his young aide Major Dwight D. Eisenhower.

In the late nineteenth century and long into the twentieth, bloody labor-management confrontations such as the Pullman Strike of 1894, the hand-to-hand fighting between management "goons" and "sit-down" strikers who seized auto plants in Flint, Michigan, in 1936, the violent clashes that left four killed and eighty-four wounded in the Republic Steel plant "massacre" in Chicago in 1937, and the pitched battle at the Ford plant at River Rouge in Detroit in 1941 stirred new fears of American class warfare.

Class conflict was at the core of the agrarian reform protest movements of the 1890s, when William Jennings Bryan rallied radical Western Democrats against the moneyed interests of the East, and when American farmers took up shotguns to protect their farms from foreclosure during the Great Depression. It was behind the extraordinary wave of fear spawned by the Wall Street bombing of 1920 and the subsequent search for anarchists and radicals. That climate formed the emotional backdrop for the arrest, trial, and 1927 execution on charges of murder of Nicola Sacco and Bartolomeo Vanzetti, the "good shoemaker and the poor fish peddler," which for years after became a symbol of class prejudice and societal injustice.

That theme of American class conflict has also dominated America's intellectual and political discourse. Recurring throughout a succession of historical periods, it has stirred controversy and created political movements, sparked reform and reaction, led to formation of new parties and radical splinter groups. Ever present in the background of these inflamed debates has been the specter, feared and predicted, of class warfare. Sometimes this expression has stemmed from idealistic beliefs and the desire to right wrongs; in others, it has taken a narrower, more destructive, nihilistic, burn-the-temple-down approach; but always the central terms of the debate are the same.

Parke Godwin, a liberal reformer imbued with Transcendental idealism and belief in Fourieristic socialism, wrote seventeen years before the Civil War about the imperfections of an American democracy that permits "a deluge of wrongs" through class oppression:

> We sometimes pride ourselves upon the equality of condition and happiness that marks the society of the United States; and to a certain extent this pride is just. Yet it is only to a certain extent. Theoretically, constitutionally, legally, there are no privileged classes in this nation; the odious laws of caste are annulled. But, practically, positively, really, we still live under a regime of caste, we are still governed by classes. . . .

It was a similar belief that led Jack London to issue his call to arms in *War of the Classes* in 1905; that prompted Mother Jones, twenty years later, to recall how she told a group of West Virginia miners holding a religious meeting, "Your organization is not a praying institution. It's a fighting institution. . . . Pray for the dead and fight like hell for the living!"; that motivated H. Rap Brown to condone violent protest by saying violence is as American as cherry pie.

Yet despite all the anger and protests that have marked American life, the United States has never fallen prey to the kinds of mass class struggles that have rent other societies, triggered violent revolutions, and led to the overthrow of regimes. The United States has never had an emperor, it has never had a king, it has never had a dictator.

In more than two hundred years of existence, the United States has experienced three revolutions—all driven by political and ideological motivations. The first, in 1776, created the nation. The second, in the Civil War, settled whether the nation would survive as a union or dissipate into separate entities. The third, in the Great Depression, preserved the U.S. capitalistic system and, through the New Deal, formed the modern American political state.

Through all those episodes, through all the turbulence bred of economic and social injustice, the United States has remained the most stable of societies: real class warfare involving the entire nation has never occurred. It has not happened because at its historic core the United States system has worked. It has not worked for every person, nor for every group, nor during every historical period, but in the main it has been a success, because America has always possessed a great safety valve.

From its earliest days, America has provided a way for those at the bottom to move up and out of poverty and hopelessness. It has taken waves of penniless immigrants unable even to speak English, educated them, and enabled them to ascend the economic and social ladder. It has responded to injustice and inequity—never swiftly enough, or perfectly, and often only after being forced by events— and ameliorated discontent. In moments of its greatest crises, it has found leaders like Lincoln and Roosevelt sensitive to America's divisions and tensions and capable of defusing them by generating public support for change.

In the end, it has worked because Americans themselves, at every level of society, have believed they are not consigned by birth and class to a permanent place whether at the top or at the bottom. With personal effort, with public and private assistance, and with the inevitable degree of luck which America is nevertheless unusually good at providing, they too can move up and out.

As the conversations of those former and present Los Angeles gang members who say they "love" the United States demonstrate, that belief still holds. But it is, at best, a more tenuous belief. At worst, the old faith is being replaced by an angry disbelief.

Much more than feelings of disbelief made Judge Demetrios Agretelis's experience so troubling, and revealing. It began when the judge's secretary told him his car was ready to be picked up. The judge thanked her, looked out the window over downtown Oakland, and made a snap decision. Instead of having someone drive him to the garage where the repair work was done, he'd walk to the corner and take a bus. It was a pleasant day; he hadn't taken public transportation in years.

The bus was crowded. As it pulled away from the corner, blacks and Asians and Latinos, young and old, jostled each other for position, shoving and bumping as the bus moved into the traffic. But that wasn't what struck Agretelis with such force. It wasn't even the way people looked at him—a well-dressed, obviously successful, middle-aged white man. Agretelis is far from insulated from society's tensions; his career as a judge in a city like Oakland has exposed him to resentment and hostility and misunderstanding. What he was now experiencing went beyond those emotions. It was the palpable anger and even hatred that enveloped the bus. "I've never seen so much hostility crammed into one moving vehicle," he remembers. "I thought, this is like those stories you read in the newspaper, where somebody pulls a gun and shoots someone because they're irritated about something."

Later, Agretelis tried to explain to friends why the experience had been so unnerving. "Jesus, you did *what*?" one of them said. "You rode on a bus in downtown Oakland? Are you crazy?"

Racial antipathy undoubtedly contributed to the hostility Judge Agretelis encountered, but another kind of resentment hung in the air as that bus lumbered through downtown Oakland. It was resentment born of class distinctions, an Us vs. Them mentality. In those few minutes on the bus, Judge Agretelis had been given a troubling glimpse into the chasm between the haves and have-nots of America.

Throughout my journey, not a day passed without my hearing some expression of fear about growing conflict between the haves and have-nots—a term that was consistently used without prompting on my part. Most of the factors contributing to these feelings have already been explored in these pages. Central among them are the long-term state of the economy and the new pressures on the diminishing middle class, conditions that led to intense emotions along class lines during the North American Free Trade Agreement debate. As America's industrial and service sectors retrench, fear over the future intensifies. It is a fear that ripples through the ranks of factory workers, farmers, and professionals alike, bringing with it realization of much tougher competition in the shrinking employment base.

Another destructive legacy of the Eighties is rising resentment toward the most favored and powerful. Again and again, when I asked people why they thought America was in trouble, they responded by saying, "The Eighties." Not Ronald Reagan, mind you, not Michael Milken or Ivan Boesky or the now-scorned yuppies whose self-centered behavior personified a distinctive era, but the Eighties as a symbol of greed and inequity—a time when those at the top profited at the expense of those from the middle income levels down. These most privileged elites are judged to have left the nation facing a mess that will take years, if not decades, to rectify. Public grievance runs deep, and is directed toward those most powerful in business, in politics, and in the media who are believed to be either unaware of or unconcerned about the plight of so many Americans.

Heightening these accumulating resentments is a deeper fear: that the unfairness of American life is producing dangerous new divisions along racial and class lines. People who once thought themselves immune from the violence of the inner cities feel a threat to their communities. Racial and ethnic polarization makes Americans apprehensive about the prospect of an explosion from below.

That is true even among those most removed from urban America. In my first conversation, in the home of Jim Tierney on Elm Street in Topsham, Maine, it was only when the subject switched to social problems afflicting America at large that his infectious optimism notably changed.

"I have a very dark view on that," said Tierney, for ten years Maine's attorney general before resuming private practice in the early Nineties. "It bothers me that I hold this view, but I think we are on our way to an underclass. I think it is large. I think it will get larger. I don't think anyone will care. I think that you will find more homeless people, not fewer. I haven't been to Mexico or South America, but I understand that the wealthy there live behind very tall walls and live very well. I don't think we'll reach that point, because you won't be able to see the walls but you'll be able to feel them. I think white police officers will continue to pick up black people who drive in white neighborhoods. And once in a while it'll get in the papers because they'll pick up a member of the Supreme Court or they'll pick up the local DA, who may be black, or, as they did in Boston not long ago, pick up and frisk Dee Brown while he was looking for a house—a Boston Celtic, rookie of the year.

"There will always be people who, for whatever reason, can make the step across, but only a few. That the Clarence Thomases of this world can say—and this is a very dark view—that you don't have to look back and take care of anybody, even if you came from that particular community . . . if that's true of his community, it can be true of others. It's hard to feel any personal connection to those people who are shooting themselves down on the streets anyway. And you never go there."

From that time forward, a wide range of people expressed similar concerns. In Waverly, Iowa, a tranquil island of tidy farms set in the rich dark soil of the Midwest prairie, the Rev. Dennis Dickman of St. Paul's Luthern Church talked about traditional shared values. "There's still a lot of that here," he said, "but that's slowly eroding, whereas my experience in other parts of the country suggests that that's gone. That's the fear I have. That we are so caught up in our own privatized, self-centered, acquisitive lives that we're blowing ourselves apart. Everybody's got their own view of everything. Very few people are willing to sit down and talk together, reason together, try to work together. It's either my way or I'll shoot you. There's a lack of trust, a cynicism. I'm fearful that the only thing that can make change happen is going to be semi-catastrophe, if not a catastrophe, like violence spreading out from the cities."

In Peoria, Illinois, Dr. David Holden talked about how abuse in the medical world sowed resentment among the less affluent. "Everyone abuses the system," he said. "Nobody's simon-pure. Doctors figure out codes to maximize their income, hospitals figure out codes to maximize their reimbursement, insurance companies figure out codes to minimize what they have to pay for, patients have different standards for their loved ones than for others' loved ones, and no one wants to pay the price.

"Interestingly, some of my doctor colleagues complain bitterly about government and taxes. I ask them where they went to medical school. They usually say the University of Illinois, which means they paid five or perhaps ten percent of the cost of educating themselves and the taxpayers paid the rest. I try to remind them of that. They remind me that they pay a lot of taxes now. They also live in suburbs, so they don't have to pay the high taxes of Peoria. When I point out to them that they live in these lily-white communities and pay the low taxes and drive for free on the government-paid-for highway, they don't like to be reminded of that."

The Los Angeles riots had flared two weeks earlier, and that subject naturally came up. America increasingly is becoming a country of service providers, the doctor remarked, where goods are produced by an expanding underclass. Inevitably, that condition will increase tensions.

Like Los Angeles? I asked.

"Sure," he said. "It's the haves against the have-nots, and it's an economic conflict, not racial."

In Peoria, too, I spoke to Jack Gilligan, president and chief executive officer of Fayette Companies, a management and business development corporation whose entities run companies that provide extensive drug-and-alcohol-abuse treatment and mental health services. He sees what he calls "a bifurcation of our society" that owes more to class than race. On the one side are blacks who are doing well and have no connection with those who live in the inner city. Aligned with them, but in a separate category, are whites who keep to themselves in suburban "medieval fortresses," often with their own private police forces. On the other side are the increasing numbers of the poor and the dispossessed. They, hit hardest by budget cuts and the declining economy, exhibit the most rage.

"There's a whole group of people we can no longer serve that we used to serve," Gilligan says. "They're shrinking out of the middle class into the lower end of the income spectrum. We have no resources to serve those people, so we're seeing more homeless. We're seeing more homelessness related to the young, and to mentally ill substance abusers, who are very difficult to manage. It isn't a pretty picture. The culture is changing in a way that has a time bomb in it. That's the terrible thing about the Rodney King situation. That thing was bound to blow; it had critical mass. Everyone's known that, but we don't look at it, in the hope that it will go away. What plays in Peoria plays in America."

In Arlington, Texas, University of Texas urbanologist Paul Geisel talks about the "Armageddon neighborhoods"—the walled-in suburban enclaves where the middle class escapes paying taxes for the impoverished central city.

"Those sections of upper-class Arlington are still building," Geisel says. "That construction goes on and on and on. At the same time, the low-income housing is coming down. The problems characteristic of a big city are increasing—murder, rape, drug abuse, homelessness. There is a homeless shelter here in Arlington now, but it's not nearly big enough. There's a new shelter here on campus for homeless families. It's here, but unless you are in immediate juxtaposition, it doesn't exist.

"I watch the crime rate go up. I see the violence rate go up. But I don't see anybody getting very excited about it. The fact is, because of the huge space that we occupy, we don't see it. So what you're getting are these Armageddons, neighborhoods that are literally walled in. And it isn't just in Arlington."

Geisel, who is white, chooses not to wall himself in. He lives in a large house in an area of Arlington afflicted with high crime rates. When we talked, he had been in his home one year. Three times he had been burglarized. Finally, he had burglar bars installed. Even then, on one occasion burglars gained entry, while he was there, by stretching the bars. Why did he choose to stay there? It's what he did for a living, Geisel said, adding:

"I adopted a motto a number of years ago. I don't want to be corny with you, but I sing it to myself. It's an old black hymn which goes: 'I will live the life I sing about in my song.' If you're committed to change, particularly for inner-city people, then you've got to be there. You've got to be in that neighborhood."

Whatever price Geisel might pay in terms of personal security is more than compensated for, he says, by the insights he gains from firsthand observation. One of those observations offers as good a glimpse as you'll get into the reality of the world of have-nots.

In Geisel's neighborhood, the grocery store stands alongside the blood bank. Before cashing checks, whether from work or welfare, the grocer requires a purchase of at least 99 cents. As a result, there are long lines of people outside the blood bank waiting to sell their blood for $20. Those same people then move to a grocery line to cash their checks, after turning over the 99 cents just received from proceeds for selling their blood. "They're very poor guys," Geisel says. "There you see the fat of poverty."

Occasionally, an incident occurs that perfectly reflects the depth of class resentment and the danger it presents to a wider society. That's what happened in Oakland after the great fires in the fall of 1991, long before the Los Angeles riots. When inner-city youths from the flatlands of Oakland swept into and looted wealthy enclaves on the hills overlooking San Francisco Bay and the Golden Gate Bridge, their "statement" was no less significant than that of the furious Los Angeles mobs almost a year later.

But theirs was not an uprising that sprang solely out of racial hatred. Many blacks lived at the top of those hills, along with the range of racial and ethnic diversity that characterizes California. Nor was it an uprising motivated by ideology. Many of the people who lived in houses that were looted were devoted to liberal ideals, to progress, to racial harmony, to economic and political justice. They not only espoused those principles. They lived them through engagement in community organizations or in philanthropic endeavors.

Quite simply, the uprising was directly related to class. The have-nots were taking from those who have. And the rift between the two societies was much deeper than the warnings about America's division along racial lines after the Watts riots a generation before.

That's what most troubled my friend, the seventy-year-old man who had sat alone in his living room with a baseball bat to ward off looters. He was concerned, he said, that for the first time America was heading toward open class warfare.*

Even for those at the bottom rung of the economic ladder, the sense that the quality of life is declining is powerfully held, and with good reason. In places like Los Angeles, more and more factory workers whose pay and benefits have been cut are existing without some of the basics like medical insurance. Typically they go to health facilities for indigent care only in cases of extreme emergency. For them, there is no such thing as preventive care. In Los Angeles alone, for instance, it is estimated that 40 percent of Latino residents do not have medical care.

Union officials who attempt to organize workers to take traditional collective action for better health and economic conditions say they increasingly encounter two conflicting reactions among the people they seek to serve. One is the overwhelming belief that the society is unjust—the few are receiving disproportionately more, the many much less. And there is the despairing belief that nothing can change. *Vali madrismo,* Mexican-Americans living in Los Angeles will say,

*Whether the devastating fires that swept affluent enclaves of southern California like Malibu in the fall of 1993 could be attributed to class resentment cannot be known, but the fact that they were set by arsonists arouses such suspicions.

meaning nothing is worth anything. Nothing has value, therefore don't expect anything to change.

David Johnson is an organizer for an international electrical workers' union that had just conducted a several-month-long drive involving some twenty thousand factory workers in the Los Angeles area. "Old-timers in the labor movement say when people were angry over social injustice they used to organize and try to do something about it," he said to me. "Now people tell us they would *like* to organize, they would like to change the situation, but they don't think they can. There's a general sense that the laws, the institutions, are all banked against them.

"The belief that there's no way to improve things explains the psychology of the Los Angeles riots. When people can't channel their energy to try to make things better, their frustration explodes in these anarchistic ways. When people got mad, they just struck the match and lit the fuse. They didn't turn to the church or the civil rights organizations or the unions. It was a spontaneous explosion, which to me is evidence that people don't believe they can make changes through any of the existing institutions."

Johnson goes on to say that when things heat up for people at the bottom, they strike out at those nearest to them, those with whom they compete most directly—hence the conflict between blacks, Koreans, and Latinos. Occasionally, though, as in Oakland, those forces coalesce. Then, instead of the have-nots fighting among themselves, they strike out against the haves.

In America of the Nineties, more people descend the economic ladder than ascend it. As they do, social and economic consequences become all too clear: the failure of public education to meet needs of the poor and the new immigrants, thereby keeping those groups locked at the bottom; the new inequities produced by the restructuring of the American economy, which create increasing numbers of disposable and temporary workers and leave white- and blue-collar workers without health and pension benefits; the inability of the social safety net to provide for those in need, which forces larger numbers out of the middle class into grim new struggles for survival.

All these forces converge simultaneously. At the same time, the ranks of a permanent and heavily armed underclass increase. So do the acts of violence that mark the fight for survival among those at the bottom—acts which increasingly become more random, striking at anyone who happens to pass by. For many in this group, the lives they see and lead make them think such violence is natural, inevitable, and justified. For others trapped at the bottom, the yearning for the life America affords its more fortunate people is poignant and heartbreaking, all the more so because they do not believe they can ever attain it.

Charles Rachal, for instance, recalls how the gangs in Los Angeles gave him something he didn't have—and wanted. "I grew attached because they were showing me something that I didn't get at home," he said. "You know, each and every one of us out there in the streets talks about, 'Man, I just wish I could go home right now and do this here. I wish I had this in my life.' We all talk about that. Even in the roughest times of my life, I talked about that. And I talk to fellows who say, 'Man, I don't care about nothing in life. I don't give a damn. I shoot to kill.' Deep down inside, I know how they feel. They want something in life. They want an opportunity in life. They just don't have the strength to tell people what they want. They don't have the words to tell people. They feel they wasting their time by telling you because ain't nothing going to come out of it."

Rachal then gave a classic expression of underlying causes for social unrest and violence that have motivated those in the revolutionary communes of the past: "You got to bring the food to the table instead of the appetite. How you goin' to bring an empty plate to the table and say now let's get to eating? Where are the food? How about such and such and such and such over there that need a slice?"

Other former and present gang members listening to him immediately picked up his theme.

"We don't have no sense of ownership in the community, although we are the ones who continue to be the consumers, the greatest consumers in the world," said Keith Washington. "We do not own nothing, really, and that's sad. If you don't have no ownership in your community, then you subject to destroy it, because there's nothing there for you. Throughout the world, you know, the whites control a lot. If you control economics you control—let's see, economics, education, and geographical location, where you live. That's what you control."

From there, the conversation increasingly turned to expressions of resentment. Carolyn Hamilton-Ballard—"Bubbles" of the Bloods—spoke of her deep resentment of Korean merchants in the aftermath of the Los Angeles riots of April 1992. "It might sound selfish," she said, "but I'm glad a lot of things were burned." She recalled going to a Korean-owned store before the riots to buy a pair of pants. She paid $14.99. Her sister liked them, so after the riots she went back to the same store to buy the identical item. This time the price was $24.99. "What the hell are you trying to do?" she yelled at the owner. "Help the ones that got looted? This shit don't cost that much. I said that's why you guys got burned out, and I said it could get started again. The Korean woman said, 'Oh, no, no, no, my mistake. Sixteen ninety-nine.' She still had to have the extra two dollars."

That led Keith Washington to add: "They don't have no respect. I mean, don't nobody really hardly respect African-Americans or whatever we want to call ourselves. You know, we have an identity crisis problem—African-American, black, whatever we are. But don't nobody really have respect for our community."

The more they talked, the more their expressions of class resentment emerged. In referring to the riots, Bubbles said instead of destroying their own neighborhoods, they should destroy those responsible. "You know, where those people who caused it live—the jurors and the police or whatever," she said. "They caused the grievance. So instead of tearing up our stuff in our own neighborhoods it should be done over there."

From there the conversation picks up on class resentment and rampant conspiracy theories. Turn on any black radio talk show in America, for instance, and you will hear repeated talk about the "white power structure" that conspires to inflict genocide on blacks in America through controlling the drug trade and the flow of weapons into the inner cities, assassinating such a black leader as Martin Luther King, and even failing to eradicate the scourge of AIDS.

The idea of a powerful unseen manipulating hand is hardly new, of course. But this belief has, clearly, become more widely accepted and disseminated. For many, particularly those at the bottom, it stands almost as an article of faith. "You blame your problems on somebody else," says Chris Womack, a young black executive who works for the Alabama Power Company in Birmingham and is one of those African-Americans who moved back to the South from the urban North. "Fortunately, I've been able to get to know quote-unquote 'folks in the white power structure' and they aren't as organized as we think they are. But it's a strong feeling. People do think there is some cartel somewhere pulling the strings."

A white social worker in Los Angeles suggested that I interview "an average guy who went out and took a TV" during the riots. "You know why he took a TV?" he continued. "Because it's not a just world. Social justice is clearly an issue on the street and in the community. Everybody understands that stealing is something you're not supposed to do, but they feel why shouldn't they do it because it's being done to us. White America has not even a clue as to what's going on, because they don't live in those communities. They don't talk to those people. They don't go to the same schools and they don't read the same books or go to the same movies."

By any standard, the greatest American success story of the twentieth century is the rise of blacks from a totally segregated society to a position in which increasing numbers have shared in the material benefits of the nation. Since 1910, the number of blacks in the American middle class has increased tenfold. But nearly all of that growth occurred in the generation that emerged from the civil rights movement of the Sixties, and, as we've seen, the economic aftermath of the Eighties has hit the middle class as a whole.

In 1940, three out of every four black persons in America were impoverished. Forty years later, it was estimated that nearly seven out of ten blacks enjoyed middle-class status. Even greater economic advances were made in the small elite of upper-middle-class blacks who held professional positions of greater prominence in corporate America, in law firms, in entertainment, in sports. The number of blacks in those categories has been doubling every decade since World War II. By the Nineties, nearly half of all blacks own their homes and one and a half million work as managers, business executives, and professionals, while the number of black elected officials increased sixfold in a generation to more than seven thousand.

The fastest-growing segment of America's population, Latinos, also recorded major gains. By the Nineties, 40 percent of Latinos owned their homes and the number of elected officials increased to 3,700. Notwithstanding such signs of minority improvement, the relative position of both blacks and Latinos still greatly suffers beside that of the white majority. Poverty rates for blacks are three times those for whites, and in any given month the Latino unemployment is 50 percent higher than for whites. On an annual basis, three of every ten minority Americans spend some time below the poverty line; the younger the minority person is, the worse those poverty statistics.

In that expanding underclass exists a world that the middle class of all races and ethnicities deals with from a distance, and with scant understanding. On any day in America in the Nineties you can go to an employment or job center and see long lines of people waiting to apply. Increasing numbers of whites are in those lines as America's economic restructuring continues, though the greatest numbers are members of minorities.

For those fortunate enough to enter a job training—or retraining—program, the prospects of good entry-level jobs are increasingly scarce. The result is that millions of Americans in that underclass turn toward a rapidly expanding underground economy to survive. They live by their wits, working odd hours and without basic health and pension benefits.

It is a cash-and-carry world in which the wages are below minimum, no taxes are paid, no records are kept, no Internal Revenue Service W-2 forms are filed, and everyone involved from high-income yuppie employer to illegal worker knowingly becomes a scofflaw.

Most of the time, this world exists out of public view—or, at least, public attention. Occasionally, an incident occurs that briefly forces the public to take note of what virtually everyone knows is happening, as in the Zoë Baird affair.

When Bill Clinton named the young $500,000-a-year corporate lawyer to be his attorney general, it turned out that neither she nor her Yale law professor husband had been paying required Social Security taxes for their illegal alien baby-sitter, or "nanny." The nomination failed. So did the nomination of the next young woman Clinton proposed to be his attorney general, Kimba Wood, a federal judge on the New York bench. Wood's nomination failed for similar reasons of appearances over another nanny who had been an illegal alien at the time Wood first employed her. A third nomination attempt was successful: that of Janet Reno, a single woman with no children who employed no illegal household workers. But the man Clinton intended to nominate as the number two person in the Justice Department, Charles Ruff, was forced to withdraw his name when it turned out that he, too, had failed to pay employment taxes as required for household workers.

All this was a study in hypocrisy, and of the world in which those at the bottom still reap less than those at the top. A more personal glimpse into the attitudes that form that world came one night in the retirement community in Santee, South Carolina. Those seated around the dining-room table were all white professionals, and they were talking about the disconnect between their pleasant world on the shores of the state's largest lake and the world of rising crime, crack gangs, poverty, and new antagonisms they felt increasing even in that more remote corner of America.

They recognized, when they thought about it, that America's have and have-not world touched them too, though perhaps only in a peripheral way. Anne Hale and her neighbors had been talking about wages for a maid they all shared, a black woman named Claire. "They said: 'You pay her five dollars an hour?' " Hale recalled. " 'No,' I said, 'I pay her seven dollars an hour.' 'You're spoiling her!' I told them this woman comes in and cleans our homes, has keys to all our homes, but she has no benefits. And they complain if I pay her seven dollars an hour instead of five!"

Hale thought a moment, then said: "How long can we continue to do well? How long can we live in our little isolated world?"

CHAPTER 11

CULTURE:
THE SALAD BOWL

*America was melting pot,
but now is salad bowl.*

—A Korean-American
in Los Angeles

In his classic *Letters from an American Farmer*, written during the American Revolution, the French-born Michel-Guillaume-Jean de Crèvecoeur described for his European friends the Americans he observed. "Americans are the Western pilgrims," he wrote, "who are carrying along with them that great mass of arts, sciences, vigor and industry, which began long since in the East; they will finish the great circle." He also wrote: "The American is a new man, who acts upon new principles; he must therefore entertain new ideas and form new opinions. . . . This is an American."

Viewed from a late-twentieth-century perspective, Crèvecoeur's elegant words undoubtedly would be criticized as sexist, perhaps racist, and certainly the product of Eurocentric arrogance. Neither politically correct nor multiculturally acceptable in today's terms, they nevertheless underscore one of the sharpest paradoxes of contemporary life. At the same time that Americans move toward a greater—and much-needed—appreciation of ethnic and racial diversity, they are riven by new ethnic and racial divisions. Instead of racial integration, there is more racial separation. Instead of an American melting pot, there is a multiculturalism that divides as well as unites. Instead of more political tolerance, there is a new political intolerance that through "political correctness" intimidates while it liberates.

The strongest example involves integration. The dream of an integrated society did not die with the murder of Martin Luther King, or with the urban riots of the late Sixties, but those events and the racial isolation that followed had a severe impact on the nation. Whether or not integration was ever a realistic goal, the degree to which the races have moved farther apart during the very period when segregation laws were being eliminated is striking, if not dismaying. In school after school from coast to coast I saw and heard the same thing. "They segregated themselves before and after the riots," said Cathy Silva, assistant principal of an inner-city public school in Los Angeles. "It was there before; it hasn't changed. The black kids sit with the blacks, the Hispanics with the Hispanics. Every once in a while you see a few intermingle, but that hasn't changed either. And the same thing with the adults when we meet with them."

Increasing numbers of blacks reject outright the concept that integration is desirable. In Los Angeles, Bondi Gambrell, an aggressive and successful entrepreneur in his early fifties who came to California from Detroit, said: "We were happier as a black people in a community. I remember growing up when our community was basically segregated but we had our own businesses and we looked to each other for help. We were more family-oriented. It was all there. Then integration came and destroyed the fabric of our communities. I guess progress is the name of the game. People want change. Change sometimes is not good for you."

America's campuses reflect all of these changes, both the good and the bad. Students of the Nineties, inheritors of the most liberal reform movements in the nation's history, could be expected to be the most tolerant collegiate generation. They never personally experienced the segregated society of their parents. Even if de facto segregation still exists, they attended public schools that in principle and legally were integrated, or private ones that made special, and successful, efforts to recruit black students. On television, in films, and in the marketplace, they saw evidence of an expanding black middle class with new models of integrated success from Bill Cosby and Michael Jackson to Michael Jordan. As heirs of cumulative protests of the Sixties, they enjoyed societal changes that vastly expanded American rights—civil rights, African-American rights, Hispanic rights, Native American rights, Asian-American rights, women's rights, gay and lesbian rights.

On campus they entered what is without doubt the most equitable environment in American society. Affirmative action programs mandated by law have gone a long way toward remedying discrimination. Intensive efforts have been made to see that all members of the college community—students, faculty, staff, administrators—are more sensitive to the concerns of minorities. Strict codes have been designed and enforced against discriminatory, sexist, or racist behavior.

Yet despite this praiseworthy effort over the space of one generation, colleges have been marked by conflicts that all too often have polarized their campuses. The most serious involve race. By the end of the Eighties, the National Institute Against Prejudice and Violence had identified a "proliferation" of racial incidents occurring over a three-year period at 160 colleges. These ranged from open racial violence to numerous acts of racial insensitivity and harassment. At the University of Massachusetts at Amherst, an argument over the World Series turned violent, triggering a racial assault in which three thousand students chased and beat twenty blacks. At Dartmouth, three editors of the *Dartmouth Review* were suspended for harassing a black professor in his lecture hall. At Yale, the Afro-American cultural center was defaced by a swastika and the words "white power." At the University of Michigan, racial jokes were broadcast on the campus radio station. At the University of Wisconsin, white fraternity pledges painted their faces black and wore Afro wigs during a mock slave auction. At Stanford, two freshmen drew thick lips over a poster of Beethoven and hung it on a black student's door after the university president had warned the incoming freshman class that "bigotry is out."

Accumulation of incidents such as these, chronicled in a brilliant *Harper's* article,* led a black professor of English at California's San Jose State University to make an intensive examination of racial conflicts on American campuses. Shelby Steele wanted to try to under-

---

*Shelby Steele's "The Recoloring of Campus Life: Student Racism, Academic Pluralism, and the End of a Dream" appeared in the February 1989 issue of *Harper's*. See also Steele's superb *The Content of Our Character: A New Vision of Race in America,* in which this essay and others appear.

stand what had happened since his mid-Sixties student days, when colleges were "oases of calm and understanding in a racially tense society."

"It was not hard to see, after my first talks with students, that racial tension on campus is a problem that misrepresents itself," he wrote. "It has the same look, the archetypal pattern, of America's timeless racial conflict—white racism and black protest. And I think part of our concern over it comes from the fact that it has the feel of a relapse, illness gone and come again. But if we are seeing the same symptoms, I don't believe we are dealing with the same illness. For one thing, I think racial tension on campus is the result more of racial equality than inequality."

Steele concluded: "What has emerged on campus in recent years—as a result of the new equality and affirmative action, in a sense, as a result of progress—is a *politics of difference,* a troubling, volatile politics in which each group justifies itself, its sense of worth and its pursuit of power, through difference alone. In this context, racial, ethnic, and gender differences become forms of sovereignty, campuses become balkanized, and each group fights with whatever means are available."

If anything, the tensions Steele wrote about had worsened by the time of my journey. To his politics of difference, I would add a *politics of intimidation* in which teachers feel forced to conform to the pressures of various political correctness groups and in which the dominance of affirmative action programs can result in the shelving of better scholars for minorities. As for the balkanization to which Steele referred, and which Berkeley's Chancellor Chang-lin Tien singled out as a main source of concern,* it was evident everywhere.

Multiculturalism is one of the reasons for this balkanization. Here, too, a strong paradox exists. Emphasis on America's multicultural background is most welcome in a society that has been awash in historical lies and myths. Greater public understanding of the economic exploitation of minorities, of the forces and motivations behind slavery and colonialism, and of the contribution of diverse racial/ethnic elements can only result in a stronger America. However, the best-intended efforts to "celebrate differences" and create better

*See Chapter 7, "Schools: The Dumping Ground," pp. 161–163.

understanding have often had the unfortunate result of celebrating *division* and intensifying misunderstanding. As minorities are encouraged to speak out against their perceived inequalities, other groups discover their minority status—and come forward with their grievances. Groups who feel they are inadequately represented ethnically or racially in the curriculum agitate for *their* department, *their* curriculum, *their* textbooks. The result is a proliferation of competing departments and, in many cases, mandatory ethnic studies requirements for a diploma.

Instead of empowering students, multicultural courses actually leave them less prepared to deal with the real world. In the 1970s, minority students discovered that the route to success was via the professions (something the Jews had recognized sixty or seventy years before). Now, many minority students are buying into programs that presumably make them race-proud or nationality-proud—but at the considerable expense of further removing them from the mainstream culture. They thus become even more alien from the everyday world of the majority, and less well equipped to compete in it. In a sense, they have become victims of new forces of division created out of a desire to make American society fairer and less discriminatory.

All this is a symptom, as historian Arthur M. Schlesinger, Jr., puts it, of "the notion that history and literature should be taught not as intellectual disciplines but as therapies whose function is to raise minority self-esteem." He goes on to say, "The attack on the common American identity is the culmination of the cult of ethnicity," and warns that if carried to its logical extreme it could result in "the decomposition of America."

To Schlesinger, "self-styled 'multiculturalists' are very often ethnocentric separatists who see little in the Western heritage beyond Western crimes. The Western tradition, in this view, is inherently racist, sexist, 'classist,' hegemonic; irredeemably repressive, irredeemably oppressive. The spread of Western culture is due not to any innate quality but simply to the spread of Western power. Thus the popularity of European classical music around the world—and, one supposes, of American jazz and rock too—is evidence not of wide appeal but of 'the pattern of imperialism, in which the conquered culture adopts that of the conqueror.' "

Out of such animus toward Europe, he adds, lies the move against U.S. collegiate courses on Western civilization. This has had such impact that 78 percent of students can graduate from American colleges and universities without taking a course in the history of Western civilization. As Schlesinger further notes, a number of distinguished institutions—he cites Dartmouth, Wisconsin, and Mount Holyoke—require courses in Third World or ethnic studies but not in Western civilization.

Colleges are not the only educational institutions affected by the new pressures for a multicultural curriculum; so are high schools, as I learned. "The students of this generation don't have the knowledge of American history that I have," says Joanne Grimm, principal of Oakland High School. "We've become so involved in multicultural education that we just teach the basic things. I'm not too sure any of them really know the presidents of the United States, for example. We haven't quite figured out how to put all these things together— the multicultural education. What we tend to do is eliminate education about anything with a European-type background. We just skip over it."

The greatest difficulties are felt on college campuses where pressures for political and ideological conformity, and for an ethnocentric multiculturalism, are still on the rise. My boyhood friend Father Bob Swain, who chairs the history department at St. John's University in New York City, reflects on this. People no longer think of America as a melting pot, he says. That's an expression you hardly hear anymore. Now—and here he unconsciously echoes what a Korean-American told me in Los Angeles—you hear more about America being a *salad.* That's fine, Father Bob says, but it also suggests greater disunity.

"I live with disunity," he says. "This very religious house I live in has disunity. We're all upset with disunity in the world today. It's in the family, it's in the religious communities, it's in the churches. Even synagogues are being ripped apart today. Our Lord Himself said that a house that's divided against itself cannot stand. And here in the United States, in this city of New York, in this Borough of Queens, on this campus of St. John's, we have disunity even as we try to create unity."

Multiculturalism was a strong issue at St. John's when we spoke.

"Maybe the melting pot, where everybody speaks English and everybody has some kind of a standardized culture, was an impossible dream," Father Bob says. "I don't know. But we don't teach Western civilization anymore as an introductory course. We've got to teach world civilization. Can you imagine trying to teach—in two semesters—all world civilization? Put on your seat belts, everybody, we're covering three centuries today and four cultures.

"All right," Father Bob says, gesturing vigorously, "you've got me turned on now. You start out, where is the world today? Where's Western civilization? All right, we say it comes from the ancient Greeks, from the Athenians to Rome, Rome spread it into the West. Germanic tribes came down to the fringes of Ireland and the Anglo-Saxons. It becomes Christianized.

"We have the medieval period. And then what happens? You have the monarchies coming in and then the discovery of America and it spreads to other parts of the world. Then you get to the French Revolution. That's my Western civilization. That's what I want to teach. But I've got to get into Asoka and the Indian Empire and the Chinese empires, which I'm not trained to do, you understand. And why are we doing all this?"

He sits back in the chair and stares out the window, seemingly lost in thought.

"By disassembling history, or by scattering history, are you trying to get unity?" he finally says. "We're diffusing it too much. We're diffusing it."

Two other campuses I visited, each with a long and distinguished tradition of academic excellence and progressive leadership, are illustrative of the kinds of diffusion Father Bob cites.

At the University of Wisconsin at Madison, where I did my graduate work in American history in the mid-1950s, it is striking to see, again, how the various groups have chosen to separate themselves. In the cafeterias at lunch, you see blacks eating with blacks, Asians with Asians, whites with whites. Rarely is there a truly integrated table. The campus in 1992 was agitated over the university's creation of an Interim MultiCultural Center (IMCC) located inside the Memorial Union that for generations served all students at Madison. Intended to improve race relations, it was perceived to be a source of division. Farzaneh Behroozi, an Iranian-American student active in student-

government-sponsored cultural events, remembers her first reaction
to the MultiCultural Center. As a freshman, she stood before the
glass-paned doors and looked inside, where a painting of Martin
Luther King hung against dark wood paneling in the long, high,
narrow room.

"I never opened those doors," she says. "I was pretty sure that it
was a black-pride place and they wouldn't appreciate my presence.
My friends agreed. Maybe they called it MultiCultural, but it seemed
definitely *minority.* Yet my friends are Indians, Chinese, Koreans,
Iranians, Hispanics, and other minorities ourselves. Hey, wait a minute! Shouldn't the MultiCultural Center be for *everyone,* majority or
minority?"

Behroozi adds: "Many people feel that it's a place for people of
color to get together with their people. In other words, a safe haven. I
disagree. This university is creating an artificial situation. The mission of the university is not to make everyone comfortable. The mission of the university is to be provocative and to provide a forum for
the discussion of ideas. Where in the real world is there a respite from
racism, sexism, and general insensitivity fueled by ignorance? What
essential social skills do we learn by practicing separatism? Why
aren't we learning to communicate and *listen* to each other?"

She and others strongly feel that the center has failed to improve
race relations or even provide a forum for conflict resolution. Instead, she argues, it has attempted to empower "minority" student
organizations at the expense of the emphatically not unitary "majority." As an example, she says the MultiCultural Center council, composed of five target groups—the Black Student Union, the Asian-
American Student Union, two Chicano groups, and Native
American students—received a $100,000 events budget from the uni-
versity to sponsor special campus events and speakers. (A $10,000
university lecture appearance by Louis Farrakhan, the black separatist leader, came from this university fund and was dispensed by the
sponsoring student group.) At the same time, the entire remaining
student government budget for *all* such special events was set at
$45,000. "That is used to empower the *entire* student body to host
speakers, hire musicians, bring in debaters, ad infinitum," Farzaneh
Behroozi says. "A hundred-thousand-dollar budget for five minority
groups is entirely out of line. They may view themselves as the cul-

tural programmers for the university, but are they serving their purpose?

"I come to the conclusion that they program for themselves and really aren't concerned with the needs of the entire student body. But, okay, what if they really are the 'cultural programmers' for the campus? Then it's time to raze the Union, because the Union has become redundant."

Behroozi would like to see the cultural center turned back into a study lounge and the Union back into the Union, a place where daylong music sessions with bands and speeches by professors and students addressing race relations would take place. Encourage ethnic student groups to set up their booths and hold their programs, she suggests, and conduct lunchtime discussions with campus and community leaders. "Programs like these should help to establish a sense of community at a campus where most students feel lost in the crowd," she says. "A few students would probably get angry enough at *our* inadequate programs to join the Union and set us straight!"

At Berkeley, Luis Guillen, a senior from San Antonio, Texas, whose ambition is to become mayor of San Antonio, speaks of the difficulties of Latinos like himself. He has a sense of confidence in the future, and great pride as a first-generation American whose father came to the United States as an illegal alien and worked in the fields as a laborer. But he also worries about ethnic separatism.

"I have a lot of friends of Mexican descent who refuse to speak English," he says. "When they got to Berkeley, they spoke English very well. Now they refuse to speak English. They only speak Spanish. They say, 'Hi, Luis, how are you doing?' in Spanish. When I respond in English, they don't accept me as well."

Guillen believes America's greatest problem is its increasing social unrest, which makes it "almost impossible for two groups of different races to sit down together and deal with problems." That same awareness of polarization worries Eunice Baek at Berkeley. "Being friends with Monica, my black friend, annoyed some people in the Korean-American community," she says. "It annoyed Monica's black friends too. At Cal you walk into a class and all the black students sit together and quite a few Asian students sit together. I don't think you should always be with your own—what they say, your own kind, your own color, your own ethnicity. It's pretty discouraging to see a large lecture class with hundreds of students and a couple of rows of just black students and a little pocket of Asian students.

"I can understand the need to be with your own people who have the same customs, but I don't think life is all about just being comfortable. If you have a cultural house it should be for people who are interested in African culture rather than just for people who are of African descent. If you have a Korean-American group it should be for all those who are interested in the culture or the language.

"The PC—politically correct—thing now is for each ethnic group to congregate by themselves. A lot of my white liberal friends are saying we've pushed immigrants so much to assimilate, we should make up for it now—because they're feeling guilty—by letting them do their own thing, speak their own language. I know it's important to keep your own language and culture, but there's definitely a limit. It's really rude when Korean students are with non-Korean students and they just jabber in Korean the whole time. That's very, very rude. Speaking Korean is fine, but speak it when you're by yourselves.

"Black students in college feel very—I don't know what the word is. Not really intimidated but like they're in the spotlight all the time because people are always pointing out how few black students there are in college. People play with numbers and they look at minorities and they say, 'Look at Asians. In California, the Asian population's not even eleven percent, but look at the colleges. Over thirty-three percent. Look how successful they are.' And then they go on through the Hispanic community and get to the black community and say, 'Well, the black community makes up this much percentile of the state and they're only this much in the colleges. What's wrong with them?' "

Blacks, not surprisingly, react intensely to such implicit criticisms of their ability and also to a tangle of other emotions and circumstances that continue to set them apart from other racial and ethnic groups. They alone among America's citizens suffered the incalculably crippling effects of two and a half centuries of slavery and another hundred years of segregation before the legal barriers to racial equality fell. Many blacks who make it to college were born into poor and troubled families in heavily stressed communities and receive special assistance in admittance and financial aid through affirmative action programs.

Acute awareness of those factors, and of the resentment their special status stirs in other groups, inevitably intensifies feelings of vulnerability and anxiety. As Shelby Steele writes, in the mutual jostling for identity and power "all that remains unresolved between blacks and whites, all the old wounds and shames that have never been addressed, present themselves for attention—and present our youth with pressures they cannot always handle." He offers a revealing example that occurred at UCLA. Steele asked a black student if he ever felt anxious about "black inferiority." The student, clearly disturbed, finally admitted he did. He then described his reaction to the behavior of black classmates who sat in the back of a large lecture hall and "acted out every stereotype in the book": they were loud, ate in class, came in late, and generally scored lower than the whites.

"I knew I would be seen like them, and I didn't like it," the student told Steele.

Seen like what? Steele pressed, though he was certain both he and the student knew what the answer would be.

"As lazy, ignorant, and stupid."

Problems over multiculturalism and moves for greater racial and ethnic separatism are compounded by the pressure to conform to imposed standards of political correctness that, at the worst, inhibit candor, debate, and free expression. Here, too, a good-news/bad-news situation exists, especially in regard to women.

In just a generation, the women's movement has transformed the university. Now women increasingly hold major positions of authority as presidents of colleges and universities, as deans, as graduate teaching assistants, and as representatives of professional schools. About half of entering law school students, for instance, are now women. The same is so with medical schools. These numbers alone guarantee that women will be more influential in American life in years to come. The women's movement can take credit for these achievements, and it is on our campuses that the women's movement has flowered most. The attitudes formed there carry over into the larger society, reinforcing a determination to fight sexism and gender discrimination not only on campuses but in communities and corporate offices. That is the good news, proof that American openness still works. The bad news—hardly surprising—is that the women's movement, like any other movement, is subject to ideological extremes and bias. It, too, is capable of exerting pressure for a conformity that can easily become another source of intimidation—and division.

A perfect example came at the University of Michigan, where a hapless sophomore's misuse of language led to his being accused of sexual harassment by a female teaching assistant. This on the basis of a hypothetical example he employed in his term paper for an introduction to American politics course, in which he wrote:

> Another problem with sampling polls is that some people desire their privacy and don't want to be bothered by a pollster. Let's say Dave Stud is entertaining three beautiful ladies in his penthouse when the phone rings. A pollster on the other end wants to know if we should eliminate the capital gains tax. Now Dave is a knowledgeable businessperson who cares a lot about this issue. But since Dave is "tied up" at the moment, he tells the pollster to "bother" someone else. Now this is perhaps a ludicrous example, but there is simply a segment of the population who wish to be left alone. They have more important things to be concerned about—jobs, family, school, etc. If this segment of the population is never actually polled, then the results of the poll could be skewed.

As *The Wall Street Journal* later commented, a neutral observer would probably conclude the student had deviated somewhat from the political science department's politically correct "checklist for nonsexist language," but had showed proper "sensitivity" in using the sexless "businessperson" term and made interesting points about the validity of polls. The teacher's reaction was hardly so neutral. She took his paper as a verbal assault on her and, employing the devices of the "language censor," wrote:

> You are right. This is ludicrous & inappropriate and OFFENSIVE. This is completely inappropriate for a serious political science paper. It completely violates the standard of non-sexist writing. Professor Rosenstone has encouraged me to interpret this comment as an example of sexual harassment and to take the appropriate formal steps. I have chosen not to do so in this instance. However,

any future comments, in a paper, in a class or in any dealings w/me will be interpreted as sexual harassment and formal steps *will be* taken. Professor Rosenstone is aware of these comments—& is prepared to intervene. You are forewarned!

The student made the sensible decision to drop the course, leading the *Journal* to comment: "It is very hard to see how this enterprise can lead to much good end. If we know anything from history, it is that such exercises in the policing of language and thought drive people into lifetime opposition."

Such examples of pressures to banish offending free expression by new Jacobins are all too common on American campuses. In the spring of 1993, for example, a group of black students at the University of Pennsylvania confiscated nearly all fourteen thousand copies of the student newspaper and dumped them in the trash. The motivation, according to a statement issued by a "Working Committee of Concerned Black and Latino Students," was not to protest specific events or individual actions on campus but to protest "the blatant and covert racism continually perpetuated by both institutions and individuals on Penn's campus."

This explanation notwithstanding, the papers were seized after a student—he happened to be conservative—wrote a column condemning "black militants [who] rail against white bigotry . . . while praising hatemongers like Malcolm X, an ex-pimp who conspired with the Ku Klux Klan." The confiscation of the student newspapers led Penn's president to comment that he regretted that "two important university values, diversity and open expression, seem to be in conflict."

Seem to be indeed! Universities have a responsibility to insist upon the right of diversity, to assure that groups and individuals have the freedom to associate as they wish, while at the same time trying to teach in ways that will lead to greater understanding and tolerance for differences. But they also have a responsibility to guarantee the right of free expression, the right to dissent, even the right to be wrong without being subjected to behavior that suppresses free expression. At Penn, two vital values—respect for diversity and the right of free expression—were not defended simultaneously as they should have been. Not only were they permitted to be in conflict, but the side that exercised the greater degree of intimidation was permitted to prevail.

The Penn case attracted even wider attention when it was followed by another highly publicized incident on that campus. A white freshman student there was cited for racial harassment by five black sorority members who were partying loudly outside a dormitory at midnight, triggering shouts from many students for them to be quiet. The freshman charged acknowledged that he had shouted out his dorm window, "Shut up, you water buffalo," but said he meant no racial insult. He was charged nonetheless with violating the school's speech code against using racial epithets to injure others. Interestingly, in all the controversy that this incident created, nothing was said about citing the students for disturbing the peace, which by their own account they clearly were. Eventually, the black women dropped the case, bitterly charging that news media accounts were biased against them.

These tensions on Penn's campus were given even greater national exposure when First Lady Hillary Rodham Clinton, in delivering the university's commencement address later that spring, referred to the university's struggles with racial tension and free speech. "We must always uphold the idea of our colleges as incubators of ideas and havens for free speech and free thought," Mrs. Clinton told the graduates, adding, "Freedom and respect are not values that should be in conflict with each other."

Hillary Rodham Clinton made another important point in her commencement address at Penn, one that applies not only to all American campuses but to the nation at large. "We must be careful not to cross the line between censuring behavior we consider unacceptable and censoring," she said. "We have to believe that in the free exchange of ideas, justice will prevail over injustice, tolerance over intolerance, and progress over reaction."

Here was a classic restatement of the oldest American belief in the power of reason, justice, and progress. It was especially notable because it came after a long period during the Reagan/Bush years in which national leaders either did not address such issues or, if they did, often contributed to greater division and tension by making ideologically divisive remarks.

Berkeley's chancellor, Chang-lin Tien, knows that many Americans are beginning to despair of creating a more inclusive multicultural society—and a truly integrated one. Those beliefs are strengthened by two factors: public awareness of racial and ethnic tensions on campuses nationwide, and the influence of best-selling books that warn against divisions created by the imposition of multiculturalism in college courses.

Tien cites three of these books in particular. The first, Professor Allan Bloom's *The Closing of the American Mind,* reflects the perspective of a political conservative. "We are used to hearing the Founders charged with being racists, murderers of Indians, representatives of class interests," Bloom writes, attacking the new scholarly iconoclasts for "weakening our convictions of the truth or superiority of American principles and our heroes." The second, offering another conservative analysis, is Dinesh D'Souza's *Illiberal Education,* which makes a strong case against the excesses of political correctness and portrays the increasing group polarization of campuses along racial, ethnic, and gender lines like those I have described at the University of Wisconsin campus at Madison. The third, Arthur M. Schlesinger, Jr.'s, *The Disuniting of America,* presents the viewpoint of a white liberal.

Chancellor Tien acknowledges all the points in these kinds of criticisms. He's read all of them, he says, and finds them factually correct; it's their basic premise about multiculturalism with which he disagrees. For the United States, he believes, nothing is more important than to demonstrate it is capable of providing excellence in public education for its immensely diverse and competing ethnic and racial components. In the outcome of that question lies the true future of the United States.

His own life strengthens his conviction on that point, for Tien's personal experience has made him a believer in the melting pot, in multiculturalism, in an integrated society, and in the American Dream. It has also put him in strong opposition to the pressures of mindless political correctness. When Tien came to the United States in 1956 from mainland China by way of Taiwan, he was nearly destitute and barely spoke English. He had to borrow money even though he received a full collegiate scholarship, and he entered a world in

Louisville, Kentucky where business, washrooms, dining rooms—everything—were segregated. Even some professors contributed to his feelings of being a member of a discriminated-against minority by continually referring to him as "Chinaman."

This was at the time when Martin Luther King, Jr., was stepping onto the American stage. Tien became an admirer from afar of the black leader as someone who demonstrated that society could be changed by using the political system through nonviolent mass pressure and by appealing to the nation's conscience.

In his own mind, Tien's life exemplifies the American Dream. Never, he says, looking back, did he think he'd become chancellor of a major university, especially a great public institution like Berkeley. The experience of his three children reinforces his passionate belief in his country's possibilities. All attended the public schools at Berkeley and graduated from its university. His two daughters earned master's degrees at Harvard before returning West, one becoming a medical doctor in Denver, the other a law student in Arizona. His son earned a Ph.D. from Princeton, as had Tien, and became an electrical engineer in San Diego. They are, Tien says proudly, "real Americans, but also very multicultural in their heritage . . . new Americans" with bright futures.

All this convinces Tien that the melting pot is far from a foolish notion of the past. He believes that integration is still a highly desirable goal, and that multiculturalism can, and should, be a means of achieving it. He is determined to make that happen at Berkeley and believes that because of world events, it is critical for us to succeed.

As he points out, America's new cultural divisions coincide with the reemergence of historic national, ethnic, racial, and religious hatreds worldwide. Compared to these, America's problems of diversity pale. "If any country can solve its multicultural problems," Tien says, "that's the United States."

What critics fail to understand, he says, is the stunning transformation already reshaping American society. The new ethnic and racial tensions, for all their problems, can bring opportunity, if the schools and the society are up to meeting the challenge.

To that end, Tien emphasizes giving special attention to freshmen entering Berkeley. Given their diverse backgrounds, they are understandably insecure when they arrive on campus and tend to associate with their own groups. "That's not wrong," the chancellor says. "In fact, you need those groups to give you pride, identity, comfort, and confidence. But it's wrong if the university is not providing the environment and the opportunity for all those groups to interact with each other. The only way you do that is with freshmen. By the sophomore year, if you cannot achieve some integration, you are out. Because they have their own groups."

In freshmen residence halls, Tien seeks to encourage students of various backgrounds to initiate discussion groups. Instead of requiring ethnic studies, Berkeley takes a different approach: a requirement for broader *American* culture courses. After one year, some eighty such pilot courses were established. As an example, Tien says a course on American music might discuss Aaron Copland and George Gershwin, but also study Latin American and Asian music and black jazz. "That's the American culture," he says, "all together. Then we have a class called Urban Politics. How can you talk about urban politics and not talk about different constituencies? So every course must have at least three different subcultures or cultural groups. They don't have to all divide along color lines. They can be Jewish, German, Italian, or Irish, but they have to have at least three. That's very exciting. I went to quite a few myself, and if I were a freshman I'd love that."

As for political correctness, Tien is determined to oppose it. He seeks to do everything he can to assist minorities and promote diversity—but he has bluntly let faculty and others know that he will not compromise standards to do so. That, he says, would hurt the very groups that the movement sets out to help by treating them as second-class or inferior.

"There are talents in blacks, in Hispanics, in Asians, in any cultural group," he says, "and we want to help develop them to their fullest capacity, but when judgment time comes, when evaluation time comes, we have to maintain the highest standards. I have to be convinced the person is absolutely of the highest quality, and I am not going to inject politically correct thinking in the promotion and evaluation process."

Tien's hope is that Berkeley's example can be a model for American education. If his approach succeeds, it also holds promise for American culture at large. Tien is determined to demonstrate that diversity can be a source of strength in a democracy that faces increasing division at every level.

The stridency of American life has its positive features as well. Certainly a society that airs its ugliest problems from racism to sexual harassment—and not only airs them but screams about them— has opportunities to be healthier than one that pretends no problems exist. But there are troubling elements that go beyond the problems we've examined here. Violence in America *is* increasing; civility and attempts to reach consensus *are* declining; racial and ethnic groups *are* becoming more polarized; the concept that rights should be expanded into notions of absolute entitlement *does* make compromise among diametrically opposing groups more difficult.

The signs are everywhere. On radio and TV talk shows the shouted racial insult and the angry ethnic epithet—and the more outrageous, the better—are staples of popular programming. This is not by chance. Such TV and radio shows encourage extreme views; they are part of the nation's new Theater of Disagreement, a theater where those who shout loudest get most access. There is no thoughtful middle, no historical context, no expression of doubt, no equivocation. It is all one-sided polemic by players picked to represent opposing sides of an ideological argument—and to do so with disregard for fact. Nor do moderators of these shows correct egregious misstatements. When a new national controversy erupts, such as an abortion ruling or a Clarence Thomas hearing highlighting the charged issue of sexual harassment, spokespeople for the competing sides are given full voice to make their partisan cases. The voices of the dispassionate middle are rarely aired. So too with news analysis programs like the *McLaughlin Group,* on which ideological posturing, a smug tone of omniscience, and absolute predictions about the outcome of controversial issues pass for serious discussion. When added to the daily reports of violence, the latest deadly outbreak of a hitherto obscure religious cult like the Branch Davidians in Waco, Texas, and the bloody scenes offered regularly by Hollywood films and TV productions, these ideological hothouse programs contribute to an impression that America has become ever more fractious and destructive.

And all this is magnified by an electronic communications revolution that changes the way Americans relate to each other and even govern themselves. In the new media age, as more groups have access to expanding electronic outlets, the tendency increases to go public with grievances rather than negotiate them. This hardens lines of conflict and makes compromise more difficult—a condition already evident in America's increasingly litigious society. Instead of trying to fashion a political deal through adoption of political strategies, competing groups either take their cases to the courts or try them in the media—or both. This, too, contributes to growing divisiveness.

More than media impressions of cultural conflict are at work here; statistics suggest that America's group conflicts are becoming more violent. Accurate figures on the number of hate crimes committed against people because of their race, religion, gender, or sexual orientation are hard to determine. They form a relatively new statistical category of national crimes. Definitions about them differ, and reporting on them has been remiss among local and state jurisdictions. Often, victims themselves are reluctant to report these crimes, particularly when attacks are against gays and lesbians who do not wish their sexual preferences publicly known. Fear of public embarrassment or humiliation also restricts the reporting of crimes of sexual harassment.

In 1993, the FBI's hate-crime report recorded 4,598 victims nationwide, but conceded that its figures were highly incomplete. Only 2,771 out of 16,000 law enforcement agencies participated in the report. There is no doubt, however, that such crimes have been increasing and that they appear to be more violent in nature.

"Gay-bashing" incidents nationally, for example, appear to have tripled from 1988 to 1993, according to figures compiled by the National Gay and Lesbian Task Force. Incidents of racial assaults, neo-Nazi "skinhead" attacks on blacks, defacing of synagogues by painted swastikas—all are on the rise. Public-school teachers also report being harassed and threatened by students who refuse to accept discipline. Any criticism or disciplinary action is seen by these students as "disrespect" toward *them,* not the reverse. This is particularly true among black inner-city youths; perceived slights, whether racial or other, are taken as signs of "dissing" them—thereby offering a license to retaliate upon the source of the imputed disrespect. Such behavior is not confined to the classrooms or schoolyards, of course. It thrives on the streets and often leads to individual or group acts of violence, providing further evidence of a world in which youths with no families and no traditional models of conduct adopt their own standards of behavior. Putting down anyone who challenges or disagrees with them is not seen as wrong. It is heroically self-affirmatory and right to punish those who dissed them. Such behavior recalls the old saying that one's country is the only possession of the poor. In time of peace, the gang thus offers a surrogate form of nation, complete with the excitement of killing and dying for it.

Keeping track of—to say nothing of examining the causes of—these symptoms of a seriously fragmented society is not easy. One of the best sources for information, and insights, I found was at the Massachusetts Institute of Technology. There, Mary Rowe's job is to collect *concerns,* and her prime concern is what she calls the rise of "meanness and mean behavior" in American life. She is in a unique position to make that judgment. As ombudsperson for MIT, she has helped establish nearly five hundred similar offices to address problems and grievances within corporations, government agencies, colleges, and universities. She is the person other ombudsmen turn to for advice. Out of such a background, Rowe has earned a reputation as one of the most knowledgeable of those who attempt to assess the strains of American life and address rising tensions over race, gender, ethnic identity, political correctness, and multiculturalism.

"About a decade ago I began to talk and write about meanness, mean behavior," says Rowe, who holds a Ph.D. in economics and a bachelor's degree in history and international relations. "As an example, I encourage institutions that are setting up an external ombudsperson office to have policies about mean behavior in general—not just sexual harassment, not just hate crimes or racism or gay-bashing, but across-the-board concern with how people deliberately or accidentally interfere with each other's lives on an unreasonable basis.

"The data in this office have shown a very sharp increase in reports of meanness. I'm always asked whether this is increasing behavior or increase in *reports* of that behavior. I personally believe that it has to be both, that the kinds of mean behavior reported all over North America simply couldn't have been out there in the 1970s and not been reported, at least to some extent."

Most common among increasing reports of "mean behavior" are racial insults, outrageous rudeness, tirades, threats, deliberately interfering with the excellence of someone else's work, petty sabotage, and what Rowe says is the "the kind of behavior which—figuratively speaking—is sticking out your foot when somebody goes down the aisle just for the pleasure of watching them stumble."

Though her office keeps track of "mean behavior," there is no body of statistical evidence that easily explains why it is increasing. Certain factors—the continuing breakdown of the American family structure, tensions related to economic stress and greater awareness of violent crime—must be considered, of course. But Rowe herself attributes the rise in meanness to a more general societal problem that she began detecting around 1980. National statistics indicate that concern for one's *own* situation, as against lending a helping hand to others, became much more pronounced sometime between 1978 and 1982 and grew steadily more alarming through the decade. A major factor, Rowe believes, is that America's leaders were widely perceived as being "out for themselves." In effect, national leaders were displaying get-it-for-me and get-it-now behavior. The public emulated their behavior. During that same period, the United States experienced increasing frictions over race, gender, nationality, and ethnicity.

To someone like Rowe, the passing of the melting pot concept is not a great concern. "All of those folks who began to talk about an American 'mosaic' instead of a 'melting pot' some years ago had it right," Rowe says. "I'm astonished at the different ways people view the same facts—sometimes I find two different points of view in the same head. Let's imagine that you're the child of one black parent and one white parent. What are you? Brought up as you and I were—I'm fifty-six today, by the way—the child of the black and the white parent is a brown child who is black, right? Not for that kid! I had a long talk about race and ethnicity with such a person and I said, 'How do you feel about yourself?' He said 'I am black and white.' An hour before, I had asked a Chinese-Jamaican student from a nearby large research university how she identified. She said, 'I am Chinese and I am Jamaican. I'm a Caribbean.' Kids tell you, 'I am black and white, thank you very much. Don't go around pigeonholing me, lady.' These are kids who are saying, within one person, 'I'm no melting pot, mister. I'm a mosaic.' "

Mary Rowe takes this as a hopeful emergence of a more mature society, even if the melting pot concept has faded. Despite evidence of new segregation and separatism, she believes that as America learns to appreciate the strengths of its new "mosaic" and the varied background from which it is formed, it will be in a better position to resolve its disputes. "My hope is there will so many cross-cultural entanglements that it will not be in anybody's interest to fight another war," she says. "I'll give you a good example of two equal and opposite points of view residing in one head—my own. My old head says I don't like it that even the English, let alone the Germans and the Japanese, are buying up my country. My forward-looking head says, why, you nitwit, if they buy up this country, and the interests become interlocking enough, nobody's going to want to fight a war!"

At the same time, she concedes that in the ever more complex American society, where so many cultures are in conflict, it is increasingly difficult to forge consensus. In fact, she believes that a mature America will have to learn to make more complicated choices based on individual and community needs as opposed to setting and achieving national goals through national consensus. As evidence that this is already taking place, she cites the "flexible" benefit plans increasingly being offered employees, in which the individual chooses what proportion of the company benefit package he or she wishes to use for vacation, health care, child care, or tuition assistance.

That may well be the way of the future, and a better one at that, but the evidence of my journey presents a more immediate concern: of an increasingly balkanized America in which consensus on the hard economic and political issues is harder to achieve. The danger is that Americans, an assimilating people whose proudest heritage has been their ability to rise above tribal differences, will become so torn by their own internal tribalisms that they will no longer be able to achieve agreement on *any* difficult question.

CHAPTER 12

MIGRANTS: BOTTOM OF THE BARREL

From the crest of the hill, brown and bare, the desolate ridgelines run east into the desert, disappearing in a hazy merging of brilliant sky and sand. A hot sun beats down, a steady wind stirs the dust. Other than the small ground squirrels scurrying from burrow to burrow beside the high corrugated-steel fence that follows the ridgelines into the desert, there are few signs of activity.

To the west, beyond where cars are backed up as far as the eye can see and the flags of two countries and one state whip in the hot breeze, the ridges run for another five miles. They cross floodplains, run before electric light towers rising every few hundred feet in the desert floor, and around steep canyons before ending at the Pacific Ocean. The same dark ten-foot-high corrugated fence, silhouetted against the skyline, meanders along the ridges into the distance; but here, close up, clusters of people perch atop it. Some scamper down the fence, others race across the open terrain toward the small single-story bungalows that stand several hundred yards away.

Mike Nicely and I had taken off for that high point on the ridge after leaving the U.S. Border Patrol station several miles to the north. We had a shotgun propped between us in the front seat of the cruiser, and a two-way radio chattered. Our route, along narrow congested streets, took us past the trolley tracks winding toward the border; past the bungalows and alleys; past the small stores, one after another, with signs in Spanish proclaiming twenty-four-hour check-cashing services, or handling of insurance and tax forms; past the rows of money-changing shops also open around the clock; past the pawnshops; past the fast-food shops, the 7-Elevens, the McDonald's; past the dense crowds lining the streets and standing on corners in groups of fifteen or twenty, waiting, it seemed, for action.

Just before the border, we swung to the left and began climbing a dirt road up the ridge. Clouds of dust followed us. At the top, we parked and looked down on the international border between San Ysidro, California, and Tijuana, Mexico. "We have only seven-tenths of a mile of border to patrol," Mike Nicely said, "and until recently this was the busiest seven-tenths of a mile anywhere in the country." It's still the busiest port of entry in the world, and nothing else comes close, he added, glancing down at the lines of vehicles inching into the United States through the San Ysidro inspection station. But for the U.S. Border Patrol, which Nicely serves as a field operations supervisor, its busiest sector has now shifted from San Ysidro to the five miles between the crossing place and the ocean.

We got out of the car, stood on the ridgeline, and surveyed the border scene. Over there, in the distance, on the other side and shimmering in the heat, a plane rose slowly. That was the Tijuana airport. To our right, to the west, we could see the dark break that indicated the ocean. To our left, to the east, was the desert, stretching hundreds and hundreds of miles from California across the Southwestern states to the Gulf of Mexico. Behind us, to the north, the freeway ran straight to San Diego, a half hour's drive away, and then on to Los Angeles and beyond.

"We have problems with everything from narcotics trafficking to other types of contraband—everything you can think of that's not supposed to be coming in," Mike Nicely was saying. "It's a multibillion-dollar-a-year business. Plus the illegal foot traffic. There may be millions of illegal aliens in Los Angeles. Most of them come through here. Illegal immigration is a symptom of the border being out of control because we lack funding and support. If we doubled the resources, would that be enough? If we did, we'd double the arrests, double the interdictions. I don't know *what* an appropriate amount of resource is. I do know that what we have is woefully inadequate. We have only two hundred people to enforce the laws of this entire border.

"In the twelve years that I've been here, I have not taken *one* person out to show him what was going on—be it at the checkpoints or on the border—and had anybody tell me this is the way it should be. People say, 'My God, what's going on down here? What do we need to do to change this?' "

Nicely pointed toward a ridge slightly to the west, where another Border Patrol cruiser was parked. That was one of the big staging areas for the illegal aliens, he explained. Until the fence went up you'd see five hundred to a thousand people staging up there. They'd wait until night to begin moving.

"It takes on a whole different look at night," he said, speaking as someone who has patrolled that ridge in the darkness but also from the point of view of the illegals who make their way to the United States from there. "These hills look pretty innocuous in the daytime. But at night there's no residual lighting. A lot of those places on the other side have no electricity, so it's very very dark, and the canyons are rugged. You can see the land, how difficult it is to traverse."

The problem for us Central Americans coming to the United States is Mexico. It's easy to get through Central America from El Salvador, but it's hard to get into Mexico. I crossed into Mexico from Guatemala in an inner tube over the river that's the border with Mexico. There were thirteen of us.

I had to leave El Salvador when I got a message saying I would be killed unless I left the country. Our soccer team beat the team of the national police, and there was a fight. I was studying law then at the University of El Salvador, and under the circumstances my family and I decided I should stop my studies and leave the country. So they contacted a fellow who knew a "coyote"—someone who passes people from one country to another. The coyote explained how the trip would be, so I took a bus to Guatemala, and then went to Mexico.

We spent the first day in Mexico trying to avoid Mexican immigration. Finally we got to a little town where we were supposed to be a little more secure, although once you leave your home and cross borders illegally you never really feel secure. We spent nine days in Mexico, sometimes taking buses, getting off buses, walking around immigration checkpoints. That was to get to Mexico City. From Mexico City to the border, all of the immigration checkpoints were Mexican federal police who would stop the buses and check people's papers. They all accept bribes from Mexico City north.

The going rate at that time was fifty thousand pesos, which was about twenty dollars, every time we got stopped. I got stopped five times between Mexico City and the border. You pay in cash. They count it and see if you have more money. They demand more, so you have to be very careful about hiding the fact that you have more money. The cost of paying the coyote and the different bribes I had to pay to get from El Salvador was about thirteen hundred dollars. My family helped me there.

You can't bring a backpack or a suitcase or anything else. You just wear jeans and tennis shoes, a T-shirt. The coyote had a suitcase and he would have one change of clothes so after you'd crossed a river you'd have a change of clothes. But the suitcase got lost, so we ended up having to wear the same clothes for the whole trip.

The coyote said you shouldn't take anything but I took my university ID and my armed forces card. But in Mexico I had to throw them out because when you cross over from Tijuana to the United States if the INS [the Immigration and Naturalization Service] catches you and you have a document proving you're from El Salvador you don't get deported to Mexico—you get deported to El Salvador. Whereas if you don't have any documents they can't prove you're from El Salvador so they deport you to Mexico and you can try again.

So we got to Tijuana and we passed those five checkpoints along the way. We got to the border at three o'clock in the afternoon and we had to wait at the border until the coyote said we could cross, which was at midnight. But Tijuana is very dangerous. There are all kinds of armed guards running around the border area, and the staging area where we were was also tremendously cold at night. Nobody had a jacket and it was really cold that night.

Well, we waited in the hills above Tijuana until midnight, until there was a whole bunch of us there. Every little group had its own coyote, and when the coyote says it's time to go, well then you see these little groups forming up and crossing through the hills. Running and then falling to the ground. Then running again. We arrived in the town on the U.S. side of the border, which is San Ysidro, and we had to run through some residential neighborhoods. Like jumping over people's yards and stuff. Once we got through the residential neighbor-

hood we got right up to the freeway. There was a driver waiting to take
us to San Diego. It was a van with like curtains around the windows.

In the world of illegal immigration, Mike Nicely was explaining, there are various levels of operations.

There are what the Americans call the "smugglers"—and the Latinos the "coyotes"—who bring the aliens and the narcotics across the border. For a single trip, like transporting the group from El Salvador the illegal alien has just described, the coyote can make as much as $30,000—not including his take from drug smuggling. Then there are the "arrangers," who never smuggle; they stay safely on either side of the border recruiting business by acting as front men or go-betweens. For fees of $25—or $250—they'll arrange transportation for illegals through their underground network to final destinations as far away as Denver or Chicago.

Sometimes the arrangers employ "guides" whose specific job is simply to lead the immigrants through or around the U.S. border checkpoints that stand as the first line of defense, and to their initial stop at one of numerous "load houses" where they huddle in San Ysidro before moving on. Money is often "laundered" there.

Finally, there are "mules," also illegals, whom the smugglers/coyotes pay to carry drugs into the United States, often in balloons they swallow. Once they have crossed, they are given plane tickets to a city—Seattle, Chicago, Dallas—where they are met and turn over their drugs to others in the criminal network.

As we drove back through the streets of San Ysidro toward the Chula Vista Border Patrol station, Nicely pointed out groups of people he identified as guides, arrangers, and smugglers, known or suspected.

The gang graffiti on building walls became more rampant the closer we came to the area Nicely wanted me to see. He swung into a maze of alleys running through an area of highly concentrated, run-down one-story homes. Many stolen vehicles are parked here for people coming across, Nicely explained. "This is the area where we're going to get most of our traffic, the area we're working in at night. You can see it's a maze if you're trying to track down people."

At that point, a tall wiry Latino in jeans and no shirt lurched toward the patrol car and flagged it down. He held a bottle in one hand. Still holding it, he grasped the open car window with his other hand and leaned forward. We could see needle marks on his arm.

"Well, good morning, good night," he mumbled in English.

"How you doin', partner," Nicely said.

"You know of course that I know Spanish and English," the man continued. "And you know the streets, like coming to the alley and then you keep going north. There's a right and a left when you get to other street then you take that to ummmm."

"What's the problem?" Nicely asked.

"I went to high school to the sixth grade, but I went more to . . ." His words became unintelligible.

"Let me see your other arm," Nicely snapped.

"Hold on," the man said. "You know when go ahead like that I do remember that that was stolen."

Nicely, growing sharper, ordered the man to move away. There was no response. Again, Nicely ordered him to move, this time dropping his hand to his revolver. The man moved.

"Have a nice day," Nicely said as we drove off down the alley.

"You can't be involved in this without being interested in why people come across the border," he was saying, "and to a certain extent it's our job. Most people will tell you it's because there's no work in Mexico. Everybody has an opinion on immigration, and most of those opinions are ill-informed. Everybody's got a good illegal alien story. 'Hey, I know this guy who came up here, salt of the earth, became a productive member of society.' Or: 'Every illegal alien I've ever seen has been on public assistance and is here to take, take, take, and get, get, get.' Well, the truth falls somewhere in between.

"People don't like to see pain and suffering. People don't like to see poverty. People like you and me who live fairly comfortably say, 'What's wrong with somebody coming over here to make their life a little better?' Well, there's nothing wrong. But there may be something wrong with millions and millions and *millions* having an impact on our society, and instead of raising their standard of living pulling a lot other people down.

"If we want to have open borders, let's have open borders. If that's the will of the people, let's open up the borders. If they want to legalize narcotics, then let's legalize narcotics. But let's not make a halfhearted stab at fixing the problem and then throw up our hands and say it's not fixable."

So we got to San Diego and waited until our coyote's contacts told him that the INS checkpoint in San Clemente was not being manned. Then they put about ten of us in the back of this pickup. They piled a bunch of plywood on us and then we drove to Los Angeles.

The thing that really worried us was that all these coyotes were all drugged up. In my country I never knew what cocaine was. It wasn't until I met the coyotes that I knew. They were always on coke or marijuana and drinking. They were always half crazy. They were young men; probably the oldest I saw was maybe thirty-five. Always armed. Always! Automatic pistols. The understanding is that if you don't pay what you owe when you arrive, then they'll kill you. It was just twelve days of suffering that we went through. It's incredible what you go through to get here. I swore that I would never go back to El Salvador until I had my papers in order, because I would never go through that again.

The Chula Vista Border Patrol station was never meant to accommodate the numbers of people it now must deal with daily. The nature of the job has become infinitely more dangerous. Attacks on agents were unusual fifteen years ago. Now they are common. Once immigrants were largely docile young Mexican laborers eager to work in the United States; now the patrol encounters increasing numbers of young illegals heavily involved in drugs. If they want to stay alive, agents are told by their superiors, they'd better not show their backs.

Danger takes many forms, from assaults with rocks on officers to increasingly frequent high-speed chases resulting in crashes. Two such happened shortly before my visit. In one, a seventeen-year-old driving a stolen car sheared a car in half while fleeing the patrol, killing two people on the sidewalk. In the other, a young driver in a stolen minivan crossed the center line of traffic and hit a semi head on, killing five.

The greatest change involves the sophistication and organization of the criminal network that traffics in people and drugs. Everything is arranged, from the route traveled, to the destination sought, to the documentation that gives an illegal alien presumed legal status. Within a few blocks of the Chula Vista station, an alien can purchase a fake birth certificate for $10. With that, the person can obtain a legal driver's license and a legal Social Security card. Some agents have arrested aliens carrying four valid California driver's licenses and the appropriate identification to go with them. None of these IDs had the person's real name. Resale of legal birth certificates is so brisk that sometimes the same document has been used by numerous people over a four-year period before being detected.

All of this is largely out of sight of the border station. Not out of sight are the numbers of people who are arrested and processed there in shifts around the clock. Through four plate-glass windows at one holding cell—a rectangular room made of cement blocks with five long benches—some thirty young men can be seen, most of them asleep on the benches and the floor. Heaps of clothing are piled around them. That cell, and others like it, is filled and emptied several times every twenty-four hours as groups are arrested, processed, and then sent back to Mexico. Over and over, shift by shift, that cycle is repeated. Most of those picked up appear young and vulnerable. Nearly all are poorly dressed. Some, though, wear well-tailored suits. Mike Nicely points to one man with expensive shoes and remarks that that one's not likely to be coming across the border to work in the fields. Nicely and other agents draw a sharp distinction between that kind of illegal immigrant and the hungry young ones lying in the holding cell.

"There's an impression that this is just a bunch of poor people coming over to the United States to work and worship—a victimless crime. Not a big deal," Nicely says. "That is so far off-base, so far off-base. These are organized alien smugglers who are preying on these people. I thought I had my prejudices pretty well thought-out before I came into the Border Patrol, but I had no idea what an animal is until I started dealing with some of these alien smugglers. The things they do. There was a situation in San Clemente where the alien smuggler got out of the van and pushed two children into traffic, knowing that the Border Patrol agents would have to try to rescue those children. It killed 'em both. The smugglers bail out of cars that are moving—they turn the wheel into traffic, get out and flee, knowing that the Border Patrol agent behind has got to be concerned with that car, with the people hidden in the trunk. Just turn the wheel and leave it and let it go out into traffic. The hell with who gets killed, who gets hurt!

"I've never seen such callousness before. It's not a small business. It's dirty, and it's very, very lucrative, and you can look at the impact they're having on schools, health services, stuff like that. To say that it's victimless is irresponsible. There are some major victims getting hurt here."

We got to Los Angeles at dawn. We couldn't see anything when we were coming in because we were, of course, covered up. I felt a tremendous sense of happiness. All the sacrifices that I'd put myself through to get here had finally paid off. I was excited that I would see my brother when I got there. I hadn't seen him in four years, and we were close. It was just a real emotional high.

Well, I felt those things, but I also felt very unsure, because when I first arrived they took us out of the pickup and they put us in a house like we were in prison. We couldn't speak, because the neighbors might think something was suspicious. We had to do exactly what the coyote said, and if we didn't pay him off, then we were prisoners. I had doubts whether or not I would be really free. So I called my brother and the coyote said we'll take you to such-and-such a place. Your brother can pick you up there. They told me they were carrying weapons and if I didn't pay they'd kill me. And I believed them, because they were half crazed.

J. W. Swanson is more laconic than the outgoing Mike Nicely. Tall, lanky, with a drooping sandy mustache, he expresses his opinions with more understatement. We were in his patrol car driving past the major staging areas where hundreds of aliens congregate and cross every night despite night scopes, new tower lights, and electronic censors implanted in the desert floor.

Already, in the searing heat of midafternoon, young men were on top of the corrugated fence. "By dark there should be several hundred people as far as you can see up to the top of that hill," Swanson said as we approached the Levee, an embankment built up before the flat Tijuana River plain through which the immigrants cross. "We won't see them now, because they'll be on the other side of the fence, but you can see a guy in the tree there. This area south of us is called the Coahulia, the name of the neighborhood. It's a traditionally violent neighborhood, a lawless part of Tijuana. Those light towers are relatively new. They don't really help us that much except as a safety factor. You used to sit over here in the pitch black and there'd be literally hundreds of people wandering around behind your vehicle. You didn't feel real safe. Agents were assaulted on a regular basis over here. With the lights, that's been cut down a bit. Also there's less robbery of the aliens by the bandits."

In addition to the people in trees, we could see others standing by the fence on the American side, staring toward us and waiting to see if the Border Patrol would arrive to head them off, in which case they would merely climb back up the fence. Farther down the fence another group of ten young men clustered together. Then we saw a group of between twenty and thirty young males—all standing illegally inside the United States in broad daylight. In the space of a few minutes, I counted approximately one hundred such people. "Again, this is small numbers," Swanson said. "The real numbers aren't even out yet. When they feel they have a chance they'll run across the river there, up the other side, and over the fence, or they'll run all the way down to where the fence ends and cross at the end of the embankment."

After the fence was erected, he said, the aliens began to cut holes in it. Some drove right through it. Others tunneled under it. But at the time we talked, neither he nor anyone else in the Border Patrol had any idea of the magnitude of the tunneling that was taking place. A year later, Mexican authorities patrolling their side of the Tijuana border discovered an extraordinary tunnel that extended from underneath a warehouse near the Tijuana airport to the outskirts of San Diego. Air-conditioned, fully lighted, with reinforced concrete walls, and constructed sixty-five feet below the surface at a cost of millions of dollars, it was a major engineering feat. And this tunnel, authorities believed, was probably only one of many along the border.

During our tour of the border, Swanson's vehicle passed two young men lying facedown in the dirt, obviously trying to escape notice from a passing patrol car. Swanson radioed for another car to back him up, then stopped his vehicle and got out. As he did, one of the youths got up and ran into the thick tangled grasses that flourish in the desert in clumps over six feet high.

The other youth stood patiently with his hands in the air as Swanson frisked him. Swanson told him to get in the back of our car, where he sat silently behind the iron mesh grating. He was only a boy, no more than sixteen, bright-eyed, wearing jeans and a thin plaid shirt and carrying a pack. He was breathing heavily, out of fear or nervousness. We exchanged a glance, and made a surprisingly personal contact—quick, intense, knowing, as if we shared a special knowledge. The boy shook his head slightly, smiled wistfully, shrugged, and waited for the other patrol car to pick him up and take him to the station for processing.

After the cruiser came and took the boy away, Swanson again got out of his car. He plunged into the thicket where the other youth had disappeared. In his left hand he held a walkie-talkie. His pistol was not drawn. Many minutes later he emerged, breathless, his face flushed and perspiration staining his uniform blouse. "He'll probably stay in the thick stuff until night," Swanson said, "then he'll cross." It's a very small section, he said, but something like half the illegal immigrants in this country come through here. About one out of ten is a criminal type. "Somewhere in that number somebody is going to give you trouble. Some nights it seems like everybody runs from you. You gotta chase everybody—on foot, usually. We work on foot."

I kept thinking about the boy with the earnest face who so briefly had passed through our lives. There was no way of knowing, of course, but I definitely put him down in the noncriminal class.

Swanson started the car and continued to cruise, heading due west beyond the Tijuana River Basin and Stewart's Bridge, a major crossing area, by Goat Canyon, a center of major drug activity, and by Smuggler's Canyon, a notorious area, until we reached land's end in Borderfield Park, where the Pacific Ocean crashes on a beautiful white beach. The fence stops before the beach. You can cross into the United States there, Swanson acknowledged, simply by walking north along the beach.

It was a clear day, no clouds, bright blue skies, a bracing west wind blowing over the surf and sand and tugging at our clothing. In the park, picnic tables set out every few feet offered a splendid view of the ocean and beach. Around them sat crowds of men, all of them appearing to be Latinos. They stared at our cruiser as it circled the park area. "Those are among the scum of the earth," Swanson said. "They're the smugglers. They're waiting for night to move."

You mean, these are the coyotes? I asked. Swanson nodded. "See that one over there?" He pointed to a man with long black hair, hard coal-black eyes, and a contemptuous expression, short-sleeved shirt unbuttoned to expose his chest. "That's one of the worst. We've arrested him a number of times."

We drove away. "My job is trying to cut down on the amount of alien criminal traffic that comes back and forth just in this one little area," Swanson said. "People have been deported as criminals and come back and commit felonies. They get thrown out of the country again and they just jump back over the fence. It's no big deal to them. My philosophy is always try to be somewhat optimistic. I've refused to burn out, and always fight it when I feel a completely negative feeling about the job coming on. I don't want to feel that way. But the constant hammering, hammering, hammering—working up against the same numbers of people all the time—that's what gets to you."

As it happened, Officer Swanson came into the Border Patrol after other career goals did not turn out, mostly because of the economy. He earned a degree in public administration and political science and became interested in geology, returning to school to pursue that field. But when he graduated, oil prices fell and he could not find work. He took civil service tests and entered the federal service in the Border Patrol.

On my prompting, Swanson spoke of his feelings about America. "I don't know where we're going," he said. "That's part of the problem with a lot of things, like immigration or Medicare and how we're going to take care of ourselves. We are mandated by Congress to do this job and we do it and carry it out to the best of our ability, but we obviously don't have close to the necessary number of people."

We drove on in silence. Then Swanson said: "You know *Forbes* magazine where they have the quotations in the back? There was one by Albert Camus a few months ago that my dad showed me. Camus said: 'The most dreadful punishment is hopeless and futile labor.' It struck a chord with what we're doing here."

I became nationalized over here on Alvarado Street. [He laughed.] A friend of my brother's told me to go look for so-and-so on Alvarado Street, and he told me the address and everything. He said you have to ask for what we call a mica—M-I-C-A—which is a green card, and they had a special price. For twenty-five dollars you can get a green card and along with it a Social Security card. He said everybody around here sells this kind of stuff. So I got to the house and found them in the middle of making them.

My brother got me a job after I came, a temporary job as a janitor, and I immediately became aware that my dream of studying would go out the window because I wouldn't be able to study with the hours that I worked as a janitor at the——Center. I work from six-thirty P.M. to three in the morning, four seventy-five an hour. No, no benefits. I clean up desks, do vacuuming. Office-cleaning work.

The only way I'm going to have any future in this country is to learn how to speak English, so a month ago I enrolled in English class. I go to bed about four-thirty in the morning and I wake up at ten and take a class from eleven to two to learn English. My dream is be able to get my papers legalized and be able to have my credits transferred from the University of El Salvador and be able to study here. But I know I can't do that without English. The real truth, though, is that I don't like living here. I don't like the system of life in this country. The pace of life is so pressured, the level of stress, the work is so consuming, that you can't enjoy life.

"As soon as the sun drops, everything picks up," says Delmar Martin, a short, compact thirty-year-old agent who speaks with a pronounced Texas twang, as befits a man whose hometown is Del Rio, Texas. "Everything starts to move. The numbers you see in the daytime pretty much double. That's the busiest time—from right when the sun drops until the early-morning hours when the sun comes up again."

In only three years with the Border Patrol, a position he sought after becoming discouraged by the uncertainty of work in the oil and gas fields of Texas, Martin has become accustomed to gunfire throughout the canyons near the fence, and to sometimes being shot at by persons unknown.

He's also aware, as are all the agents, that the potential for violence increases the closer one gets to the fence. But he's a confident, if not cocky, young man who believes he can handle any situation. He also likes his work and is proud of the record compiled by his station—the Imperial Beach—and its adjoining rival at Chula Vista.

As his car moves toward the ocean, Martin says: "Our one station is by no means large, but we get the highest number of apprehensions in the entire Border Patrol. This little spot here, from the port west, is the busiest crossing for illegal alien traffic in the entire border—the entire border."

The greatest problem, Martin says, stems not from potential violence but from the attitude of people who live in the small homes and apartments closest to the fence, at one point barely a hundred yards away. Most of them are Mexican-Americans who either are citizens or hold resident alien cards.

"We're not well liked in there," he says. "We've come to near riots by going in there and trying to apprehend aliens that are running through there. A lot of those people are very sympathetic toward the aliens, and we get no respect at all.

"That's a perfect spot for them to mingle, being so close to the fence, and they try to hide in the complexes. If we go in, people come out of the apartment buildings and throw stuff at us and yell and scream and mob us. Actually, at one point there was an agent on one side of the fence and an alien on the other and there were people from the apartment complex trying to pull him away from the agent— telling him to run."

Even American tourists heading south into Mexico tend to look on the Border Patrol as a joke, Martin says. When they see agents chasing aliens in San Ysidro, near the border port of entry, they even cheer—not for the agents but for the aliens.

"Run! Run!" the tourists yell as the aliens attempt to escape on foot.

"It's pretty frustrating," Martin says. "We didn't make these laws, we didn't write them or anything. We're just trying to enforce them and do the job we're sworn to do."

Probably ninety percent of the janitors I know came in exactly like I did—illegally. The other ten percent got some kind of a visa and then stayed illegally beyond the expiration of their visa. All the janitors are here that way, you know. They ask to see your documents when you're hired but they don't check them with the INS. As I understand the laws of this country, the employers are not the INS, so they can't tell whether the document is true or false. And also it's an advantage for the companies because we're cheap labor. If the janitor companies were paying good wages then probably it'd be Americans working there. But now we see that even Americans are asking for quarters in the streets.

I was going to be an attorney in business—a business attorney. It still might be possible to do it here, but the only way for me to do that would be for me to stop working, and if I stop working I don't eat. So the only way for me to do it would be to have a scholarship—which I can't get. And I can't qualify for any of the social welfare programs. If I don't work, I don't eat.

Oh, yes, about the coyotes. The reason they are called coyotes is because el coyote *hunts chickens for his food and they call us—those who are crossing the borders—they call us chickens. Coyotes are also scavengers. They eat the food that other animals have hunted. That's why we put that name to these people. We're the chickens that they hunt.*

Between 1830 and 1914, 35 million immigrants poured across the Atlantic Ocean and into the United States. In sheer numbers, it was the greatest migration in history—a human tide that moved west from the Eastern Seaboard and across the Appalachians and plains for some twelve hundred miles, and then flowed another eighteen hundred miles to cross the Rockies and reach the Pacific.

It was this outpouring of diverse cultures that made America unique, that created its special character, its complex mixture of myth and reality so interwoven that even dispassionate scholars have difficulty distinguishing between the two. Waves of immigrants, generation after generation, made the nation. And it was the constitutional system of checks and balances that made possible the free but protected intermingling of so many races and religions without the violence that has divided and destroyed less diverse societies.

If America was always "promises," as the poet Archibald Mac-Leish wrote, America was also the nation that turned its back on the past. It was the continual renewal of the American Dream through scores of immigrants—the opportunity to make a new and better life for yourself and the generations to follow—that validated those promises. Not by happenstance did Americans choose as their motto *E Pluribus Unum:* Out of Many, One. For most of its citizens, at least until recent decades, that motto symbolized, and was acknowledged to be, the central core of an American faith.

It was a faith, though, that applied largely to whites of Western culture.

At the time of the American Revolution, in 1776, 60 percent of the white colonists in America were of English descent. Another 18 percent came from a Scotch-Irish background, and of those by far the greatest number were Scots whose ancestors were settled in Ireland by Cromwell. Germans, at 9 percent, many of them made homeless by the wars that had rent the European continent, made up the next-largest population component. Those three groups—English, Scotch-Irish, Germans—constituted 87 percent of the white American population. The remaining 13 percent came from many lands. Prominent among them were French Huguenots driven from France by royal persecution, and Spaniards already long occupying what became American territory.

Not until the 1830s did that demographic background begin to change, rapidly altering the American mix. Of the more than thirty million immigrants between 1860 and 1930, when unrestricted legal immigration came to an end, only four and a half million were from England, Scotland, and Wales, while four and a half million came from Ireland alone and a similar number from Germany. Two and a half million were Scandinavians, more than four and a half million were Italians, another four million came from Austria-Hungary and the Balkan states, and nearly four million came from Russia and Poland. Thus, the concept of the melting pot came into being. By the mid-1960s, Germans, Russians, and Poles were the single largest ethnic minorities.

Throughout all that history, of course, blacks remained the people apart in America—economically, socially, politically. After 1619, when the first slave ship anchored off Jamestown, Virginia, blacks became an increasing proportion of America's population. Of a population of 5,308,483 persons counted by the 1800 census, nearly one-fifth were black slaves. Not until the closing decades of the twentieth century did blacks begin to decline proportionately in the American population and lose their rank as the nation's fastest-growing minority group. In percentage of increase, as we have seen, they are being outstripped by Latinos. Their relative numbers are also being diminished by increasing numbers of Asian immigrants.

Never has America experienced such an explosion of legal and illegal immigration as that which now reshapes the nation's population and racial/ethnic composition. The decade of the Eighties saw the single largest flow of immigration in U.S. history—some nine million who entered legally and at least two million illegally. The number of illegal aliens in the United States is impossible to determine, but some demographic studies estimate it to be as high as eight million—and rising. The lowest estimate is two million. These numbers pose a complex problem that threatens all the comfortable assumptions of the old status quo—and not only the shrinking White Anglo-Saxon Protestant (WASP) component of America that grudgingly gave way to new influxes of largely Catholic and Jewish white Europeans. Blacks who battled longest and hardest for racial and economic equality find themselves facing new competition from those of other races and ethnicities. This competition lies at the root of many of the questions raised earlier in this book about schools, public services, race, class, crime, and increasing cultural tensions. These problems will not dissipate; they are destined to be our dominant concerns well into the next century. A central question becomes not whether *E Pluribus Unum*—Out of Many, One—still applies as an operative philosophy for America. It is whether the new operative motto—Out of One, Many—will permit a society capable of addressing common national concerns.

Of all the challenges, one of the most crucial involves illegal aliens. In Los Angeles alone there are estimated to be between 300,000 and 500,000 illegal aliens from El Salvador. Like the twenty-five-year-old law student whose story I have just chronicled, they are economic slaves. I say that calculatedly. They arrive with stars in their eyes, having often experienced abuse and exploitation at the hands of their coyotes, and are thrown into a situation from which it is almost impossible to escape legally. The 1986 Immigration Reform and Control Act was supposed to stop the flood of illegal immigration by making it illegal for employers to hire undocumented—i.e., illegal—workers. The act provides for employer sanctions against businesses that fail to adhere to the law. It is a huge failure. Worse, it's a sham.

Those who work with undocumented workers in Los Angeles say that aliens are deliberately recruited to come to the United States to work in factories even though everyone involved knows it is against the law for them to be so employed. A union official who attempts to organize factory workers in Los Angeles and Orange County, where up to *half* of the work force is believed to be composed of illegal aliens, says that employers let their foremen, who are often Latinos themselves, know that they welcome people willing to do factory work for $4.25 an hour and no benefits, but don't want to know anything about hiring undocumented workers. That's up to the foreman to arrange.

The foreman then handles the hiring directly, sometimes by recruiting in his own village in Mexico. Once in the United States, through the illegal network, the foreman refers the undocumented workers to the street corner where they can buy a false Social Security card for $25. For fancier fake work permits, the charge can be up to $300.

Essentially, all that's needed is a photo ID like a driver's license and a Social Security number. The personnel department of the plant then fills out the required I-9 immigration form. The personnel department does not know whether the documents are valid or not; all it knows is that the foreman has provided them. Thus, the legal requirements are presumably met. If challenged, the plant officials from employer to personnel can maintain a know-nothing attitude; the foreman feigns ignorance even as he pointedly warns the illegal aliens whom he has assisted in finding work that if they complain about their wages or benefits or working conditions—or if they attempt to join a union—they will either be fired or, worse, reported to immigration authorities as illegals and deported.

The workers are willing to pay this terrible price to escape even worse conditions in their homelands. So they continue to arrive in huge numbers through the land route via that narrow corridor at the southernmost point of California—primarily from Mexico and Central America but increasingly from South America. Peruvians, for example, are known to have been arriving in significant numbers. They take their place alongside the swelling ranks of illegal aliens who compete in a tougher economic market with other new immigrants: Vietnamese, Filipinos, Cambodians, Koreans, Chinese. (The flow of Chinese immigrants attracted national attention when boatloads bearing illegal aliens were turned away from California ports in Clinton's first year, and after a particularly heartbreaking example when hundreds of Chinese jumped into frigid waters off Long Island beaches only miles from the Statue of Liberty after their vessel foundered. Many died. It turned out that those Chinese had been charged up to $30,000 apiece by the smugglers who brought them to the United States, a price they would be forced to pay off through years of forced, and illegal, labor approaching the worst of nineteenth-century conditions.)

Despite their vast numbers, and whether they come legally or illegally, these people are the new Invisible Americans, omnipresent but ignored by the middle and upper classes whose work they do and whose unwanted—and underground—tasks they perform. They are the housekeepers, the cleaners, the street vendors, the janitors, the child-care helpers who work for the Zoë Bairds. They are the highly energetic ants of American society.

Their problems and the burdens they impose on society aside, they are also a great potential resource.

"If you set aside the issue of the Third World angst that is out there, and try to look at California as a country, we're not doing too badly." Those are the words of one of the most knowledgeable observers of grass-roots democracy in California, a man who for political reasons was one of the few who did not want to have his name in this book. "Go down to Mexico and ask somebody where they want to go and they'll tell you point-blank: California! They don't care that we have a deficit, that their kids aren't going to go to UC Berkeley. They couldn't care less. That's not the issue. Talk to the Koreans, talk to the Filipinos, talk to the ones that are here, talk to all the people that are coming here: they'll all say the same thing. They're coming here because for them it's the best place to be. We've got the youngest work force in the Western world. California. Oh, yes. This is it. Look to see how many nineteen- and twenty-year-old men and women are here of all races. You'll find out the best Koreans are here, the best Mexicans are here, the best Filipinos are here, the best Chinese are here. The best Japanese want to be here but we don't want 'em because they have to be upper management before they get here. But everybody else is getting here any way they can. All roads lead to California. The reason is that you can scrounge here, you can scrounge in California like you cannot scrounge anywhere else."

Discounting a certain bravado, that is an accurate view, and one not often heard publicly. In fact, most of the public commentary about immigration woefully misses the mark, either by failing to understand what is really taking place day after day or by ignoring the implications for the long term. Millions of immigrants are already here, legally or illegally, and they intend to stay—especially the younger ones. I met young people who said their parents might return to Mexico upon retirement, but not they. They were Americans. Two examples:

In Berkeley, the twenty-one-year-old political science student, Luis Guillen, who wants to become mayor of San Antonio, was talking about how his father planned to move back to Mexico when he retires. He still thought of himself as Mexican.

Luis, on the other hand, says, "I'm a Texan first. This country has given me enough so that I can probably say that I am an American. This country does have a lot of problems, and as soon as we take care of one there seem to be ten others. But regardless, it is still a country where there are many opportunities. If I had been in Mexico, I would never have been able to come here to Berkeley, one of the best schools in the world. I mean, the United States is great. It has its problems, but it's great."

In Los Angeles, María Elena Durazo, a daughter of Mexican farm workers, who has become one of the city's important labor leaders and was one of the most compelling people I met on my journey, was equally clear about her American outlook.

"In spite of the fact that we went through the riots in L.A. in which half or more of the participants and the victims were Mexican and Central American and Asian and the other half were African-Americans," Durazo said, "there is still this denial and refusal to deal with immigrants. They are the future of this population in L.A. and southern California. This city, this leadership, is not dealing with that reality. It tries to think of Mexicans, for instance, as immigrants who are illegal who just need an immigration policy and that's it. And that's not true. We're here. We're here to stay. Mostly everyone who's coming here is here to stay—and their kids, too."

Of all the immigrant groups that have affected American life in recent decades, two in particular illuminate one of the oldest traditions in the nation's history: providing a new life for those fleeing oppression. In the case of Cuban-Americans and Southeast Asians, the American government made a special effort to help them enter the United States and to assist them after their arrival. It did so not just for altruistic motives—the United States owed each group a special debt.

With the Cubans, it was the bitter legacy of the Bay of Pigs invasion of April 1961, in which the U.S. government, through the Central Intelligence Agency, secretly formed, financed, trained, and drafted battle plans for the Cuban Brigade 2506. The result was humiliating defeat and captivity for those who survived. The U.S. government ultimately ransomed those survivors and brought them back to the United States. Amid emotional promises by President John F. Kennedy in the Miami Orange Bowl, they were told that the brigade flag their leaders had just presented to the president would be returned to them in a free Havana.

Out of that came a continuing connection between many Cuban-Americans, the CIA, and the secret operations that have fueled so many poisonous conspiracy theories—including those concerning the assassination of JFK. Bay of Pigs veterans played prominent roles in other U.S.-backed clandestine adventures in Central America, such as the support of the contra forces during the years of Ronald Reagan's presidency.

With the Southeast Asians, Vietnamese and Cambodians, it was another sense of historic debt—and guilt—that prompted American policymakers to give special sanction. During the Vietnam War, the United States had again committed its honor and treasure—and this time its own blood—to help people win their battle against communist regimes. Like the Bay of Pigs failure, but with enormously greater impact, the U.S. failure in Vietnam spawned bitter divisions and more destructive conspiracy theories—not only about the true nature of America's leaders but, especially among blacks, about a

society that practiced genocide by consigning its poorer racial
minorities to the slaughter fields of Southeast Asia. These wounds,
plus continuing accusations of U.S. abandonment of people the U.S.
government had pledged to support, have haunted us for a generation. They remain unhealed even into the mid-Nineties. For obvious
reasons, they have also had special impact on the two immigrant
groups most affected, so many of whom saw the United States not as
a permanent home but as a temporary haven.

That sense of waiting to return—of plotting and planning and
hoping—most powerfully characterizes the Cuban-Americans.

By any measure, Cuban-Americans form one of the great American success stories of the last thirty years. In the immediate aftermath of the Bay of Pigs, when I first became intimately acquainted
with Cuban refugees while living in Miami, traveling to Central
America, and working daily with Bay of Pigs leaders and their families on research for *The Bay of Pigs,* * Cubans virtually thought of
themselves as awaiting their imminent return to Cuba. They were not
immigrants; they were *exiles.* That distinction colored their attitudes
and affected their behavior.

At the same time, they did not sit idly dreaming of that homecoming. With drive and panache, they elevated themselves from near
poverty to a prosperity that has been matched by few.

By pooling their resources, by remaining tightly knit as a community, by sheer hard work and dedication, they transformed southern
Florida—and especially Miami—into a Cuban-American enclave.
From the small cantina operations that I had seen there in the early
Sixties, the Cuban colony expanded its business and economic reach
until it possessed a combined annual income of some $9 billion. Cu-
bans became the leading players in the city's real estate business, in
merchandising, in the professions. They headed—if they did not own
outright—large banks and commercial houses. They were entrepreneurs, venture capitalists before that term came into vogue in the
Eighties, and increasingly affluent.

They also swiftly grasped another lever of American power—
politics. Cuban-Americans became mayors of communities large and

*I began work on this book immediately after the Orange Bowl ceremony in December
1962, and it was published in 1964.

small in Florida's Dade County, occupying city halls from Miami to Hialeah. Their swelling political influence extended into the state's house and senate. Though already solidly Republican in political affiliation, they were singled out by every Republican president from Richard Nixon to George Bush and given positions of influence greatly disproportionate to their numbers in GOP national gatherings. But they also exerted influence over the Democrats. A Bay of Pigs veteran, for example, headed Florida's Democratic Party.

Despite their success and their prominence in American life, Cubans still dreamed of the day when Fidel Castro would be overthrown and they would return to Cuba. Increasingly, it was a dream more observed in its retelling—in its myths—than in the reality of its prospect. Now, with Castro's long reign visibly waning, if not by natural causes then by economic and political pressures arising out of his status as the last client of the once-powerful communist bloc, Cuban-Americans exhibit conflicted emotions when they consider whether they really will go back.

As I reconnected with many of the Cubans whom I had known so well in the Sixties, and talked to their children and even grandchildren for this book, not a single one failed to say that, in their own minds, they still thought of themselves as Cubans. "Yes, yes, I'm still a Cuban," was the common response. But the idea of leaving the United States permanently was difficult to contemplate.

"We have no place to go back to," said Tere Zubi, who heads a multimillion-dollar advertising firm in Miami. "In our real minds, Cuba died in 1959, and even if there is a comeback it's not going to be the same. It cannot be the same. What it's going to represent to a lot of Cubans here is an investment opportunity and nothing else.

"I have to travel extensively, and if I go to Colombia or some such place and the pilot says if you look to your left you're going to see the island of Cuba, I literally crush my face on the window and I start crying and crying and crying. Then I run to the back of the plane to catch that last glimpse from thirty thousand feet up. If Castro falls tomorrow and you ask me are you going back to Cuba, I will tell you exactly where I'm going to open Zubi Advertising in Cuba. That doesn't mean I'm going to close Zubi Advertising *here*. It means I'm going to commute back and forth. It is my duty as a Cuban to bring the knowledge that I have acquired here to make my country better. There is a materialistic edge also, because Cuba stood still more than thirty years ago and I can just see the Burger Kings and the McDonald's and the Pizza Huts and the Sinclair Oil stations and the supermarkets—all of which are my clients! The opportunities are immense. So I am going to open my office at Arampa. I'm going to paint a big Z on the roof so that the planes see it when they fly over."

When I first knew her, she was Theresa Zubizarreta, a twenty-four-year-old housewife with two small children whose husband was one of the Bay of Pigs prisoners. She lived in modest circumstances with her parents, drove a used car, could not afford to purchase a pair of shoes, and regularly stood in line on Miami's Fifth Street to receive big bars of cheddar cheese, powdered milk and eggs, cans of Spam and peanut butter, provided by the U.S. government.

Thirty years later, assessing her own success, she also offers a shrewd analysis of why Cubans did so well in the United States. They are, she believes, different from other immigrant groups in this century: they came as political refugees, not as economic refugees, and they were fortunate enough to arrive on the eve of the Martin Luther King civil rights movement.

"Many people consider that to be the salvation of blacks," she says, "but it has been for all minorities. People don't realize that. Before the civil rights movement, the Hispanics here were also considered second- or third-class citizens. If you look at Hispanic pockets in Texas and California, the children weren't even allowed to speak Spanish at school. They were reprimanded and punished. They all wanted to become part of the so-called melting pot, because it was the way to belong. Then we arrived in the early Sixties, and Cubans benefited from the Martin Luther King movement. Cubans benefited from that, but they don't realize it. The quotas, the EEOC [U.S. Equal Employment Opportunities Commission], apply to us also—and they apply to women, too. They benefited both blacks *and* Hispanics."

Tere is another who rejects the melting-pot image—and who, interestingly, once more uses the analogy of a salad bowl to express her view of the Cuban-American immigrant status:

"In a salad bowl," she says, "all the ingredients are present but not one becomes part of the other. The tomatoes remain tomatoes and the lettuce remains the lettuce and the scallions remain the scallions. You can enjoy them, but they don't have to meld. The Cuban community tries very hard not to meld. We brainwash our children not to meld, because the Cuba we knew only lives in our minds. It doesn't live anywhere else. And if we don't preserve those memories they will be lost forever. So we try to maintain *la cubanía,* which is Cubanism, by passing on these things to our children."

In talking to Cubans, a curious disconnect emerges. The old emotions still flare in all the conversations, but now there is a more muted troubled strain. Cuban-Americans are beginning openly to question not only what it might be like to return to Cuba but also what it might be like to stay in the United States. For Miami has been shaken by the economic downturn, and the most prominent Cuban-Americans find themselves suddenly confronting disturbing long-term questions.

"We are going through a peculiar economic crisis," says Luis J. Botifoll, chairman of Republic National Bank of Miami, a man regarded as the single most powerful and influential member of the Cuban-American community. "This is not the typical recession that we used to have in the past. This country was living too much on its credit, and the credit has gone to the limit. You have to do it yourself, and that is applicable to government and to business and to individuals. Individuals have to go to Chapter II and start a new life. Government has to do exactly the same thing. And business is going through the same thing. A lot of businesses are going broke. All the businesses are being reorganized. Miami has lost its financial leadership. We had the airline business. We had Pan American. We had Eastern. We had Northwest. Big businesses here. We lost that. The real estate business is in crisis. The two biggest financial institutions here are gone. The institutions are from out of state. We are the biggest local bank here and we are a billion-dollar institution, but compared to big ones out of state, that's small. That's bad for Florida."

Botifoll, too, sees a change in ethnic and cultural assimilation. "This country is facing a different situation—of people who come here and don't intend to stay and still think their country is better than the United States," he says. "They're arrogant. They don't want to be confused with the American. They say, no, I'm not American, I'm a Cuban-American. I speak Spanish, even though I can speak

English. How long that situation is going to remain, I don't know. But in Miami, that's the situation. In Miami, the people do not want to meld." (To underscore his point, a year later citizens of Dade County voted to make Spanish an official language; no longer was English the required language at official proceedings.)

For the Cubans, the tug between cultures and countries often becomes emotional and confusing. Two younger professionals, each highly successful, still wrestle with their complicated feelings about being uprooted and then feeling adrift in the United States.

Rene V. Murai, a lawyer in his forties, remembers how it was when at age fifteen he fled Cuba with his family. "It's like you're in the middle of a sea," he says, "and believe me, it felt very, very disruptive. I do not look at those years with any kind of pleasure. I really felt cheated in a sense." When he went to college in the East, he immersed himself in American culture—dating American girls, wanting to feel "completely American," and, after working in New York, thinking of Cuba as existing in another world. Then he returned to Miami to practice law, married a Cuban-American, and slowly reentered the world of his birth. He became, again, a Cuban-American. "For someone who has been displaced and doesn't really know quite where he is or where he fits in, this is a wonderful city," he says of Miami. "I have Ecuadorian friends, Venezuelan friends, and Spanish friends and clients. We talk about a global city and a global world, and it takes place in Miami."

Now, Rene Murai finds himself increasingly depressed about the United States—but even more threatened by the prospect of Castro's demise. "I went through a disruption once before," he says. "So I'm a little threatened by a Free Cuba—please understand that has nothing to do with my desire to see Cuba free. The threat is, is my world going to collapse? Am I going to have these conflicts between staying and going and between family and friends? All of a sudden, my whole world divides itself."

Raul Rodriguez, an architect, also in his forties, remembers a similar wrenching experience. "It's awful as a kid to have barely tasted your own culture and your own place, but you're a kid and can survive," he says. "But for my parents' generation it was terrible." His father played piano in Miami hotels, and then he and the family moved to New York "and started in the rag game, as they call it, basically selling, which they knew how to do."

They, too, prospered, so they could send Raul to college. The experience did not diminish his cultural feelings. "I have always been a Cuban and I am still a Cuban," he says. "But now I have lived thirty-three years in a world in which the U.S. and the country of my birth are sworn enemies. In my ideal world, those two peoples are the best of friends. It pains me to see the U.S. government pass bills aimed at making people who are still in the island suffer. Why does the United States want to punish Cuba beyond what it's punishing Vietnam? I'm not trying to elongate Fidel's term. I don't have love lost for the revolution, I don't have any red dye in my blood, but I just can't believe the incredible effort the U.S. puts on that island."

Rodriguez is troubled by something else—the increasing hostility between blacks and Cuban-Americans in Miami. It is a situation filled with ironies. As he says, Cubans came to the United States after having been burned by the left with Castro at the same time that blacks were being helped by the left here—and quickly adopted the belief that Martin Luther King was a communist, a belief, he adds, that was inspired by FBI Director J. Edgar Hoover. To Rodriguez, out of this mistaken belief have come the tensions between Cuban and American blacks. Cubans also, he believes, adopted prejudices against blacks held by many Americans thirty years ago. "The only thing Cubans were doing," he says, "was becoming American—accepting the values that this society was placing on them. It is tragically true that a segment of a country that is by and large African in its own descent—albeit the lighter portion of that country—comes into another country with a huge black population. The Cubans and the blacks have many things in common, yet by fate and by international political maneuvers they are cast as enemies. Now that Cubans are the majority in Miami, we have to take responsibility to help the black problem."

He made another point, never addressed publicly, so far as I am aware. "There are two exiles," he says. "Those who cannot go to Cuba and those who can't get out. They're also segregated and alienated."

And when Castro goes, that internal Cuban population lying

ninety miles offshore inevitably will present another challenge for both Americans and the Cuban-American immigrants who even yet have not come to terms with their split identities.

Of the Southeast Asians who sought refuge in the United States after the wars that ravaged their nations, no group experienced more hardships than the Cambodians. Between one and two million of their fellow citizens were slaughtered by the most systematic practice of genocide since World War II. To flee the horrors of their homeland, which had left a quarter of the population dead, they were forced to embark on desperate marches through jungles, crossing other national boundaries, before finding sanctuary in a U.S. embassy. Countless thousands never survived their overland flight to freedom; others were lost at sea in overburdened boats that capsized and sank.

Many Cubans spoke English upon their arrival in America, but few Cambodians did. Neither did they feel the same close connection to the United States. Before Castro's rise to power, Cubans and Americans regularly traveled back and forth between their two countries, which were separated by only ninety miles of ocean from Key West to Havana. The Cubans also had a much greater appreciation—even admiration—for American culture, having adopted such sports as baseball as their own long before Castro's revolution. The Cambodians arrived in America as total aliens—penniless, unable to speak the language, having no personal or cultural ties with the land in which they found themselves. Despite all these handicaps, for the most part their American experience has been one of remarkable success. Just how much they have been able to achieve in a relatively short period, and with what complications, can be seen in the old mill town of Lowell, Massachusetts.

In 1982, the first wave of an extraordinary Cambodian migration began arriving in Lowell. They were lured there by the most familiar of motives—jobs, better economic opportunities. Wang Laboratories, headquartered in Lowell, was hiring, new businesses were burgeoning, and Lowell still had many cheap housing units available.

The Cambodians came to Lowell as extended families. One person would arrive from the West Coast or the Southwest, settle in, then send for the next group, brothers and sisters, uncles and aunts, mothers and fathers. In just three years, Lowell had 3,500 Southeast Asians, most of them Cambodians. In four more years, that number had increased to 17,000. By the late 1980s, Lowell had 25,000 Southeast Asians out of a population of approximately 100,000. Each week, thirty-five to fifty Southeast Asian children were entering its public school system. By then, Lowell's Cambodian population had become the second-largest in the United States, exceeded only by that of Long Beach, California, where many Cambodians first arrived.

The impact of this enormous and rapid population change was immense. Because many of the new immigrants could not speak English except to say "thank you" and "yes," Lowell's school system had to institute English as a second language. Bilingual programs were begun, assisted with federal school aid grants.

The programs were a great success. "Each year at high school graduation it's the function of the mayor to give the class speech," former mayor Richard Howe recalls. "So I attended the last four. This last high school graduation was the best that I ever attended. The first youngster on the speaking program was of Vietnamese heritage. She made a wonderful appearance, she spoke well, she was well versed in the English language. The second youngster was a Cambodian. And the two of them really reflected how well Lowell has done. That's why America is the greatest country in the world, because all these different bloodlines flow into it."

But there were problems, stemming in part from prejudice, in part from new tensions over the burdens of taxation in a worsening economy, in part from problems with certain Southeast Asian gangs that took root there. "It takes time to assimilate," says Bill Taupier, former Lowell city manager and leading entrepreneur, "and this is why I hate bad economics, and bad economies. When there are bad economies, the last-guy-in-the-barrel syndrome takes place, and the last guy in the barrel is the last immigrant who takes the hit and falls. During the booming times here, no one seemed to complain about Southeast Asians in town. We've had a tremendous amount settle in our community. They're now acclimated, they're educated, they're becoming readers, they're becoming the valedictorians, they're gobbling up business, they're buying up real estate. They're doing extremely well. But lately public officials have been making horrible, horrible remarks about them here in Lowell: how they're a major,

major problem, how we should have English only in the schools. We have politicians who talk about 'those people' and all the ugly things that happen. What's caused it? They're afraid that person is going to take their job." Many Lowell citizens resented the extra public expense needed to educate "them." Some reacted by sending their children to private schools; they were even less inclined to support school bond issues.

Joe Tully, sixty-six, a former city manager of Lowell whom I had also met ten years before, talked about some of the implications of that Cambodian influx. "I'll be blunt," he said. "Any time you have people from another country who don't speak English—and the majority don't when they first come here—then that has a negative effect on the city. I don't care whether they're Cambodians, Laotians, Rumanians, Bulgarians—whatever they may be—when they come in those numbers it's a problem. When you have to have two teachers for those kids, when they live in conditions where they rent an apartment and have twelve people living in it, that puts a strain on neighborhood values and the taxes to support them."

At the same time, Tully points to something often ignored in the continuing debate over taxation vs. public services: that citizens over the years, especially those with large families, receive far more benefits from their taxes than what they actually pay. "My good friend, who is a big, big, big accountant and lawyer, educated five kids in the public school system, and four of them became lawyers," Tully says. "He says he believes in public education. That's twelve years the Lowell public schools paid to educate his kids. If you multiply what it cost per year to educate them, the total comes to three hundred thousand dollars. He lives in one of the nicest houses in Lowell, and he probably pays three thousand dollars a year in taxes. Forget what the city pays for the roads and the driveways and the cops and firemen that serve him, we can't get even with him on what we spent to educate his five kids for one hundred years. Put that philosophy in your mind."

The Cambodians have their own philosophy, and it turns out to be one that every immigrant before them would instantly recognize: hard work leads to success.

I experienced this personally when, early on a Sunday morning, a Cambodian took me on a tour of his community, where bustling commercial enterprises flourished. It was like entering another world. There in the heart of downtown Lowell, in an area where buildings had been vacant and some of them burned, Cambodian marketplaces of wide variety were attracting large numbers of customers, and all while much of the city of Lowell slept.

My guide, Chanrithy Uong, was a guidance counselor at Lowell High School. As we drove through deserted downtown streets toward Palin Plaza, a Cambodian shopping center, he talked about his experience, which seemed to be typical. He had escaped from Cambodia by walking through the jungle to a border camp. He made his way to the U.S. embassy, applied for a visa, and arrived in Fort Worth, Texas, in November 1981. He could not speak English. After saving money earned as a factory computer assembler, Uong moved to Boston, studied English, and entered Boston University under a special program for immigrants. The rest of his story was familiar: more hard work, more study, two degrees, one in electrical engineering, another a master's in education. He moved to Lowell as a math teacher, then became a guidance counselor. In the meantime, he married an American and started his own family.

We pulled into the small parking area before the Palin Plaza and went inside. It was a self-contained city: restaurants; video stores; beauty parlors; barber shops; jewelry, grocery, and clothing stores; offices of lawyers and dentists and tax consultants; a driving school. All of these enterprises were Cambodian-owned, all served a Cambodian clientele, all were started within the last ten years, all were open seven days a week, from early morning until late at night, holidays included.

Inside, we were met by Rapha Yem, a Cambodian lawyer on the staff of the Massachusetts attorney general's office in Boston. He was thirty-eight, and his odyssey was similar to Uong's. After fleeing through the jungle from Cambodia to Thailand, with twenty-seven other Cambodians, he entered the United States in 1979. Two years later he relocated from California to Boston, where he worked for a Cambodian refugee resettlement program. He spoke with a simple eloquence. "I am an American citizen," he said. "I became a citizen in 1986. I think this is a great country, and that's the reason I came here. Is an opportunity, freedom, especially freedom. You know freedom is that you are free from being harassed, you're free from being killed, free from government persecution and all of that. And also opportunity, as long as you working hard, pursue your ambitions, I think you fit, you know. So that's why I came."

In Cambodia, Yem studied law. Many of his classmates went on to study in France. Yem never wanted to go to France. "I always wanted to come to the United States because it's just my favorite country, even though not everything that I perceived it would be."

I asked him to explain.

"The perception that, you know, Americans are an educated people and are more tolerant and everything," he said. "That's the reason I did not want to go to France, because the French people are not particularly fond of other nations besides their own people, and I thought the United States would be different. But, you know, quite the contrary. There is prejudice and all of that. In some areas I think it is worse than the French people. Still, the majority of people are very nice."

I asked Yem to draw a portrait of America as he sees it, with both its strengths and weaknesses.

"Okay," he began. "The strength is that the United States it's free, opportunities are there. It's up to you to make it happen, to make it become reality. Everything you dream, you know. The sky's the limit, you know, they always says. But on the other hand you have to pay the price as a minority. If you're too poor as a minority they would say, well, because he is too lazy, he's not working hard enough. When you become successful, people are jealous of you because they think, oh, he's successful, or they're successful, because government give them handouts and all of that, you know, which is not true at all.

"But we in trouble, yes, I think we in big trouble. We in trouble because the management, picking auto as one of the example, the management never listen to the people. And then the competition coming in listening, you know, to the need of the people and be able to adapt to that need. Unless the management change their attitude and listen more to the consumer they going to be in big trouble. We've fallen behind, you know. Yes, we feel that. We see that. I'm an American, you know, even though I came from Cambodia, but that Japan-bashing make me feel uncomfortable. Why? Because general public don't know and can't distinguish Cambodians from Japanese.

I'm afraid of being attacked physically because of my appearance."

I heard similar comments from many of the merchants with whom we spoke during the day. Something Uong said summed up their feelings:

"I travel to other countries in Europe, France, and Germany, and I still like nobody else like America. Nobody in the world. And I feel so awful to hear all these problems now, with all the cars that are going bankruptcy, all the airline company going bankruptcy. It hurt me because this is my home. If something happen to this country it will affect my life, my family, and my country also. So there is a lot of tension and there is a lot of problems, yes."

Both of these men married Americans. In so doing they continue the long pattern of assimilation. One wife is Jewish, the other of Irish background.

Even as we spoke another old American pattern was beginning to repeat itself. Many of the Lowell Cambodians were relocating again. As the jobs that drew them to Lowell disappeared, they looked for other opportunities. Already, I was told, the Cambodian grapevine, relayed by phone from family to family, had settled on another outpost of opportunity.

This time it was a continent away in the state of Washington. There, it was said, the jobs were more plentiful and the environment more hospitable. So they were beginning a westward trek that countless Americans before them had undertaken. But this time, it was along a path they had covered once before.

CHAPTER 13

VALUES: THE AGE OF ANXIETY

Not long after Amy Dickenson started work at NBC's Washington newsroom, the newscaster Roger Mudd asked her help in preparing a story for that night's network telecast. A "rare form of cancer" is reported to have been discovered in San Francisco, Mudd told Dickenson. Find out if we should spell out the name given to the new disease, A-I-D-S, or say it as one word: AIDS. The decision was to do both—spell it and say it.

That was in 1983, and Dickenson was then in her twenties. She remembers the moment vividly because of her challenging new job, but even more because of the impact the new disease would have on the lives of Americans. Ten years after that first report was aired nationally, nearly fifty thousand Americans a year were contracting HIV, the AIDS virus. That means that fifty thousand Americans a year will soon be dying of AIDS, unless a cure can be found. Once diagnosed, AIDS victims have a life expectancy of between eighteen months and two and a half years.

"When you ask me what concerns me most about our future," Dickenson says now, "the spread of that disease is at the top of the list. This is what I think about: the strain on our medical services and the strain on the economy. The cost of maintaining one American with AIDS is now thirty-eight thousand dollars a year. That's over one hundred and two thousand dollars spent on a person with AIDS during their all-too-short life. We spent ten billion dollars last year, and the cost is going up as treatments increase and more and more people get the disease. I think about the massive losses. Soon it will be like a Vietnam every year!"

Dickenson also reflects on the toll for American culture as AIDS strikes young writers, musicians, designers, dancers, actors, opera singers, and sports figures, all of whose potential contributions are lost when they die—and, of course, on the sorrow felt by families and friends who lose someone they love to AIDS.

Awareness of a new life-threatening menace like AIDS, striking suddenly and spreading throughout the culture, intensifies apprehension and stress felt by numerous Americans. Much more than fear of a new disease for which no cure has been found prompts these emotions; they are part of a national uneasiness that reshapes attitudes, affects lives, changes behavior. It also leads to a search for values, something firm to cling to in a time when everything seems more complicated and confusing, less secure and more threatening.

The fear of AIDS heightens existing fears—of violent crime, of further economic restructuring and job losses, of natural disasters from earthquakes (the Big One!), hurricanes, fires, and floods, of depletion of the earth's ozone layer and asteroids crashing into the planet. All this gives Americans more reason to fear they're losing control over their lives and facing forces beyond society's ability to handle. Life as they've known it appears to be heading toward breakdown. We are all anxious Americans living in an age of anxiety. And in our anxiety, we seek other sources of support.

Among Americans I met, the quest for values goes far beyond the political realm and represents much more than the term politicians use to claim superiority for *their* values over their opponents' unworthy values. As someone said to me, in discussing family values, "I often think if we can have healthy families, we can ensure the future of our country. But I'm afraid 'values' is turning into another Nineties 'thing,' and if it never goes deeper than that we're sunk."

For some, the search for values takes the form of a new yearning for spiritual reassurance, whether from organized religion, popular media-age spiritual "gurus," or cults whose messiahs promise new forms of salvation. For others, the search leads toward a return to tradition, to strict "rules," to literal "truths" of the Bible. For still others, those same "rules" do not apply, nor can they rely on the traditions of the past as guides to the future. Fears of a disintegrating society make some people yearn for escape, for security, for more time for themselves. As only one sign of that hunger, two-thirds of Americans questioned in one national survey say they are so desirous of more time with their families or by themselves that they would happily trade a portion of their paychecks for an extra day off. Reporting those findings in *The Washington Post,* Barbara Vobejda concludes: "In a society that has always coveted wealth, the finding that time has become more valuable than money is a telling signal that Americans feel besieged."

Adding to these feelings of being besieged is the knowledge that few safe havens exist. Here again, AIDS provides a metaphor for the times as the disease spreads alarmingly, extending beyond its original host groups of homosexuals and drug users. Now, the disease is being spread increasingly through *heterosexual* transmission. By 1993, in little more than a decade since the disease was first diagnosed, a quarter of a million cases of AIDS had been reported in the United States and 158,000 persons had died from it. The trend from homosexual to heterosexual transmission is pronounced and accelerating. By 1993, the greatest proportional increase—17 percent—of AIDS cases was from heterosexual exposure to high-risk individuals. (This increase in heterosexually acquired AIDS cases is most marked in the South and Northeast, with lowest increases in the West and Midwest.) Worse, U.S. health officials at the Centers for Disease Control in Atlanta say the number of people with AIDS will increase several percentage points annually. By 1994, 70,000 persons are expected to be diagnosed with the disease. By January 1995, the number of living Americans with AIDS is expected to jump from 90,000 to about 125,000.

Already, for Americans between the ages of twenty-five and forty-four, AIDS-related conditions are the *second* leading cause of death for men and the *fifth* leading cause of death for women. In several major cities—San Francisco, Los Angeles, New York, and Baltimore—AIDS has become the *leading* cause of death among young adult men, surpassing heart disease, cancer, and homicide. In New York City, AIDS has become the leading cause of death for women aged twenty-five to forty-four. Terrible as these figures are, the disease also has spread rapidly worldwide. Official estimates of all the cumulative AIDS cases by 1993 show a total of two and a half million, of which 71 percent are in Africa. The United States stands second, with 13 percent, followed by the Americas, 9 percent; Europe, 5 percent; Asia, 1 percent.

Fear of discovery of other horrific diseases heightens the public uneasiness. In the spring of 1993, Americans suddenly learned of a "mystery epidemic," apparently caused by an unknown virus with flulike symptoms that was bringing quick death to relatively young, healthy people, mostly Navajos, living on or near a 24,000-acre Indian reservation on the New Mexico–Arizona border. Like AIDS, this disease seemed to spring out of nowhere. It began when a thirteen-year-old Navajo girl collapsed at a Saturday-night party at a state park and then died. Within days, at least eleven people had died. All succumbed after experiencing high fevers, muscle aches, coughing, redness of the eyes, and such severe trouble breathing that they suffocated before they could be put on respirators. Death came as quickly as within a day after the first symptoms were detected. U.S. health officials suspected that the source of the virus was airborne transmission of dried urine from field mice and other rodents. That finding was hardly reassuring.

Nor is such a new threat the only cause for alarm. Americans of the electronic information age learn that even their computers can develop dangerous "viruses." In 1992, the entire nation—indeed, much of the world—reacted to the news that a computer virus dubbed Michelangelo was about to destroy data stored in the memory of any infected computer. This new virus was said to threaten not only sixty million individual personal computers but also those in government offices and commercial houses. This could cause companies to lose all their account records and governments at all levels to lose records that enable society to function. While that calamity did not occur, Americans learned that such computer viruses *are* a reality and not just the figment of a sci-fi scriptwriter's imagination.

In the brief hysteria over Michelangelo, Americans learned that more than a thousand such computer viruses, engineered to seek out and destroy data in what one expert calls "the digital equivalent of germ warfare," have been identified. It was yet another source of the new anxieties that drive Americans to be more watchful and wary.

Only in America, and perhaps only in the Nineties, would "anxiety boutiques" flourish as they do on Manhattan's Upper West Side. In one such "safety store," the owners offer cards to customers warning that "2,204,000 children under the age of 5 are injured in their homes every year." Thus, parents would be wise to purchase stove-knob covers, anti-scald valves, cord shorteners, window guards, and lead-testing kids. They also can purchase "Baby on Board!" bumper stickers, warning other drivers to be careful.

Similar stores offer denim jackets that are custom-bulletproofed. There is the Video Probe, a device to detect hidden cameras in hotel rooms; earthquake safety kits; "antiviral" computer software security devices to guard against new Michelangelos; microwave leak detectors; personal alarms and Mace; a briefcase, bearing an internal label "Citizen Defense Shield," that is bullet-proofed; and another briefcase that emits an alarm if stolen and fifty thousand volts of electricity, all triggered by remote control. All these are part of what *New York Times* writer Rick Marin, in a sprightly but sobering account, describes as the New Paranoia induced by our "doomy times." It is a high state of collective paranoia that induces Americans to spend more than $50 billion a year for security material to protect themselves and their property.

Passion for safety—for safe sex, safe enclaves, safe schools, safe streets—collides with fear that safety may be unattainable. This drives people to become ever more wary of taking risks or of trusting others. At a time when people hunger for new security and a stronger sense of the old connections of community, their many fears force them away from community rather than toward it. So increasing numbers turn to new forms of security that are peculiar offsprings of the electronic age: to "virtual reality," to phone sex like the kind depicted in the popular novel *Vox,* to computer hookups that allow people to exchange intimate conversations through modems. All of these permit people to experience contact on a totally isolated and impersonal—thus safe—level, satisfying their need for excitement but removing them from the objects of their fears.

In the Broadway satire *Search and Destroy,* the playwright Howard Korder portrays two anxious yuppies exchanging intelligence.

Robert: Tell you what my broker says.
Martin: What?

Robert: Fear.

Martin: What about it?

Robert: He thinks it's going to be very big. He thinks we're going to be hearing a lot from fear in the Nineties. It's going to be the Fear Decade. And he says now's the time to ground-floor it.

Martin: Fear?

Robert: Fear-related industries. Blood analyzers. Viral filters. UV screens. Total security systems. Impact-proof leisure wear. Very cutting-edge. Very hot.

In such a climate, personal relationships become especially stressful. What's "expected" of both men and women changes so rapidly that nearly everyone—including those leading movements for greater sexual freedom—feels bewildered about where the life-style changes ultimately will lead.

Everything is more open—and more constricted. Tune in any TV talk show morning or night and you'll see audiences nod gravely and applaud as children turn on parents or parents turn on children over abuses each has suffered at the hands of the other. Transvestites describe their lives, gays and lesbians and straights talk openly of their needs. Soldiers with medals come out of the closet on the Donahue or Oprah TV shows. Everyone is coming out, and even those who don't want to may be forced to, in the process called "outing."

At the same time, a strong backlash accompanies these public confessions and private-life disclosures. Radical feminists take out after men, "traditional values" fundamentalists attack what conservative talk show host Rush Limbaugh derides as "feminazis," skinheads attack blacks, some blacks attack Jews. Everybody, it seems, is roiling with inner conflicts and eager to express them to the widest public audience. As we have seen, speech codes on campus and political correctness often penalize free expression as much as they celebrate it.

Questions of race become even more complex and confounding. Black women find themselves in conflict with black men and grappling with troubling new questions about race and gender, sex discrimination and racial discrimination. Lisa Evans, a young black woman about to graduate from the Duke Law School, asks: if you're a black and a woman how do you resolve where you stand between

Anita Hill and Clarence Thomas or between the white Central Park jogger and the blacks charged with her rape? "There aren't any easy answers," she says. "Sometimes your feeling about your sex overcomes your feeling about your race, and sometimes your feeling about your race overcomes your feeling about your sex."

Younger women, whatever their race or background, find themselves threatened by the tone of a nasty backlash against women and feminism, and also by the increasing violence that makes them feel like special targets. "As a woman, I'm very worried about the night, just going out alone at night," says Sandy Galbis, another Duke Law School graduate whose family lives in Texas. "It bothers me that my male friends can go running at night and I can't do that. And I won't. There's a certain fear that women have that doesn't go away. There's definitely a sense of unease. I remember never locking our doors as a child. That's just disappeared. It doesn't exist anymore."

Young men or women of the "twentysomething" or "thirtysomething" generation wrestle with questions unimaginable to older groups. Women worry about pressures they feel as their "biological clock" ticks down. They discuss whether to have children without marriage and whether to raise them as single parents without fathers. Concepts of "love" are even more confounding and elusive; now members of both sexes may focus more on questions of "commitment" rather than romance, and on whether men and women can really trust each other in long-term "relationships." Couples tacitly acknowledge the prospect of failed marriages and take steps to protect themselves. Prenuptial legal agreements, spelling out terms of marital breakup before the marriage has occurred, are in wide use.

What is "acceptable" behavior between males and females becomes infinitely more complicated—and sometimes more threatening—as standards change over what constitutes sexual harassment, raising questions as to whether a casual touch or teasing friendly remark might become the basis for a lawsuit and destruction of career and reputation. Even one's name assumes a certain challenge. Should a woman who marries keep her maiden name, drop it, or join it to her husband's name with a hyphen? As if divorce were not painful enough, fear of "palimony suits" further complicates living together, and no longer only among the celebrities where that practice began. Such breach-of-affection suits are now more common among couples with no claims to public fame.

Families strain under new pressures. One of every two marriages ends in divorce. Between 1970 and 1990, census figures show America's marriage rate fell nearly 30 percent while its divorce rate increased nearly 40 percent. In that same period, another dramatic change in family structure occurred: the number of children who live with a single parent doubled, rising to one-quarter of *all* American children. That's three times as many as in 1960. The number of Americans who never marry, long increasing, has accelerated sharply: the Census Bureau reports that the number of Americans aged eighteen and older* who have never married has risen from one in six in the early Seventies to one in four in the early Nineties. Working mothers struggle to find affordable child care or, for the more affluent, live-in nannies for their children. In whatever economic circumstance, the problem of dealing with two careers and small children creates intense daily pressures.

On my journey, hardly a day passed without people citing this pressure as one of their greatest personal concerns, if not the greatest. The problem of raising small children is most severe, of course, for single women. It's infinitely more difficult for such women struggling to bring up children in the inner-city worlds of drugs and guns. There, merely getting the child to school safely takes courage and tenacity. But the new pressures also affect the lives and the attitudes of young professionals, who, however more fortunate their lot, find themselves facing stress they had not anticipated. Burdened with heavy debt from college educations that in the past provided a surer ticket to a more prosperous and leisurely future, they face additional financial burdens in pursuing their professional careers and raising their families—and all in a personal environment that offers less time for themselves.

Typical of many such young couples I met are Kirk Read and Camille Parrish, both highly educated professionals in their thirties. He's a professor of French literature at Bates College in Auburn, Maine, and she's a nitro-geologist for Maine's Department of Environmental Protection, specializing in hazardous wastes and waste

---

*Eighteen is the age at which "adult" demographic statistics begin, and at which one assumes the right to vote and serve in the armed forces.

water management. They have two small children. The couple went through long and nerve-wracking job searches before settling in Maine. Kirk found that even private New England colleges were scaling back benefits, while Camille discovered that a high-paying private-sector job she had been offered in Maine was not as flexible about permitting career women with children to work reduced hours. As a result, she took a lower-paying state job. "I've had to compromise between my career and my family," she says. "Women my age are wrestling with this a lot these days. How much of your career can you give up for your family, and what's the importance of that?"

The state job allows her to work four days a week, giving her more time for her family, but it also requires her to commute two hours each day by car between Auburn and Augusta, the state capital, a trip that can be arduous in Maine's severe winter weather. To arrive at work on time, she leaves home before the children are awake, and she doesn't see them until she returns at night. Before going to his job at the college, Kirk takes one girl to nursery school, the other to the home of a woman who cares for children of other working parents. Theirs is hardly a life of despair, but it is stressful, and the gloomy economic conditions, especially state layoffs because of Maine's budget crisis, heighten their feelings of stress. As someone near the bottom of the civil service seniority system, Camille says, "I'm always worrying about my job. Every Sunday I look at the want ads to see what's out there—just in case." For all their hard work and careful planning, they're acutely aware that it takes both their incomes to live reasonably well. More than half her income goes to pay their mortgage and taxes. More than a quarter of his take-home pay goes for day-care costs for their daughters. When they add in additional regular expenses—food, clothing, heat, insurance, car payments—their financial margin grows slim. Loss of one of their jobs would be a disaster; their standard of living, their life-style, their ability to provide for their children all depend upon that second income.

Their experience is no different from that of millions of young American couples who, born at the tail end of the baby boom, have an uneasy sense that their children may not have things as good as they did, that somehow something has gone wrong. They, too, feel anxious. They wonder if the middle-class positions for which they indebted themselves will enable them to enjoy the life-style that Americans in the past expected to achieve, and did.

It's not just *their* life-style that worries them; it's their children's prospects. For many of the people I met, those fears force them to reexamine their values, and the values they want to instill in their children. Again, my first conversation with the Tierneys of Maine set the pattern for all that followed.

"There's no way that my children will be able to achieve the degree of financial success I have, and I'm not a wealthy guy," Tierney says. "I don't think my kids are going to have a house as big as mine unless they end up with this one, because I can't sell it to anybody else because of the real estate market! They've been able to live in nice houses and go to good schools, and it's an open question whether they can continue to do that." To their immense credit, Jim and Susan Tierney accept that knowledge but do not worry about it. They're the kind of parents who try to give their children a sense of self-worth and spiritual well-being so that even if the children do not enjoy economic success it will not destroy them.

"If you live your life for your week in the Caribbean and you lose your job so you can't go to the Caribbean, you have a miserable life," Jim Tierney says. "If you live your life so that you take pleasure from, as my daughter, Josie, said the other day, writing for herself and her audience, that's okay, because she doesn't need to go to the Caribbean to see the world and to sense emotions and feel things. Or that my son, Matthew, who loves the theater, will always be able to be in community theater, if not Broadway. So that's how we have opted as parents."

I met many like them, and in so doing found reason for reassurance about the solid values Americans continue to hold. That, of course, does not eliminate the anxiety and doubt felt even by those who appear to have the soundest, and strongest, sense of values.

Nothing is simple anymore, if ever it was. Even children become players in life dramas no American would have dreamed in years past. Those who advocate children's rights—the latest manifestation of Americans' urge to extend "rights" to previously uncovered groups of people, even animals—press for what would have seemed radical revision of the laws, and succeed. In Florida, a juvenile judge rules that an eleven-year-old boy can legally seek a "divorce" from his parents so he can be adopted by a foster family. The ruling is taken to mean a child has the same constitutional right to protect his or her fundamental interests in court as an adult. And it's hailed by children's rights groups as paving the way for similar disowning suits in other states. In America's increasingly litigious society, children are now suing their parents for abuse and maltreatment. In some ways, this extension of rights is an offshoot both of political correctness and of the American tendency to believe that legal remedies, or new laws, can solve deeply complex societal problems. Yet it's also a response to greater awareness of terrible abuses in the society—and, at the least, a belated public recognition that things like child abuse *do* exist, *are* rampant, and require stronger action to remedy them.

Adults, whether men or women, find the rules governing relationships have changed, or that there are no rules at all. Does a woman carry a condom? Does she insist the man use it—notably, as in a Texas criminal case, that a rapist use one? In the Texas case, the woman was both smart and courageous. She was determined to protect herself from possible life-threatening disease, even if forced to submit to rape, and even if her persuading the rapist to use a condom made him think their sexual act was consensual.

What about the man? What of his responsibility, and how does he exercise it? Does he react as one male student I met at Bridgeport University did and boast about having a "sex addiction" and of refusing to use a condom? "I'm trying to have that invincible air," he says. "It's from the way I was raised. I know better, but I feel like, okay, I can do anything, I could jump off the top of the building and not be hurt." Or does he pay attention to a female student who, listening to him, says, in disgust, that "there's a lot of people around campus who like to sleep around with as many people as they can, but I don't feel that way. I'm dead afraid of diseases like AIDS and will not have sex with anyone who doesn't wear a condom."

Then there is the now quaint notion of "dating." It, too, becomes laden with new concerns. Debbie Quisenberry, the young Peoria teacher who lost her job, talks about beginning to date again after her marriage to her high school boyfriend failed. "The rules have changed," she says, describing her "panic attack" after learning from a friend that a young man was interested in taking her out. "Dating!"

she exclaims. "I don't know how to date. I don't know what's expected anymore. Sexually, what is expected? Now you have to worry about all sorts of things. Who pays? What does he expect at the end of the evening? You hear a lot about date rape these days, and AIDS is a factor now. Definitely! I would have to know a person very, very well before I would consider a sexual relationship in this day and age.

"Most of my friends are married, but since I've gotten divorced we've talked about these issues, and they say, 'Oh, I would hate to be single now. It's scary.' It's scary because of all of these things. I don't know that it's more scary for women than men, but being a woman adds to it. You just don't know what's out there. I find myself being very picky about people."

All these concerns have an impact not only on the way people think, but on how they relate to each other. Awareness of so many societal dangers does change behavior. "You hear older people talk about some wild flings they had in college," says Eunice Baek at Berkeley. "You hear them, and think, no way! There is not a single chance you would do anything that stupid anymore. We in college now realize the magnitude of AIDS, because we have friends and relatives with AIDS. We all know of someone who either has it or who has died from it."

Americans are anxious about another kind of threat—environmental dangers leading to some ultimate the-way-the-world-ends calamity. Since Earth Day signaled the emergence of an environmental movement in the United States and then around the world in the early 1970s, a growing sense of the danger of global warming and the depletion of the ozone layer has taken hold. Environmental concern is no longer limited primarily to college students and committed activists; Americans in general are increasingly aware of the long-term effects of nuclear accidents like that at the Soviet plant at Chernobyl and the dangers of contaminated food and polluted water and air. Such concerns are everywhere, many expressed in areas where life seems most secure and protected.

In the retirement community of Santee, South Carolina, Dick Miller, a former international paper company executive, gazes over his patio at the lakeshore that graces his home. Here it is, he reflects, the reward of years of hard work. But now that scene no longer appears so reassuring. He worries that the water could be contaminated forever by radioactive waste seepage from the world's largest hydrogen bomb plant in Aiken, South Carolina. The plant is located on the Savannah River, which flows into his lake. His fears have a basis in reality; the plant was closed because leakage from its reactors raised questions about safety. "We've got dangers," Miller says. "These little time bombs sitting around and ticking. It could hit this water system just as soon as not. I'm not anti-nuclear-reactor, but I feel we're creating our own doom—and I'm a very positive person. I've always been a big optimist. In a selfish way, by the time all this happens I'm going to be gone. If it wasn't for kids and grandkids and loved ones, you could be selfish and withdraw within yourself. But you can't be a caring person and not think about these things."

It's strange, he says, but when he retired in the early Nineties he believed the world was on the brink of a new era of peace after the collapse of communism. It seemed, too, as if America's brightest period was about to begin. Instead, the American economy is in serious condition and new wars are ignited throughout the world, making him suddenly more concerned about the future. "But my *biggest* worry is the environment," he says. "I worry about things like the ozone layer. I worry about radiation. I recall seeing a film at World War II's end when they tested an atomic bomb. They had these soldiers all standing in trenches, with goggles on, looking at that bomb. As soon as the bomb went off and the dust cleared, they went charging in. It was a maneuver. They also had a bunch of generals watching the bomb go off. Nobody had any idea what the hell they were doing—that they were marching these people right into radiation. Now, I think, how many times a day are we ingesting things that we don't know what the effects are going to be on us?"

Younger Americans are even more highly attuned to environmental issues, judging by the ones I met. They're quick to talk about ozone-layer depletion and destruction of the Amazon rain forests, as well as problems in their own areas, whether erosion of the Great Plains, damage to the Great Lakes, flooding of Mississippi Valley farmland, or, in the case of Amy Dickenson, the landfills, toxic and otherwise, that dot the countryside in upstate New York where she was raised. "I no longer worry," Dickenson says, "that there will be a nuclear war in my lifetime. But I know that the world I knew as a child, living on a small dairy farm, has disappeared as surely as if it were blown off the planet. I don't know which dies first, the land or our connection to it. But I think about the generation just behind me—the teenagers and the twentysomethings—who have embraced the environment as the cause of their era—promoted by McDonald's and Burger King and The Gap and Benetton—and I wonder how deep their commitment can possibly go when chances are they grew up around shopping malls. Surely the natural world exists as more of an abstraction to them, as it increasingly does for me."

To Americans like Dickenson, the "environment" means much more than the condition of the air and water, of course. It also means the environment in which people must work and live. But even if one's own life is relatively free of stress—a dubious proposition, however fortunate the individual circumstance—the electronic communications revolution that instantly links all Americans to outside forces and events makes it virtually impossible to escape from terrible scenes that shake confidence and increase anxiety. In the age of television, every American has reacted in horror to the explosion of the space shuttle *Challenger,* has been to south-central Los Angeles during the riots, has experienced the shells raining on innocent women and children in Sarajevo, has felt the terror of the flames consuming the men, women, and children in the Branch Davidian compound in Waco, Texas.

So it's not surprising that Americans have been turning inward. Their hunger for self-improvement—shown by strenuous diets and fitness classes, self-help books and videotapes—reflects that desire. In a related way, so does the yuppie phenomenon. The line between selfishness and self-interest is exceedingly fine; both qualities are driven by a belief that one's fate is increasingly in one's own hands— or, to put it another way, that the best chance of surviving is through one's own efforts. Americans no longer believe they can expect the kind of support they once received from leaders or institutions, whether in politics or in the workplace. Distrust is profound. Bonds of loyalty, from top down to bottom and the reverse, are broken. In the absence of faith in the "system" or its leaders, people naturally turn to themselves. This is not all bad. Self-reliance leads to initiative. But it also can make it more difficult to unite for new common goals. Nor is it surprising, in such circumstances, that increasing numbers of people yearn for spiritual fulfillment. Along with this yearning comes renewed interest in miracles, visitations, visions—a state of mind that always accompanies periods of great change, when uncertainty, confusion, and fanaticism inevitably flourish.

Amy Dickenson, in talking about her hopes for her small daughter, admits to a strong personal pull toward spirituality and miracles. "We've been so lucky as Americans that we've never had to look beyond our TV screens for meaning," she says. "Now we're digging deeper, looking for signs, looking for answers, looking for our one last hope. If you're lucky enough to survive these periods of deep distress, you find yourself forever changed."

Of course, such feelings are hardly new, nor is yearning for spiritual fulfillment and salvation merely a "Nineties thing." Throughout their history, Americans have been swept by mass spiritual movements—by Great Revivals and Great Awakenings, by preachers shouting warnings of hellfire and damnation at firelight tent camp meetings, by sinners seeking redemption after hearing evangelists proclaim the evils of contemporary life and the erosion of moral values. From the Brook Farm idealists who withdrew from the world to establish Utopia in communes outside Boston in the 1840s to the flower children of the 1960s who sought spiritual rebirth by fleeing the materialism and corruption of the Establishment for their own rural communes, Americans have always sought escape in mass movements and causes. They have found, too, convenient signs of God's hand to justify actions that might not be considered so heavenly. Pioneers bent on seizing territory in the West claimed to have seen the image of an American eagle spread across the sun after a violent prairie thunderstorm. Surely a signal that the Lord beckoned them on. So westward the divinely sanctioned path of American Manifest Destiny progressed, through the lands occupied by the Indians, the Mexicans, and the Spaniards. And Americans throughout their history have joined cults and celebrated faith healers, been seduced by religious hucksters and charlatans who energetically save souls while passing offering plates to the beat of tambourines.

It's also true that the present yearning for spiritual rebirth, or rediscovery, springs from a long and growing concern over the nature of modern life—what Walter Lippmann, writing at the end of the 1920s in *A Preface to Morals,* called the "problem of unbelief." He meant the increasing numbers of people "who feel that there is a vacancy in their lives" and who, "having lost their faith, have lost the certainty that their lives are significant, and that it matters what they do with their lives." To Lippmann, here lay the reason for "modern man's discontent." As he defined it: "At the heart of it there are likely to be moments of blank misgiving in which he finds that the civilization of which he is a part leaves a dusty taste in his mouth. He may be very busy with many things, but he discovers one day that he is no longer sure they are worth doing. He has been much preoccupied; but he is no longer sure he knows why. He has become involved in an elaborate routine of pleasures; and they do not seem to amuse him very much."

If Americans were experiencing these kinds of doubts at the end of the Twenties, they still had many more reasons to believe in their, and their country's, destiny. The great majority then believed in progress, in tomorrow being brighter than today, and in their ability to overcome the problems of modern life through the invention or discovery of new methods and new technologies that would continually improve the quality of life. By the 1990s, all of these beliefs had been shaken.

You cannot spend a day talking with Americans without hearing over and over that America's problems stem from its lack of "values." *Loss* of values would be more accurate. But what's wrong takes many forms, and is open to many interpretations. There is no single definition of "values," and those that exist are often in direct conflict.

To some Americans, "values" are related to the American work ethic. Depending on the individual viewpoint, that value has either eroded or is still there. In either case, Americans tend to be irate over claims that their work ethic is declining or that they have become "lazy," the term used by a Japanese political leader to characterize American workers. Days after that widely publicized remark by Yoshio Sakurauchi, speaker of Japan's lower house of parliament, a businessman in Bridgeport, Connecticut, bought billboard space on I-95, crossing the heart of downtown Bridgeport, to post this message: COME WORK FOR ME IF YOU THINK AMERICANS ARE LAZY. It was still there when I arrived in Bridgeport. Yet among themselves many Americans express those same criticisms, and in equally harsh terms.

Opinions conflict when values are considered from ideologically differing viewpoints. "Traditional values" and "family values" became the politically charged slogans of Republicans during the 1992 election, though Republican candidates and strategists had been successfully using such terms during previous election cycles. The "right" traditional moral values are contrasted with the "immoral" values of the "liberals," who are depicted as antifamily and as holding extreme positions labeled "pro-gay," "pro-lesbian," "pro-abortion," and, generally, "pro-radical." Such polarized ideologies remain in the Clinton era as conflicts over gays in the military, abortion, and racial quotas continue to serve as rallying points for opposition to Clinton.

For election after election, the Republicans turned the supposed liberal excesses of the Sixties into a referendum on the Democratic Party's national leadership. By 1992, many of their positions—especially as articulated during the 1992 Republican convention—were seen as too extreme and divisive.

Clinton's victory, in no small measure, came from the support of people of his generation who, like him, had been forged in the bitter polemical disputes of the Sixties, and who, in many cases, were returning to political activism after having dropped out. "I remember the values we had then," says Sarah Colvig, who was one of the "flower children" of the Sixties and left Houston to live on a commune in California, "and a lot of people think it was just a fad, those who became immersed in the consumerism of the Eighties. I don't think my values have changed that much. I'm for universal peace and against war—unless you're actually attacked—and for civil rights and protecting the environment. My values haven't changed. Except maybe now I work more with the political process. I try to get other people to vote; if you don't vote, I don't see how you can complain about what's happening in America."

Many such Clinton supporters were joined by others who reacted against another kind of excess, that of the televangelists of the religious right, whose rise to political power was stimulated by their far greater access to television. The public downfall of many of their leaders—Jim Bakker after criminal fraud and conspiracy conviction, Jimmy Swaggart after acknowledged involvement with a prostitute—lessened the political power of the televangelists. Still, they remain a potent force, especially in the Republican Party.

A visit to a former Moral Majority stronghold in rural Rocky Mount, North Carolina, provides a glimpse of the ideological stance of the right. Seated in the pastor's office are church leaders and parishioners of the fundamentalist Parkwood Baptist Church. "This church hasn't changed in the belief that the Bible is truth from cover to cover," one woman says. "We believe every word in the Bible."

Nodding in agreement, a man adds: "There are two churches in our state now, in Chapel Hill and in Raleigh, and one is involved with the ordination of homosexuals as priests or ministers and the other with the blessing of a homosexual union. In our church, those are not questions that are open to debate. The Bible says homosexuality is a sin, and while God loves these people, there's no way under heaven this church could ordain them. We would not even discuss it."

The pastor, the Rev. Hank Sanders, says: "God's values never change and they're never in jeopardy. What's in jeopardy are the people who are moving away from it. That's the danger, yes sir, that's the danger. Whether folks are willing to admit it or not, our adherence to His word and our basic Christian ethics have been the basis of the success of our country."

Most Americans are not so absolute in their beliefs. They struggle to adhere to their personal values somewhere in the murky middle, expressing concern over eroding values yet still having tolerance for opposing views. Still, such Americans—and in my experience they are the great majority—find their values best expressed by mainstream American groups, whether representing organized religion or not. However, increasing numbers gravitate toward a different kind of spiritual support. One of the most memorable experiences of my journey occurred on a winter night in Manhattan when I sat among HIV-positive men and women who had come to hear a popular New Age guru conduct a long emotional session of shared experiences. As people related their stories, they often broke down in tears.

The guru is Marianne Williamson, a slight, dark-haired young single mother whose books have become huge national best-sellers,* and who has founded two nonprofit organizations—Centers for Living on the East and West Coasts devoted to the care of AIDS patients. Those who filled the room—and every seat was taken, with more people standing by the windows and at the back of the hall— joined in holding hands, in prayer, and in sharing their fears and frustrations as they talked about the deaths of their friends and their own mortality. "Is this your first time here?" the man sitting next to me whispered as we all held hands and bowed our heads. "Don't worry; you'll like it." He gave my hand a reassuring squeeze.

Williamson, from a theological standpoint, is ecumenical. The daughter of Jewish parents in Houston, she bases her lectures on something called "A Course in Miracles" and cites the example of Jesus in exploring what she calls "spiritual psychotherapy." During the long session, she maintains a low-keyed manner. Her intent appears to be to let members of her audience express themselves as she shares reflections from her personal history of divorce and drug addiction that led her to find spiritual comfort through the "healing power of love."

Despite my considerable doubts about one person promoting the healing power of love before wide audiences and profiting from it, I found Williamson understated and thoughtful both during the group session and later when we spoke. Most interesting was how the themes she expressed were virtually the same that others kept articulating throughout my journey. The powerlessness that people feel, the belief that conventional politics no longer seems the primary vehicle for change in America, the fears about crime and drugs and disease, the search for new meaning, for inner peace and security, for alternative ways of acting, for new thinking—all these are central to her message.

"People don't need to be awakened to how bad things are," she told me over dinner after the group meeting. "People know how bad things are. The news today is not how bad things are but how good

*At the time we talked, the best-seller lists provided an insight into what topics Americans felt of greatest interest. Williamson's *A Return to Love* was the number one nonfiction best-seller, followed by Gloria Steinem's *Revolution from Within: A Book of Self-Esteem* and Susan Faludi's *Backlash: The Undeclared War Against American Women.*

they could be. A Course in Miracles addresses itself very profoundly to violence. The goal is the attainment of inner peace. A doctor said to me recently, 'You're not sick, but that doesn't mean you're healthy.' America's not at war, but that doesn't mean we're at peace. We are in a very insidious war. It's right here. The violence is practically on every street corner. People who thought drugs would never come to our neighborhood, who thought guns would never come to our elementary schools, who never thought violence would come to our homes, are wrong. I don't see myself saying anything that anyone doesn't know. What I *do* think bears repeating is how much difference we can make contrary to the delusion that we are powerless."

You need not be a believer in miracles—and I am not—to recognize that even at the levels of American life where exploitation has often existed, serious reexamination appears to be underway.

Another theme, expressed widely in the culture, reflects the anxiety of Americans about violence and lack of control. In *Fatal Attraction, The Hand That Rocks the Cradle,* and countless "copy-cat" films, the child-as-innocent-victim is the subject of abuse and terror from adults who threaten the family itself. Victim films of the past, such as *Bonnie and Clyde,* dealt with people on the fringes of society. But by the Nineties, the victim stood in the center of what had been believed to be the most secure place in America—the family. Suddenly, that sense of security seems shattered. Protection of the threatened child becomes a symbol for the menace of contemporary life—of violence in schools and on the streets; of aberrant behavior in which previously unmentionable acts of sexual and child abuse become subjects of common concern; of more census evidence of the crumbling family structure.

These disturbing cultural changes are far removed from the gently deprecating self-portrait America presented to itself during the Depression years when Shirley Temple danced and Jimmy Stewart wisecracked through the hardest of times or from the saccharine innocence projected over TV by Ozzie and Harriet of the Fifties ("Hi Mom," "Hi Dad," "Hi Ricky," "Hi Dave"). Those naive images of ourselves failed to reflect the grimmer realities of the United States, of course. Lynchings and chain gangs and organized crime and professional murderers were part of the backdrop of the Thirties. The supposedly innocent Fifties were stained by the mass character assassinations and ideological witchhunts of McCarthyism and the building of bomb shelters to withstand the anticipated nuclear assault of Soviet communism. And throughout their history, Americans have always succeeded in masking the harsher aspects of their national experience by viewing events through a sentimental and romantic haze. Cowboys were good; Indians were bad. Americans didn't take territory by conquest; it was God's will, Manifest Destiny, that drove them West to their promised lands. But at no point have they felt so besieged by so many forces that seem beyond their control—and so driven to try to escape from new threats by withdrawing into their own lives and creating the safest and most secure environment possible for their family and children.

In the case of Steve and Lynne Spickard, the young couple in Oakland, California, who reluctantly decided to place their children in private school rather than public, this leads to fashioning a self-contained interior world. Their home is equipped with the best that the new electronic world of computers and VCRs can offer. "The only way we have to maintain some quality of life is by creating a kind of private wealth that you can put inside the walls of your own little house," Steve says. "So we have all these CDs and TVs and electronics. Yet you can't go walking outside your house. You're not safe. You can't walk in the parks. You're not safe. So we're building our own private safe world." Within this world, they do the best they can as parents to teach children strong personal values.

Yet, there are no guarantees. "We can do a great job of educating our kids, and provide all this," Steve says, gesturing around his living room, "but you can't help thinking that they can step out that front door and be blown away by random violence on the street."

CHAPTER 14

POLITICS:
AWAY FROM ROME

Now had been divulged the secret of the empire, that
emperors could be made elsewhere than at Rome.
—Tacitus, *The History*

Ross Perot is an unlikely emperor. In a nation that cele-
brates youth and glamour, invariably picks the taller over the shorter
candidate, distrusts great wealth and power, and prefers charm to
sarcasm in its leaders, the bantam Texas billionaire with the big ears
and even bigger ego would seem to have had only minimal political
prospects. Yet more than any of the 1992 presidential candidates,
Perot symbolized how the American people felt about their political
system and the need for change. When the election was over, Perot
also best symbolized the dangerous potential for greater fragmentation of the political system if real changes do not occur during the
Clinton presidency.

Perot, not Clinton, became a more dominant political figure as
Clinton encountered early difficulty in securing passage of his program. Increasingly harsh in his denunciation of the new president,
Perot lashed out at Clinton for weakness and vacillation on Bosnia,
for being a "tax-and-spend" politician, for failing to act boldly to end
the capital gridlock and reform the workings of Washington, for
supporting the North American Free Trade Agreement (NAFTA)
with Mexico and Canada. Most of all, Perot assailed Clinton for
producing an economic program that, he argued, would neither reduce the deficit nor restore America to health and prosperity.

Deficit reduction was Perot's ace, the card he had played more
successfully than anyone else during the campaign, as he hammered

and hammered at the dangers of the rising debt. He had succeeded in linking this in the public mind with America's decline. He also had the advantage over the president in not having to propose hard remedies to bring down the debt; he could simply respond to public demands for immediate action to get the economy moving again. That, of course, meant creating jobs—now. Where Clinton tried to implement a more balanced, long-term approach, in which spending for needed investment in infrastructure or job retraining or high-tech research and development was accomplished along with deficit reduction, Perot stuck to a single theme—and scored repeatedly with the public.

Perot had another advantage: he did not have to indulge in the acts of compromise and persuasion necessary to any party leader in a democracy. Ross Perot is the classic lone wolf. Freed of political affiliation and of the necessity to win tough votes in a bitterly divided Congress, freed too of the need to pacify clamorous constituents who had elected him, Perot presented himself as a decisive problem-solver. He was the straight shooter whose blunt talk and no-nonsense manner inspired, if not affection, at least respect and public interest. Nor did Perot have to explain his actions, or even answer questions about how, precisely, he would accomplish his goal of deficit reduction. When pressed during television interviews to specify what taxes he would raise, what programs he would cut, where his economic ideas differed from Clinton's, he filibustered or fumed. And he got away with it. He simply brushed aside tough questions that suggested his own published economic plan was grossly inaccurate and would result in a $400 billion budget shortfall. Even more caustically than during the presidential campaign year, Perot was contemptuous of the president. Emboldened by his own rise in public opinion polls, Perot came more frequently to Washington on highly publicized political missions to challenge Clinton. He met privately with Republican freshmen members of Congress and derided Clinton's proposal to form a "trust fund" into which tax funds earmarked to cut the deficit would be placed and protected by law. That was a "whitewash," Perot told the Republicans. He continued to buy television airtime and to use the free exposure networks granted him. In his most personal assault on the president, Perot used national television to accuse Clinton of being unprepared for the presidency and incompetent in exercising power. Clinton was doing things the "Arkansas way," Perot sneered; so bad was the new president, the Texan went on, that he would not even be hired as a middle manager in a respectable business firm. And all the while Perot courted his citizens' grassroots movement nationally. It was called United We Stand America. "United" was a misnomer. Perot was, in fact, an agent more of national division than of unity.

Not since Huey Long challenged Franklin Roosevelt during the early New Deal days has there been such a spectacle. And even there the analogy is not apt, for Long, the legendary "Kingfish," was an accomplished legislator of proven political skills, first as governor of Louisiana, then as a dynamic United States senator whose lunge for the presidency was cut short by an assassin's bullet in Baton Rouge. Ross Perot has never held elective office, but he was—and is—a symbol of, perhaps an omen for, the future. For Ross Perot did not spring into public consciousness by happenstance. The conditions that created his opportunity, whatever it may prove to be, were there to be exploited. If not Perot, others would have grasped that chance. They are still likely to if Clinton fails. In this, Perot symbolizes not a new political force but the deep distrust that pervades the political system.

For at least a decade, and in reality far longer, people at the bottom have grown increasingly alienated from those at the top, and especially from leaders who seem unable and often unwilling to address their concerns. Over the last generation, surveys on public alienation have tracked America's steadily eroding confidence in its leaders and institutions—a decline so uniform and so steep that it raises the most serious questions about public faith in the democratic system and therefore the ability of that system to function.

In Gallup surveys from 1975 to 1991, the polling firm asked Americans whether they had "a great deal or quite a lot" of confidence in major institutions. The findings revealed sharp drops in public confidence in banks and banking, public schools, big business, organized labor, organized religion, Congress, newspapers, and the Supreme Court.

And those findings were recorded before the recession of the Nineties further weakened public confidence in the American system.

For some of these institutions, the decline is even more striking, because the level of public confidence was low in 1975 and kept falling thereafter. Big business, for instance, had the confidence of only 34 percent of the public in 1975. By 1991, that figure had dropped to 22 percent. Similarly, confidence in organized labor and Congress began at low points in 1975—38 and 40 percent respectively—and sank to only 18 percent for Congress and 22 percent for labor in 1991.

Those few institutions in which a majority of Americans expressed confidence in 1975—banks at 55 percent, newspapers at 51 percent—declined sharply in public favor by 1991. Banks then had only a 29 percent confidence rating, newspapers only 32 percent.

Only one major American institution that enjoyed strong public confidence in 1975 registered greater public favor by 1991. That was the military, which had rebounded from the demoralizing effects of the Vietnam War. It rose from a 58 percent confidence level in 1975 to 69 percent in 1991.

With the fear stirred by the recession during the election campaign, these feelings of alienation worsened. Consumer confidence indices plunged to all-time lows, and, as we have seen, when polled throughout the year seven of ten Americans repeatedly said they believed the nation was heading in the wrong direction. That sense of something amiss did not develop suddenly. National measurements of consumer confidence had been declining since the 1950s and early 1960s, leading to what Richard T. Curtin, director of consumer surveys at the University of Michigan, calls a collective state of mind of "diminished expectations" and other scholars describe as "resigned pessimism" that government is not likely to make things better. Still, Americans had not entirely lost their traditional belief in their capacity for change. With Clinton's election and inauguration, a surge in confidence was recorded. One survey taken then—the "Consumer Confidence Index," based on nationwide interviews for ABC News's *Money Magazine* to measure attitudes toward the national economy, personal finances, and the buying climate—hit its highest point in two years. Exactly a year before, it had stood at a record low. But even then, despite clear evidence of renewed confidence in and hope for the new president, there were deeper signs of trouble.

A Harris poll, released to coincide with Clinton's inauguration, showed that public confidence in U.S. institutions was still sinking.

Of all institutions examined—the military, the Supreme Court, major colleges and universities, television news, the White House, medicine, major corporations, the press, the federal executive branch, Wall Street, Congress, law firms—only one, again the military, registered an improvement from a similar survey in 1988. As for the other institutions, fewer than one out of four Americans had a great deal of confidence in any of them. For many of the institutions—major companies, the press, the executive branch, Wall Street, Congress, and law firms—the confidence levels sank into the low teens. At the bottom in public esteem were law firms, with only 11 percent of Americans expressing great confidence in them. Barely above them was the Congress, at 12 percent.

Feelings about the way Washington works continued to be sharply negative. A month after Clinton's inauguration, a *Washington Post*/ABC News poll found that only 17 percent of adults trusted the federal government to do what was right most of the time. That was a drop from 38 percent in 1985. When asked how many cents are wasted of every dollar the federal government collects in taxes, the estimates of half those sampled averaged 39 cents. And when asked whether they favored smaller government with fewer services or larger government with many services, 67 percent of Americans chose the latter and only 30 percent the former.

This signaled another sharp change in public attitudes about the political system. Nine years before, when Ronald Reagan was beginning his second term, the American public was nearly evenly divided on that question, with 49 percent favoring smaller government but 43 percent wanting larger.

That national sample of opinion did highlight two strong feelings about what the public wanted. When asked whether America needs to make major or minor changes in the way the federal government works, by an overwhelming majority of nearly four to one—71 percent as opposed to 18 percent—Americans wanted *major* changes. They also strongly believed then that Clinton was trying to make those major changes—56 percent thought the changes the president proposed were major, and only 36 percent thought they were minor.

Those last findings provided the basis for Clinton's opportunity. They also suggested the magnitude of his task, and the urgency of the public's desire that problems be resolved.

Traditionally, American politicians are driven by the short-term approach. From city council members to members of Congress, emphasis is on the "quick fix" to complex problems and on claiming political credit for responding to immediate needs. The result, as we have seen, is postponement of decisions on major long-term issues. Thus, the real size of the budget deficit is masked. Genuine attempts to reduce it are put off to the next session of Congress—and the next and the next. Action is not taken today; it is always planned for tomorrow, to take place in what Washington policymakers, in typical semantic obfuscation, call "the out years." The out years never quite arrive; they continue to lie beyond grasp. So the debts increase and the charade continues with each new congressional session. The same was true with Clinton, whose budget calls for increases in spending during his first four years with actual deficit reduction not to come until later.

Lawmakers under pressure to "do something" *now* pacify this or that powerful interest group. This is not inherently wrong, nor is it necessarily damaging. The damage comes when national leaders fail to build support for long-term policies that will lead to a sounder future. That is the essential challenge of presidents. Great presidents—Jefferson, Jackson, Lincoln, the Roosevelts, Truman—rise to it and articulate a national vision that engages the people and forces the political system to respond. Ineffectual or weak presidents accept the politics of the status quo and accomplish little.

A month after he became president, I asked Gerald Ford what he would like people to say he had accomplished ten years after his presidency. He looked blank. It was clear that he had not thought of it. That was not his fault, nor do I intend a judgment on his intellect and ability. He was a creature of Congress, a skillful legislator accustomed to the daily give-and-take of the legislative process. He had not sought the presidency nor, it seemed, given it much thought. His was an accidental presidency—he was the first man ever to gain both the vice presidency *and* the presidency without being elected by the people.* He could not be fairly blamed for lack of national vision,

*Ford was appointed to the vice presidency by Richard Nixon after Vice President Spiro T. Agnew was forced to resign when Agnew was indicted for criminal income tax evasion in 1973. One year later, Ford succeeded Nixon after Nixon was forced to resign under threat of impeachment.

and his brief transitional presidency served the country well in a difficult period.

That was not the case with Ronald Reagan, a strong president with wide public backing and a clear vision for America. But it was a do-nothing vision, according to which government was the problem, not even part of the solution. He exemplified the spirit of laissez-faire to an extent not seen since the Coolidge presidency in the Twenties. Let things take their natural course. Let the marketplace work its will without the stifling hand of regulation. Let there be an end to national planning and national goals, of social programs and political tinkering. Let individualism thrive.

Reagan's vision was not entirely wrong. Government cannot solve all of society's problems. It cannot change the human character, legislate morality, impose standards of thought and conduct by fiat. As the Founding Fathers understood, too much reliance on governmental solutions weakens the individual initiative essential to a self-governing society. The Founders also understood the wisdom of not acting precipitately or according to the dictates of the groups that shout loudest. At its best, Ronald Reagan's vision appealed to our desire for independence of action, our appreciation for entrepreneurship and risk-taking, our need to be free of oppressive bureaucrats and bureaucracy. He appealed to the traditional hunger of Americans to have mastery over their fate.

The problem was that his vision created the comfortable illusion that nothing *needed* to be done. All was well in America. In cases where it was not, society had no responsibility—indeed, no capacity—to find the remedy. And the ruins of the Great Society to some degree bore him out. Individuals—and minorities—and migrants—and cities—and the poor and the infirm and the dispossessed—should solve their own problems, as had Reagan's own family sixty years before. (They didn't, of course. Reagan's father benefited from the New Deal's Works Project Administration, which gave him a job.)

When carried to its extreme, as it was, Reagan's vision epitomized short-term thinking with long-term consequences. To a public weary from the exertions and heavy expenses of the Cold War, the frustrations of Vietnam and domestic strife, and the loss of leaders in the Sixties and Seventies who left a legacy of high hopes unfulfilled, his was a seductive vision: live for the moment, don't worry about tomorrow, because tomorrow surely will be better than today. America is number one and always will be.

It was especially appealing to a people whose mass culture intensified both a desire to "seize the day" and to escape—and it provided those opportunities to degrees never before experienced.

Through the constant media focus on today—not yesterday, not tomorrow—every issue was magnified and simplified. Politicians were under constant media pressure to respond immediately to short-term problems. And woe to them if they didn't; failure to react brought a chorus of media criticism. All this strengthened an already powerful American impatience, a characteristic that has always typified this restless nation.

Along with this attitude was a corresponding desire for escape. Through the expanding sports and entertainment business, whose stars were rewarded far more lavishly than the nation's scientists, teachers, and doctors; through the diversions of television and VCRs and Walkmen, Americans were able to retreat into their own worlds. They were *encouraged* to think that nothing needed to be done for their long-term future.

Herein lay the tragedy that paved the way for the problems of the Nineties. At a time when the nation was in the best position economically to begin dealing with long-term questions, it pursued a reckless and irresponsible policy of official passivity—of doing nothing.

Rhetoric aside, the nation developed no plans for conversion from defense to civilian needs; adopted no strategy to retrain workers and create jobs for a challenging economic future; launched no common effort to aid the cities, rebuild its deteriorating infrastructure of highways and bridges and water systems, restrict the growth of weaponry, or deal honestly with the problems of immigration, inner-city education, and abysmal public services.

Neither did it seriously address racial and ethnic polarization. It ignored signs of environmental dangers—disposal of nuclear waste, destruction of rain forests, depletion of the earth's ozone layer, over-development of coastal areas and floodplains. It also shamefully refused to join international efforts to control population growth in a world where famine and disease were rampant.

When America awoke from its slumber in the Eighties, it was to a world suddenly grown more menacing, and a world in which many of our comfortable assumptions no longer applied. Awareness that the recession represented more than a temporary, though difficult, passage struck with full force among people at all levels, from senior executives to blue-collar workers. New feelings of vulnerability, new uncertainties, abounded. As Chris Womack, a young black business-man in Birmingham, Alabama, put it, "There is no blueprint any-more. You can't just say, 'Okay, go to school, get a good job.' That's not a guarantee. You can't guarantee anybody anything anymore."

All these were among the consequences of America's failure to adopt long-range strategies to deal with what clearly were long-term economic and social problems. That was not the only failure. The public as well as the politicians had failed to insist on accountability for the short-sighted policies and actions that produced and exacer-bated the problems.

If the system had been working as it should, political parties and politicians would have been held accountable for their failure to stem the historic rising annual budget deficits and long-term escalating national debt. Despite repeated attempts by congressional leaders to check the hemorrhaging debt, the upward pressures continued year after year, administration after administration. Not since 1969 had any Congress or any president been able to balance the annual bud-get. The result, as we have seen, was an ever-rising price extracted from every American worker just to pay interest on his or her share of the federal government's debt.

Similar lack of accountability was responsible for other signs of political breakdown. For years, the government played a cynical game with the public in which major spending items totaling hun-dreds of billions of dollars (as in the savings and loan bailout) were declared "off budget" and therefore not accountable in legally re-quired actions to reduce the budget deficit through either spending cuts, increased taxes, or a combination of the two. So, too, growing surpluses accumulated in the Social Security trust funds have been used to hide the real deficit. Instead of preserving those funds, as was intended by law, for the large numbers of baby boomers when they reach retirement age in the next century, the federal government spends them to meet daily demands.

Real political accountability would have extracted a price for the

Housing and Urban Development scandals, for the failure to exercise proper oversight over the machinations of the Ivan Boeskys and Michael Milkens on Wall Street in the Eighties, for the savings and loan debacle and its raid on the federal treasury, and, perhaps even more dismaying, for the inability of political Washington to break the financial hold of lobbyists and political action groups that provide the immense sums needed to run for and hold public office.

For years, members of Congress have professed disgust with the necessity to raise campaign funds—a process that compels them to set the weekly schedule of Congress not by deliberation of issues but by political fund-raising. Congress normally schedules no votes on Mondays or Fridays so that the members can raise money at functions in the capital or in their home districts. Each campaign year requires greater amounts of campaign money.

In 1976, the average cost of winning a U.S. Senate seat was $600,000. By 1990, it was over $4 million—nearly a sevenfold increase in just fourteen years. In 1992, the cost continued to rise. A single congressional race in California, for instance, cost a challenger more than $1.5 million. Yet despite all the wailing about the grip of the "interests," neither party has acted to change the way this system operates. Nor, despite promises for real campaign reform by Clinton and Democrats in Congress, did the Democrats act either swiftly or decisively once they controlled both White House and Congress for the first time since the Jimmy Carter years.

Clinton's experience in attempting to fulfill his campaign reform promise typifies the difficulties of creating other fundamental changes. He did propose a bill that would restrict the influence of political action committees, but it fell far short of his public claim, at a televised Rose Garden ceremony when he made public his plan, that it would "change the way Washington works." First, the proposed legislation, if passed, would not even take effect until the 1996 elections. This example of Washington again putting off until tomorrow what needs to be done today came because Clinton's own Democratic Party, controlling both houses of Congress, wanted to maintain the advantages of incumbency. Incumbents benefit most, because they receive by far the greatest share of PAC contributions. Democratic members of the House of Representatives, who face election every two years and thus feel a more pressing need to raise money immediately for their reelection campaigns, were particularly insistent to move the effective time for the legislation to after their 1994 races. This was not the only concession wrung after months of private deliberations between the White House and Democratic leaders. Another concession was even more telling. Despite Clinton's campaign pledge to reduce from $5,000 to $1,000 the amount a PAC can give to a candidate, his proposed legislation kept the $5,000 amount for House members. The contribution limit for senators, who hold six-year terms, was lowered to $2,500.

The "reform" bill itself was riddled with other loopholes. Yet it did propose genuine changes that could lessen the power of the PACs. It sought to eliminate "soft money" in presidential campaigns—wealthy donors evade limits on direct contributions to presidential candidates by funneling their money through the political parties, who then legally make it available to the campaign committee. It offered public subsidies to defray the extraordinary expenses of TV commercials to those congressional candidates who adhered to voluntary spending limits of $600,000 established by the campaign reform bill. It also would provide similar federally financed vouchers to be used for postage and printing costs for candidates who accepted the same overall voluntary campaign spending limits. And, in a major breakthrough, Clinton proposed to prohibit lobbyists from giving money to any lawmaker they had lobbied within the previous twelve months.

Imperfect though Clinton's campaign reform proposal was, it did represent a serious attempt to make significant changes. Its outcome was uncertain, however, and the effects of the changes, even if all of it became law, would not be felt until after another election cycle.

At the same time, the special interests were demonstrating that their power remained great in Bill Clinton's "era of change." Virtually every one of his new proposals, from health care to new taxes on energy and Social Security benefits, attracted fierce lobbying opposition that imperiled them. Despite intense efforts to maintain a unified Democratic position in the face of already-successful Republican filibusters, Democratic ranks were sundered by all the old special-interest politics that had doomed other attempts at reform. Opposition from Democratic senators in oil-producing states to Clinton's energy tax threatened passage of his entire budget, and therefore his presi-

dency. Power of the "interests" was vividly displayed when Democratic congressmen and senators, reacting to middle-class anger at
new taxes, proposed shifting the burden from wealthier constituents
to poorer ones by placing a "cap" on spending for "entitlement"
programs such as unemployment, welfare, food stamps, and Medicaid.

This was only the latest example of the way in which powerful
narrow interests usually prevail over larger national ones. Another
classic example of the power of the lobbies to block the public interest involves gun control. Despite the rise of violence in American life,
not only daily shootings in the nation's cities but the assassination of
some of its most promising young leaders; despite the broadest public
consensus about the need to control the flow of weapons across
America; despite the new president's own strong support for such
controls, one lobby representing seventeen million Americans has
thwarted the vast majority that favors *real* gun control.

While the National Rifle Association (NRA) continues to have
sufficient power to defeat genuine legislation on this subject, America
experiences a mounting outflow of blood and the further sophisticated armament not of deer-hunting storekeepers but of Little Cae-
sars of the drug world and street-corner psychopaths. Anyone who
believes that all but a fraction of the 200 million and more weapons in
America are in responsible hands has not lived long in America. The
outrage this issue stirs was expressed memorably to me by Police
Chief Sweeney in Bridgeport.

"Gun control, as far as I am concerned, is all political bullshit,"
he said. "I've heard all the arguments espoused by people who want
the weapons removed from the street. And I've heard all the malar-
key from the NRA about 'punish the people who misuse the guns
and don't penalize the gun owners.' You've got an open sewer dumping guns on the streets of America with a lot of money and a lot of
competition to sell drugs. Why are you surprised there's violence?

"I've heard the same arguments since King and Kennedy were
assassinated in 1968, and the politicians haven't moved one iota to
choose either one of the two courses: punish the offender who uses
the gun or remove the guns. But stop talking. Pick one of them. Am I
optimistic they'll do either? No. 1990 was the bloodiest year in the
history of America, and I suspect that 1991 topped it, although I

haven't seen the final tally in that regard, and 1992 is sure well on the way."

Sweeney is one who acts as forcefully as he speaks. In the year after we met, he became a central player in a drive to ban semiautomatic assault rifles in Connecticut. As a result, he was denounced publicly as a "liar" by the state's largest gun owners' group. That charge came after Sweeney disputed the claim that the Sporter, a modified assault rifle made in Connecticut by Colt, was really not an assault weapon. Sporter bullets, he was tactless enough to point out, can rip through bulletproof vests and the officers behind them.

The Connecticut battle over gun control came when it looked as though the efforts of people like Sweeney were finally beginning to have an impact. The proposed Connecticut ban was the third major state battle the gun lobby faced, and it had lost the first two. First, in Virginia, the National Rifle Association failed to defeat a proposal by Governor Douglas Wilder to limit handgun purchases to one a month. Despite an aggressive campaign, the NRA suffered a second setback in New Jersey when it was unable to stop a ban against a more restricted definition of semiautomatic weapons. Connecticut ultimately dealt the NRA a third major defeat when the legislature passed the similar ban on semiautomatic rifle sales. These were hopeful signs, but, like the Clinton attempt to reform campaign financing, they were at best limited. So was the congressional legislation to require waiting periods for the purchase of handguns in order to allow police enough time to check criminal records—the "Brady Bill"—which, if passed intact, as Clinton urged it should be, would still not stop the flood of further weapons throughout America.*

The proliferation of these weapons and the ease with which they can be obtained are evident to anyone who turns on a daily TV newscast and hears of still more deaths from guns—to say nothing of

*In the closing hours of the 1993 congressional session the extraordinary power of the gun lobby was again demonstrated. After years of fruitless debate and rising national concern over murders related to handguns, a Republican Senate filibuster once more blocked the passage of the Brady Bill. The impasse continued even after Republican moderates shifted votes to send the measure to a joint House-Senate conference. Yet again, agreement could not be reached. Sarah Brady, wife of James Brady and leader of Handgun Control Inc., said that she had "never seen such obstructionism," adding bitterly: "This is gridlock at its worst." Finally, with nearly all members of Congress absent, the Brady Bill was passed. Clinton signed it into law November 30, 1993.

a Branch Davidian cult in Texas that is able to amass an armory of high-powered deadly weapons. A vivid example of the difficulty in achieving strong measures to stop the mayhem caused by guns came toward the end of Clinton's first year when Congress began deliberating on his health care reform plan. Daniel Patrick Moynihan, chairman of the powerful Senate Finance Committee which will have a major role in the outcome of the health legislation, attempted to link its passage with a huge increase in federal taxes—in certain cases as high as 10,000 percent—on handgun ammunition. Moynihan's idea was to make the cost of obtaining particularly lethal ammunition prohibitive, saying, sensibly: "Guns don't kill people, bullets do. It is time the federal government began taxing handgun ammunition used in crime out of existence."

Immediately, his proposal was derided as "laughable" by the NRA. Within twenty-four hours, Democratic leaders of the House let it be known they would not support Moynihan's idea, thereby demonstrating anew the reluctance of national legislators to confront such a powerful interest as the gun lobby. Once again, Moynihan's was a lonely voice in trying to focus national attention on the causes of underlying social problems, and once again his call was not heeded, further adding to public frustration with the performance of political leaders on such a critical issue.

The ability of the gun lobby to withstand national campaigns backed by the great majority of Americans mocks the power of the people to force change on a major national issue. As such, it creates greater pressure for more radical attempts to "change the system."

Public indignation already exists over perceived abuses of an all-incumbent Congress. It is this growing resentment that produced widespread public anger against special privileges enjoyed on Capitol Hill, where lawmakers seemed able to bank without paying fees or being penalized if they wrote bad checks. Out of such abuses came the national term-limitation movement, which coincided with the desire for change at all levels of leadership.

Strong anti-incumbent feelings were expressed by voters in 1992 (and again in 1993), resulting in the greatest turnover of members of Congress through resignation or defeat since 1948. Term-limitation initiatives on state ballots uniformly passed across the nation. The movement itself continues to gain in strength in the Clinton presidency (and did again in the elections of 1993). It is a terrible idea, for it penalizes the best and most experienced legislators and would mean that unelected staff people and consultants inevitably would have even *greater* influence over congressional action than those elected under the present system. But it has powerful appeal to citizens who feel, rightly, that their system has been neither accountable nor responsive.

Just as Ross Perot casts a long shadow—or the specter of more protest movements led by outsiders like him—over American politics, the term-limitation movement represents another sign of Americans' unhappiness with their political system and growing desire to change it.

These are among the many reasons the political system remains under siege. A more elemental one involves the public conviction that the American political system has produced a generation of politicians in both parties who can't, or won't, tell the truth, because if they do, they will not win; and that lies permeate American politics.

It is a harsh indictment, unfair in many individual cases and probably among a majority of all public servants, but there is enough truth to give it special force. The problem goes beyond individual politicians. At least since the Sixties, and certainly in many cases before, the government has increasingly turned to falsehoods to buttress its official positions. Much of this stemmed from fears of espionage and uninformed public reactions during the Cold War, and indeed in the years before Pearl Harbor, when clandestine international operations also flourished. Maintaining security to protect these covert operations and safeguard lives was essential. But inevitably there were excesses. As the Cold War lengthened and the National Security State became more of a power unto itself, governmental secrecy became more pronounced. Increasingly officials covered up their mistakes by classifying actions they launched or policies they approved as "top secret." There were gross examples of manipulation of facts and outright lying: the false CIA estimates of the Soviet economic and military threat in the 1950s that influenced American policymakers and resulted in needless expenditure of money for defense;* the false official accounts of the 1964 Tonkin

---

*Democratic Senator Daniel Patrick Moynihan of New York was again a lonely voice trying to call national attention to this historic false estimate through sparsely attended Senate hearings. See Moynihan's book *Pandemonium* (New York: Oxford University Press, 1993).

Gulf incident that became the rationale for greater U.S. involvement in Vietnam; the false Pentagon reports that "we're winning the war," complete with body counts to prove it; the daily lies put forth by the White House month after month during the Watergate cover-up; the concerted lying about the arms-for-hostages deals made by senior officials of the Reagan administration in sworn testimony to Congress during the Iran-Contra affair.

By the Nineties, the public had either become so conditioned to the Cold War arguments of officials about the need for greater secrecy and security—or so cynical about government officials—that there was little outcry over the spread of absurdly high and overcomprehensive classifications of public documents. In the past, Americans had reacted with outrage to governmental attempts to operate in secret. If they are not docile toward such bad habits of the state, Americans now tend more to see excessive security classification as not that significant, given the range of their other concerns; and besides, they will say, you can't trust government anyway, so why should you be surprised that officials try to cover their tracks or lie?*

No small part of the problem involved in individual political lies and incomplete, misleading statements stems from the increasingly combative tone of political discourse and the often hostile nature of journalistic reporting that assumes—and implies—the worst about the politician or the candidate. Political commercials assault character and distort issues and records and force the opposing candidate to respond in kind. All this places special pressures on the political candidate. While much of the public reacts with disgust to assault tactics, the sad truth is that in many cases they work. The liars—and the campaign consultants who devise the strategies and are paid handsomely for them—are rewarded by winning the most votes.

As an example of how strongly some people from within the system itself feel about this subject, consider the indignant comments of the first person I met on my journey, Jim Tierney of Topsham, Maine, as optimistic, thoughtful, and informed a person as you will meet.

Tierney's decade as attorney general of Maine earned him bipartisan respect for honorable conduct and dedication to public service.

---

*Clinton did make a welcome beginning in much expanding the declassification of government records, but his action attracted relatively little public notice.

So when he expresses a passionate conviction that American politics are permeated by a culture of lies, one listens. When he says lies, he doesn't mean evasions or sugar-coating or creating of illusions or falsehoods uttered in an attempt to lift people's spirits in a time of crisis. Those have been the staples of American politics—of representative government—throughout American history. He means deliberate, repeated public falsehoods.

"I'm talking about flat-out lies," he says. "Saying to people there isn't a budget deficit when there is. Saying that you are for something when you're not. Saying that the umpteen thousand dollars you took from a contributor didn't influence your judgment, when you were signed, sealed and delivered. . . . I mean, there are just flat-out untruths, because a successful career is defined in terms of being elected at any cost and reelected at any cost. To that degree the increased cynicism is well learned by the people. I mean, I share it and a lot of other people share it for good reason. Truth is not rewarded. My basic belief—and it pains me a great deal to say this—is that you've got to lie to get elected. I talked to a former governor of a nearby state about this last week and he said, 'You can't win without lying.' Flat out! 'You can't win without lying.' Former governor of a state. And that's true. If you're campaigning, you've got to tell senior citizens that you're going to pay their bills. You're not going to say, 'Listen, I'll be honest with you. Senior citizens are getting a disproportionate share of the budget pie compared with children, and if we really care about our future we're going to have to do something about that.' No politician in America will say that, but it's clearly true. That would infuriate people. And so it goes on and on. You can be a radical left-winger in a primary and be a conservative in the general election. You can do it in a matter of weeks, and many do.

"What candidate dares to run on his *real* record, even if it's a very solid record? In order to win, you have to attack the system. So you attack the system, you lessen the respect anyone has for it, you make it more impossible to build bridges and build coalitions and actually resolve the social problems. Then you lay wire on top of that and you've got yourself a serious breed of new politicians."

Therein, as Tierney sees it, lies the greatest danger.

"It's very scary, because what you're really taking apart is the ability to solve problems," he says. "If you develop a generation of elected officials who can only face the voters with nontruths and attacking the very system of which they are a part, then how do you do what has to be done?"

That last point is most serious, for it touches on perhaps the most significant failure of the political system—the public misunderstanding of the ways the American system was *designed* to operate as opposed to the way people think it *should* function.

As Berkeley political scientist Bruce Cain points out, what political scientists define as good politics—indeed, essential politics—is the ability of opposing camps to sit down and forge common interests through debate and arduous efforts to arrive at consensus. Americans increasingly do the opposite. They attempt to resolve questions by taking them to the courts instead of permitting the political system to solve them. Thus, litigation strategies replace political strategies; too often, conflict rather than compromise is the chosen political path. A large, politicized middle class has acquired a taste for both denunciatory and "feel-good" politics: Norman Mailer did not run for mayor of New York in vain. The media reward such postures. The pressure to compromise, arising out of the clash of material interests, is trumped by more special individual or group demands. The result is further divisiveness, more hardened positions among competing groups, less willingness to yield. Thus: more division.

All of which leads to what Cain calls the decline of effective politics through greater polarization on issues dividing public life, a polarization in which well-financed groups representing sharply differing ideological positions dominate the increasingly rancorous debates. At the most extreme are groups of true believers so convinced of the rightness of their causes—and of their right to impose their beliefs on others—that they take matters in their own hands. In the Sixties, this mentality led to the bombing of draft offices and ROTC units. In the Nineties, it led to the murder of a Florida doctor who performed legal abortions at a public clinic after that doctor's photograph was distributed on a "Wanted" poster by anti-abortionists, and to the spiking of trees to damage saws and milling machinery, if not injure loggers.

Two other factors exert powerful influence over political life and American attitudes in the Nineties: the electronic media revolution, which heightens and quickens all conflicts and offers symbols over substance; and the public's woeful misconception of how their system was designed to operate.

"People confuse the lack of consensus with the breakdown of the system," Cain says. "They don't understand that the system is designed to operate a certain way when there is disagreement—namely, that it's designed *not* to do anything. We regard that as a good feature of the system rather than lurching ahead when there's no agreement. It's an especially good way to operate when you have a big society with so many different groups of people in it. So there's a misunderstanding about the system that is *extremely* frustrating.

"I work with editorial boards to try and head off ill-considered attempts at reform, and I am getting very disillusioned. There are strategic manipulators of the parties who see short-term political gain from their 'reform' ideas, and they're abetted by people who write op-ed pieces. So I see enormous frustration among political scientists who are concerned about the present assaults on the political system. I'm not sure what we can do about it. A lot of public education about how the political system works is out of our hands. We get students for a couple of classes when they're in the university. After that, they basically get their understanding of the system from talk radio stations. There are so many other outlets that purport to teach people about the system."

And those outlets, as he says, are increasingly dominated by the whoever-talks-the-loudest form of political discourse that passes for serious discussion of complicated issues—or, worse, by the intolerant ideologues so certain of their causes that they are willing to silence dissent by whatever means necessary.

Cain is correct about the failure to educate Americans about the true nature of their system. For years, public opinion surveys have shown that Americans would not pass their Bill of Rights if it were put to a present vote. That suggests only one more reason to beware of Ross Perot's proposal to conduct instantaneous electronic "town hall" democracy sessions. In these, citizens meeting in public forums "vote" by pushing buttons allegedly to let their representatives know what they want them to do. Thus issues inevitably would be decided by passions of the moment instead of by the serious analysis of the best experts available. Qualification and compromise are strangers to this new "talk-show democratic" system; they are undercut by new push-button sovereignty and fly against the very reason for constitutional democracy. Constitutions are about giving room for second thoughts, for deliberation, for due process. A century and a half ago, with the coming of the first instantaneous electronic device, the telegraph, Thoreau asked what would happen if Maine should be able to speak to Texas but have nothing to say. As it turned out, they had too much to say to each other but little grounds for agreement as the slavery and secession arguments were rapidly transmitted throughout the nation. Now, in the new era of vastly swifter instantaneous mass communication, Perot, a Texan if ever there was one, wants the whole country to speak out at once, possibly drowning out hard-won sense in short-term clamor.

That this idea strikes many as appealing—proof of grass-roots democracy at work in the electronic-talk-show age—is all the more cause for concern. It underscores the appalling lack of understanding of why and how the American system was designed, and for what purpose. In my experience, even presumably well-educated people often do not appreciate why that system was fashioned to check the excesses of the majority while at the same time guaranteeing majority rule; to place numerous checks on the potential abuses of power whether in the legislature, the executive, or the judiciary; to attempt to protect the citizens in their communities and states from the oppression of a federal government by making the powers of that government few and defined while those of the states numerous and undefined; to make the great end of justice the substitution of the notion of right for that of violence; to seek always to reduce the dangerous factions that might destroy the democratic experiment; and, finally, to ensure that the real strength of the nation be vested not in the federal government but in the local ones.

In recent years some of the most creative aspects of American government have taken place at state levels. Governors have had to deal with the basic problems that affect people's lives—schools, police, fire, welfare, public health, parks and playgrounds—and with raising taxes to support all these. They have done so amid the most difficult constraints since the Great Depression while required by their state constitutions to balance their budgets. As a group, they have had to be ingenious problem-solvers. Bill Clinton emerged on the national scene out of that background, and with a solid record of achievement in education reform and job creation accomplished in a poor state with a legislature historically dominated by major interest groups.

At the same time, the successes of state and local governments and of community-involvement movements across the nation do not hide their failures. The weaknesses of local government are all too evident, as seen in the failure of communities to provide adequate funds; in the public indifference—as in Lowell, Massachusetts—to the cutting of services vital in the long term but prompting instant anger if trash is not picked up; in the kind of middle-class denial that leads the citizens of Arlington, Texas, to reject school bond issues that would assist minority students; in the polemical disputes entangling an Oakland, California, so mired in political correctness debates that its school board could not agree on choosing history textbooks to the point that fourth-, fifth-, and sixth-grade students had none; in the scare politics of some racial and ethnic groups that find inflaming new hostilities easier and more rewarding—for the moment—than seeking to achieve consensus to deal with the most basic concerns.

One of the most serious failures, already noted, is the growing division between cities and suburbs, leaving the cities poorer and burdened with higher taxes and fewer services while the wealthier suburbs enjoy lower taxes and better services. It is a condition ripe for revolt—and more violence. Once again, Bridgeport, Connecticut, provides an unenviable, but common, example.

"The legislature and the Congress are controlled by the people who live in the suburbs," says Lawrence Merly, for four years Bridgeport's city attorney. "The political power structure, the economic power structure, the judicial power structure lie in the suburbs. They pass the laws and they set the policy. They tell us we should have such things as welfare, public housing. They tell us the levels of welfare. They tell us all social institutions that ought to exist. They tell us how we can raise money in the city—and the only way we can raise money in the city is with property taxes—and then they exclude from their own residential communities all of the things that they create.

"So they force all of the poor, the public housing, the welfare, the social institutions into the city on tax-exempt property, which means

that the rest of the properties have to subsidize it. The heavy concen-
tration of the poor people in the public housing breeds crime, drugs,
burnt-out neighborhoods. It damages the image of the city, it dis-
courages development, it lowers the quality of life. Literally, we are
driving out the middle class. It looks like we're making these cities
sacrificial areas for society."

The need for a regional approach is obvious, and efforts along
those lines are being attempted in various places. Still, divisions at
the local level remain largely unresolved problems for an American
political system plagued by similar divisions in its national legislature.

In a dour mood during the forging of the Union, John Adams
wrote to John Taylor of Caroline: "Remember, democracy never
lasts long. It soon wastes, exhausts, and murders itself. There never
was a democracy yet that did not commit suicide."

What Adams and the Founders feared most was the power of
"faction," the eighteenth-century term for the passion of narrow interests that operate against the common good. If anything, factions
pose greater difficulties in late-twentieth-century America. They are
better organized, better financed, better skilled at the politics of persuasion through pressure. That's especially so in an electronic age
when public response can be mobilized instantly through nationwide
computer networks and the assistance of call-in radio or TV shows,
all of which can result in the flooding of congressional offices with
expressions of mass support for or against specific bills, policies, and
nominees to high positions. Clinton found this to be a major problem
in the plucking apart of his legislative proposals by organized lobbyists in such battles as raising taxes on energy and Social Security
benefits, and in the overnight collapse of support for his first attorney
general–designate, Zoë Baird, whose nomination evaporated after a
storm of popular opposition, engineered in large part through the
talk-show call-ins, broke over Capitol Hill and the White House.

Clinton was also bedeviled by another old problem of presidents:
that of dealing with the mass media. Relations between political leaders and the press have always been, at best, adversarial, and, more
often, hostile, as the experience of the nation's first three chief executives demonstrates. Washington went to his grave despising the ex-

cesses of the press. John Adams shared these feelings. Even Jefferson, whom journalists quote approvingly for his oft-cited remark that given a choice between having a government without a press or a press without a government, he would prefer the latter, came to a very different view of the press once he became president. In office, he bitterly resented its excesses and falsehoods, and he mused about the proper form of punishment that could be meted out to this turbulent estate, concluding that perhaps the best remedy would be the contempt in which his fellow citizens would ultimately come to hold it.

Nor did Jefferson nurse these resentments privately; he took them directly to the people. In his second inaugural address, this architect of American liberty and exponent of the press's constitutionally protected liberties said: "During the course of this administration, and in order to disturb it, the artillery of the press has been levelled against us, charged with whatsoever its licentiousness could devise or dare. These abuses of an institution so important to freedom and science, are deeply to be regretted, inasmuch as they tend to lessen its usefulness, and to sap its safety; they might, indeed, have been corrected by the wholesome punishments reserved and provided by the laws of the several States against falsehood and defamation; but public duties more urgent press on the time of public servants, and the offenders have therefore been left to find their punishment in the public indignation."

With the emergence of television, with its emphasis upon the immediate quick point, and amid a briar patch of doubts about presidential credibility sowed during the Vietnam-Watergate-Reagan years, by the time Clinton became president media/executive relations were more difficult, and, in Clinton's case, more complex. During his presidential campaign, Clinton and his aides had deeply resented the extensive media exposure given women who claimed to have had sexual relationships with him, thus raising the "character issue" more than with any president since Grover Cleveland, who was accused of fathering an illegitimate child while in the White House. Even more than usual, press coverage of Clinton exhibited the deepest ambivalence. At times during his campaign, defeat for Clinton was predicted by a broad spectrum of leading Washington commentators and analysts. Then, when he demonstrated remarkable staying power, Clinton was hailed for his resourcefulness, his tenacity, his political talent—so much so that George Bush and his campaign operatives bitterly accused the press of open partisanship.

Clinton faced another media problem. In the communications age, with national coverage of presidential campaigns beginning at least two years before the election, increasing press attention is paid to the candidates and to the pollsters and consultants who devise the daily strategies that enable their player to maintain a lead by counter-punching a rival. Even more than in the past, the emphasis is on *now*—today's polls, today's charge, today's counterattack. The up-and-down rhythms of the permanent campaign carry over into the presidency, and are magnified by the size of a media corps whose members both compete for a distinctive angle on the inside workings of a new administration and simultaneously are more removed from the actual operations of the new presidential team—indeed, more removed from the vast, intricate government as a whole and, except only in most special cases, from the president himself. All this strengthens the already-noted short-term mentality that drives the news business, especially in an age when coverage of personality— and specifically the presidency—takes precedence over institutional reporting of government and other complicated issues.

The same wild swings characterized Clinton's coverage once he was in office, veering between adulation and antagonism, praise and ridicule, one endlessly following on the heels of the other. Even before he was inaugurated, at a time when his cabinet and White House appointment process seemed to lag, the press was debating whether "the honeymoon was over." Barely in office a week, with the gays-in-the-military and Zoë Baird issues dominating the news, Clin-ton and his new operatives were derided as "the gang that couldn't shoot straight" and as political professionals who "didn't know how to play the game." A mere *two days* after his inauguration, NBC's Lisa Myers told network viewers: "From up close, the Clinton White House has looked like the 'Not-Ready-for-Prime-Time Players.' " One day later, Fred Barnes crowed on *The McLaughlin Group:* "He hit the ground backpedaling." After his nationally televised eco-nomic message to Congress led to swift enactment of the general—as it proved, *very* general—framework of his four-year budget propos-als, Clinton was hailed in the press as one of the most skillful politi-cians Washington had seen in years, master of all he surveyed, a new king of Congress, destroyer of gridlock. This, of course, was followed by increasingly negative coverage as, first, his stimulus proposal was stymied by Republican resistance and his own missteps, and then the overall economic program came under open attack from his own party in both House and Senate.

The New Yorker, addressing the latest stampede of journalistic herd mentality at work in the volatile first spring of Clinton's presidency commented: "During the last few weeks, Americans have had a chance to witness one of those great migrations of columnists, reporters, anchors, commentators, and guest experts which are the media world's answer to the wildebeests crossing the plains of Africa. When it began, we were just getting used to the idea of a new President with some new ideas, and our opinion-molders, like the country at large, seemed unsure where they stood. By the time their journey was over, they had arrived at a place where they looked more comfortable: confident unanimity. Bill Clinton, we were told by authorities too numerous to mention, had bungled things—bungled them so badly that, according to Ted Koppel on *Nightline,* the question being asked by 'Washington insiders' (a group not easily distinguished from those who, like Koppel, report on them) was whether his problems were 'still soluble.' " The magazine concluded: "A four-year term may seem very short when it's measured against the problems facing the country, but four years is nowhere near short enough, evidently, for many of those who cover our government for a living. To judge by their current fixation on how, rather than what, the President is doing, they want to turn every year into an election year."

Clinton compounded his problems. On the very day after his inauguration, the White House press corps was enraged to discover that the door from their briefing room to the press secretary's office had been barred to them for the first time in more than thirty years, and perhaps ever—an action taken on the advice of the outgoing Bush team in order to protect the comings and goings of senior officials who had found themselves facing unwanted questions in the corridors.

On its face, this was a frivolous issue. It would not stop the media from doing their job, as some journalists claimed, although it would be more constrictive; but it was a needless decision by the Clinton group that produced ill will, guaranteeing more critical coverage and underscoring the wisdom of Walter Mondale's observation that Clinton needed to be served by people of tested White House experience. In fact, a similar proposal had been made when Ronald Reagan took office, and it was agreed to by Reagan's principal image-maker, Michael Deaver. In recalling that incident after the Clinton imbroglio, Deaver told me how he had mentioned his intention to Reagan's then chief of staff, James F. Baker, later Reagan's treasury secretary and Bush's secretary of state. Baker, who had served in the Ford and Nixon White House and run Reagan's presidential election campaign, immediately vetoed the idea: it would needlessly alienate the press and rebound against the president. The idea was quietly dropped.

Far more damaging were two episodes likely to have more lasting public impact. Just when Clinton was again attempting to regain the initiative over his economic program and reverse the slide in his public ratings, it was disclosed that his plane had been held for forty minutes at Los Angeles International Airport so that the president could have his hair cut by a Hollywood barber who charged members of the public $200 for the service. While Cristophe of Beverly Hills cut the presidential hair, planes seeking to land at LAX reportedly were forced to circle the airport awaiting the presidential departure. (In fact, as *Newsday* reported months later after examining airport records, they were *not,* but this fact came too late to undo the damage.)

No sooner had that incident drawn intensive press criticism, prompting jokes about "Hairforce One" on late-night TV and giving columnists like William Safire of *The New York Times* rich material for satires about "Scalpgate," than ever sourer commentary arose after the White House announced it had fired all seven members of its travel office. They were career employees, and some had worked for presidents for thirty years. The travel office handles arrangements for members of the press accompanying the president. The official reason was the discovery of mismanagement and even perhaps criminality in the office's operations. In place of the veteran staff, all of whom serve "at the pleasure of the president," a new team headed by a distant cousin of Clinton's was chosen; and the new travel agency to be used was an Arkansas one that had served the Clinton presidential campaign. This led to a real fiasco when it was swiftly revealed that the cousin had written a memo two months earlier recommending elimination of the old team, in part because they were "pro-press," and the appointment of herself and other Clinton supporters to take over the operation. Worse, another memo came to light showing that a Hollywood producer friend of the president's, Harry Thomason, who had staged the nationally televised Clinton pre-inaugural events and whose interests included a travel agency of his own, sought to open the White House travel business to other bidders, including the firm in which he was an investor. The Clinton team made a bad matter infinitely worse by bypassing the attorney general and seeking to have the FBI give color to the purge by documenting illegality.

Red meat for the press: intimations of venality, abuse of power, cover-up. In the frenzied reporting, the CBS Evening News posed a correspondent reporting the latest on "travelgate" as he stood before the Watergate. Then, as if the invidious linkage to a true national scandal were not clear enough, the network news program went on to interview people who had figured in the Nixon White House crisis that actually destroyed a presidency. On that same broadcast, the CBS correspondent obligatorily noted that "travelgate isn't Watergate"; but the clear impression left was otherwise.

Measured against the great issues facing the nation, from the economy and crime to Russia and Bosnia, these were hardly matters of major significance. Yet they represented much more than a public relations disaster, striking sharply at both the president's judgment and that of his aides, planting new questions about his character and believability, and inspiring new feelings of distrust at the very moment when the public was becoming more skeptical of the not-quite-so-fresh face and his ability to fulfill his many ambitious promises. The drumbeat of critical reports, prompting such things as a *Time* magazine cover with bold headlines proclaiming "the incredible shrinking presidency" hanging over a diminished figure of President Clinton, came amid poll results showing Clinton holding the lowest public approval ratings of *any* of his presidential predecessors at that point in office. Everywhere, news reports trumpeted another "failed presidency." A "Style" article by Joel Achenbach in the *Washington Post* was typical. Under the headline "Just Another Failed Presidency?" the reporter breathlessly (and embarrassingly) wrote: "Almost everyone in town is wondering the same thing: Will this be just another failed presidency? It's the word every Democrat fears. Failed! It has haunted and mocked so many recent inhabitants of the Oval Office. Failed! . . ." Editorials questioned whether Clinton could survive. One such report I heard speculated that Clinton would not even last out his first term.

It was against this background that the president brought aboard David Gergen, a key "image maker" in three Republican administrations (Nixon's, Ford's, Reagan's), to assume the strategic role held by Clinton's young communications director, the thirty-two-year-old George Stephanopoulos. Gergen was assigned even greater responsibilities as a counselor to Clinton and given the task of attempting to quell not only critical coverage but the increasing public skepticism. His appointment did not end Clinton's problems. Within days after the president announced Gergen's return to the White House, in a nationally televised event with the new veteran at his side, an even more damaging episode occurred.

For weeks, while Clinton and his staff struggled to win passage of his budget in the House of Representatives, opposition had been mounting on another front. On April 29, Clinton had nominated Lani Guinier, a black woman and career civil rights lawyer, to head the Justice Department's Civil Rights Division. Guinier, a professor at the University of Pennsylvania, had come under sustained right-wing criticism as a racial radical—a "Quota Queen," one conservative political activist called her—who was antidemocratic and whose legal writings branded her as an advocate of special racial treatment and entitlement. The White House failed to respond to these well-orchestrated attacks, in part because Guinier was a good friend of both President Clinton and his wife, Hillary. The Clintons had been her classmates at Yale Law School, had attended her wedding, were well acquainted with her character and, it was assumed, her legal credentials. Nor did Clinton aides charged with "vetting" this nomination raise alarms after reading Guinier's law-journal articles. But these were also being circulated to members of Congress, the press, and other interest groups by some of the same right-wing organizations that had defended Robert Bork in his failed Supreme Court nomination fight and Clarence Thomas in his tumultuous passage to confirmation. When it became clear—as it turned out, too late—that

Guinier was in serious trouble on Capitol Hill, and not least among some Democrats whose support Clinton desperately needed for other battles, the White House began to leak news that the president would withdraw the nomination. But no action was taken. Nor would Guinier go quietly, as the White House wished. Stung by her portrayal as a radical racial polarizer and determined to answer back, she wanted nothing less than the opportunity to defend her reputation and competence in hearings such as those accorded to Robert Bork and Clarence Thomas.

She did not get it, and in the single most humiliating moment of his presidency, Clinton was forced to announce from the White House in prime time that he was regretfully withdrawing her nomination. Only after reading her articles *that* day, he said, had he concluded that her views about race and democracy did not entirely reflect his.

Immediately, he came under the most severe criticism, this time from some of his strongest supporters. Civil rights groups, liberals, blacks in Congress and throughout the country, women's organizations still upset by the mishandling of the earlier Zoë Baird and Kimba Wood nominations, liberals—all were outraged and accused Clinton of betraying a friend and not standing by someone he had praised publicly only weeks before. Some accused him of cowardice and of caving in under pressure.

Exacerbating Clinton's problems was the contrast between his actions and those of Guinier. In a televised press conference at the Justice Department, she defended herself with disturbing eloquence. In a low-keyed but strong manner she insisted she had never been in favor of quotas, and never could be. She declared her commitment to civil rights, to democratic fair play, to cross-racial coalition-building, and to a vision of an integrated legislature "where all of its members work together for the common good." Refuting her critics—and implicitly the president—she said: "I have always believed in democracy, and nothing I have ever written is inconsistent with that. I have always believed in one man, one vote, and nothing I have ever written is inconsistent with that. I have always believed in fundamental fairness, and nothing I have ever written is inconsistent with that. I am a democratic idealist who believes that politics need not be forever seen as an 'I win, you lose' dynamic in which some people are permanent monopoly winners and others are permanent, excluded losers. Everything I have written is consistent with that."

And she left with words that will linger after her: "I hope that what has happened to my nomination does not mean that future nominees will not be allowed to explain their views as soon as controversy arises. I hope that we are not witnessing the dawning of a new intellectual orthodoxy in which thoughtful people can no longer debate provocative ideas without denying the country their talents as public servants. I also hope that we can learn some positive lessons from this experience, lessons about the importance of public dialogue on race in which all perspectives are represented and in which no one viewpoint monopolizes, distorts, caricatures, or shapes the outcome."

With the Guinier episode, Clinton had succeeded in raising the heat of every possible group of supporter—conservatives, moderates, liberals, minorities, women. Coming after all the other missteps and the repeated promises to regain "focus" and to reshuffle the staff, the handling of this case embarrassingly demonstrated how few clear lessons had been learned. Poll ratings plummeted even further; but even so, Americans said they still believed in giving him more time to prove his capacity for leadership. Once more, Clinton made a "beginning." He bargained openly with Democratic senators to gain their support for his budget proposals, and accepted a new formula to cut spending by every dollar that taxes were raised—by further compromising on his energy tax proposals and by postponing public consideration of his still-uncompleted health care plan. Attempts were made to bridge the gap between Clinton and the press. Gergen ordered that the door to the press secretary's office be reopened, and called it, somewhat too obviously, the turning of a new page. Attempts to turn other new pages were made through more staff changes and new outreach to Congress. At the same time there were renewed criticisms and repeated assertions of a failed presidency—a presidency only months old and one not beset by a calamity like a Bay of Pigs or a Watergate break-in or the commitment of troops to an unending war. Problems notwithstanding, there was little acknowledgment of his attempt to address major issues that had not been dealt with for years, or decades.

Clinton's difficulties began to take on a familiar pattern. Even when his decisions proved to be right, the process by which he arrived at them reinforced the impression of White House disorganization and presidential vacillation. This was forcefully demonstrated in the process of replacing the retiring Justice Byron R. White.

Filling a Supreme Court vacancy is the single most significant appointment of a president, the one with the greatest potential for long-lasting effect on the nation, the one that most often outlasts a president's time in office. Clinton's opportunity was even more significant than usual. Not for twenty-six years had a Democratic president had such a chance. In those intervening years, the court process had become bitterly politicized, especially during the Reagan and Bush presidencies, when strongly ideological justices went on the bench. Two months after Clinton became president, Justice White announced his intent to retire at the end of that court term. White, who had been appointed to the court by John F. Kennedy in 1962, said he was making his plans known to give the new president ample time to fill his seat. Clinton welcomed the opportunity, saying publicly that he intended to nominate someone of such distinction and public prominence that Americans would respond by saying "Wow!" and acclaim his choice as having been the equivalent of hitting a home run.

But once again, the Clinton nomination process became bogged down in self-inflicted controversy. Three months later, with the court term nearing its end, the president still had not made his choice. Taking time was not the problem. The problem was that the White House publicly floated names and then, as in the Guinier, Baird, and Wood cases, humiliatingly abandoned them after questions arose about them. Here the president was initially rebuffed by Governor Mario Cuomo of New York and then turned down by former governor Richard Riley of South Carolina, his education secretary. Next the White House let it be known that the president's preferred choice was former Arizona governor Bruce Babbitt, by now secretary of the interior. Babbitt wanted the job, believed he had it, and let friends know it. But after a week in which Babbitt, like Guinier and the others, was left dangling alone in full public glare, Clinton dropped him in the face of threats of Republican opposition on the grounds that he was too political a choice and after protests from environmental groups that he was too valuable in his present position.

With the clock now ticking rapidly, Clinton's aides surfaced the name of the next leading contender, Federal Judge Stephen G. Breyer of Boston. Amid intense public attention, White House aides accompanied the judge from Boston to Washington for a meeting with Clinton. Here, it seemed, was the perfect choice, a judge hailed by Republican conservatives and Democratic liberals, someone with wide Washington experience as staff director of the Senate Judiciary Committee and distinguished service on the bench. The judge, who was literally escorted to Washington from the hospital bed where he was recovering from a traffic accident, stayed in the capital with friends after his meeting with Clinton, drafting an acceptance speech. But once more, a last-minute problem arose—and one that stirred all the memories of past appointment disasters. It turned out that the judge had failed to pay Social Security taxes for a household worker. The White House knew this when aides brought him to Washington and did not consider it to be nearly as serious as the earlier incidents. But in the end, Breyer was abandoned as the president stunned the capital by naming someone he had previously considered and rejected, and whom he had met only the day before his choice was announced—Ruth Bader Ginsburg, a federal appeals court judge in Washington, D.C.

As it turned out, Clinton made a superb choice. Judge Ginsburg was, as he said accurately in naming her, a legal pioneer, a distinguished jurist who had played a major role in expanding the rights of women. But at the same time, Clinton allowed needless public controversy to seep through his appointment process, leaving many of those involved bitter and initially detracting from the larger good he eventually achieved. It was a pattern that kept plaguing the president as he struggled in his early months to set the correct course. Bill Clinton did the right thing in the wrong way.

A deeper problem was reemerging, one that long predated the television age and its swift spreading of new and often critical public impressions which have lingered long enough to blast many a useful career. That is what Charles Dickens described as the single greatest national character flaw of the Americans he met during his long journey throughout America in the 1840s: "Universal Distrust." To Dickens, herein lay the "one great blemish in the popular mind of America, the prolific parent of an innumerable brood of evils" and a danger for the future. He concluded his memorable *American Notes,* speaking in friendly warning to Americans whom he otherwise much admired:

> "You carry," says the stranger, "this jealousy and distrust into every transaction of public life. . . . It has rendered you so fickle, and so given to change, that your inconstancy has passed into a proverb; for you no sooner set up an idol firmly, than you are sure to pull it down and dash it into fragments. . . . Any man who attains a high place among you, from the President downward, may date his downfall from that moment. . . ."

Whether the ancient cycle was renewing itself, whether a fickle public was beginning to look elsewhere for change, perhaps paving the way for another outsider like Ross Perot, could not be known. As Clinton ended his first presidential year, his popularity was rising and there was a record of significant achievement. But the elements were there, threatening the promise of another presidency and suggesting that our political system continues to face turmoil and division.

CHAPTER 15

LEADERS:
THE REFORMER

It was late afternoon of an August day and, as usual, the president was behind schedule—first thirty minutes, then an hour, then nearly an hour and a half. Twice he started toward the local and national officials, assorted politicians, admirals and generals, cabinet officers, members of his personal staff, and other invited guests who formed a long line before Air Force One at the Alameda Naval Air Station in Oakland, California. Each time, he turned back for a final word and a handshake with police officers and others who had escorted him, reaching out endlessly, it seemed, for one last personal encounter.

The president was about to begin his first real vacation in four years. It was sorely needed. No president in the modern era had experienced so many difficulties during the critical first phase of his term. None, at a comparable time nearly seven months in office, ranked lower in the public opinion polls that constantly track the standing of a president. Nearly half of Americans had a negative view of Clinton's performance, while only 44 percent polled gave him favorable ratings. Not only was the public more negative toward the president's leadership, attitudes about the future were again becoming more despairing. After he had been in office only five months, one national poll (*Washington Post*/ABC News) found that 56 percent of voters interviewed across the country agreed with the statement "The problems this country faces today are so large that no president could do much to solve them." In the ten years that this question had been asked, the response to it in the summer of 1993 was the most pessimistic ever. Even worse in the public mind was the standing of Congress. At that moment, reflecting the newly intensified plague-on-all-your-houses feeling of the public toward Washington and the workings of government, only 23 percent of the American people credited Congress with doing a good job; 69 percent believed Congress was *not* doing a good job. Those negative attitudes extended to both political parties, with Republicans in Congress viewed even more critically than Democrats.

These dismal findings followed an extraordinarily divisive congressional debate over final passage of the president's budget, a process decided only days before by a single vote—and that vote cast in the closing moments of deliberations that had run virtually around the clock for two days. Not a single Republican in either congressional chamber voted for the budget containing tax increases and spending cuts projected over the next four years. By contrast, twelve years earlier, Ronald Reagan's budget with its massive tax cuts and defense-spending increases had passed easily with the support of Democrats in both House and Senate. The remarkably narrow margin of victory on so critical a political test drove analysts to the history books. They found few comparable examples: the single vote that saved Andrew Johnson from impeachment in 1868, the single vote that authorized creation of a military draft in 1940 on the eve of America's entry into World War II.

That such an important issue hung in the balance until the final seconds in a Congress strongly dominated by Democrats, and reached its moment of decision only after the Democratic vice president cast the vote to break a tie in the Democratically controlled Senate, testified powerfully to the divisions that continued to afflict American government from Capitol Hill to White House.

The debate itself, months in the making, was embittered, intensely partisan, filled with misleading statements and, often, flat-out untruths so flagrant in their misrepresentation of facts and figures that even usually well-informed people were confused over what was actually true or false about the budget package. Republican opponents depicted the budget as another installment in a decades-old Democratic political ploy: the latest example of tax and tax and spend and spend and soak the rich; but postpone action on any real cuts in government spending, especially for "wasteful" social welfare programs. Even many Democrats who eventually voted with the president agreed that the budget did not propose nearly enough spending cuts. Other Democrats gave it their grudging support after expressing unhappiness for its failure to make greater spending investments in people, or for asking either too much or too little sacrifice from the middle class.

Through hour after hour of rancorous speeches and inflamed tempers, prompting at times jeers and childish catcalls from legislators, deep national conflicts—sectional, regional, racial, ideological—were exposed. Urban vs. rural interests, oil states vs. Midwest manufacturers, consumers vs. producers—all were at war with each other.

Of all the issues debated, none more perfectly demonstrated the difficulty of accomplishing the kind of change Bill Clinton had promised than his proposal for a broad-based tax on energy. The so-called BTU (for British thermal units) tax would impose a levy on the energy content of all fuels. It was a tax that would raise some $70 billion and be applied most evenly on all elements of society. It had the further advantage of reducing America's again-growing dependence on foreign energy sources, the very force that nearly brought the United States to its knees during the oil embargo of the Seventies and was the critical factor in igniting the Persian Gulf War of the Nineties. But in the crucible of special-interest maneuvering in Washington, the BTU tax was quickly rejected for a less fair, and less income-producing, gasoline tax.

During the presidential campaign, Ross Perot had called for a 50-cents-a-gallon gasoline tax increase, but the tax that emerged for final debate in the Clinton budget package was for only 4.3 cents a gallon. This at a time when America enjoyed by far the lowest gasoline taxes of any industrial nation and when other U.S. competitors were increasing their gas taxes. Even the minuscule increase of less than a nickel a gallon, representing on average no more than $30 a year in additional costs to Americans, almost scuttled passage of the budget. Lobbyists, backed by angry citizens, persuaded members of Congress that their constituents would not tolerate a higher levy.

The result was a classic example of shortsighted, and selfish, interests prevailing over long-term ones.

The debate also demonstrated the distorting influence of the radio and TV talk-show hosts. National talk-show hosts, especially those like Rush Limbaugh and Paul Harvey on radio, tend to be strongly conservative, expressing highly partisan views and provoking ideological listener responses. They practice the politics of division—mobocracy, as opposed to democracy. Their audience, it also appears, is far more conservative than the general American public. A Times Mirror Center national survey describes call-in radio listeners who contact their congressional representatives or respond to 800 or 900 phone surveys as a "vocal minority." They also express their views with greater "intensity" than most Americans. The survey, made public during the budget debate period, finds these call-in listeners—"the voices of the vocal few"—to be predominantly wealthy, white, elderly, male, and Republican. By ten percentage points, they are also more hostile to Bill Clinton than the general public and more opposed to liberal positions on such issues as abortion, gays in the military, gun control, and the influence of the religious right. They are also conditioned to instant mass mobilization by the talk-show hosts—a process that leads, the Times Mirror survey concludes, to public opinion "being distorted and exaggerated by the voices that dominate the airwaves of talk radio [and] clog the White House switchboard when a Zoë Baird stumbles."

During the budget debate, listeners were urged to register their protests immediately by calling their leaders in Washington. Call-in hosts such as Limbaugh, reaching audiences of millions daily, exploited fears that massive taxes were about to be levied on middle-class and lower-income Americans. So emotional was the public response that by noon on the day before the budget votes were cast, congressional switchboards were flooded with more than a million calls. Before the final votes were cast that week, the Senate switchboard alone logged an extraordinary 3.6 million calls. Most of the callers were highly critical of the president's budget. Some Democratic senators and congressmen who helped answer calls told me they were stunned by the vehemence of many of the remarks—and by the misinformation expressed. Once again, such responses suggested that substantial elements of the American public were still all too ready to swallow simplistic slogans—"tax and spend"—that defeat concerted efforts to deal decisively with major national issues.

In the end, the Clinton budget passage permitted the president to hail it as a great victory, an end to gridlock, the foundation for a better American economic future. It was hardly that. The hairbreadth victory saved Clinton's presidency and gave him time to remobilize for greater—and tougher—battles to come. The congressional vote did signal that a majority, however slim, was willing to risk political retribution at the hands of voters by reversing the policies of the past twelve years, to raise taxes, and, on paper at least, to cut spending. Also true, the budget represented the first honest attempt to deal with the deficit and long-term national debt in years; but it was only a beginning—and one with uncertain final results.

This was not the only hard lesson Clinton had to ponder as he set out for the West Coast after Congress finally recessed, stopping first to meet Pope John Paul II in Denver, then paying a political call in Oakland. From almost the president's first day in office, even his successes seemed fated to be overshadowed by new controversies and, in one terrible moment, by tragedy. Just three weeks before leaving Washington for the West, Clinton's lifelong friend and personal counselor Vincent W. Foster, Jr., was discovered shot to death in a secluded park overlooking the Potomac River north of Washington. The death of Foster, the deputy White House counsel, transfixed Washington and seemed to call into question the culture and values of the political capital as well as the pressures that weigh so heavily on ranking officials.

At forty-eight, Foster had been a widely admired Arkansas attorney—first in his law school class, first in the bar exams, leader of the state's most prominent firm, which had employed not only Bill Clinton but his wife, Hillary—when he accepted his boyhood friend's offer to accompany him to Washington.

Foster had never worked in Washington and was unprepared for the experience. His office became intimately involved in the controversies—the Zoë Baird nomination, the Lani Guinier choice, the Supreme Court appointment, the travel office fiasco—that kept engulfing the White House and, through all the attention they received, detracting from the presidential effort.

In the process, Foster, a quiet, self-effacing man of honor, found himself subjected to unaccustomed public criticism, especially in the sternly ideological and combative editorial pages of *The Wall Street Journal,* where he was depicted as a shadowy figure of influence, part of the Little Rock "legal mafia" pulling strings on behalf of his clients, the Clintons, and perhaps covering up White House misdeeds and even, it was implied, illegalities. Whatever demons possessed Foster will probably never be known, but he was the kind of private figure who took his responsibilities with utmost seriousness and prided himself on protecting those he served. Finally, he broke. On July 20, six months to the day after he sat behind his friend Clinton on the inaugural platform, after a moment of triumph for himself and the president while watching Clinton name a much-praised Louis J. Freeh to head the FBI in a sunlit Rose Garden ceremony, after accepting congratulations for this "home run" choice following the equally acclaimed Supreme Court choice of Ruth Bader Ginsburg, Vince Foster returned to his office and ate a sandwich alone at his desk. Shortly after one o'clock he told his secretary he was going out and left. Some five hours later his body was found a few yards from an old Civil War cannon. A vintage Colt revolver was still clutched in his hand. He had shot himself in the mouth.

For the next three weeks, the mysterious circumstances of the Foster death—no suicide note was found, and nothing initially to indicate the reasons for his death—hung over the White House, almost overshadowing the critical budget showdown vote on Capitol Hill. A poignant handwritten note was found in Foster's briefcase, torn into twenty-eight pieces; it had been overlooked on a first search of his office. On the day Clinton left for Denver on the first leg of his trip to Oakland, the note was made public by U.S. Park Police, who investigated the case and concluded it to be a suicide. "I made mistakes from ignorance, inexperience and overwork. I did not knowingly violate any law or standard of conduct," Foster's opening lines read. "No one in the White House, to my knowledge, violated any law or standard of conduct, including any action in the travel office. There was no intent to benefit any individual or specific group." The note went on to accuse the FBI of lying to Attorney General Reno in its report to her on the travel office incident, to accuse the White House press corps of covering up illegal benefits it had received from the travel staff,* to accuse *Wall Street Journal* editors of lying "without consequence." It ended with words that could serve as an epitaph for some who, like him, came to Washington to serve the public:

"I was not meant for this job or the spotlight of public life in Washington. Here ruining people is considered sport."

News reports about the Foster case, and more critical and speculative commentary on it, followed Clinton as he flew west across America. He could not escape other reminders, either, of the range of problems that continued to plague the country and confront him as president.

As the president awoke that morning in Oakland, preparing for visits to defense bases slated for closing because of military budget cuts, a front-page editorial in *The Oakland Tribune,* splashed above the masthead, warned the president that the circumstances of his visit "leave a lot to be desired." Even though he would be among political allies, the paper commented, "you're going to need their support when you try to put a positive spin on the impending loss of 33,000 jobs"—the number the Bay area stands to lose from the closing of naval bases there. "Here in the East Bay," the paper went on, "the closings will wipe out 1 of every 20 jobs, according to the Pentagon's own estimates. It's a staggering blow to our hopes for economic recovery in California, where the unemployment rate for July leaped to 9.8 percent. That's 3 percentage points higher than the national rate. . . ." The paper recalled Clinton's campaign pledge to offer a plan to convert from a defense to a civilian economy, adding caustically: "What troubles us 16 months later is not so much that we're proceeding with the transition, but that we haven't seen the plan."

As if that weren't enough, the president only had to glance at the paper's second section for compelling evidence of the further deterioration of inner-city areas like Oakland, where I had spent so much time during my own journey nearly a year before. "Woman Stabbed to Death While Chanting Mob Watches," read the headline over the lead local story, an account which began: "While a dozen frenzied drug dealers chanted 'kill her, kill her, kill her,' a knife-wielding woman pinned another woman down on a busy Oakland street

*This allegation has not been sufficiently examined at this writing, but in years past some journalists covering the president on overseas trips cleared customs without paying duty on such personally acquired items as Persian rugs and caviar.

Wednesday night and killed her with a flurry of deadly blows, police said." The slain woman had been running from her assailant when she was surrounded and tripped by drug dealers who prevented her escape. This came after she had sought refuge in a nearby liquor store only to have the door slammed in her face.

A secondary story served as another grim update. A local school district board had just voted unanimously to purchase and install fifty-five metal-detector machines to make it more difficult to smuggle weapons onto school grounds. This action was prompted, the paper reported, by the rising number of weapons being confiscated on school grounds.

Up early as usual, after another late arrival from his visit with Pope John Paul II, the president left his hotel shortly after seven o'clock to jog around Oakland's Merritt Lake, in Lakeside Park. When he finished, a crowd of well-wishers gathered around him. But this pleasant moment was cut short when one woman in the crowd suddenly shouted: "What about the middle-class tax cut? You lied to the American people."

The president proceeded on his tour of naval installations, and thereby provided another strong reminder of the difficulties he faced in fulfilling his political promises. Fear about the economic future, fueled by deep cutbacks in America's post–Cold War defense base, had formed his opportunity to be president. Hope that he would be able to move the nation forward, creating new jobs as the United States converted from defense to civilian needs, was largely responsible for his victory. But now, nearly a year later, the revitalization of the economy had not occurred—and nowhere less so than in California. The vaunted new partnership he sought to forge between federal, state, and local officials to ease the pain of conversion remained more slogan than fact. The suspicions about his motivations among career military ranks were greater than ever.

While the president was getting ready to deliver his prepared remarks at Wharf Three at the Alameda Naval Air Station, three young naval enlisted men were chatting among themselves, and with me, about their uncertain futures. They didn't know how to plan, the young sailors were saying, for the short term or for the long; whether they would stay in the service, or, more likely, if they returned to civilian life, what kinds of jobs they could expect to have. They worried aloud about the economy, about the cost of living, about what was happening to the country. One of them asked about Washington. He'd heard Rush Limbaugh talk about the guy who killed himself in the White House. What was the real story on that? Was it about that travel scandal, or that haircut from that Hollywood barber? Another said he was the personal driver for a three-star general at the base, and had driven the general to meet Clinton at the airport arrival ceremony the night before. The general didn't like Clinton, the young man said; he didn't even want to go meet him. A three-star general said that? one of the others asked. Yeah, the sailor replied. That's what the general said.

Then the president began to speak. Clinton's theme, again, was "the wave of change that has washed over our shores" after the Cold War, and the opportunities—and the traumas—change brings. He spoke of the difficult period of national transition, of the uncertainty faced by the military in this time of relocation, and of the need for all Americans, whether in the military or not, to adapt and plan for change. He recalled a remark of President Kennedy's: "Those who think only of the past and present will miss the future." Clinton, nodding in agreement, said, "That has happened." Americans, he added, "have not done very well" in facing the future and planning aggressively for change. As for himself, he said he had met earlier in the day with community leaders devoted to revitalizing the Bay area's economy. "Presidents would do better if they spent more time listening to people at the grass-roots levels," he said. "And that's one of the lessons I'm trying to learn and teach to Washington." But his principal message was more general, and broader. "I am determined," he said, "not to let the American Dream founder. What a tragedy it would be if the aftermath of winning the Cold War were a legacy that we left millions of Americans who won that war out in the cold. What a tragedy it would be if, because we did not have the discipline and will to change, we hung on to our outmoded ways of doing things. . . ."

His formal business was done. The thick low-lying clouds, driven by stiff west winds, scudded even more swiftly across the naval base, rippling the waters of San Francisco Bay and tugging at the clothing of the party gathered to see him off for a week-end of golf in the Rockies and then, days later, the real vacation on Martha's Vineyard. Still, the president lingered. There were more hands to shake, more people to talk with, perhaps more lessons to be learned before boarding the plane for the flight east that marked, in literal and symbolic ways, the conclusion of the critical first segment of his presidency. Even the date was a reminder of problems he had encountered. It was Friday the 13th when the president bounded up the steps leading to the forward stateroom of the massive blue-and-white aircraft bearing the words THE UNITED STATES OF AMERICA.

The president was wearing his navy-blue windbreaker with the presidential seal on the right breast and the name "Bill Clinton" in white letters over the left. His blue commander in chief's cap, with the gold braid splashed across its bill, was tipped over his eyes as he thumbed through a first edition of Mark Twain's *Huckleberry Finn,* wearing the narrow-rimmed reading glasses he never uses in public. Look here, he said, turning in his swivel chair to greet me in the forward stateroom of Air Force One, isn't this great? He pointed to Twain's opening words: "Persons attempting to find a motive in this narrative will be prosecuted; persons attempting to find a moral in it will be banished; persons attempting to find a plot in it will be shot." Then he turned to the business at hand, a conversation with me that he knew was arranged solely to address the themes of this book and the lessons learned thus far in his presidency. We faced each other across a small table, while a White House stenographer stood nearby and a press aide sat on a sofa against the cabin wall.

From that point on, while Air Force One flew over California to Denver, bucking in crosswinds so severe that my tape recorder was knocked over several times, the president spoke with an intensity and passion that belied his public image as the laid-back, soft-spoken, smiling chief executive. He was remarkably candid about mistakes made and lessons learned in dealing with the press, with the "culture of Washington," with "the other players" of the capital, with his own staff, with contributing to public cynicism and disbelief, with what he believed would be the outcome of "the great gamble Bill Clinton is taking with history." While he was sharply critical of what he regarded as unfair press coverage and a general media "willingness to believe the worst," there was no attempt to shift blame. More than once, in one way or another, he said, "I hold no one responsible but myself." Nor, despite the critical cast of many of his remarks, was he defensive about being wronged by enemies. Instead, he seemed eager to analyze his own performance, to draw lessons for the future, to assess what had been done right—and wrong. So intent was he on the conversation that he barely touched a tray of food brought by a steward. Although he seemed somewhat drawn after a twenty-one-hour workday preceding his long day in Oakland, his words tumbled out, anticipating almost every question or topic I intended to raise.

"One thing I have learned," he said, leaning forward, a position he held throughout our conversation, "is that in spite of having spent a lifetime observing the presidency and observing the way Washington works—although I've only lived here as a student and worked for two years in the Congress and that was more than twenty-five years ago—an enormous part of being president is being able to speak to the American people through the prism and lens of a press corps . . . and against a cacophony of noises from your adversaries and your friends, all of whom not only see the world differently maybe, but also have different interests. It doesn't make them bad, just different.

"What that means to me is that the mistakes that I thought were, frankly, nowhere near as significant as the things I did *right* tended to be much larger and to deprive me of the honeymoon that every other president in my lifetime has gotten, and we didn't. It tended to feed into this public cynicism that none of us could be trusted to be different or to really effect change. And in that sense, I've paid a high price. In a larger sense, it happened because we pushed our product—that is, all the change I wanted to bring—before we had our processes as well organized as they should have been and as clearly attuned to the culture of Washington."

This was a theme he returned to several times. "Most of my errors grew out of two things," he said at another point. "Pushing too hard to get the product in place. That was the cabinet, the bills, the budget. And not working enough on process—organizing the staff, working on how you're going to handle these things, being attuned, thinking about the ragged edges of how we were relating to the press. And the second thing was just not thinking in terms of the imperatives of the other players in the town. I use the press because it's an obvious example, but there were also other players. And I lost some goodwill and fed into the public cynicism and I got soaked up."

Later, he said, "This whole thing was to me extremely disorient-
ing. . . . I did actually make some mistakes that I think we could have
corrected because I worried more about pushing the product—because I was obsessed with trying to make these changes as quickly as
possible. And because I wasn't finely attuned to the Washington
culture. And I paid a terrible price because, in some ways, people put
up their blinders on what I was substantively doing and achieving. So
there was no perception that it was a big deal when we passed family
leave, or motor voter [enabling people to register to vote while getting driver's licenses], or reversed the environmental policies of the
last twelve years, which we largely did by executive action.

"There was a willingness to believe the worst when we said we
were pulling the grazing-fee issue out of the budget bill because we
didn't have any votes to spare on the budget bill. Now everybody
knows we *literally* didn't have any votes to spare. And we could do it
without that. Here was [Interior Secretary] Bruce Babbitt with a
lifetime of environmental work, and people still didn't believe us. Yet
he did it last week, just like we said we were going to all along.

"We weren't in sync. And I have no one to blame; I hold no one
responsible but myself. But on the other hand, I think when the
historians look back on the first six, seven months of this administration, they'll have a very hard time finding any presidency in the
modern era where more actually got done that was exactly consistent
with what I said I would do in the election—whether it was institu-
tionalizing choice, or repealing the ban on fetal tissue, or changing
the environmental policy, or having a cabinet that was both the most
diverse in history and still unquestionably excellent and pragmatic
and progressive in outlook. Or even all these initiatives. We even
managed to get campaign reform, lobby reform, and the modified
line-item veto through one of the two houses—all of this stuff. An
incredibly active thing."

Whatever the problems, though, and however deep his personal
introspection, the president appeared absolutely confident about the
outcome of his attempt to create change. "Now, the up side is this,"
he said. "I still believe that in the end, by having a vision about where
the country ought to go and having it be the right one, and by pursuing policies that are consistent with it, by actually getting things
done, [our efforts] will win out.

"In the long sweep of history, in terms of being effective in the last six months," the president said, "it was at least significant that I became the first president of the modern era to have all of his cabinet but one confirmed the day after I was sworn in as president. That hasn't happened in a very long time. One of the people I proposed had to be pulled down, but the one that I pulled down became a hundred times bigger story—or a thousand times bigger story—than the fact that I had appointed a cabinet that was not only diverse but excellent. And it was all confirmed. But instead of being seen as early, prompt, and excellent, I was seen as being late and ragged. That was a different sort of story in a town that really is obsessed with the process."

He wasn't blaming anyone, Clinton repeated. "I mean, I did make a mistake in the vetting of Zoë Baird. I feel badly for her. She's a fine person and in some ways was an innocent bystander because she never attempted to cover anything up. And I could give you other examples."

He had been astonished, he went on, by the media handling of the death of David Koresh and his cult followers in Waco, Texas. "I was stunned that anyone would think because I did not issue a definitive statement when Koresh was killed [hours before], until five-thirty p.m. or something, that I was somehow trying to make Janet Reno take the fall for it. I mean, I was shocked, because from my perspective, first, the president is responsible for anything that happens on his watch—especially something he knew about and signed off on and made to go forward—and, secondly, I asked three times that day, which we duly reported, whether I should go out and make a statement and talk to Reno during the day. The consensus was that I shouldn't until we knew whether the kids were alive or not. I wasn't thinking about the fact that if I didn't make the news deadline it would be interpreted as attempting to lay more of the blame for it off on her."

That was an example, he continued, of how his political antenna was not adjusted to the way Washington thinks. "It should have been," he added. "After all, Washington has put up with presidents they were convinced were violating the law and covering up things and stiffing them." The Waco story was also a vivid example of his failure to appreciate the different demands of the news cycle in

Washington, Clinton reflected, and what he had been accustomed to in Arkansas. An example, too, of where his state-level experience hurt him when he came to Washington. At home, he recalled, if he put out a statement at nine o'clock at night it would be reported on the ten-o'clock newscasts. In Arkansas, unlike in Washington with its focus on the network news telecasts, making the ten-o'clock time slot was as good as the six-o'clock.

Similarly, he said, when his friend Vince Foster committed suicide he had been thrown off by the suspicion that his White House was attempting to cover up some wrongdoing. The president fully understood that Foster's death was a compelling story. As he said, he was aware that it had been nearly thirty years since anyone who worked for the White House had committed suicide.* And, he added, he also realized that Foster was probably the highest-ranking official to kill himself since James V. Forrestal, Harry Truman's secretary of defense, jumped out of a window at the Bethesda Naval Institutes of Health, where he was being treated for depression. But the notion that the Clinton White House or even the president himself and his wife, Hillary, were trying to cover up misdeeds of Foster, or others, deeply disturbed him. "We were all, I thought—clearly—just grieving," he said.

Another incident that still rankled involved the famous haircut episode at the Los Angeles airport; air traffic reportedly was delayed while a Hollywood stylist cut the president's hair aboard Air Force One. The express purpose of the Los Angeles visit, all but ignored by the press, was to signal that a president connected with, and stood by, people in the inner city; that, as president, he wanted to make a difference in their lives. In fact, as he said, he had been the first president in a very long time to walk the streets of the inner city— and not just to stage a presidential photo opportunity.

He had also gone to an inner-city sporting goods store in Los Angeles owned by two former gang members, and used the occasion to announce a major part of his economic package (later lost when the "jobs" bill was defeated in Congress). This was an "empowerment zone" proposal that Republicans such as Jack Kemp had been

*He referred to the death in 1964 of Walter Jenkins, LBJ's chief of staff, after Jenkins had been arrested for engaging in homosexual acts in a pay toilet at the YMCA two blocks from the White House.

advocating for years; but Clinton believed the proposal he made public that day was even broader and better.

Instead of reporting on his ideas to aid the inner city, journalists made the Clinton airport departure haircut the story of the day—and for days and weeks to come. "And it wasn't even a true story," the president said, "and we said it wasn't a true story. We said we asked if anybody would be delayed and they said no, and we certainly didn't pay two hundred bucks for the haircut."

As that story kept dominating the news, the president said he had given a lot of thought to whether he should call the head of the Federal Aviation Administration and have him publicly correct the false reports about airport delays at Los Angeles International Airport. But in the end he concluded it wouldn't make any difference. "There was not even a presumption of good faith [in the press]," he said. "They just blew it off as if we were not telling the truth. It now turns out that somebody at the FAA lied to them. Just lied to them—for whatever reason."

Clinton then recalled another example of the vastly different manner in which his actions were judged during his years as governor of Arkansas. It was not the harshness of criticism that struck him, but the different standards applied. When the newspaper wars in Little Rock ended in the 1980s, with the progressive *Gazette* folding and leaving the ultraconservative *Democrat* the sole paper in the capital, he had been subjected to intense daily editorial criticism. "But even though they were trying to kill me—because they didn't agree with me or like what I was doing—there was never the presumption that I or my administration would lie," he said. "I always got a straight shot at my side on the news pages and the corollary on the evening news." That had not been so in Washington.

Again, the president did not say this in a bitter tone. He was trying to understand the process and what seemed to him to be a fundamental change in the nature of press coverage—a change, as he put it, "where people don't get the benefit of the doubt, where there's an obsession with little things that look big and controversial, where big things that are important go unnoted." It raised a question about how to overcome coverage that "is obsessed with the moment, and has no memory—no memory, no realism. I don't know what to do about that except to keep talking about it."

"If you were to ask me what my two major frustrations have been," he said, "one is trying to catch my process up to my product. That's my problem. And we're working on it, doing a lot better. The other is trying to get some perspective on the way people are told about what I'm doing. It must have something to do with the way I communicate or relate to the press. I know I've got a higher percentage of my plan passed than Reagan did of his in '81. And I know we're moving faster and doing more than any president has in the modern history of the presidency. And I know the Democrats are voting for me a higher percentage of the time than they have in previous presidencies—than they did for Kennedy, Johnson, Carter. Yet that would surprise a vast majority of the American people because of what they have been told."

The budget battle that had just been concluded was a perfect example of the degree of public misinformation, the president remarked. Until the White House launched its own information campaign to counter attacks on its budget package, a majority of Americans had been persuaded that the budget contained no spending cuts and no deficit reduction. That this belief was held until the final days before the Congress voted on the budget "just shows you how deepseated the cynicism is," the president added. It also underscores how intensely the daily spotlight shines on momentary events. The result of all this made Clinton think that "people may know more and understand less than ever before."

In his mind, *that* was the problem, the reason why what a president did, or was attempting to do, as reported through the media to the people, was vital to a leader's success or failure. Clinton acknowledged that he had tried to do too much too fast, and that he should have spent more effort on sharpening his focus and ensuring that staff work was better coordinated. "While ninety percent of what affects people's lives may come from the White House to the cabinet," he said, "ninety percent of how people interpret the White House comes directly out of how people perceive what's going on inside the White House." That was his responsibility to fix; he was determined to do it, and believed he was succeeding. Still, the larger problem of getting through to the public, and of being understood, remained.

He told a story to illustrate his point. In the hectic days before the congressional vote on his budget, he received a call at the White

House from Bernard Sanders, a freshman congressman from Vermont (raised in Brooklyn and educated at the University of Chicago) who ran and won as the only Independent in the U.S. Congress.

For the only time during our conversation, the president permitted himself a grin. "Do you know Bernie?" he asked. "He's a real piece of work."

Sanders told Clinton on the phone, "God, I have really shafted you."

"Bernie, what are you talking about?" the president said. "You voted for me every time."

"That's the problem," the congressman said. "You did something I never thought I'd see in my lifetime. You convinced every liberal in the Congress that we should reduce the deficit. And not a one of us uttered a peep out of all these budget reductions. None of us. Nobody did. As a result, because there was no fight about it, there is no perception that you cut spending. So what I should have done is burn you in effigy, hold three days of demonstrations, then the American people would know we cut spending."

Here's what he meant, Clinton said, offering another example. Suppose someone wanted to write a genuinely critical article about his economic plan, but at the same time meant to be fair to him. Here—and he began motioning vigorously with his hands, as if tallying a balance sheet, and referring to himself in the third person—we have the first budget to be passed since Reagan in '81 to be taken seriously. It's the first budget since Reagan to be passed by the August recess. It has a higher percentage of what the president originally recommended than Reagan's budget did—Clinton got 85 percent of what he wanted, Reagan only got about 60 percent. Therefore—Clinton continued to refer to himself in the third person—his budget is a unique document in modern times. And he had to do it all with Democrats. Even though people say he doesn't twist arms, he's gotten a stronger level of support than his three Democratic predecessors.

What no one knows, he went on, is whether or not you can reduce the deficit by cutting spending and raising taxes in a weak economic period without slowing the economy further. He has taken a chance. He has made a deliberate decision. He argues you *can* reduce the deficit by cutting spending and raising taxes if you keep interest rates down and if you have targeted investments for government spending. Traditional economic theory, from both Republican supply-siders and Democratic progressives, is that when you've got an economy this sluggish you need to go light on taxes and spend more money.

"This," he said, gesturing strongly, "is the serious question. *This* is the great gamble Bill Clinton is taking with history."

Continuing his third-person analysis, he said here you have people on the right and people on the left who disagree with him. Then here's the other serious question: could he have done this with fewer taxes and more spending cuts? Here are the people who argue that. "In other words," the president said, "people would see the big picture, the historical context. They would see the positive things we have done and understand the major policy questions that are still unresolved. If I were doing a story criticizing me, that's what I would have written."

As for his "great gamble with history," he understood that "only time will prove whether we were right or not." But he was convinced that fighting for that budget and getting it passed—thereby reversing the trickle-down economics of the Reagan era—was a major achievement and one that, at the very least, was seen by the experts as having restored the credibility of the national budget process.

He was also convinced that this long, bitter, and divisive struggle had set the stage for greater future achievements. The budget victory, however slim its margin, had anchored his administration and given it a stronger base from which to pursue the great challenges that lay before it—health care reform, the North American Free Trade Agreement with Mexico and Canada, welfare reform, crime legislation. All these, he said, represent the larger changes he seeks: to try and help "America adjust to the external pressures and the internal pressures that are bearing on our lives today."

Months before, in an Oval Office interview, he had read aloud from *The Prince* and implicitly compared himself with Machiavelli's example of the political leader as "the reformer." Now, to me, he articulated a major goal of his presidency as enabling Americans to address those external and internal pressures in ways that will lead to "a more active government but also produce a more responsible citizen." Clinton added: "I think we're positioned to do that."

We had reached the point of examining the larger concerns I

have attempted to address in this book. I raised the question of the American people first, their character and their willingness or unwillingness to change. How did Clinton assess the current public mood? The hope for him, I suggested, recalling the people I met on my journey, was that he represented the chance to end national divisions and put America's house in order. What's your reading of the people now, I asked, as we fly across the United States and down below us is that elusive something—"the people"?

"I think one of the things the public wanted from me," he replied, "was some sort of immediate action—immediate action in Washington that they could feel in their own lives. And in that sense, even though I said until I was blue in the face in the campaign, this won't be immediate—it won't be easy, it won't be quick—I think . . . they question whether anybody could get it done, or whether I could get it done. I think there was this inchoate idea that if they gave me a chance to govern with a Democratic majority in both houses, I would be almost like a prime minister; that whatever I wanted, Congress would do and we would see whether it would work."

That clearly had not happened. The president said he had thought a lot about how he could do a better job of forging public consensus and help create a more realistic understanding of the time it will take to resolve national problems. People must understand that "we can't make unemployment go down and incomes go up overnight." He hoped to be able "to tell people that my job is to advance the ball," but that "not every aspect of every issue can or should be a moral crusade in a democracy where honest debate is important and where the future is uncertain." That's what he meant about forging a new link between "a more active government" and "a more responsible citizen." Although he did not make this specific point, he seemed to suggest that a new kind of partnership between the people and their government and elected officials is needed.

There was a larger question; it concerned his own leadership. Let me take you back to the campaign, I said. Do you think that the public was ready for sacrifice during the campaign? Do you think you could have asked the middle class to take more pain? Had he missed a moment to be bolder by misreading public hunger for action and by not asking the middle class to bear more of the cost of change instead of promising them a tax cut?

"Maybe," he said, "but let me respond to that. First of all, I really believed, when I put out the first version of my [economic] plan in New Hampshire and we'd had basically almost flat job growth for three years, that in that environment there was a limit to how quickly, or by how much, the deficit could be reduced. "I also always believed," he said, "that I could get a health care reform package through that—over a ten-year period—would do more to balance the budget than we're doing."

It had become obvious, he said, after the Bush administration's projections of a higher budget deficit in August 1992, "that there was a good chance that we'd have to defer" a middle-class tax break. "But I still felt that I could do it during my term." He never thought that asking the middle class to shoulder more burdens was either good politics or good economics, especially in view of the conditions America faced after the Eighties: a period of steady erosion of income of workers because of stagnant wages, higher taxes, and explosive health care costs. He had always argued that additional revenues should be raised by moving the tax system away from consumption toward investment—and that there ought to be "an offsetting break for the great, vast mass of consumers because they didn't have enough to help contribute to the economy."

"So I don't belong to the school," he said, "that says that clearly the best economics is to squeeze the middle class further, because I think one of the reasons for our anemic job performance is the fact that there is already a middle-class squeeze on. On the other hand, I do feel more strongly than I did at some points in the campaign that without taking firm control of the budget, you run the risk of further erosion—higher interest rates, stagnant growth, and all of that."

There was another aspect of his leadership to which he had already alluded several times during our conversation: the charge that he compromised too much, wasn't tough enough. Bill Clinton, the cave-in president. A prince, to be effective, Machiavelli said, must act both as a lion and as a fox. Was Bill Clinton too much the fox and not enough the lion? By way of response, the president recalled an incident from just the night before. During dinner at a restaurant in Berkeley, he had been impressed—and obviously pleased—when a woman came up to him and complimented him for the way he had worked through the budget process, as well as the gays-in-the-military issue. "I read about all these people saying that you gave in to people who weren't going to vote for you anyway," the woman told the president. "What is this giving in? You have no stick that you're holding over them. In the world we're moving toward, being able to engage in dialogue and keep pushing forward on a range of difficult issues will be the ultimate test of leadership." He didn't have a lack of courage, she added, but courage in tackling tough issues.

"That's another thing that's perplexed me," the president told me. "When I'm out here taking on these tough issues that have been dodged for a decade, and I get most of what I want, and the story is I didn't get everything I wanted—am I weak because I didn't beat somebody up or something, and talk mean to them? I mean, it's sort of a weird deal." Especially, he repeated, when the record showed that he had received higher voting percentages in Congress than those enjoyed by Kennedy, Johnson, and Carter.

The president understood that his future efforts would be imperiled—my term, not his—unless he could find ways to overcome the deeply partisan atmosphere in Washington that had led to defeat of his jobs program early in his presidency and almost to loss of his budget package. He laid much of the blame for those problems on the unified Republican front. "Dole's conservative wing in the Senate caucus got them all to swear on a blood oath that they would not negotiate with the enemy, basically," he said, and they were followed in lockstep by House Republicans.

But there was a deeper question about the political divisions that have racked Washington. Are they merely reflective of a difficult phase in American life, or do they represent underlying structural problems with the present two-party system? In 1946, I recalled, the president's mentor, Senator J. William Fulbright of Arkansas, had stirred national controversy when he called for adoption of a parliamentary system like that of Great Britain to provide greater unity and the ability to accomplish national goals.* Fulbright's proposal came at another moment of great turmoil and division. Harry Truman was encountering enormous difficulties in the new postwar America. His popularity, like Clinton's, was sinking to historic lows.

---

*A more complete description of this appears in my biography, written with Bernard M. Gwertzman, *Fulbright: The Dissenter* (New York: Doubleday, 1968), pp. 98–106.

Republicans had just enjoyed their best day at the polls since Herbert Hoover's landslide victory in 1928, gaining control of both houses of Congress, holding twenty-five of the forty-eight governorships, and moving to block every Truman initiative and roll back the long New Deal–era gains of the Democrats. It was against that background that Fulbright made his famous proposal, one that in years since has attracted more attention from political scientists as they watch the growing divisions of Washington. Did Clinton, the new reformer-president, who had studied at Oxford on a Rhodes scholarship as had Fulbright, ever wonder if America would be better served by a parliamentary system? I asked. He emphatically did not.

"If the United States had a parliamentary system," he said, "there wouldn't be room for the conservative Democrats, the progressive Republicans, the ultraliberal Democrats, the ultraconservative Republicans. We might wind up with four parties and more paralysis. What has happened in rare moments of American history—what happened when the Republicans replaced the Whigs—is that neither party could accommodate the realities of the present and move to the future. So one gave up the ghost and was replaced by another in a relatively short period of time, maybe ten or fifteen years.

"That," the president said, "could still happen here if we don't do what we have to do."

And that, naturally, raised the subject of Ross Perot.

"I've got to ask you about Perot," I said. "Where do you see that specter, not just for you but for the system historically?"

Without pause for reflection, the president addressed a subject that he clearly had been thinking about.

"I had believed for a long time," he said, "that there was room for another party or an independent candidacy if it had a consistent program—and a way to reach the people. The problem with the [George] Wallace candidacy was that it rose on an issue"—race—"that was ultimately unsustainable in American life. The problem with John Anderson's candidacy, a very attractive man, was that it rose basically out of the conflicts of the moment so that the reformist ideas couldn't carry it on.

"The virtue of the Perot candidacy was that it rose out of people's accurate sense that America wasn't working, that we needed political reform in order to get economic change, and that both parties in Washington bore some responsibility for the fact that we had not adequately responded to the economic challenges in the last twenty years. Those things were all true.

"Then he had the money to reach out to people, to organize them on a mass basis, and he had a coherent program. Then he collapsed, when he went from first to third in the polls [and] before he ran out because of problems with his program and problems with execution and questions about whether he should be president."

But the president believed the Perot phenomenon had not run its course, either for Perot or for somebody like him. There is still space in American life for another political party, or an independent presidential candidacy, he said, "and that space will be here unless we Democrats conclude that we can build coalitions with Perot people and Republicans of goodwill, and that we can change ourselves."

That was why he believed it most important that the House of Representatives take up campaign finance reform, and lobby reform, after returning from its recess. It was equally important for the Senate to pass a bill giving the president modified line-item-veto power.* "If both houses would pass the other's action on those two things," the president said, there would be a strong signal to "the American people that maybe there was room in one of these parties for this kind of change. I then think the Republicans would have to be more forthcoming on things like health care and other reforms. I think that the two parties might once again take up the American landscape."

That was part of the great challenge. If the challenge were met, faith in government and political leaders would be restored and the stability of the two-party system strengthened. If not—well, there was Perot, and at the moment, in the president's mind, Perot's prospects were very much alive. "There will be an opportunity for him or somebody else that people can imagine being president," Clinton said, for one good reason: "We haven't done enough yet to meet the frustrations and disillusionment of those people who vote."

In the end, he remained confident that sufficient change would occur to forestall that kind of greater, and potentially historic, political crackup. Things would finally tend to come together, he repeated.

*Campaign reform bills passed both houses before Clinton's first year ended.

As the Congress acted and piled up a record of achievement, particularly if it produced political reforms along with other major changes—removing free trade barriers and achieving universal health care—conditions would gradually improve.

He had another hope: to find a way to launch his health care reform plan in a way "that will create an environment in which it will become impossible for the thoughtful Republicans not to engage in the dialogue so that we can produce something together."

There are a lot of good people in the Republican Party and in the Congress who really want health care, he went on. If their cooperation can be won, it could initiate a pattern for other common action and "maybe set the stage for all future budgets."

So you think health care is going to be the defining issue for you in the next phase of your presidency? I asked.

"Well, I think it's something that I have to deliver on or die trying," the president said, speaking with even more urgency. "Not just for me, but because I think it's so important for America. It's a health care issue. It's an economic issue. It's a government-worker-ordinary-people issue. It's a can-we-pull-together issue—can we build a sense of community? My belief is that the American people—families, workers, business people—need something done on this so badly that we have a real shot to have a bipartisan consensus and move toward something that will be much better."

Air Force One was beginning its descent into Denver. Before we landed, I told President Clinton about the question I had asked Gerald Ford shortly after Ford became president: if we met ten years from now, what would you like it said that you accomplished as president? Ford, a product of Congress accustomed to dealing with daily legislative issues, had looked blank. When I asked Clinton what he would say to the same question, he responded without a second's hesitation.

"I would like for people to say that I was able to restore possibility in American life, that I got the American people to confront the challenges of the last twenty years, that we met those challenges, and that because of our administration and what we did, America moved into the twenty-first century with a sense of possibility, with a sense of opportunity. And furthermore, because of what I did as President, the American people had a much deeper sense of community . . . and as a result of that we seriously dealt with things like teen pregnancy, teenage violence, and all these social problems. That's what I would like people to say—that I gave people back a sense of possibility and a sense of community and moved into the twenty-first century basically with America still as the greatest country in the world because of that."

Minutes later the plane landed. The president was about to begin his vacation, and the first phase was a round of golf with Gerald Ford at Vail in the Rockies, an outing that would provide a public example of bipartisanship and perhaps an opportunity to compare presidential lessons learned.

CHAPTER 16

PEOPLE:
CLOSING THE CIRCLE

The critical period in the life of a national society comes
when it has to learn new habits, acquire new emotional
attitudes, possibly unlearn some old lessons. . . . Such
necessary change is painful for an individual and
for a people. . . . It means personal risk, personal
discomfort, personal stock-taking.

—D. W. Brogan

After my conversation with the president, I felt the need to reconnect with some of the people I had met during my journey. I wanted to close the circle, as it were, after the major events of the Clinton first year had taken place. My cross section, I was fascinated to discover, turned out to be representative of the electorate in two ways. First, in how people had voted—for Bill Clinton, George Bush, or Ross Perot. Second, and more significant, in how they felt about the nation and the performance of their political leaders. So while the jury is still out on whether President Clinton can forge public consensus, whether his proposed policies are equal to the task, whether he himself possesses the necessary leadership qualities, and whether the public has the will to break the political gridlock and demand real change, the responses of my national sample strongly suggest that an interim verdict is already in.

Many of the people I interviewed now express disappointment, not only with Clinton himself but even more with the performance of Congress and Washington in general. Senate Minority Leader Bob Dole and the Republican Party come in for special criticism for being too negative and obstructionist; this complaint also extends to conservatives who admired Dole in the past. As for Clinton, there is sympathy for him personally and an appreciation of the difficulties he faces. Even those most critical of his leadership still hope he will be successful. But the dominant impression is fear that a great opportunity for change may be lost—a feeling that inspires greater concern about America's problems.

These people, at least, are more eager for change than when I first spoke with them nearly two years before. They were ready for strong action then and frustrated now by the failure of national leaders to take it.

"Congress and the president are not reading the mood of America very accurately," says George Duncan, the Lowell, Massachusetts, banker. "I thought the Perot phenomenon was going to make them sit up and think, but it's been politics as usual. They put a budget bill before the Congress and nobody really understands it. People still think there's gross mismanagement in Washington and gross overspending. Whether it's Perot or somebody else, the stage is being set for someone with a message, someone who wants to make the hard calls and decisions. What's happening in Washington is forcing people to look for a Perot-type guy."

George Duncan sees Clinton as being "over his head." "He's like a fighter who gets hit hard in the first round and hasn't recovered yet. My hope is he can still provide leadership, but my concern is that he seems too anxious to please everyone."

His greater concern is that New England is sinking into a ten-to-twelve-year "down cycle." It's estimated that another fifty thousand to seventy thousand defense jobs will disappear within a hundred-mile radius of Boston. What's going to take their place? Duncan wonders. And what about the next generation? Duncan's daughter had recently graduated from Brown University. "She and her friends are all bright, honest, hardworking," Duncan comments, "but they can't find decent jobs. When they do find jobs, there's no challenge. My son's just starting college. Even so, he says, 'Gee, Dad, with all these layoffs, and jobs going to Mexico and Asia, what's America going to be like when I get out of college?'

"I can't help thinking what happened in 1929. It took all of the hard times of the Thirties, a ten-year period, for America to recover. I can't help wondering if history is repeating itself." At the same time, he sees signs of growth. Throughout New England, hundreds of small companies are springing up, begun or staffed by people who lost their jobs—people with new ideas who are seizing the moment. Many of the companies are high-tech, with people from computer backgrounds trained in the great educational institutions around Boston; they are in strong positions to succeed in that highly competitive world of the future. Duncan cites three in the Lowell area enjoying quick success: a computer network company, which after only three years made the *Fortune* magazine list of America's fastest-growing companies; an energy management firm, also reliant on computer technology; and a new brewery formed with local risk venture capital.

In New York, Bob Kiley feels a sense of letdown. He's the construction company executive who led the city's effort to improve its subway system and is an expert on the nation's infrastructure of deteriorating bridges, airports, dams, reservoirs, rail and sea facilities, highways, and sewer systems. "We had the language of crisis in the campaign," he says, "and Clinton did focus on the infrastructure. But there was only a tepid effort to put together a stimulus program, and that quickly collapsed."

It was Kiley's hope, when we first talked, that a major investment of government public works spending would strengthen the base upon which the U.S. economy would rest for the next quarter century and facilitate the shift from Cold War expenditures to essential domestic needs. Even with such a commitment, much more would have to be done. Because it has failed to invest adequately in new technology, the United States has fallen a generation behind its foreign competitors. In Southeast Asia, for example, Indonesia, Thailand, Malaysia, Singapore, and Hong Kong have all been spending heavily on improving infrastructure. The Vietnamese are beginning to invest in similar rebuilding. Taiwan alone, a country with a population approximating that of Pennsylvania, spends more on infrastructure development than the United States of America.

In the year since the election, Kiley says, public works activity is way down. "There were lots of expectations," he adds. "They've all been deflated."

Kiley is disappointed with Clinton and with his lifelong political party, the Democrats. "There's no *there* there," he says of the Democrats. Of Clinton, he observes: "Not only is there some question about what Clinton really believes, but there is some question about what he thinks needs to be done. So there's enormous frustration." He worries that all of America's institutions, public and private, are failing to provide leadership. "They're too isolated," Kiley says, "especially the Congress. Leadership is just not coming from traditional quarters."

Yet he, too, retains hope. "We keep getting messages from pollsters that people are divided about sacrifice," he says. "The polls may be misleading. Maybe people are ambivalent, but that doesn't mean they don't want leaders to strike at our problems. I see this as an opportunity missed. My sense is that Perot really tapped into deeper feelings. It wasn't just his money or his ability to get on television. It was what he was saying, how he was saying it: that it was not going to be easy, that it was going to be painful, but that it *could* be done."

To Jack Gates, Ross Perot seemed the best hope for new national leadership. Gates, a retired lawyer, organized the Perot chapter in Santee, South Carolina, and proclaimed his preference with a Perot sign on his front door. When Perot withdrew from the race, Gates was outraged. A Republican, he wound up voting for Clinton and feels sympathetic to him. "I think he wanted to be bolder," Gates says, "but he had to be practical. He realized if he did not make some compromises he'd get nothing. As it was, the budget he did get was a squeaker, and though it didn't go far enough, trying for anything more would not have got through the people of his own party. But I'll tell you I'm irritated with Washington, and I'm irritated with Senator Dole, who seems to be against anything the president is trying to do about the deficit. At least the president's trying to do something about it. I'm pleased that people are finally beginning to realize that the deficit isn't just going to take care of itself.

"A lot of people get a big kick out of the polls. It's like being in candy land. Are you in favor of more health care? Yes. Are you in favor of paying for it? No. How are we going to get rid of this big deficit without paying for it?"

In Charleston, South Carolina, Father Sam Miglarese, the priest whose heroes were Martin Luther King and Robert Kennedy, had flirted with supporting Perot. "I loved his witty one-liners," he says. "I enjoyed his performance in the debates. There was a believable quality about him." In the end, though, he voted for Clinton. Now he says, "Whatever fascinated me about a bold third-party candidate has lost luster. Perot's no longer a credible candidate, though he may still represent something important to the American people."

Father Sam had just returned from a trip to Italy. While there, he rented a car and paid $45 for a tank of gasoline. The Italians have been living with high gasoline prices for years without damage to them or their country, he says, and here our Congress thinks even a nickel-a-gallon increase is too much to ask.

"We missed the boat," Father Sam says. "We seem to be stuck in a governmental system that's wrong. Those two close votes in Congress—it was very partisan. Bob Dole, a man I have great respect for, I always thought he had a measure of statesmanship that allowed him to rise above the fray and do what's best. But he now seems geared to self-interest. I feel like writing him to tell him he's been very vindictive."

When we first talked, Father Sam had fears that America was going to reach the millennium and "still allow the differences among us . . . to become sources of division rather than diversity." More than a year and a half later, he still felt America lacked a sense of community. "I still think the American people are motivated to change," he says, "but I guess it will take a longer time."

In Selma, Alabama, in one of the biggest upheavals in the city's history, blacks had just seized control of the city council when I spoke again with J. L. Chestnut, the leading black lawyer. For the first time, voters in a special election had ousted four city council members to give blacks a majority on the nine-member council. Three women, the most ever, were also elected. Mayor Joe Smitherman, the former white segregationist who was reelected for an eighth term with the support of black voters on election day, was quoted in that day's paper as saying: "We are going to be the most multicultural, politically correct council in Alabama. I don't think any city in the state will be able to match us in those terms."

Despite this striking new evidence of black political advancement, Chestnut was disturbed by the failure of the Clinton Justice Department to understand that blacks in Alabama faced serious new voting rights problems. Promises to act swiftly to strengthen the Justice Department's civil rights division had not been fulfilled. Most notably, the position of assistant attorney for civil rights—for which Lani Guinier had been nominated—was still not filled. "We can't wait on Washington for action," Chestnut says, "because we're still facing setbacks in programs that it took us thirty years to win."

Before the election, Chestnut had asked two of his law school classmates, both blacks and both well known nationally, for their assessment of Clinton. Virginia's Governor Douglas Wilder was dubious about Clinton, while Vernon E. Jordan, Jr., who eventually headed Clinton's presidential transition team in Washington, was highly enthusiastic. Bill Clinton will be the best thing that has happened to America, and the best thing for black Americans in particular, Jordan told Chestnut. Now Chestnut says: "My own sense is that the truth lies somewhere between Doug's position and Vernon's. I have serious reservations about Mr. Clinton's commitment to a struggle that I have given my life to. All the more because he is Southern himself. When you have a white Southerner who is *for* you, he understands the landscape—like Lyndon Johnson did, for example. When you have one who is not really with you, you have problems for the same reasons. So I'm apprehensive about Mr. Clinton, and what is going on in the Justice Department tends to confirm my worst suspicions.

"I do think Bill Clinton has brought forth an honest discussion on the deficit issue. I never thought I would live to see the day that I was happy to pay taxes, but my wife and I are both happy to pay them. Mr. Clinton has genuinely forced honest debate about honest problems—health care and all that. He deserves great credit."

Chestnut, joining all the others with whom I renewed contact, was most concerned about worsening economic and social problems. "In Alabama we have all of the problems peculiar to America economically," he says, "but in addition now we have this army of uneducated, unskilled people and we don't know what to do with them. Whites have left the public schools, which are now all black. You can't get tax measures passed to help public education. So we are going backward rather than forward. I do not yet see any leader in Alabama, black or white, who is prepared to bite the political bullet and stand up and tell these folks the truth. We have a governor down here now who is about to call a special session of the legislature to authorize gambling casinos in the state. That is hardly an answer to the serious economic problems we have here."

In Peoria, Illinois, Jack Gilligan sees the country still badly divided, as he continues to travel nationally as chairman of a management and business corporation. "I see so much trouble across the nation in our local communities," Gilligan says. "I think it comes from a lack of sense of who we are as Americans. What does it mean to be an American today? It's very confusing to lots of people. So there's a rallying around whether you're Irish, or black, or Hispanic, or Asian. That's okay. What concerns me is the polarization. We're not talking as much to each other as we used to. We're just going about our business, and there's a lot more pressure to do your business now. There's so much focus on survival and making it, and less on building community and what it means to be a community."

Gilligan voted for Clinton (his wife voted for Perot) in the hope that he would make a difference. "Some of the excitement associated with Clinton was that he could bring some of these diverse groups together," Gilligan says, "that he could breach that. All of that remains to be seen."

Debbie Quisenberry, when we first met, had just answered an ad for blackjack operators on a gambling riverboat, the *Paradise,* in the Illinois River off Peoria. Her aim was to save money to go back to school after losing her teaching job.

She completed her blackjack training, then began working on the gambling ship. "I hated it from the moment when I walked on that boat," she said in our talk later. "From the moment I got on, I realized who I was and that the only thing I wanted to be was a teacher; but I didn't have much hope."

Six weeks later, her luck turned and she filled an opening for a sixth-grade public school teacher and coach of the girl's basketball team, in Bartonville, Illinois. "It's a wonderful school," she says. "The children are well-behaved, the teachers are dedicated, the parents are really involved. I feel very much at home. I'm in my second year now and it feels very secure there. Yes, I'm still living with my parents, and I'm still not making a lot of money, but I'm very happy and doing what I want."

She realizes, though, that she's lucky. "I still see lots of people my age with college degrees not getting jobs and not being able to live the American Dream," she says. "I see it changing the way people think, and I don't think it's getting any better. We're in for a long haul of rough times, and not just for teachers and people like me."

Debbie voted for Perot. "I was going for a big change in America," she says. "But I don't have any major problems with Clinton; I don't see anything terrific happening, either. I see a lot of conflict between the two parties in Washington, and of course in some ways government acts like a child. It wants it done its way instead of working for the good of everyone. That bothers me."

In northeastern Iowa, around Waverly, the Winners' Circle of farm couples still meets to support each other as new problems arise in the Farmbelt. Now natural calamity rather than human specula-tion in land rivets their attention. The rains that came with the spring of 1993 brought record downpours—thirty-four inches in only a few months, exceeding the annual Iowa rainfall of thirty-two inches, and continuing to fall. Then the great floods began as the Mississippi and the rivers that flow into it—the Missouri, the Yellow, the Turkey, the Maquoketa, the Wapsipinicon, the Cedar, the Iowa, the Skunk, the Des Moines—rose to levels not experienced in at least a hundred years (some government climatologists said five hundred years).

The farm of Fran and Howard Mueller, where I had met with the members of the Winners' Circle more than a year before, was spared the worst of the flooding; but every field was sodden, every farmer faced severe problems with prospects for fall tillage in land so wet that even with an unusually long dry spell, which had not material-ized, they would still be forced to harvest what crops they could in seas of mud. All the members of the Winners' Circle were left to ponder again their dependence on forces over which they had no control, and all were left with a new awareness of how increasingly dependent American farmers are on international trade—a reality hammered home by the closing of the Mississippi and the Port of New Orleans to their products in the world market.

In his wry, understated manner, Howard Mueller expresses the view of America from beyond the Farmbelt: "partly cloudy." He's a lifelong Republican who thinks of himself as a "liberal-conserva-tive," but who worries about the growing influence of the ultraright. Mueller voted for George Bush, although he was disappointed with Bush, especially in the closing days of the campaign when he seemed to "run out of gas." That isn't Bill Clinton's problem. "His prob-lem," Mueller says, "is he doesn't know when to shut up. The guy can't stop talking. He's going to overexpose himself."

Fran Mueller feels much the same. Like her husband, she voted for Bush; but, as she says with a laugh, out of "backward reasoning."

In a lesser-of-evils choice, she favored Clinton, but when she saw that Clinton would carry Iowa easily she voted for Bush so Clinton "wouldn't have a mandate to think he could go and do anything he wanted." She had hoped, too, that the Republicans would step forward and demonstrate greater leadership. "I still see the same old foot-dragging, especially among the Republican leadership. Clinton didn't have that great a mandate, and the Republicans could have stepped in and cooperated. Bob Dole is very astute, but I don't really trust him now. He could do something very noble for the United States if he wanted to, but I think he's more interested in what's good for himself."

Howard Mueller says America is not rudderless but directionless. It's impetuous. It gets excited momentarily, then moves on to something else. "I am not positive about our leadership, either of our administration or of our Congress," he says. "It's business as usual. Perot? I think Ross Perot relishes and enjoys the spoiler role. He has a Napoleon complex—a small man with a billion bucks absolutely enjoying what he's doing. His message is 'Trust me; I've got a plan; I don't know what it is, but trust me.' He will continue to play the spoiler role as my dissatisfied contemporaries throughout the country keep looking for immediate solutions. He will continue to louse things up for everybody, both liberals and conservatives."

The Muellers are Americans who place their trust more in the strength of individuals—in their son, who will follow them into farming, and in their neighbors—than in the collective strength of political bodies and public institutions. They also believe that America's greatest strength lies in the personal ties that bind communities together. They do worry, however, about the encroachment of dangerous elements on their safe community. "We're seeing a lot of gang activity in Iowa now," Fran says. "That's scary. That worries me a heck of a lot more than the economy."

In Piedmont, California, a similar concern affects Lynne and Steve Spickard. They're the young couple who reluctantly moved from their old Oakland neighborhood into a more expensive area where public schooling promised to be better for their children. That turns out to be so. Their new pleasure has a bittersweet quality, though, as they see conditions changing in their former community. Crime is rising in Oakland, there has been a recent shooting at an automatic bank teller machine, community tensions are increasing. And they, too, have an uneasy sense of encroachment. More graffiti appear in the new neighborhood. Theft of equipment from school playgrounds has forced the school to remove basketball hoops after hours.

The Spickards have a hard time with higher mortgage payments, and the shaky northern California economy adversely affects Steve's consulting business. "To sum it up," Steve says, "what had been imposed as temporary reductions at the beginning of the recession have become permanent. I have serious concerns about where America is headed in the long run. Will we be competitive in the world market? We're already approaching a serious point with Japan. People have to look at the big picture and not expect things to be the way they were."

Both Lynne and Steve voted for Clinton and remain supportive of him; both are disgusted by the partisanship in Washington. "I've never been partisan before," Lynne says, "but I'm getting very angry with the Republican Party. It's all negative." She's equally disturbed by the news media. They're the most negative of all, she thinks. "I hate all the polls and all the comparisons of Clinton with other presidents at this point and that point. It's such a herd mentality at work. I can't imagine why anyone would want to be president now."

Steve shares her feeling about press preoccupation with Bill Clinton's performance: after a week . . . after a hundred days . . . after six months . . . after a year. Then he adds, "I hope Clinton has the patience himself to stay with it." At the same time, he realizes that it isn't only the president who needs patience in meeting the challenge of change. The people need it too.

EPILOGUE

JOURNEY'S END

At St. John's University in Queens, my boyhood friend Father Bob Swain stands before the blackboard and draws an arc, stopping from time to time to write specific dates and events: 3000 B.C., the invention of writing . . . 443 B.C., the Age of Pericles and the crest of Athenian democracy . . . A.D. 476, the fall of the Western Empire of Rome . . . A.D. 814, the death of Charlemagne . . . 1453, the fall of Constantinople . . . 1776, the American Revolution . . . 1789, the French Revolution.

Upward he draws his arc, noting the American Civil War, the Spanish-American War, World Wars I and II, and on to the present. As he does, he talks about the cycles of history, of the rise and fall of empires and of the historians who chronicled them—Gibbon and Spengler and Toynbee. Then he asks his students to compare the birth and maturity of great civilizations with the lives of humans. Where is America? he challenges them. Where are we in this arc? Is the arc rising or falling? Is America on the way up, or down? Are historians someday going to say: 1989–90, the fall of the Soviet Empire? Or are they going to say: 1989–90, the beginning of the fall of the American Republic?

Ordinarily, the students don't offer much response. "They just look at me," Father Bob says. "I don't think they want to think about it."

When I press him for his own response to his questions, Father

Bob says he thinks America reached its zenith in the years between the end of World War II and the early 1960s. The country was united then, it believed in itself, its industry was unmatched, its currency the world's soundest, its standing around the globe never higher. More important, America had a strong sense of those great possibilities that President Clinton speaks of, a belief that nothing was beyond its grasp, that it could right old wrongs at home, safeguard the world abroad, and lead the way to a brighter future through exploration of the heavens and reliance upon its own energy, inventiveness, and technology.

Many share Father Bob's view of an America whose best period is behind it, an attitude that makes the stakes even higher as the nation faces its current challenges. Americans may not think these are the worst of times, but they do feel these are the most unsettled of times. Where once they felt like fortune's darlings, now they feel more like hostages to fortune, swept by new forces rather than creating and controlling them. For the first time they worry that instead of being ahead of the curve of history, they trail behind it. They must race to catch up. The promises of the past have not worked out as expected. After forty years of seemingly quick fixes—of fighting this revolution and that over civil rights, women's rights, political reform, environmental reform, and educational reform, of battling racism and stopping war—Americans discover that things really aren't fixed.

The nation whose efforts over the last half century helped create conditions that led to the collapse of communism finds itself not reaping the anticipated benefits. Rather than a new world order, America faces a new world disorder, and its own place in that world has been diminished. Ancient religious, racial, ethnic, and national hatreds erupt in a globe that seems teetering on a new age of barbarism, from "ethnic cleansing" in Bosnia to famine and collapse of all authority after civil war in Somalia. In the vacuum created by the end of the Cold War, new problems arise; but glittering new possibilities are also present. In South Africa, hopes rise for easing of the racial hatreds that have so divided that troubled land as black and white leaders—two of whom won Nobel Prizes for peace—signal a desire to work together to rebuild their country. Perhaps even more hopeful was the dramatic signing of an Israeli-Palestinian peace accord in Washington, an event witnessed around the world, which symbolizes what Clinton perfectly characterizes as "a great occasion of history and hope" and a "brave gamble that the future can be better than the past." Yet even as this tantalizing prospect renews dreams for a new era of international cooperation, political instability continues: governments totter, leaders are replaced, hopes for European unity fade, Russia veers away from democracy toward dictatorship, factionalism increases. This takes place at a time when the world economy is bound together as never before and when recession and rising unemployment raise new concerns in markets from London to Tokyo.

For the first time in living memory, increasing numbers of Americans feel that the world is acting more on them than they are acting upon the world. They understand their lessened ability to exercise American authority, or American will, abroad. They fear the world has changed, and we have not changed with it. In some ways, America is the sorcerer's apprentice. It unleashes new forces, rebuilds its former enemies from the ruin it rains upon them, then finds itself threatened by those very foes-turned-allies. America, a westward-looking land, for the first time sees the west extending beyond its grasp. And as it warily looks over the ultimate western frontier, it confronts what may prove to be the new forge of the future: Asia. If the twentieth century was American, the twenty-first promises to be Asian.

The profound uneasiness that spread over the land when I began my journey still exists. Nearly two years later, despite signs of a better economy, the restructuring of America accelerates. Now, as then, corporate giants—IBM, Kodak, Johnson & Johnson, Prudential, General Dynamics, DuPont—announce permanent layoffs for additional tens of thousands of employees. Now, as then, more people find themselves among the ranks of "temp" workers with lower pay and fewer, if any, benefits. To sharpen the frustrations, corporate profits rise as a result of further "downsizing" but personal problems mount. More Americans feel like the proverbial frog in a deep, slippery well: the higher it leaps in attempts to get out, the heavier its fall back to the bottom. Crime and random violence proliferate. Immigration is even more a national issue than it was when I stood on the Mexican border and watched those hundreds of illegal aliens pour into the United States. The plight of the public schools grows more severe as the struggle for scarce tax funds intensifies. Those gaps between haves and have-nots continue to widen, and so do new concerns over growing class conflict as evidenced by arsonists destroying homes of the wealthy in southern California.

All the problems of the political past have resurfaced—the difficulty of creating a bipartisan approach to national problems; the impatience of public and press with failure to achieve quick success; the growing criticism and cynicism that make achievement of consensus more difficult; the tendency of people to say raise *your* taxes but cut *mine,* cut spending but not when it affects me. And all of these have raised the prospect of another failed presidency, coming after an early surge of hope.

Politically, the real verdict on President Clinton and his "great gamble with history" will not come until after the presidential results of 1996, although the 1993 elections signaled bad news for the Democrats and the White House. Voters, expressing even greater unhappiness with incumbents, continued the trend of a year ago by replacing the ins with the outs. As a result, Republicans became mayors of the nation's two largest cities, Los Angeles and New York, Democrats lost Senate seats in Georgia and Texas, the GOP candidates replaced governors in New Jersey and Virginia. All this further accelerated a 1996 presidential election process that has already begun. Even before Clinton had served six months, prospective Republican opponents flocked to New Hampshire to set the groundwork for the presidential campaign then more than *three years* away.

In the 1993 election aftermath, Ross Perot began to loom larger, especially after the Texan accepted a White House challenge to debate the North American Free Trade Agreement. Perot's performance in that televised "debate" with Vice President Albert Gore— where personal assault and misstating of fact overrode serious discussion of issues—was uniformly judged by political commentators to have depreciated the Texan. Subsequent polls confirmed those impressions. Some leading political analysts believed that Perot's manner, even more contemptuous than usual, removed him, finally, as a serious national force.

That assessment was probably premature however, especially when measured against the repeated misjudgments of Perot. Besides,

Perot is (and has been) only the most visible symbol of discontent with the political system—a discontent that resurfaced during the embittered NAFTA fight. Again, Clinton's presidency was imperiled; and this time, Democratic defections were the greatest threat to his authority. Clinton wryly acknowledged his problem on the eve of the NAFTA vote, predicting that he would win another razor's edge victory and saying, "It's going to be another landslide in paradise."

NAFTA produced some of the most intensive lobbying in years. Numerous examples of pork-barrel politics were recorded as the White House cut protectionist deals with members of Congress representing a rainbow of special interests. The lobbying also exposed deep fissures—ideological and economic—in Republican as well as Democratic ranks. In the end Clinton prevailed on NAFTA, winning by a comfortable sixteen-vote margin but carrying only 40 percent of Democratic members of the House of Representatives with him.

Again, Clinton won on an intensely controversial issue, one that leaders of his own party thought was doomed only weeks before. In the process, he demonstrated tenacity and formidable political lobbying skills. He also demonstrated that he had learned from his faltering early months in office: he focused sharply on the NAFTA issue, framed the debate for the public effectively, showed the capacity to forge new political coalitions, and led a White House staff that performed flawlessly. But his victory also carried a possible future price, in further disaffection among supporters when Congress returned in 1994.

But however Clinton's administration is judged in years ahead, he represents a departure. He is a president with a sense of history, and one who asks himself what Lincoln or Franklin Roosevelt or Truman—the models he cites—would have done when faced with difficult judgments. At the least, he is the president who challenged Americans to rethink their future. His presidential agenda remains the most ambitious in decades. Despite the difficulties of the first year, his record of legislative success was the greatest since Dwight D. Eisenhower—and, for the second time in sixty years, was achieved without the use of a presidential veto. Not only is he gambling with history when he attempts to reduce the deficit by simultaneously raising taxes and cutting spending in a weak economy. He also rolls the dice in his health care reform plan—the boldest, most visionary domestic initiative since the 1930s, and one that ultimately tests the American political system's ability to overcome its many divisions.

In presenting his health care plan during a nationally televised address to a joint session of Congress three weeks after he returned from his vacation, Clinton rose to the challenge of what he called a "magic moment" for America. Speaking passionately, urgently, as he had during our Air Force One conversation, the president struck a note of bipartisanship as he appealed for immediate action. Afterward, a Democratic senator who has been critical of Clinton's performance—and in particular of his health care plan—told me that Clinton's speech was the best he had heard any president deliver in more than twenty years in Washington. The initial public response was equally positive. Suddenly, as Republicans rushed to present their own health reform plans to guarantee universal coverage, it seemed as if one of the goals Clinton articulated to me for his presidency—restoring a sense of possibility—was closer to realization.

Clinton began articulating, too, a theme that I'm certain resonates among Americans I met: that of restoring a sense of security— health security, job security, personal security from random violence. Then, as happened so often in his first year, just when his fortunes were improving he became diverted by foreign policy crises in Somalia and Haiti. Americans watching TV were horrified to see dead American soldiers being dragged through the streets of Mogadishu after a company of Rangers suffered grievous casualties in attempting to capture leaders of a Somali warlord clan. Stirring national memories of past presidential failures was the scene of an American military hostage being questioned for the TV cameras by captors. The ensuing political debate about the president's foreign policy goals and his exercise of power made it more difficult to refocus public attention on the domestic initiatives at the heart of his promise.

As for those other goals he articulates for America—rebuilding a sense of community; rekindling public faith in a more active government; helping produce a more admirable citizen—they are shared by virtually everyone I met. The problem is, these goals remain generalities. Desire for change and willingness to pay the price for it are distinctly different. And at present, the forces that divide America are greater than those that unite us. An absence of larger institutional loyalties characterizes our times. Loyalty to corporations has diminished in the wave of layoffs following restructuring and downsizing; the example of the once most-admired IBM typifies the standing of corporate America. Unions long since have fallen out of favor among their own members and the general public. Colleges and universities, great law firms, and Wall Street investment houses no longer are held in as high public esteem. Now, it's not so much national identity that unites and defines Americans but identity within one's gender, ethnic, and racial group—identity as women, blacks, Asians, Native Americans, Latinos, gays.

Diversity is a source of strength. But at its most extreme, compartmentalization lessens a sense of solidarity, the special pride in being an American that once inspired national purpose and achievement. The differences extend beyond the already examined haves and have-nots. Divisions between military and civilian life are the sharpest in my lifetime—which is due in part to the long rise to power of a permanent military class in the Cold War era, and in part to the misunderstanding and ill will between civilian and military leaders, even more pronounced in the Clinton era. Campus "cultural wars" waged by education critics on both the right and left exacerbate another kind of fragmentation. Not so well noted is the degree to which these intellectual battles are conducted from secure academic perches that are often well endowed by foundation and corporate grants from "conservative" or "progressive" groups. Neither side in the debate really seeks to engage the general public, and certainly not with the clarity that would attract and inform a national audience. Too often, these critics write for, and speak to, each other, deliberately employing a vocabulary so filled with jargon that it illustrates what intellectual historian Russell Jacoby calls "a widely accepted proposition: clear language undermines critical thought." Too often their works, incomprehensible to the general educated public, aren't even geared toward that audience. Consequently, there is less emphasis on larger themes dealing with public well-being and a better society.

Admittedly, major issues have become increasingly complex, and there is greater disbelief in the ability of the public processes, especially politics and government, to solve them. Then, too, we live in an age of specialization, in which specialists are in greater demand than generalists. But when ideological factors are introduced into scholarly writing and intellectual debate, the divisions in the public mind become even more extreme.

Both at home and abroad, Americans live in a time of greater uncertainties. The energizing slogans of the past—Making the World Safe for Democracy, the Domino Theory, the Evil Empire, the New World Order—ring hollow in light of present more sophisticated knowledge of history. When it comes to finding ways to deal with today's ambiguities and uncertainties, a new politics, or a new leadership, has not yet evolved. Nor have Americans yet come to terms with their conflicted feelings about government. In past decades, Americans probably looked too much to the federal government for answers. They no longer do; now, probably they look to it much too little. The idea that government will not—cannot—deliver as promised, or that its programs are wasteful, is still deeply embedded in the American consciousness.

Despite some early disappointments with the Clinton presidency, however, and the renewed evidence of how difficult it is to end political divisions, a different national feeling about the role of government is beginning to emerge. The most lasting legacy of the Eighties is the belief that rewards for the powerful went too far and came at the expense of the rest of the country, thereby contributing to national decline. Appreciation of the need for *certain* kinds of greater governmental action—for health, public safety, job creation and security, the very kinds of themes Clinton began to sound—is now more widely shared.

This is perhaps Bill Clinton's greatest challenge: to convince Americans that the actions he proposes are worth additional cost and sacrifice. They must work as advertised, thus demonstrating that national government, instead of being the problem, is part of the solution.

The "solution" has nothing to do, in the public mind as opposed to the Washington mind, with whether Bill Clinton is a "New" or "Old" Democrat. Predictably, political insiders began debating this once the fall election results were tabulated. What people want is something that works; most people I met care little which party gets the credit. Indeed, such talk about partisan gains or losses disgusts and further alienates them from Washington. They want to celebrate *American* successes and *American* efforts.

So, too, with increased emphasis on "community," which Clinton rightly cites as one of his major goals. Many times, in many places, I heard how irrelevant Washington was to people's deepest concerns, how distant they felt from the capital and how disillusioned by the political "attack" talk on television. Such attitudes seemed reminiscent of the earliest national debates between Jefferson and Hamilton about communities vs. the central government. What I was hearing seemed to suggest that more Americans are thinking about, if not returning to, the Jeffersonian view: it's what happens *outside* of Washington, not in it, that ultimately makes the difference. In the end, the most important question is not how the "government" addresses—or fails to address—major issues, but how communities do. This idea comes through repeatedly when people talk about their work, their families, their desire to solve problems in their own communities even if the "government" seems unwilling or unable.

Such thinking has created a new political movement. It calls itself "communitarianism" and comes with a "communitarian agenda" to restore family structures, provide safe and livable communities, and encourage increased civic responsibility and civility, all motivated by the strongest human impulse—self-interest.

It was this theme that Hillary Rodham Clinton, the First Lady, articulated in the spring of 1993. The essence was a call for a national spiritual renewal. America, she said in a speech in Austin, Texas, was suffering from a "sleeping sickness of the soul." People were missing a feeling that "our lives are part of some greater effort, that we are connected to one another, that community means that we have a place where we belong no matter who we are."

In supercilious Washington, Mrs. Clinton's comments were quickly mocked. What was all *that* supposed to mean? *The New Republic* sneered. What it meant is that countless Americans are endeavoring to articulate the same feelings as Mrs. Clinton, and often by using the same "spiritual-type" words. Cynics notwithstanding, Hillary Rodham Clinton was expressing the very concerns

I heard day after day across America. The Americans I met would instantly understand what she is groping toward.

The problem is that while the desire to tackle local problems is producing successes around the nation, the efforts remain mixed. Citizens rail against the heavy hand of the federal government, but their own actions often emphasize local failure. While they claim to yearn for community, their parochialism often further divides their communities. As we have seen, this is especially true when it comes to taxes. Instead of facing this issue squarely and raising needed taxes for local services—from schools to police and fire departments and libraries—state and local governments increasingly turn to lotteries, gambling ships, and casinos on Indian reservation land for sources of revenue.

A vivid example occurred after the Clinton budget barely passed in Washington when Michigan became the first state to eliminate local property taxes as a source of funding for public schools. This took place even though two-thirds of the money spent for elementary and secondary education comes from property taxes, and no other sources of income had been provided for the schools. Once again, antitax and antigovernment forces prevailed in a direct test over public school funding. Earlier that year, huge school funding gaps had led to closing of schools in Michigan. And Michigan voters, by 54 to 46 percent, had rejected a statewide referendum for a sales tax increase that would have guaranteed a minimum of $4,800 per pupil to equalize spending between rich and poor school districts. Without such equity, the distance between the have and have-not communities will continue to widen.

At the end of my book *Sleepwalking Through History,* I concluded that America's greatest test lies not beyond its borders—as two generations were taught during the Cold War era—but within. I saw America as threatened by four internal factors: festering social and economic problems and growing divisions among its citizenry; subversion of its constitutional system, as in the Iran-contra affair; governmental corruption and ineffectiveness; and the cynicism and inattention of its people. "All these elements are present in the Nineties," I wrote then, "and neither public will nor political consensus has formed on how to address them."

While those elements certainly still exist, change already is occurring in the way Americans think, as I found on my journey for this book. People are taking stock of themselves and finding it painful. In their introspection, they are grappling with an uncharacteristic notion: to set long-term goals instead of following short-term impulses. For a people conditioned to live for the moment, this is a difficult adjustment. Never in the past, when interviewing Americans, have I heard people *uniformly* say they are concerned about the nation's failure to address long-term issues—and state those concerns explicitly. That's the case with union members who acknowledge their complicity in greedy bargaining and in demanding work practices that jeopardize their, and their companies', future. It's also the case with corporate executives who criticize excessive compensation for chief executive officers and their own preoccupation with quarterly profit reports rather than long-term planning and investment.

There are other things I began to hear that bear noting: what seems a serious questioning of whether the old ideal of college-for-everyone is still relevant in today's harshly competitive environment; and a questioning of the belief that America's economic recovery and future job base depend largely in its ability to compete with its foreign rivals. "Why do we consider them competitors?" asks Jay W. Forrester, whose development of the Whirlwind Computer at MIT led to the modern high-speed digital computer and whose "limits to growth" thesis in the 1970s brought him world renown. "Why do we have to compete with them? Why are they relevant? Why aren't we just putting our own house in order and developing *our* standard of living? Our future does not depend on selling the Japanese something they don't want. Our future depends on making things that *we* want. The whole idea of having to be competitive starts the thinking off on the wrong track."

Such thinking is encouraging, even impressive, but something more must be acknowledged. If Americans and their leaders were sleepwalking through history in the Eighties, even more so was the entire nation deluding itself for at least a generation before that decade. No thinking American can have been unaware of the long accumulation of national problems that have converged in the closing years of this century. Since the Russian Sputnik first orbited the earth in 1957, Americans have been talking about the need to be more

proficient technologically and scientifically. Even before that, they
were warned about the inability of Johnny—and Jane—to read. The
deterioration of cities, rising rates of crime, ever-spreading possession of guns, racial and class tensions—all have been evident for
years. Americans knew these things, and more—and knew, too, that
their relative economic position was weakening in the world as their
manufacturing base declined and their industries and jobs moved
offshore. Nevertheless, they and their leaders failed to act, partly
from a false sense of security—"We're number one"—but even more
from unwillingness to come to grips with problems they knew to
exist.

Twice before, Americans have gone through periods like the
present when they knew, deep in the bone, that their world was
changing forever. The first was in the years between 1846 and 1861. As
the Civil War drew closer and closer, new forces collided, forcing
decisions about old questions: whether America would be an agrarian or industrial nation; whether it would be one nation or a loose
confederation of independent states; whether it would sanction slavery or uphold the principles of freedom and equality explicit in its
founding charters. The second period came after the financial crash
of 1929 ushered in the Great Depression and subsequently World
War II. Americans emerged from those challenges aware that they
and their country were forever changed. Never again would they be
as insular, never again could they cling to the isolationism of their
past, never again could they brush aside the pressures for racial and
social change within their own society. With the signing of the World
War II peace accords aboard the battleship USS *Missouri* in Tokyo
Bay on September 2, 1945, the United States stepped fully onto the
world stage, enjoying a time of unbounded confidence in the American future, a time that gradually gave way to the present doubts over
America's prospects, not only for competing abroad but for binding
itself together at home.

Against this awareness, the new introspection flourishes. In another change from the past, I found Americans no longer assigning
as much blame to the usual suspects: to Japanese . . . to welfare
"cheats" . . . to "shiftless" members of this or that minority . . . to
liberals or to conservatives. More and more, Americans are affixing
responsibility for the nation's troubles on the country and its lead-

ers—*and* on themselves. They do not need to be told that their country no longer enjoys the unsurpassed position it held for a generation after World War II. Everyone knows this. Yet they also know America still possesses enormous resources, backed by an energetic, resourceful people. As the historian D. W. Brogan noted long ago, the hardest task for a people forced to change is to acquire new attitudes and unlearn old lessons. Americans I met understand this; they say it, in private conversation, over and over again. I am convinced they are eager to respond to a strong challenge for unified action—and, yes, willing to sacrifice to achieve clearly defined national goals.

In all, I traveled to fifteen states—Maine, Massachusetts, Connecticut, New York, North Carolina, South Carolina, Alabama, Florida, Iowa, Illinois, Michigan, Oklahoma, Texas, New Mexico, California—and spoke with people in cities as large as New York and Los Angeles and as small as the rural communities of Selma, Alabama, and Waverly, Iowa. After listening to these people, and especially after hearing some of them again nearly two years later, I do not feel that I have been writing the obituary of the American Dream. I believe I have been writing about an interlude in the reclaiming of that Dream.

Perhaps I am wrong. Perhaps the challenge will not be met. Perhaps it is not America's most mature period that beckons, as I hope and believe, but its further decline. Perhaps the people are, in the end, unwilling to break with the habits of the past, rethink their future, and act anew. Perhaps I believe what I want to believe—that the only solution to America's problems is to be faithful to the best traditions of its past: to be open and tolerant, to celebrate diversity, but also to accept that progress requires willingness to compromise and negotiate disputes. Perhaps Americans will fail to act to put their house in order. Perhaps they will further divide and fall.

If so, the people and those they choose to lead them will deserve to fail. American democracy was always only an experiment, the American Dream always only an unfulfilled promise. No one ever guaranteed its ultimate success.

THE CLOCK

Midtown Manhattan, high noon, January 20, 1994:

Now the National Debt Clock registers $4,510,237,023,528. In the year since Clinton's inauguration it has risen by $332,871,285,202 and in the two years since my journey began by $705,584,022,560. The average American family's share of the national debt now stands at $58,098, up $2,382 from a year ago. The clock still runs, the numbers still rise.

NOTES AND SOURCES

Unless otherwise attributed textually, or in these source notes, all quotations in this book are from my tape-recorded interviews. Transcripts were made of all these conversations. I have edited the transcripts to remove redundancies and clarify meaning, but in every case have retained the actual language of the person speaking. There are no composite characters in this book, no made-up names, no stitched-together conversations; all of the conversations took place at specific times and places as described herein, and with the people whose names are attributed to them, with the exception of an illegal alien from Salvador whom I interviewed in Los Angeles and agreed not to use his name, and a similar source there who did not wish his name used. When people's thoughts are recalled in the manuscript, they stem from what the person said he or she *remembered* thinking at the time.

Written sources not otherwise attributed follow.

QUOTES BEFORE PROLOGUE

"In America, I saw more than America . . .": Alexis de Tocqueville, *Democracy in America* (New York: Colonial Press, 1900), p. 14. *"The genius of the United States . . .":* Walt Whitman, Preface to *Leaves of Grass,* in *The Harvard Classics. Prefaces and Prologues* (New York: P. F. Collier & Son, 1969), p. 389.

PROLOGUE: THE JOURNEY

p. 17 *"Counting the cars . . .":* Simon & Garfunkel, *Bookends* (Columbia Stereo Records, 1968).

p. 18 *"make or break time . . .":* "Remarks and a Q.-and-A. Session on the Economic Plan in Chillicothe, Ohio," *Public Papers of the President,* 29 Weekly Compl., Pres. Doc. 232., Feb. 19, 1993.

BOOK ONE: THE PEOPLE AND THE DREAM

THE DREAM

p. 32   *"Restructuring,"* it's called . . . : I have relied here upon statistics and analysis from testimony by Stephen S. Roach, of Morgan Stanley & Co., Inc., before the U.S. House Ways and Means Committee in Washington, D.C., Dec. 18, 1991. His prepared statement, "Policy Changes in an Era of Restructuring," provides much provocative analysis, and I have drawn on those data for this segment on restructuring.

p. 38   *"Unless we have . . .":* President Clinton's State of the Union address to joint session of Congress, Feb. 17, 1993.

pp. 38–39   *"at the third great moment . . .";* *"Whether we see . . .":* President Clinton, address, American University convocation, Washington, D.C., Feb. 26, 1993. Text, *New York Times,* Feb. 27, 1993, p. 6.

p. 45   *"There is no . . .":* Mark Twain, *Following the Equator: A Journey Around the World,* vol. I (New York: Harper & Brothers), p. 80.

p. 51   *"I was dismayed . . .";* *"shake off cold war . . .":* Admiral William J. Crowe, Jr., *The Line of Fire: From Washington to the Gulf, the Politics and Battles of the New Military* (New York: Simon & Schuster, 1993), p. 340.

p. 52   *"largest crush of the . . .":* Philip Hamburger, "Our Man Stanley. The Inauguration," *The New Yorker,* Feb. 8, 1993, p. 76.

p. 58   *"Mickey Mouse stuff";* *"You're going to sacrifice . . .":* Ross Perot, from interview with David Frost, broadcast, PBS, May 28, 1993.

p. 58   *"catastrophic failure":* Perot, interviewed over CBS-TV's *This Morning,* May 11, 1993.

p. 58   *"a whopping 46 percent . . .":* quoted, *Washington Post,* May 4, 1993, p. A6.

p. 60   *"tighter focus":* New York Times, May 5, 1993, p. 1.

p. 61   *"It must be considered . . .":* Washington Post, May 14, 1993, p. A10.

BOOK TWO: WINNING WARS, LOSING EPICS

"THE JOBS AREN'T THERE"

p. 65   *"It's like nobody's . . .":* John Updike, *Rabbit at Rest* (New York: Alfred A. Knopf), p. 353.

p. 68   Footnote: *"reinvention of Wang":* Glenn Rifkin, "Bankrupt Wang Planning to Lay Off 3,300," *New York Times,* March 17, 1993, p. D5.

p. 74   it would be *"cruel"* . . . : as quoted by Al Bilik, president, public employment department, AFL-CIO, in op-ed article, "Too Many Temps," *Washington Post,* April 30, 1993, p. A25.

p. 75   *"the new silent majority . . .":* Stephen S. Roach, "The New Majority: White-Collar Jobless," *New York Times,* March 14, 1993, op-ed page.

CALIFORNIA, HERE WE GO

p. 100   the state's Demographic Research Unit reported . . . : cited in a Reuters dispatch from Sacramento quoting figures compiled by Elizabeth Hoag, a state demographer, and the Demographic Research Unit of the California Department of Finance. Reuters wire, Feb. 16, 1993.

p. 100   As the recession lengthened . . .; a record influx of immigrants: Paul Feldman, "Golden State Losing Some of Its Luster, DMV Data Shows," *Los Angeles Times,* Sept. 2, 1992, p. 3.

p. 101   *In the five-year period . . . :* California Industry Migration Study, "Recent Trends in California Industry Migration, 1987–1992," a Joint Project of Los Angeles Department of Water and Power, Pacific Gas and Electric, San Diego Gas and Electric, Southern California Edison, based on California Industry Migration Study (submitted by Bules & Associates), Oct. 19, 1992.

p. 102   *"unless California recovers":* nationally televised address to the nation, Feb. 15, 1993. See "Letter from California," *Washington Post,* Feb. 17, 1993, p. A3.

p. 103   *"unless California is renewed . . .";* *"This whole part . . .":* Clinton, "Remarks on the Economic Plan in Santa Monica, CA," *Public Papers of the President,* 29 Weekly Compl., Doc. 275, Feb. 21, 1993.

BOOK THREE: AMERICAN FABRIC

SERVICES: FALLING THROUGH THE NET

p. 131   *"Over the years . . .":* Kenneth Reich, *Los Angeles Times,* May 6, 1993, p. 3.

p. 131   *"The middle class probably . . .":* Jim Simon and Barbara A. Serrano, *Seattle Times,* May 6, 1993, p. C1.

p. 133   *"Like any other state . . .";* *"We are not dumping . . .":* William Claiborne, " 'Quaint' Maine Battles Urban Problem as Facilities Release Mentally Ill Patients," *Washington Post,* March 9, 1993, p. A9.

SCHOOLS: THE DUMPING GROUND

p. 139   *First footnote.* Business–Higher Education Forum, *Three Realities: Minority Life in the United States* (Washington, D.C.: American Council on Education, 1990), p. 46. Hereafter cited as Forum, *Realities.*

p. 139   *Second footnote.* *"Even in prosperous . . .":* Kevin Phillips, *Boiling Point: Democrats, Republicans, and the Decline of Middle-Class Prosperity* (New York: Random House, 1993), pp. 133–34.

p. 145   *"an efficient system . . .":* Sam Howe Verhovek, "Texans Reject Sharing School Wealth," *New York Times,* May 3, 1993, p. A12.

p. 154   *"the new depression . . .":* Association of Governing Boards of Universities and Colleges, *Trustees and Troubled Times in Higher Education* (Washington, D.C.: Association of Governing Boards of Universities and Colleges, 1992), p. 2. Hereafter cited as Boards, *Times.*

p. 156   *"It will be cheaper . . .";* *"Regardless of whether . . .";* *"the bad news . . .":* Daniel S. Cheever, Jr., "Tomorrow's Crisis: The Cost of College," *Harvard Magazine,* Nov.-Dec. 1992, pp. 40–41.

p. 157   *"The number of advanced . . .":* Boards, *Times,* pp. 11–12.

p. 163   *"We are facing . . .":* Chancellor Tien, news conference, Berkeley, quoted in *New York Times,* May 12, 1993, p. B6.

RACE: "CAN WE ALL GET ALONG?"

p. 169   *Footnote.* The most detailed accounting of the statistical toll of the riots I've seen was in the *Los Angeles Times.* See, for example, the major recounting, "A City in Crisis: Days of Devastation in This City," *Los Angeles Times,* May 3, 1992, p. 12.

p. 183   *"People, I just want to say . . .":* "A Plea for Calm; Rodney King Speaks Out: 'Can We All Get Along?' " text, *New York Times,* May 2, 1992, p. 6.

p. 183   *"The ordinary American . . .":* Gunnar Myrdal, *An American Dilemma: The Negro Problem and Modern Democracy* (New York: Harper & Brothers, 1944), p. xlvi.

p. 186   *"penny-countin' motha fuckah";* *"Nigga mad enuf . . .";* *"their little Chop Suey . . .";* *"the black fist";* *"to a crisp":* Ice-Cube, "Black Korea," *Death Certificate.*

CRIME: FROM THE STREETS

p. 196   *By the Nineties, its annual murder rate . . . :* An extraordinary article, "The Story of a Gun," by Erik Larson, in the January 1993 issue of *Atlantic Monthly,* provides the best overview of this subject, with careful use of statistics, that I have seen.

p. 202   *By the Nineties, the statistics . . . :* Forum, *Realities,* pp. 33–34.

p. 204   Footnote. *"great crisis of the spirit . . . ":* Douglas Jehl, "Clinton Delivers Emotional Appeal on Stopping Crime," *New York Times,* Nov. 13, 1993, p. A1.

p. 205   *For generations, these gangs . . . :* Herbert Asbury, *The Gangs of New York. An Informal History of the Underworld* (New York: Garden City Publishing, 1928). See especially "The Cradle of the Gangs," pp. 1–11, and "Gangs of the Bowery and Five Points," pp. 12–45.

CLASS: AMERICA DIVISIBLE

p. 225   *"a deluge of wrongs"; We sometimes pride . . . ":* Parke Godwin, *Democracy, Constructive and Pacific* (1844), as quoted in *American Issues,* vol. 1, *The Social Record,* edited by Willard Thorp et al. (New York: Lippincott, 1944), p. 414. Hereafter cited as Thorp, *Issues.*

p. 225   *"Your organization is not . . . ":* Mary Harris Jones, *Autobiography of Mother Jones* (1925), quoted in Thorpe, *Issues.* p. 714.

CULTURE: THE SALAD BOWL

p. 239   *"Americans are the Western pilgrims . . . ":* J. Hector St. John de Crèvecoeur, *Letters from an American Farmer,* Letter Three, "What Is an American?" (New York: Penguin, 1981), p. 70.

pp. 241–42 *"bigotry is out"; "oases of calm . . . "; "It was not hard . . . "; "What has emerged . . . ":* Shelby Steele, *The Content of Our Character: A New Vision of Race in America* (New York: St. Martin's Press, 1990), pp. 128–30, 132. Hereafter cited as Steele, *Content.*

p. 243   *"the notion that history . . . "; "The attack on . . . "; "self-styled multiculturalists . . . ":* Arthur M. Schlesinger, Jr., *The Disuniting of America: Reflections on a Multicultural Society* (New York: W. W. Norton, 1992), pp. 17, 119, 123. Hereafter cited as Schlesinger, *Disuniting.* The quote Schlesinger cites about European classical music and "the pattern of imperialism, in which the conquered culture adopts that of the conqueror," is from Clyde Moneyhun's letter "Culture Schlock," *New Republic,* March 4, 1991.

p. 249   *"all that remains . . . "; "acted out every . . . "; "I knew I would be . . . "; "As lazy, ignorant . . . ":* Steele, *Content,* pp. 131, 135.

pp. 250–51 *"Another problem with . . . "; "checklist for nonsexist . . . "; "You are right . . . "; "It is very hard . . . ":* Wall Street Journal, Jan. 5, 1993, editorial page.

p. 251   *"the blatant and covert . . . "; "black militants"; "two important university . . . ":* Mary Jordan, "Black Students Dump Campus Newspaper at Penn," *Washington Post,* April 17, 1993, p. A5.

p. 252   *"Shut up, you . . . ":* Washington Post, May 18, 1993, p. A8.

p. 252   *"We must always . . . "; "We must be careful":* Hillary Rodham Clinton, commencement address, University of Pennsylvania, quoted, ibid.

p. 253   *"We are used . . . ":* Allan Bloom, *The Closing of the American Mind,* quoted in Schlesinger, *Disuniting,* p. 57.

MIGRANTS: BOTTOM OF THE BARREL

p. 275   *Between 1830 and 1914 . . . :* Three excellent historical overviews of American immigration patterns are in Alastair Buchan, *The U.S.A.* (London: Oxford University Press, 1965), pp. 8–24; D. W. Brogan, *The American Character* (New York: Alfred A. Knopf, 1944), pp. 5–33; and *U.S.A. An Outline of the Country, Its People and Institutions.* (London: Oxford University Press, 1944), pp. 12–26.

p. 282   *By any measure, Cuban-Americans . . . :* See my *The Bay of Pigs* (New York: W. W. Norton, 1964).

VALUES: THE AGE OF ANXIETY

p. 296   *"In a society . . .":* Barbara Vobejda, *Washington Post,* March 8, 1992, p. A3.

p. 296   *By 1993, in little more . . . :* from a paper, "Dynamics of the HIV Epidemic in the United States—1993," by Dr. Thomas C. Quinn, at a medical conference on AIDS at Johns Hopkins University, April 23, 1993.

p. 297   *"the digital equivalent . . .":* John Burgess, " 'Michelangelo' Scare Stirs Fears About Computer Viruses," *Washington Post,* Feb. 17, 1992, pp. A1, A25.

p. 298   *"doomy times":* Rick Marin, "Please Panic," *New York Times,* July 26, 1992, p. 6.

p. 298   *"Robert: Tell you what . . .":* Quoted in ibid.

p. 309   *"problem of unbelief"; "who feel that . . ." etc.; "At the heart . . .":* Walter Lippmann, *A Preface to Morals* (New York: Macmillan, 1929), pp. 3–4.

POLITICS: AWAY FROM ROME

p. 315   *"Now had been divulged . . .":* Tacitus, *The Complete Works of Tacitus* (New York: Modern Library), *The History,* p. 421.

p. 324   *"change the way Washington . . .":* "Remarks on Campaign Finance Reform and a Q.-and-A. Session," *Public Papers of the President,* 29 Weekly Compl., Pres. Doc. 774, May 7, 1993.

p. 328   *"Guns don't kill . . .":* Adam Clymer, "Moynihan Asks Big Tax Increase on Ammunition," *New York Times,* Nov. 4, 1993, pp. A-1, B-20.

p. 336   *"Remember, democracy never lasts . . .":* cited in Richard Hofstadter, *The American Political Tradition* (New York: Alfred A. Knopf, 1948), p. 13.

p. 337   *"During the course . . .":* The Writings of Thomas Jefferson, vol. 3 (Washington, D.C.: Thomas Jefferson Memorial Association of the United States, 1903), p. 380.

p. 338   *"From up close . . ."; "He hit the ground . . .":* Quoted in Elizabeth Kolbert, "The News Media's Rush to Judgment on Clinton," *New York Times,* Jan. 31, 1993, p. 20.

p. 339   *"During the last . . ."; "A four-year term . . .":* "Stumping for Substance," *The New Yorker,* May 31, 1993, pp. 6, 8.

p. 341   *"the incredible shrinking . . .":* Time, June 7, 1993.

pp. 341–42   *"Almost everyone in town . . .":* Joel Achenbach, "Just Another Failed Presidency? Sure, It's Early. But What's That Sound of No Hands Clapping?" "Style," *Washington Post,* May 27, 1993, p. D1.

pp. 343–44   *"I have always believed . . ."; "I hope that . . .":* Guinier press conference, text, *Washington Post,* June 5, 1993, p. A10.

p. 347   *"Universal Distrust"; "one great blemish . . ."; "you carry . . .":* Charles Dickens, *American Notes for General Circulation and Pictures From Italy* (London: Chapman & Hall, 1913,) p. 203.

LEADERS: THE REFORMER

p. 348   *"The problems this country . . .":* "Most in *Post*-ABC Poll Believe Presidency Too Big to Handle," *Washington Post,* July 4, 1993, p. A-16.

p. 351   *"vocal minority"; "being distorted . . .":* cited, *The Economist,* Aug. 14–20, 1993, p. 22. The full study is entitled "The Vocal Minority in American Politics," by Times Mirror Center for the People & the Press, July 16, 1993, Washington, D.C.

pp. 353–54   *"I made mistakes . . ."; "without consequence"; "I was not meant . . .":* text, *New York Times,* Aug. 11, 1993, p. A-12. See also, R. W. Apple, Jr., "Note from White House Aide: A Mixture of Fury and Despair," ibid., pp. A-1, A-12.

p. 354   *"leave a lot . . ."; "you're going to need . . ."; "Here in the East . . .": "What troubles us . . .":* "Welcome, Mr. President—This One's for You," editorial, *Oakland Tribune,* Aug. 13, 1993, p. A-1.

p. 354   *"Woman Stabbed to Death . . ."; "While a dozen . . .": Oakland Tribune,* Aug. 13, 1993, p. B-1.

p. 355   *"What about the . . .":* White House Pool Report # 1, Aug. 13, 1993, Oakland, Calif., written by Jack Farrell, *Boston Globe.*

p. 356   *"the wave of . . ."; "Those who think . . ."; "Presidents would do . . .":* "Remarks by the President to the Workers and Community of the Alameda Naval Air Station and Oakland Naval Supply Center," Wharf # 3, Alameda Naval Air Station, Alameda, Calif. Text, The White House, Office of the Press Secretary, pp. 2–3, 5.

PEOPLE: CLOSING THE CIRCLE

p. 373   *"The critical period . . .":* D. W. Brogan, *The American Character* (New York: Alfred A. Knopf, p. 1944), p. 167.

EPILOGUE: JOURNEY'S END

p. 387   *"a great occasion . . ."; "brave gamble . . .":* text, President Clinton, statement at the signing of the Mideast Peace Accords, *New York Times,* Sept. 13, 1993, p. A-12.

p. 391   *"a widely accepted . . .":* Russell Jacoby, *Dogmatic Wisdom: How the Education and Culture Wars Have Misled America* (New York: Doubleday, 1994), p. 295.

p. 393   *It calls itself "communitarianism" . . . :* see Amital Etzioni, *The Spirit of Community: Rights, Responsibilities, and the Communitarian Agenda* (New York: Crown, 1993).

p. 393   *"sleeping sickness of the soul"; "our lives are . . .":* Hillary Rodham Clinton, quoted in Michael Kelly, "Hillary Rodham Clinton and the Politics of Virtue," *New York Times Magazine,* May 23, 1993, p. 25.

p. 394   *"All these elements . . .":* Haynes Johnson, *Sleepwalking Through History: America in the Reagan Years* (New York: W.W. Norton, 1991), p. 464.

BIBLIOGRAPHY

I have drawn on a number of varied volumes for this work, ranging from novels to histories and scholarly treatises. Among those I found useful are the following.

Adams, Henry. *The Education of Henry Adams.* Boston: Houghton Mifflin, 1918.

Allen, Frederick Lewis. *Only Yesterday: An Informal History of the Nineteen-Twenties.* New York: Harper & Brothers, 1931.

————. *Since Yesterday: The 1930s in America, September 2, 1929–September 3, 1939.* New York: Perennial Library, 1972.

Asbury, Herbert. *The Gangs of New York: An Informal History of the Underworld.* New York: Garden City Publishing, 1928.

Association of Governing Boards of Universities and Colleges. *Trustees and Troubled Times in Higher Education.* Washington: Association of Governing Boards of Universities and Colleges, 1992.

Baker, Nicholson. *VOX.* New York: Random House, 1992.

Barlett, Donald L., and James B. Steele. *America: What Went Wrong?* Kansas City: Andrews and McMeel, 1992.

Beard, Charles A., and Mary R. Beard. *The Rise of American Civilization.* New York: Macmillan, 1930.

Bloom, Allan. *The Closing of the American Mind.* New York: Simon & Schuster, 1987.

Brogan, D.W. *The American Character.* New York: Alfred A. Knopf, 1944.

————. *U.S.A.: An Outline of the Country, Its People and Institutions.* New York: Oxford University Press, 1941.

Bryce, James. *The American Commonwealth.* 2 vols. New York: Macmillan, 1889.

Buchan, Alastair. *The U.S.A.* London: Oxford University Press, 1965.

Business–Higher Education Forum. *Minority Life in the United States.* Washington, D.C.: American Council on Education, 1990.

Califano, Joseph A., Jr. *America's Health Care Revolution: Who Lives? Who Dies? Who Pays?* New York: Random House, 1986.

Chartrand, Robert Lee. *Critical Issues in the Information Age.* Metuchen, N.J.: Scarecrow Press, 1991.

Commager, Henry Steele. *The American Mind: An Interpretation of American Thought and Character Since the 1880s.* New Haven, Conn.: Yale University Press, 1954.

Crèvecoeur, J. Hector St. John de. *Letters from an American Farmer* and *Sketches of 18th-Century America.* Ed. Albert E. Stone. New York: Penguin, 1981.

Curti, Merle. *The Growth of American Thought.* New York: Harper & Brothers, 1943.

Dickens, Charles. *American Notes.* London: Chapman & Hall, 1913.

Dionne, E. J. *Why Americans Hate Politics.* New York: Simon & Schuster, 1991.

Dos Passos, John. *U.S.A.* New York: Washington Square Press, 1961.

D'Souza, Dinesh. *Illiberal Education.* New York: Free Press, 1991.

Eberle, William D., Richard N. Gardner, and John V. Moller. *Present at a New Creation: America's Role in the World Economy.* Queenstown, Md.: Aspen Institute, 1993.

Edsall, Thomas Byrne. *The New Politics of Inequality.* New York: W. W. Norton, 1984.

———, and Mary D. Edsall. *Chain Reaction: The Impact of Race, Rights, and Taxes on American Politics.* New York: W. W. Norton, 1991.

Etzioni, Amital. *The Spirit of Community: Rights, Responsibilities, and the Communitarian Agenda.* New York: Crown, 1993.

Faludi, Susan. *Backlash: The Undeclared War Against American Women.* New York: Anchor, 1992.

Franklin, John Hope. *The Color Line: Legacy for the Twenty-first Century.* Columbia, Mo.: University of Missouri Press, 1993.

Fulbright, J. W. *The Arrogance of Power.* New York: Random House, 1966.

Galbraith, John Kenneth. *The Affluent Society.* Boston: Houghton Mifflin, 1958.

———. *The Great Crash, 1929.* New York: Avon, 1980.

———. *The Culture of Contentment.* Boston: Houghton Mifflin, 1993.

Gardner, John W. *Self-Renewal. The Individual and the Innovative Society.* New York: W. W. Norton, 1981.

Gibbon, Edward. *The Decline and Fall of the Roman Empire.* 3 vols. New York: Heritage press, 1946.

Goldman, Eric F. *Rendezvous with Destiny: A History of Modern American Reform.* New York: Vintage, 1956.

Gunther, John. *Inside U.S.A.* New York: Harper & Row, 1947.

Hacker, Andrew. *Two Nations: Black and White, Separate, Hostile.* New York: Scribner's, 1992.

Hamilton, Alexander, John Jay, and James Madison. *The Federalist: A Commentary on the Constitution of the United States.* Ed. Henry Cabot Lodge. New York: G. P. Putnam's Sons, 1904.

Handlin, Oscar. *The Americas: A New History of the People of the United States.* Boston: Little, Brown, 1963.

Heat-Moon, William Least. *Blue Highways: A Journey into America.* Boston: Houghton Mifflin, 1982.

Hoffer, Eric. *The True Believer: Thoughts on the Nature of Mass Movements.* New York: Harper & Brothers, 1951.

Hofstadter, Richard. *The American Political Tradition.* New York: Alfred A. Knopf, 1948.

———. *The Age of Reform: From Bryan to F.D.R.* New York: Alfred A. Knopf, 1955.

Hughes, Robert. *Culture of Complaint: The Fraying of America.* New York: Oxford University Press, 1993.

Jankowski, Martin Sanchez. *Islands in the Street: Gangs and American Urban Society.* Berkeley: University of California Press, 1991.

Johnson, Haynes. *Sleepwalking Through History: America in the Reagan Years.* New York: W. W. Norton, 1991.

———. *The Bay of Pigs.* New York: W. W. Norton, 1964.

———. *In the Absence of Power: Governing America.* New York: Viking, 1980.

Johnson, Malcolm. *Crime on the Labor Front.* New York: McGraw-Hill, 1950.

Kennedy, Paul. *The Rise and Fall of the Great Powers: Economic Change and Conflict from 1500 to 2000.* New York: Random House, 1987.

———. *Preparing for the Twenty-first Century.* New York: Random House, 1993.

Lippmann, Walter. *Public Opinion.* London: George Allen & Unwin, 1922.

———. *A Preface to Morals.* New York: Macmillan, 1929.

Link, Arthur S. *American Epoch: A History of the United States Since the 1890s.* New York: Alfred A. Knopf, 1955.

Machiavelli, Niccolò. *The Prince.* New York: Mentor/New American Library, 1952.

Magaziner, Ira C., and Robert B. Reich. *Minding America's Business: The Decline and Rise of the American Economy.* New York: Arbor House, 1982.

Manchester, William. *The Glory and the Dream: A Narrative History of America, 1939–1972.* 2 vols. Boston: Little, Brown, 1973.

Moyers, Bill. *Listening to America: A Traveler Rediscovers His Country.* New York: Dell, 1971.

Moynihan, Daniel Patrick, and Nathan Glazer. *Beyond the Melting Pot: The Negroes, Puerto Ricans, Jews, Italians and Irish of New York City.* Cambridge, Mass.: MIT Press, 1970.

———. *Came the Revolution: Argument in the Reagan Era.* New York: Harcourt Brace Jovanovich, 1988.

———. *Pandaemonium: Ethnicity in International Politics.* New York: Oxford University Press, 1993.

Myrdal, Gunnar. *An American Dilemma: The Negro Problem and Modern Democracy.* New York: Harper & Brothers, 1944.

Osborne, David, and Gaebler, Ted. *Reinventing Government: How the Entrepreneurial Spirit Is Transforming the Public Sector.* New York: Plume, 1992.

Parrington, Vernon Louis. *Main Currents in American History: An Interpretation of American Literature from the Beginnings to 1920.* 3 vols. New York: Harcourt, Brace, 1927.

Peirce, Neal R. *The Megastates of America: People, Politics, and Power in the Ten Great States.* New York: W. W. Norton, 1972.

Phillips, Kevin. *Post-Conservative America: People, Politics and Ideology in a Time of Crisis.* New York: Arlington House, 1969.

———. *Boiling Point: Democrats, Republicans, and the Decline of Middle Class Prosperity.* New York: Random House, 1993.

Rostovtzeff, M. *The Social and Economic History of the Roman Empire.* Oxford, England: Clarendon Press, 1926.

Schlesinger, Arthur M., Jr. *The Age of Roosevelt: The Crisis of the Old Order, 1919–1933.* Boston: Houghton Mifflin, 1957.

———. *A Thousand Days: John F. Kennedy in the White House.* Boston: Houghton Mifflin, 1965.

———. *The Cycles of American History.* Boston: Houghton Mifflin, 1986.

———. *The Disuniting of America: Reflections on a Multicultural Society.* New York: W. W. Norton, 1992.

Schlesinger, James. *America at Century's End.* New York: Columbia University Press, 1989.

Shorris, Earl. *Latinos.* New York: W. W. Norton, 1992.

Steele, Shelby. *The Content of Our Character: A New Vision of Race in America.* New York: St. Martin's, 1990.

Steinbeck, John. *Travels with Charley.* New York: Viking, 1962.

Stone, I. F. *The Haunted Fifties: 1953–1963.* Boston: Little, Brown, 1989.

———. *In a Time of Torment: 1961–1967.* Boston: Little, Brown, 1989.

Tacitus. *The Complete Works of Tacitus. The Annals. The History. The Life of Cnaeus Julius Agricola. Germany and Its Tribes. A Dialogue on Oratory.* Trans. Alfred John Church and William Jackson Brodribb. Ed. Moses Hadas. New York: Modern Library.

Tannen, Deborah. *You Just Don't Understand: Women and Men in Conversation.* New York: Ballantine, 1990.

Terkel, Studs. *Race: How Blacks and Whites Think and Feel About the American Obsession.* New York: New Press, 1992.

Tocqueville, Alexis de. *Democracy in America.* 2 vols. New York: Colonial Press, 1900.

Turner, Frederick Jackson. *The Frontier in American History.* New York: Holt, 1920.

Updike, John. *Rabbit at Rest.* New York: Alfred A. Knopf, 1990.

White, Theodore S. *The Making of the President, 1960: A Narrative History of American Politics in Action.* New York: Atheneum, 1961.

———. *The Making of the President, 1964.* New York: Atheneum, 1965.

———. *The Making of the President, 1968.* New York: Atheneum, 1969.

———. *The Making of the President, 1972.* New York: Atheneum, 1973.

———. *Breach of Faith: The Fall of Richard Nixon.* New York: Atheneum, 1975.

———. *In Search of History: A Personal Adventure.* New York: Harper & Row, 1978.

ACKNOWLEDGMENTS

I owe a debt greater than I can express to those hundreds of Americans who took time out of their busy lives for the conversations, many of which lasted for hours, that form the heart of this book. My only regret is that space limitations make it impossible to convey more of the flavor of our talks. For those whose conversations wound up on the cutting-room floor, I apologize for failing to include them; the omission was not for lack of interest, but, again, for lack of space. Many people who contributed to this book deserve more than a brief mention here, but I want to express special appreciation to these few out of so many. First, to my editor at Norton, Carol Houck Smith, who is everything a writer wants in an editor: always challenging, always supportive. Once again, Donald S. Lamm, Norton's chairman, provided a source of strength, personally and professionally. I'm grateful to my agent, Bill Leigh, for all his efforts on my behalf. At *The Washington Post,* I want to thank Leonard Downie, Jr., its executive editor, and Robert G. Kaiser, its managing editor, for granting me a leave of absence. At the *Post,* too, Jennifer Belton, director of information services, once again was most helpful. Olwen Price was indispensable in processing the tape recordings and producing transcripts. So were Karen Guzman, Melissa Mathis, Kerry Topel, and Marilee Stevens. I owe a special debt to Amy Dickenson, my editorial assistant, who not only provided important background material and data but even more critically contacted and arranged in advance many of my interviews around the country. Her ability to find exactly the right person made my task much easier. Lucy Shackelford was also of great help in setting up interviews and providing research material. At Berkeley, where my appointment as a Regents Lecturer gave me the freedom to conduct interviews throughout California, I am indebted to many people, but most particularly to Professor Adrienne Jamieson of the Institute of Governmental Studies for invaluable assistance in many areas; she deserves much more than a brief mention here. Also at the institute, Professor Nelson Polsby, its director and distinguished political scientist, once more provided insight and ideas. I want to thank institute librarians Marc Levin and Ron Heckart and researchers Margarita Najar and Mary Walther. Also at Berkeley, my special thanks to Dean Tom Goldstein of the Graduate School of Journalism and to the Jefferson Lecture Committee. Many more people than I can possibly acknowledge were of help in specific areas of the country, but I want to thank these particularly: in Oakland, Diane Dickstein of the Oakland Police Department, Jim Keddy of the Oakland Community Organizations, and Randy Hamilton; in Los Angeles, Jim Wisely and the late Professor Byran Jackson, a political scientist with acute insight into the black community, and Eunice Baek, who helped me understand the Korean-American community; in Dallas, Allen Pusey of *The Dallas Morning News,* who renewed my faith in the business of daily journalism and probably knows more than anyone about the savings and loan mess; in Miami, my old friend and colleague from Bay of Pigs days Enrique Ruiz-Williams, who reconnected me with Cuban-Americans there; in Santee, South Carolina, Anne Hale and John Miglarese, who helped connect me with the wonderful people there; in San Ysidro, California, Verne Jervis of the U.S. Immigration Service, who once more made it possible for me to see the border up close through the eyes of those charged with maintaining it; in Bridgeport, Connecticut, Ken Dixon of *The Bridgeport Post,* a superb reporter; in Youngstown, Ohio, Libby Holman, who was so good a guide to that region; in Peoria, Illinois, Tom Pugh, former editor of the *Peoria Journal Star;* in Iowa, Mary Thompson, formerly of Waterloo, later managing editor of *AgriFinance* and then of *Farm Journal Publishing,* for help in contacting people in the Farmbelt; in Madison, Wisconsin, Ken Sacks, chairman of the University of Wisconsin's history department, for stimulating conversation and historical perspective; in New York, Martha K. Ritter, who led me through the labyrinth of the world below the city, and Trish Moore, who helped me understand the infrastructure that sustains urban life; in Cambridge, Massachusetts, Ken and Suze Campbell, who guided me through MIT and provided good company along the way. In Washington, once again I benefited from conversations with Timothy Dickenson. Finally, every writer must acknowledge the support and counsel of special friends like Christie Basham, Jonathan Rinehart, Florence and Peter Hart, Susan Zox and Hedrick Smith, and Marcia L. Hale.

H.J.
January 1994
Washington, D.C.

INDEX